S0-BDP-313

Irritable Bowel Syndrome

Psychosocial Assessment and Treatment

Edward B. Blanchard

American Psychological Association • *Washington, D.C.*

Published by
American Psychological Association
750 First Street, NE
Washington, DC 20002

Copies may be ordered from
APA Order Department
P.O. Box 92984
Washington, DC 20090-2984

In the U.K., Europe, Africa, and the Middle East, copies may be ordered from
American Psychological Association
3 Henrietta Street
Covent Garden, London
WC2E 8LU England

Typeset in Goudy by EPS Group Inc., Easton, MD

Printer: United Book Press, Inc., Baltimore, MD
Cover Designer: Berg Design, Albany, NY
Technical/Production Editor: Jennifer Powers

Library of Congress Cataloging-in-Publication Data
Blanchard, Edward B.
Irritable bowel syndrome : psychosocial assessment and treatment / Edward B. Blanchard.
p. cm.
Includes bibliographical references and index.
ISBN 1-55798-730-0 (alk. paper)
1. Irritable colon—Psychological aspects. 2. Psychotherapy. I. Title.

RC862.I77 B56 2000
616.3′42—dc21

00-040583

British Library Cataloguing-in-Publication Data
A CIP record is available from the British Library.

Printed in the United States of America
First Edition

CONTENTS

PREFACE

A few years ago, a local reporter wrote an article about some of the irritable bowel syndrome (IBS) research being done at the Center for Stress and Anxiety Disorders and included our center's telephone number. The story made it onto the AP wire service and was reprinted by a newspaper in Oklahoma. Suddenly, we were flooded with calls from IBS patients in Oklahoma. Fortunately, a former student of mine was in Tulsa, so we referred the callers to her. When I heard from her, she was considering starting groups as a way of dealing with the demand. The point of this example is that IBS patients are out there and looking for good psychological care.

Although IBS is a widespread functional disorder (see chapter 2), it has attracted little attention within psychology from either clinical researchers or practicing clinicians. I hope this book may change that situation in part by showing psychologists the potential for both research and practice with this widespread, needy population. The book is written for practicing psychologists who may be interested in adding a population to their practice base and for clinical researchers seeking a readily available clinical population to study.

This book is organized into two parts. Part I pertains to assessment and assessment-related issues of IBS patients from the perspective of the psychologist or other nonphysician therapist. The first three chapters cover the definition of IBS and the changing diagnostic criteria, the magnitude of the problem presented by IBS as indicated by epidemiological and follow-up studies, and detailed instructions for the nonmedical therapist in how to take a comprehensive history of IBS patients. In chapter 4, I describe the GI symptom diary, a critical assessment tool.

In subsequent chapters, I address the psychological features of IBS as noted by standardized psychological tests and by psychiatric interviews. Also included is information on the potential role of early abuse in IBS and on the psychological differences between those with IBS who seek treatment and those with IBS who do not. Chapters also address psychophysiological testing, inflammatory bowel disease, and recurrent abdominal pain in children.

Part II (chapters 14–21) is devoted primarily to the treatment of IBS. Four broad categories of psychological treatment have been evaluated in controlled trials with IBS: brief psychodynamic psychotherapy, hypnotherapy, cognitive–behavioral treatment packages, and pure cognitive therapy. Fortunately, in Albany, we have published studies with the last three of these treatments and have detailed treatment manuals to share as well as the results from these controlled trials. For each psychological treatment modality, I summarize the existing research from both the Albany studies and other existing research. Detailed treatment manuals are then presented. There are separate chapters devoted to long-term (6 months or more to the end of treatment) follow-up of treatment results and to the prediction of treatment outcome. I also comment briefly on drug treatments and dietary treatments (primarily studies of bran added to the diet). This latter chapter is not definitive.

All of my conclusions are based on my reading of the empirical literature, with a special emphasis on the Albany studies, which represent 15 years of clinical research with this population. Throughout the book, the reader will find brief sections labeled *Clinical Hints*. These represent ideas and conclusions that are clinically relevant and useful, but for which I have no solid empirical support. I believe they are true and await confirmation or disconfirmation by the clinical research community. The appendixes include a rather lengthy clinical hint on how nonphysician therapists might approach physicians, especially gastroenterologists and internists, about referring patients, as well as a collection of forms that may be useful for diagnosis and treatment.

ACKNOWLEDGMENTS

Many people have contributed to this book and the work it describes. First and foremost are the many doctoral students who performed the work of assessing and treating IBS patients and whose dissertations and theses are described herein. The list is long, beginning with Debra Neff, Shirley Schwarz-McMorris, Maryrose Accera Gerardi, Cynthia Radnitz, and Lisa Scharff, and continuing with Barbara Greene, Annette Payne, Alisa Vollmer, Shannon Turner, and Tara Galovski. Special thanks are due to Ann Taylor, Laurie Keefer, and Tara Galovski for compiling all of the data from our many studies and to Laurie Keefer for the literature retrieval.

My research on IBS at the Center for Stress and Anxiety Disorders, University at Albany, SUNY, and preparation of this book was supported in part by National Institute of Diabetes, Digestive, and Kidney Diseases Grants DK-38614 and DK-54211.

I also want to thank two faculty colleagues, Dr. Jerry Suls, currently at the University of Iowa, and Dr. Jim Jaccard, for their contributions to the IBS research and two gastroenterologists, Dr. John Balint and Dr. Howard Malamood of the Albany Medical College.

Two others deserve special thanks: Ms. Sandra Agosto, who prepared the many drafts and versions of this work, and my wife, Dr. Cris Blanchard, who provided support and tolerated my work habits during the preparation of the book.

I

ASSESSMENT

In this first portion of the book, I have tried to cover all of the descriptive material about irritable bowel syndrome (IBS) within a framework of psychological assessment so that the reader has a sense of who the IBS patient is and how he or she will present to the nonmedical therapist or researcher. Most of the material is directly related to assessing the IBS patient prior to beginning teatment with a strong emphasis on practical matters such as taking a gastrointestinal (GI) symptom history (Chapter 3), testing with standardized psychological tests (Chapter 5), assessing for psychiatric comorbidity (Chapter 7) and possible early sexual or physical abuse (Chapter 9). There are also chapters which seemed to me to best fit into the broad descriptive or assessment framework including attention to epidemiology (Chapter 2) and to a possible developmental precursor, recurrent abdominal pain (RAP) in children (Chapter 13).

1

DIAGNOSIS: WHAT IS IRRITABLE BOWEL SYNDROME?

What we currently call irritable bowel syndrome (IBS) has gone by several names over the years: irritable colon, spastic colon, mucous colitis, and spastic colitis. The suffix in the latter two terms (*-itis*) connotes an inflammatory process, which IBS is not. IBS is now the accepted term in the gastroenterological and medical communities. IBS is a functional (i.e., no structural abnormality, leaving only disordered bowel function to account for symptoms) disorder of the lower gastrointestinal (GI) tract, characterized by abdominal pain and other GI symptoms. It is probably related to disordered colonic motility. Psychologists and other mental health professionals have been relatively slow to take on this disorder, especially in the United States. It is hoped that this book will help change that.

Clinical Hint

I firmly believe that psychology and other mental health disciplines have a great deal of knowledge and expertise to offer patients with IBS. Not everyone with IBS seeks medical care (see chapter 6). Moreover, of those who seek medical care, most probably do not need psychological treatment (see chapter 14). However, those 20–30% who do, whom Drossman and Thompson (1992) labeled as having moderate to severe IBS, can benefit a great deal from psychological assessment and good psychological treatment. They are likely to have noticeable psychological and psychiatric distress (see chapters 5 and 7) that are also the province of psychology and other mental health disciplines.

CLINICAL CRITERIA: DIAGNOSIS BY EXCLUSION

For a long time IBS was diagnosed by the so-called clinical criteria listed in Exhibit 1.1. There are several factors in the clinical criteria that warrant comment. The diagnosis of IBS, like that of some psychiatric disorders (e.g., generalized anxiety disorder; GAD) that are listed in the *Diagnostic and Statistical Manual of Mental Disorders* (*DSM–III*; American Psychiatric Association, 1980) is a residual diagnosis. That is, one diagnoses IBS when the inclusion symptom picture is present and all other medical diseases that might present with these symptoms have been excluded. The need to exclude other medical diseases that share IBS's primary symptoms has two important related implications for psychologists and other nonmedical mental health professionals (e.g., social workers). They need to work closely with the gastroenterologist or internist to assess or treat IBS patients to ensure that the physician orders and evaluates the medical tests needed to exclude the alternative diagnoses, nonmedical mental-health professionals need to be wary of accepting potential IBS patients who have not been evaluated medically.

Clinical Hint

In my experience, gastroenterologists are pleased to refer their chronic IBS patients to psychologists, because they have little to offer in terms of con-

EXHIBIT 1.1
Clinical Criteria for Diagnosing IBS

1. Recurrent abdominal pain or extreme abdominal tenderness.
2. Accompanied by disordered bowel habit:
   a. diarrhea
   b. or constipation
   c. or alternating diarrhea and constipation.
3. Present for at least 3 months or longer, much of the time.
4. Diagnosed after appropriate medical tests have ruled out
   a. inflammatory bowel disease
   b. lactose intolerance or malabsorption
   c. intestinal parasites
   d. other rare GI diseases.

Note. From *Functional gastrointestinal disorders: A behavioral medical approach*, by P. R. Latimer, 1983, New York: Springer. Copyright 1983 by Springer. Adapted by permission.

sistently successful drug or surgical interventions, leaving both the patient and the physician frustrated. One of my first IBS patients was a woman referred by a senior gastroenterologist at the local medical school. After a course of cognitive–behavioral treatment, the woman was at best marginally improved, based on her GI symptom diary. Nonetheless, the gastroenterologist became an enthusiastic supporter of the research because the patient stopped calling him weekly to complain of GI symptoms. *The psychologist should insist that patients, who potentially have IBS, have a thorough medical examination (to exclude alternatives) before engaging the patient in treatment.*

In our various research studies we have sometimes (when grant funds were available) been able to pay for physical examinations and laboratory tests. At other times we have sent a letter to the patient's physician asking for a list of diagnostic procedures that the patient has received and for a diagnosis (see Exhibit 1.2, Physician Evaluation Form). In about one case in 30 to 40, we have learned of a diagnosis other than IBS, usually inflammatory bowel disease (IBD) that we had not detected by interview and the patient failed to mention or was unaware of.

This anecdote illustrates another point about IBS: There are at present no definitive tests for it. Thus, one is forced to rely on the patient's account of symptoms to make a diagnosis and measure improvement. Pain is, of course, a subjective phenomenon for which systematic self-report is the only measure. Although it is theoretically possible to assess altered bowel habits objectively (by sending a research assistant to inspect the toilet bowl after each bowel movement), one would rapidly lose research assistants and patients with such a procedure. Thus, we have to rely on self-report of symptoms.

Other Symptoms of IBS

In addition to pain and altered bowel habits, there are a number of other GI symptoms that may be present with IBS: Chief among these is bloating. In fact, after recurrent pain, patients are as likely to seek help for bloating as they are for diarrhea or constipation. Other symptoms include flatulence and belching, as well as nausea and noticeable bowel sounds (borborygmi). We ask patients to monitor these symptoms in a GI symptom diary (see chapter 4).

TOWARD A POSITIVE DIAGNOSIS: THE MANNING CRITERIA

Gastroenterologists interested in IBS have long been aware of the problem of diagnosing by exclusion. In the late 1970s, a group led by A. P.

EXHIBIT 1.2
Physician Evaluation Form

Re: ______________________ Physician: ______________________

______________________ ______________________

______________________ ______________________

______________________ ______________________

(1) Is there any medical information which would indicate that this person not be permitted to participate in the program outlined in the accompanying letter?
NO _____ YES _____

If yes, please specify: ______________________________

____

____

(2) Diagnosis of gastrointestinal problem. Check all which apply.

_______ Irritable bowel syndrome

_______ Peptic ulcer

_______ Duodenal ulcer

_______ Gastroenteritis

_______ Crohn's Disease

_______ Ulcerative Colitis

_______ Other gastrointestinal problem (please indicate) ______________

____

_______ Other medical problem (please indicate) ______________

____

(3) Date of last complete physical examination: ______________

(4) What diagnostic tests have you conducted? ______________

____

____

(5) Is there anything of importance you can tell us about this patient? _______

____

____

______________________ ______________________

Physician's Signature Physician's Phone Number

Date: ______________

Manning (Manning, Thompson, Heaton, & Morris, 1978) addressed this issue through the use of a questionnaire administered prior to the initial examination. Manning et al. asked 109 patients complaining of abdominal pain, constipation, or diarrhea about the occurrence of 15 symptoms over the past 12 months. All chart notes were reviewed independently 17–26 months later by two gastroenterologists to arrive at a definitive diagnosis of the presenting complaint. This was possible in only 79 cases (72%). This led to 32 patients being diagnosed with IBS and 33 with organic disease; 14 cases with diverticular disease were excluded.

The four symptoms that significantly ($p < .01$ or better) discriminated between those with IBS and organic disease, as well as the three symptoms for which there were trends, are presented in Table 1.1, along with frequency of occurrence. Several things are apparent. First, there were *no pathognomonic symptoms* of IBS. That is, there were no symptoms that occurred only for IBS and in no other disorder. With the best single discriminator (looser stools at onset of pain), there were 8/30 (26.7%) false positives (patients with organic disease who reported the symptom) and 6/31 (19.4%) false negatives or misses (patients with IBS who did not report the symptom). Thus, differences in symptom prevalence that were highly statistically significant on a group basis have an uncomfortable error rate at the level of the individual patient.

Given the failure of any single symptom to reliably discriminate, Manning et al. (1978) then took the important step of determining whether the presence of two or more symptoms improved discrimination between those with abdominal pain and IBS and those with pain and organic disease. According to Manning et al., if one asks for three or more

TABLE 1.1
Manning Criteria for Diagnosing Symptoms of IBS

Symptom	Frequency in organic disease	Frequency in IBS
Pain	30/33	31/32
Looser stools at onset of pain	8/30	25/31
More frequent bowel movements at onset of pain	9/30	23/31
Pain (often) eased after bowel movement	9/30	22/31
Visible distension (bloating)	7/33	15/32
Feelings of distension	15/33	23/32
Mucus per rectum	7/33	15/32
Feeling (often) of incomplete emptying	11/33	19/32

Note. From Table 1 of "Towards a positive diagnosis of the irritable bowel," by A. P. Manning, W. G. Thompson, K. W. Heaton, and A. F. Morris, 1978, *British Medical Journal, 2,* 653–654. Copyright 1978 by BMJ. Adapted with permission.

symptoms, then 27 of 32 (84%) of IBS patients will be correctly identified, whereas 25 of 33 (76%) of those with organic disease will also be identified, leaving a false positive rate of 24% for those with organic disease who are termed IBS. Thus, the Manning criteria are useful in establishing a positive diagnosis of IBS but even at their best do not yield absolute certainty.

A more recent effort to evaluate the Manning criteria was reported by Talley et al. (1986) in a study of 395 consecutive patients assessed at the Mayo Clinic, including 82 with IBS, 33 with nonulcer dyspepsia, 101 with organic GI disease, and 145 healthy control participants. Most (n = 361, 91%) answered a GI symptom questionnaire of established reliability and validity independently of their examination by board-certified gastroenterologists. For IBS patients with more than six episodes of abdominal pain per year (n = 66; 80.5%), the presence of three or more of the six Manning criteria, in comparison to those with organic GI disease, revealed a sensitivity of 58% (the percent of agreed upon cases that were identified by Manning criteria as having IBS) and specificity of 74% (the percent of agreed upon cases that did not have IBS that were identified by Manning criteria as not having IBS). Sixty-one percent of pain-predominant IBS patients admitted to three or more symptoms, as did 26% of those with organic GI disease (and 7% of healthy control participants).

This larger, more recent study leaves us with the same problem posed by Manning et al.'s (1978) work: Statistical separations improved between those with IBS and those with organic GI disease; however, the level of false positives and misses at the individual level remained uncomfortably high. Talley et al. (1986) also reported that reliability of an alternative set of symptoms proposed by Kruis et al. (1984) fared even worse than the Manning criteria.

THE ROME CRITERIA

The international gastroenterology community began to come to grips with IBS diagnosis in the late 1980s and issued a report to the Thirteenth International Congress of Gastroenterology in Rome, Italy, in 1988. In their first published report, Drossman, Thompson, et al. (1990) identified and proposed criteria for a wide assortment of functional GI disorders including IBS. Functional GI disorders were defined as "a variable combination of chronic or recurrent gastrointestinal symptoms not explained by structural or biochemical abnormalities" (p. 159).

A later paper from this group by Thompson, Creed, Drossman, Heaton, and Mazzacca (1992) spelled out the current working definitions for functional bowel disorders (FBD, a subset of the functional GI disorders). It included IBS as the most prominent example. The Rome criteria (see Exhibit 1.3) represent an incorporation of some of the Manning criteria

EXHIBIT 1.3
Rome Criteria for Diagnosing IBS

At least three months continuous or recurrent symptoms of

1. Abdominal pain or discomfort that is
   a. relieved by defecation
   b. and/or associated with a change in the frequency of stool
   c. and/or associated with a change in the consistency of stool.
2. Accompanied by two or more of the following, at least a quarter of occasions or days:
   a. altered stool frequency (more than three bowel movements per day or fewer than three bowel movements per week)
   b. altered stool form (lumpy/hard or loose/watery stool)
   c. altered stool passage (straining, urgency, or feeling of incomplete evacuation)
   d. passage of mucus
   e. bloating or feeling of abdominal distension.

into the basic clinical criteria. Thus, there is abdominal pain (1) accompanied by diarrhea and/or constipation (1b, 1c, 2a, or 2b). Hence, satisfying the clinical criteria could also satisfy the Rome criteria, exclusive of any of the Manning criteria. The Manning symptoms are represented by 1a, 2c, 2d, and 2e. Thus, it would also be possible to meet the Rome criteria for IBS without the presence of altered bowel habit (diarrhea and/or constipation).

Empirical tests of the Rome criteria, in a fashion similar to the work of Manning et al. (1978) and Talley et al. (1986), have not, to the best of my knowledge, been reported. Such studies could solidify the value of the Rome criteria. Nevertheless, these criteria are the closest things there are to a gold standard and do represent a sound step in making research more comparable and a positive diagnosis more possible. *The authors of these criteria do recommend a physical examination, sigmoidoscopy, and blood assays for complete blood count and erythrocyte sedimentation rate. Probably, examination of a stool sample for parasites and occult blood would be wise.*

Clinical Hint

The procedures just described should have been performed for potential IBS patients by their physician before you, as a nonmedical therapist, begin treatment. This will prevent you from misapplying your psychological therapy.

ROME II CRITERIA

Although the Rome Criteria for IBS have not been rigorously tested empirically, a revision labeled as Rome II was recently published (Thompson, Longstreth, et al., 1999). Comparing Exhibit 1.4 to Exhibit 1.3, one can see that the Rome II criteria appear to be less restrictive than the original Rome criteria. Moreover, the strict inclusion of a number of the Manning criteria symptoms has been relaxed. Thus, the Rome II criteria could be reduced to the older clinical criteria (see Exhibit 1.1): Under Rome II, only abdominal discomfort or pain and altered bowel habit ("change in stool frequency and/or consistency" and "change in form or appearance of stool") are required for diagnosis. The list of supportive symptoms is helpful and includes some required symptoms of the Rome I criteria.

My complaint about these criteria is the same as raised earlier about the Rome criteria: To the best of my knowledge, no one has shown that IBS patients selected by Rome II criteria are different in important ways from patients selected by the clinical or Manning criteria. Future studies need to include patients with IBS diagnosed by clinical criteria who met Rome II criteria, as well as patients diagnosed by clinical criteria who failed to meet Rome II criteria. Comparison of these two groups on natural history, psychological morbidity, and treatment response would go a long way toward validating the criteria.

EXHIBIT 1.4
Rome II Criteria for Diagnosing IBS

At least 12 weeks, which need not be consecutive, in the preceding 12 months, of

1. Abdominal discomfort or pain
2. accompanied by two or more of the following:
   a. relieved by defecation
   b. onset associated with change in stool frequency and/or consistency
   c. onset associated with change in form or appearance of stool.

Supportive symptoms of the irritable bowel syndrome:

1. fewer than three bowel movements a week
2. more than three bowel movements a day
3. hard or lumpy stools
4. loose (mushy) or watery stools
5. straining during a bowel movement
6. urgency (having to rush to have a bowel movement)
7. feeling of incomplete bowel movement
8. passing mucus during a bowel movement
9. abdominal fullness, bloating, or swelling

2

THE MAGNITUDE OF THE PROBLEM

It has long been recognized by gastroenterologists and primary care physicians that IBS is a widespread disorder. Surveys of varying levels of methodological sophistication from the early 1980s, summarized in Table 2.1, yielded prevalence rates of 8% to 17% among American adults, with a value of 13.6% for a British sample. These early studies have a number of methodological difficulties, including nonrandom sampling (Drossman, Sandler, McKee, & Lovitz, 1982; Thompson & Heaton, 1980), reliance on an unstandardized questionnaire (Drossman et al., 1982), and reliance on answers to only two questions in a telephone survey (Whitehead, Winget, Fedoravicius, Wooley, & Blackwell, 1982). The diagnostic criteria were probably satisfactory in studies by Thompson and Heaton (1980) and Drossman et al. (1982) but relatively weak in that of Whitehead et al. (1982). Despite these shortcomings, these early studies showed three clear points: IBS is a widespread disorder, women are much more likely to have IBS than men (1.4 to 2.6 to 1), and most individuals with IBS do not seek medical help for it.

Use of Specialty Care

Another way of viewing the magnitude of the problem represented by IBS can be found in surveys of what kinds of patients are seen as outpatients by gastroenterologists. For example, Switz (1976) surveyed all of

TABLE 2.1
Summary of Results of Early Epidemiological Studies of IBS Prevalence

Authors	Sample Description	Method of Diagnosis	Results		
			% IBS	% Female	% Other
Thompson & Heaton, 1980	301 "apparently healthy participants" (54% female); 104 naval technicians and nurses (17–27); 97 clinic attendees for coronary artery disease (45–65); 100 elderly living in community flats (60–91). 14 refused; 96% compliance.	Standardized questionnaire administered by two gastroenterologists. Questions to tap Manning criteria—restricted to last year.	13.6	63 (IBS)	30.2% with a functional GI disorder
Drossman, Sandler, McKee, & Lovitz, 1982	789 non-health care seeking adults; 382 new students; 218 new employees; 189 second year medical students. 57.5% female; mean age, 24; 80% compliance; "young, White, middle-class."	Self-administered questionnaire alternating constipation; diarrhea, abdominal pain, and Manning criteria; and diarrhea or constipation.	17.1	72.6 (bowel dysfunction)	30% with bowel dysfunction; 85% of IBS group believed stress played a role in bowel symptoms
Whitehead, Winget, Fedoravicius, Wooley, & Blackwell, 1982	832 adults from Cincinnati, random sample. 41.3% completion; 25.7% actual refusal rate. 52.9% male, overrepresented unemployed and housebound, average age 50.	Telephone interview with 80 questions. IBS diagnosed if patient had abdominal pain and constipation or diarrhea often in the past year (very limited assessment).	8.0	58.2 (IBS)	More illness impact on life

the gastroenterologists in Virginia in 1973. He found that 19% of the diagnoses given by this group were functional GI disorders. Harvey, Salih, and Read (1983) reviewed the charts of 2,000 new patients referred to a British gastroenterology clinic over a 5-year period. They identified 888 (44.4%) of the patients as having functional disorders (absence of positive organic findings); 449 (22.5% of the total) of those had a diagnosis of IBS.

Finally, Mitchell and Drossman (1987) surveyed a 20% sample of the American Gastroenterological Association (*N* = 1,000) with a 70% rate of return. This large group of American specialists identified 41% of their patients as suffering from functional GI disorders; 28% were seen as having IBS. Thus, it is found repeatedly that functional GI disorders are very common, even in the practices of specialists, and that IBS probably accounts for 20% to 30% of new-patient visits to gastroenterologists with all of the diagnostic expense a new case may entail.

The Olmsted County Studies

Two more recent epidemiologic surveys, using stronger methodology, have been published in the last 10 years. One is the Olmsted County study by Talley, Zinsmeister, van Dyke, and Melton (1991). Talley et al. (1991) obtained an age- and sex-stratified sample (*N* = 1,021) of residents between the ages of 30 and 64, of Olmsted County, Minnesota, in the southern part of the state. They were sent a previously validated self-report questionnaire (Talley, Phillips, Melton, Wiltgen, & Zinsmeister, 1989) that identified GI symptoms experienced over the past year and functional GI disorders. Follow-up mail reminders were sent at 2, 4, and 7 weeks, and a telephone call was made at 10 weeks. Altogether, 835 participants (82%) returned usable surveys. There were no age or gender differences between respondents and nonrespondents. This sample thus represents a primarily middle-class, White, middle-aged population.

Overall, 68% of the sample had experienced at least one GI symptom in the past year: 26% reported abdominal pain more than 6 times per year, 17.9% reported chronic diarrhea, and 17.4% reported chronic constipation. Using the definition of IBS—presence of abdominal pain more than 6 times per year and two or more of the Manning criteria symptoms—Talley et al. (1991) found an overall prevalence of IBS of 17.0% (14.4–19.6; 95% confidence interval). Prevalence was greater for women than men (18.2% vs. 15.8%), although the 1.15 to 1 ratio was lower than commonly found. Of the 329 individuals with a functional GI disorder (39.4%), chronic constipation, chronic diarrhea, and/or IBS, only 14% (*n* = 46) had seen a physician in the past year because of GI symptoms. *Clearly, most of this sample suffered in silence.*

In a similar, but larger, study, Talley, Gabriel, Harmsen, Zinsmeister, and Evans (1995) surveyed 4,108 residents of Olmsted County between the ages of 20 and 95 using similar methodology. Excluded from the study were any who had a history of psychosis or dementia (n = 195), lived in a nursing home (n = 252), or had undergone major abdominal surgery or currently had organic medical disease (n = 236). Similar follow-ups were done and yielded a response rate of 74% (N = 3,022). All outpatient medical records were available from the Mayo Clinic.

They identified 17.7% as having IBS (using recurrent/abdominal pain and Manning criteria), whereas another 56.6% had some GI symptoms. Of those identified as having IBS, 41% were men (1.44 to 1) of an average age of 53, 69% were married, and 54% had education beyond high school. Those with IBS had median medical expenses (1992 CPI-corrected dollars) of $742 per year, as compared to $429 for those with no GI symptoms. Eliminating those with no medical charges (12%), the median per year medical costs were $893. As the authors noted, *this extrapolates to about $8 billion yearly in medical costs in the United States that are attributable to IBS.*

U.S. Householder Survey of Functional Gastrointestinal Disorders

The second recent epidemiologic stydy, and by far the most ambitious study of functional GI disorders including IBS, is that of Drossman et al. (1993). A random sample of 8,250 U.S. householders, stratified to be similar to the U.S. population according to geographic region, age, population density, and household size, was surveyed by questionnaire for 20 different functional GI disorders. The return rate was 65.8% (51% women; 96% White).

Overall, 69.3% (3,761) respondents acknowledged one or more functional GI disorders. IBS was diagnosed, using Rome criteria, in 606 individuals (11.2%), yielding a national estimate of 9.4%, about one-half of the rate reported by Talley et al. (1991). The gender ratio was 1.88 to 1, women to men. Another interesting finding of this survey was that an average of 13.4 days of work or school were missed in the past year because of the disorder. Finally, Drossman et al. (1993) reported that about 40% of those with IBS had seen a physician for GI problems.

What *is* the magnitude of the problem? The two best studies (Drossman et al., 1993; Talley et al., 1991) give noticeably different answers. Drossman et al. (1993) put the one-year prevalence rate at 9.4%, whereas Talley et al. (1991) placed it at 17.0%. This translates into a difference of 19 million to 34 million adults with IBS in the United States. Both numbers are large!

The difference could be due to population differences. The Olmsted County sample is all White and from the upper-Midwest with a restricted age range (30–64). The U.S. Householder sample was nationwide with a wider age range, but 95.5% was White. The Olmsted County survey had a slightly better return rate (82%) than the U.S. Householder survey

(66%). As best as I can tell, the same diagnostic criteria and essentially the same question format were used in both studies. Interestingly, the rate of functional GI symptoms was about the same in the two studies (68% in Olmsted County vs. 69.3% in U.S. Householder survey).

Regardless of the true answer, these reports make clear that IBS is a large-scale problem, affecting 19 to 34 million American adults, costing almost $10 billion in medical care costs annually, and leading to more than 250 million lost work or school days per year. To say the least, IBS has a sizable impact on American society, in addition to affecting many individuals.

Evidence for a Genetic Basis for IBS

Given the magnitude of the problem IBS represents both in terms of number of patients (in the millions in the U.S. alone) and the cost of their medical care (in the billions of dollars in the U.S.), a question of some interest is whether it is an inherited or genetically based disorder. A recent study from Australia by Morris-Yates, Talley, Boyce, Nandurkar, and Andrews (1998) has addressed this issue. Using data from an Australian twin registry (186 monozygotic and 157 dizygotic twin pairs), they assessed twins for FBD symptoms that caused them "a lot of trouble" and led them to seek medical attention. (Thus, the threshold for a symptom's being included was fairly high.) They found that 4.8% of each twin group had one or more functional GI symptoms, a low value from a population perspective. The low prevalence may be due to the high threshold for a symptom's being reported. Nevertheless, their analysis of the data led them to conclude that the heritability of FBD was 0.579; that is, about 58% of the variance is explained by genetic factors. However, there is no clear answer to the question of whether IBS is an inherited disorder, because data to make a diagnosis of IBS were not available. The present study is a fair approximation and does seem to indicate that functional GI symptoms, the underlying basis for IBS, do have a fair degree of heritability.

FOLLOW-UP STUDIES OF IBS

Given the magnitude of the IBS problem, a question of some interest is what happens to IBS patients over time or what is the natural history? This question is important because one would like to know what might happen to IBS patients if they received either no treatment or conservative medical treatment. If most IBS sufferers improve, or become symptom free over a follow-up interval, as one can find with phobia in children and adolescents (Agras, Chapin, & Oliveau, 1972), then one might consider not treating this group of patients and instead let nature take its course. It would also mean that the goal of treatment might be to speed up recovery. Alternatively, if most IBS patients are unchanged or worse over a follow-up interval, then the case for treating IBS patients is strengthened. A number of follow-up studies of IBS have been conducted over the years; they are summarized in Table 2.2.

With the exception of a recent large-scale study by Talley, Weaver, Zinsmeister, and Melton (1992), all of the follow-up studies were done outside of the United States, predominantly in the United Kingdom. Most were relatively long-term (about 5 years) and had the retrospective design of trying to reassess a set of IBS patients who had been carefully diagnosed and characterized in a GI specialty clinic many years earlier. An exception is the one- to two-year prospective follow-up study of 50 patients by Waller and Misiewicz (1969). Beyond this latter study's 100% follow-up rate (at 12 months), the average rate of follow-up has been about 82%—a remarkably good rate in my opinion.

The most interesting finding from these studies is that 24% to 57% of IBS patients 5 years later were unchanged or worse. In the two shorter term follow-ups (Talley et al., 1992; Waller & Misiewicz, 1969), about 13% of patients were essentially symptom free at a one-year follow-up. These studies deserve special comment. Waller and Misiewicz (1969) saw patients every 2 months for brief visits. This may have served as a form of supportive psychotherapy that could account for 48% reporting themselves as improved (36%) or symptom free (12%) and for the whole sample's reporting that they felt better and were better able to cope.

Talley et al. (1992) is a prospective follow-up of the Olmsted County epidemiological study described earlier. An attempt was made to contact the 835 initial respondents 12 to 14 months later. They received responses, after several prompts, from 690 of the original participants. Three things stand out in this large-scale study. First, this study was of the general population, not a treatment-seeking sample as in all of the other follow-up studies. Second, approximately 14% of those who met Manning criteria for IBS at Time 1, no longer met the criteria at Time 2. (Although Table 2.2 lists them as symptom free, this may not be correct and cannot be determined from the published results. It is known for certain only that they dropped below the threshold for diagnosis but could still have had some symptoms.) Third, it is of interest that some individuals who did not meet the criteria at Time 1 did meet criteria at Time 2, thus representing new cases. This amounted to the equivalent of 6% of those who initially met criteria for IBS. These new cases, added to the 86% who did not remit, meant that there was no significant difference in prevalence between the two points in time. It thus seems clear that IBS is a chronic disorder with naturally occurring exacerbations and remissions in addition to possible long-term treatment effects. All of the samples except Talley et al.'s Olmsted County sample were follow-ups of those in active treatment.

TABLE 2.2
Summary of Follow-up Studies of Natural History of IBS

	Sample description and selection							Results		
Authors and Country	*N*	% female	Age	IBS criteria selection	Length of follow-up	% followed	Method of follow-up	% symptom-free	% same or worse	Other
Waller & Misiewicz, 1969 (United Kingdom)	50	60	39 (18–65)	clinical—seen every 2 mo for brief visit in GI clinic	12–27 months	100	seen at clinic every 2 months	12	52	36% improved; most patients felt better and better able to cope.
Holmes & Salter, 1982 (United Kingdom)	91	58	57 (22–86)	clinical—follow up of GI clinic patients	6 yrs	84.6 (n = 77)	recalled to clinic	38	57	5% changed diagnosis.
Svendsen, Munck, & Andersen, 1983 (Denmark)	112	76	54 (19–84)	clinical—follow up of GI clinic patients	5 yrs	80.3 (n = 90)	questionnaire	N/R	49	51% felt improved; the unchanged, more likely had previous surgery.
Harvey, Mauad, & Brown, 1987 (United Kingdom)	104	56	40–50 (16–81)	Manning—follow up of GI clinic patients	5–8 yrs	88.5 (n = 92)	questionnaire	27	24	49% improved. Men were constipation-predominant and had shorter history associated with good outcome.
Fowlie, Eastwood, & Ford, 1992 (United Kingdom)	75	63	39	Manning—follow up of GI clinic patients	5 yrs	73 (n = 43)	questionnaire	N/R	35	65% improved; pain less in improved; no other GI symptom difference; improved were less anxious initially.
Talley, Weaver, Zinsmeister, & Melton, 1992 (United States)	835	Age and sex stratified for Olmsted County, MN (30–64)		Manning—random sample	14 months	83 (n = 690)	questionnaire at initial and follow-up	14	86	About 6% new cases in the year; "complainers" more likely to emerge; women more likely to disappear.

Although in the Albany studies, we have never conducted a long-term natural history follow-up of IBS patients, we do have some interesting data on short-term variation for untreated patients who have been assessed and who kept a GI symptom diary while awaiting treatment over a 3- to 4-month interval (in a wait-list condition). The results for this intensive short-term follow-up condition in the Albany studies are presented in Table 2.3.

One can see that if patients are actively awaiting treatment and are monitoring GI symptoms daily, a small average reduction may be seen in the level of diary-validated symptoms (about 5%). Moreover, about 15% of patients make a substantial recovery from IBS from active monitoring alone. Interestingly, the largest fraction of a wait-list sample to improve by at least 50% occurred with the largest sample (Blanchard, Schwarz, et al., 1992, Study 2); in this instance almost one third of the sample showed substantial improvement.

TABLE 2.3
Short-term Follow-up of Symptom Monitoring Controls from the Albany Treatment Studies

			Results for untreated control participants	
Study	Sample size	Active treatment conditions	average CPSR score reduction	% of sample improved
Neff & Blanchard, 1987	9	cognitive–behavioral package	15.4	11
Blanchard, Schwarz, et al., 1992 (Study 1)	10	cognitive–behavioral package, psychological placebo	9.5	20
Blanchard, Schwarz, et al., 1992 (Study 2)	31	cognitive–behavioral package, psychological placebo	6.4	32
Blanchard, Greene, Scharff, & Schwarz-McMorris, 1993	8	relaxation training	−1.4	13
Greene & Blanchard, 1994	10	cognitive therapy	2.0	10
Payne & Blanchard, 1995	10	cognitive therapy, psychoeducation	10.0	10
Vollmer & Blanchard, 1998	10	cognitive therapy	−4.0	10
			5.4 (mean)	15.1% (mean)

Note. CPSR = Composite Primary Symptom Reduction (see chapter 4). It represents roughly the percent reduction in primary GI symptoms of IBS. Patients are labeled as improved if CPSR score equals 50 or greater.

Speculation

It may be that carefully attending to one's GI symptoms and the other things happening in one's day-to-day affairs may lead some IBS patients to identify triggers for attacks and lead them to some self-initiated behavior change. There is no research on this point to the best of my knowledge.

Clinical Hint

If you are overextended and cannot begin treatment with an IBS patient right away, the data summarized in Table 2.3 suggest that a small fraction of patients, who are asked to monitor GI symptoms daily, may improve noticeably from this activity alone. Thus, the short-term follow-up data echo Talley et al.'s (1992) one-year data: Some IBS patients do improve without treatment in the short term and also in the long term. I say again, IBS is a chronic disorder with a variable course over time.

3

TAKING THE IBS HISTORY

As was made clear in Chapter 1, the diagnosis of IBS is primarily based upon the patient's history and presenting symptoms. The nonphysician therapist will need to work in close collaboration with a physician so that the appropriate physical examination and laboratory studies can be performed to rule out other explanations (e.g., organic diseases) for the symptom picture. Suggestions for the minimal laboratory studies are given on page 11.

Clinical Hint

Your collaborating physician may be able to spare the IBS patient the financial costs and the stress of repeating many laboratory tests if he or she can obtain previous medical records. The patient *will probably* have to undergo some level of laboratory testing under certain circumstances: (a) if the symptoms are of relatively recent onset (less than 6 months) and do not represent the return of a previous bout of similar GI symptoms; (b) if the symptom picture has changed appreciably from the patient's usual GI symptoms; (c) if the patient is passing blood in the fecal material (either dark, tarry stools or some bright red blood is evident on the toilet paper).

In this chapter, I present the detailed Albany IBS History. I felt it was better to include it here in the chapter, rather than in an appendix. It has three parts: I. The detailed history and description of GI symptoms, II. A fairly elaborate psychosocial history and description of current psychosocial functioning and potential problem areas, III. A brief mental status examination. We used the entire history in our research. Clinician readers may want to omit the mental status examination in favor of their own version of it.

The GI symptom history is designed to permit one to make either a clinical diagnosis (Exhibit 1.1) or a Rome criteria diagnosis (Exhibit 1.3) of IBS once one is certain that competing organic diagnoses have been ruled out. Care is taken to obtain a fairly full description of each symptom and to conduct a behavioral analysis for antecedents and consequences (i.e., what situational factors precede the onset of a symptom and what happened after the symptom began) of each symptom. The latter can be helpful in the cognitive–behavioral therapy (CBT) treatment (Chapter 17) or in the pure cognitive therapy approach to treatment (Chapter 18).

The Psychosocial History starts by covering the history of GI disorders and diseases in the extended family. It addresses potential problem areas in the patient's daily life (i.e., relationships with peers, coworkers, classmates, and spouse or significant other; performance problems at work, home, or school). These areas are assessed to gain a picture of how the patient is functioning and where the problems and stresses in his or her life are. This latter portion of the Psychosocial History was designed to elicit material for use in the CBT, especially the focus on developing coping strategies for stressful situations.

The third section is a brief mental status examination. As noted on the interview schedule, if one plans a more detailed psychological or psychiatric evaluation as part of the total assessment (see Chapter 7) of the patient, this part could be omitted.

Clinical Hint

As you read through the history, you can see that it goes from direct questions about GI symptoms—the reason the patient is being evaluated—to how IBS affects the patient's life, and then into other related psychosocial factors such as family history. There is a bit more of a shift when the mental status examination begins and the patient is alerted to the shift of focus. I have never had a patient balk at answering any of these questions and attribute that to the order in which various parts are asked.

Clearly, one can use any or all parts of the Albany IBS History for assessment. The form is also set up to make it easy for one to code the data and enter it into a computerized data base. This was done because of my research interest in IBS. Even if one is not interested in assembling such data, the information from the interview should provide a good, comprehensive history.

In the Psychosocial History section, reference is made to several cards to be given to the patient. Samples of these are given at the end of this chapter as Exhibits 3.1, 3.2, 3.3, and 3.4. We have found that having the answer options in front of the patient speeds up the interview because we do not have to take the time to repeat them after each question. We also realize that we have constrained answers somewhat by forcing the patient to use our categories.

In our experience, this complete IBS history takes about 45 minutes. We believe it is a good first step in the total assessment of the IBS patient because it starts the assessment with a focus on the presenting GI problems that brought the patient to you. Later chapters cover psychological testing (Chapter 5), psychiatric status (Chapter 7), and psychophysiological testing (Chapter 10). Information gleaned from this interview can be used in conjunction with information supplied by the patient's physician, using the Physician Evaluation Form (Exhibit 1.2), to gain a more thorough assessment of the patient's need for therapy.

THE ALBANY IBS HISTORY

General Coding:
1 = Yes; 0 = No; Blank = Missing Data; 8 = Don't Know; 9 = Does not apply

Physical Factors

(1) When did GI distress first become a problem?

No. years ______

(2) When did you first seek medical attention for abdominal problems?

No. years ______

(3) Which of the following medical professionals have you consulted about your problem?

Family physician 1 = yes, 0 = no ______

Internist 1 = yes, 0 = no ______

OB/GYN 1 = yes, 0 = no ______

Gastroenterologist 1 = yes, 0 = no ______

Other 1 = yes, 0 = no ______

(4) What kinds of diagnostic tests have you been given?

Upper GI series (barium swallow) 1 = yes, 0 = no ______

Lower GI series (barium enema) 1 = yes, 0 = no ______

Abdominal X-rays 1 = yes, 0 = no ______

Gall-bladder series 1 = yes, 0 = no ______

Sigmoidoscopy 1 = yes, 0 = no ______

Colonoscopy 1 = yes, 0 = no ______

Negative lactose tolerance test 1 = yes, 0 = no ______

Neg. response to lactose-free diet 1 = yes, 0 = no ______

Neg. stool for ova and parasites 1 = yes, 0 = no ______

Neg. stool for occult blood 1 = yes, 0 = no ______

Other ____________________ 1 = yes, 0 = no ______

(5) Have any of your IBS symptoms ever caused you to see a physician?

1 = yes, 0 = no ______

(6) Approximate date first saw a physician for IBS symptoms: ______________

(7) Have any of your IBS symptoms ever caused you to take prescription medication?

1 = yes, 0 = no ______

(8) What? ______________________________

(9) When were they first prescribed? ______________________________

(10) Have any of your IBS symptoms ever caused you to take nonprescription (over-the-counter) medications?

1 = yes, 0 = no ______

(11) For which symptoms?

____

____

(12) What medication(s) have been *prescribed* for your IBS symptoms?

	Name of drug	Taken in the past	Currently taking
Minor tranquilizers/anxiolytics			
Antidepressants			
Analgesics			
Antispasmodics			
Anticholinergics			
Antidiarrheals			
Other (list)			

(13) What nonprescription medication(s) have you taken for IBS?

	Name of drug	Taken in the past	Currently taking
Analgesics (aspirin, Tylenol, etc.)			
Enemas			
Bulk agents			
Antacids			
Antidiarrheals			
Fiber supplements (Metamucil)			
Other (list)			

Gastrointestinal Symptom Questionnaire

From what you have told us thus far, we believe you have a disorder that is called irritable bowel syndrome, or IBS for short. People who suffer from IBS may have a wide array of symptoms. For this reason, I want to ask you a series of questions about your possible gastrointestinal (GI) symptoms.

I. PAIN

First I want to ask about pain in your abdominal region, that is, from the area below your chest or rib cage.

1. Do you *frequently* have abdominal pain?

   1 = yes, 0 = no ______

2. (If no) if you do not have pain, do you frequently have abdominal discomfort or abdominal tenderness?

   1 = yes, 0 = no ______

3. (If no to 2) do you *occasionally* have abdominal pain, or discomfort or tenderness?

   1 = yes, 0 = no ______

(If no to 3, then patient does not have IBS. Go to II Altered Bowel Function.)

4. Depending upon the patient's term (i.e., pain, discomfort, tenderness), use his or her term for all of the next questions.

Over the last year, how often was abdominal pain present? (Check one)

Constant ______

Daily ______

Weekly ______

Monthly ______

Other ______

Over the last *2 weeks*, on about how many days was abdominal pain present?

No. of days ______

On about how many days was abdominal pain a problem?

No. of days ______

Now, ever since you have had IBS, about how frequently has abdominal pain been a problem? (Have patient give an estimate of the percent of time.)

% of time ______

5. Does the abdominal pain ever awaken you from sleep?

1 = yes, 0 = no ______

(If yes) about how often? ______________________________

6. Does your abdominal pain usually occur in a specific location?

1 = yes, 0 = no ______

7. (If yes) can you (show me) (point to) where it generally occurs? (Record location)

____

8. Does it also occur regularly anywhere else? (Record location)

____

9. (If no) is there some area where it is more likely to occur?

1 = yes, 0 = no ______

10. (If yes) please show me where? (Record location)

____

11. Has the location of the pain changed at all over the past year?

1 = yes, 0 = no ______

12. (If yes) describe how that occurred. ______________________________

13. Is your abdominal pain fairly *constant*? 1 = yes, 0 = no ______

Or does it come and go? 1 = yes, 0 = no ______

14. (If constant) are there times when the pain disappears?

1 = yes, 0 = no ______

15. (If no) is the pain with you almost all of the time?

1 = yes, 0 = no ______

16. Does it fluctuate in severity?

1 = yes, 0 = no ______

17. How? Describe ______________________________

____

____

18. How intense is your abdominal pain usually? (Check one)

Mild ______

Moderate ______

Severe ______

Debilitating ______

What is the worst pain of any kind you ever experienced? ______________

____

19. Compared to the worst pain you have experienced [call it 100]:

(a) how severe is your usual abdominal pain? ______

(b) how severe was the worst abdominal pain you can remember? ______

20. (If yes) what kinds of things seem to lead to the pain's becoming less or disappearing?

Psychological event ______

Physical event ______

Both psychological and physical ______

Nothing ______

Don't know ______

21. (If intermittent) for the last 2 weeks, about how many hours per day did you have noticeable pain?

No. hours ______

22. What kinds of things seem to cause the pain to begin? ______________

____

____

(CHECK FOR THESE POSSIBLE TRIGGERS)

Does the pain *sometimes* or *regularly* start shortly after you eat a normal meal?

____

____

Does the pain *sometimes* or *regularly* start shortly after you eat certain specific foods?

1 = yes, 0 = no ______

Describe. ______________________________________

____

Does the pain *sometimes* or *regularly* start

after you have had a stressful situation? 1 = yes, 0 = no ______

or had to rush too hurriedly? 1 = yes, 0 = no ______

or do things which were unpleasant? 1 = yes, 0 = no ______

23. What kinds of things seem to relieve the pain? ______________________

____

____

24. Does having a bowel movement *usually* or *occasionally* relieve the pain?

1 = yes, 0 = no ______

Do you take any medicine to relieve the pain? 1 = yes, 0 = no ______

Does the pain seem to ease on its own over time? 1 = yes, 0 = no ______

If yes, how long? Duration ______

25. When you have abdominal pain, do you ever notice that you may need several bowel movements before the pain is relieved?

1 = yes, 0 = no ______

Describe ____

____

26. (If bowel movement relieves pain) when you have a bowel movement that relieves abdominal pain, does it tend to be:

relatively hard and well formed ______

soft and not well formed ______

loose and watery ______

pellet-like (little small pellets) ______

27. Does your abdominal [pain] ever interfere in your life or cause you to avoid activities?

1 = yes, 0 = no ______

Elaborate ____

____

28. For women only—is your abdominal pain at all related to your menstrual cycle?

1 = yes, 0 = no ______

29. Do you ever get cramps or pain associated with your menstrual cycle?

1 = yes, 0 = no ______

30. Is this menstrual pain different than IBS pain?

1 = yes, 0 = no ______

Elaborate ____

____

II. ALTERED BOWEL FUNCTION

1. For the last 2 weeks, about how many bowel movements do you have per day? ______

   If very irregular, what is the range of daily BMs over the last 2 weeks? ______

2. Is the pattern over the past two weeks fairly typical for you and your IBS?

   1 = yes, 0 = no ______

3. (If no) what is the more typical pattern? ______________________________

   ____

   ____

(Probe to see if patient alternates between periods of frequent BMs or diarrhea and periods of infrequent BMs or constipation.)

4. Has this pattern changed over the course of your IBS?

   1 = yes, 0 = no ______

   How? ____

   ____

   ____

III. DIARRHEA

1. Do you ever suffer from diarrhea? Is that a big part of your IBS?

   1 = yes, 0 = no ______

2. (If yes) about how often (how many days per week) have you had diarrhea over the past two weeks?

   No. of days ______

3. Is this fairly typical of your IBS over its lifetime course?

   1 = yes, 0 = no ______

4. (If no) how is it different? ______________________________

   ____

5. Different people describe diarrhea differently (everyone has different definitions). When you have diarrhea, what do you mean? ________________

____

Soft, semiformed bowel movements ______

Frequent, small bowel movements ______

Loose, watery stools ______

Passage of gas, mucus, and liquid with little solid stool ______

6. Do you take anything or do anything to try to stop the diarrhea?

1 = yes, 0 = no ______

7. (If yes) what? ____

8. Are there any things regularly associated with diarrhea? (Certain foods, eating too much, abdominal pain, stress, etc.)

1 = yes, 0 = no ______

____

9. Do you ever have a sudden strong urge to have a bowel movement?

1 = yes, 0 = no ______

10. (If yes) is this usually accompanied

by pain? 1 = yes, 0 = no ______

or by diarrhea? 1 = yes, 0 = no ______

Describe ____

____

11. About how often does this occur? ____________________________

12. Have you ever had an accident where you soiled your underclothes because of sudden, strong urges to defecate?

1 = yes, 0 = no ______

13. (If yes) about how often has this occurred in the last year? ______

14. (If hasn't occurred in last year) about how many times in the past 5 years?

______

15. Have you had a lot of close calls?

1 = yes, 0 = no ______

16. (If yes) do you take special precautions to avoid a repeat of the accident (i.e., not eating)?

1 = yes, 0 = no ______

17. (If yes) do you avoid situations where a toilet is not available (generally restrict activities, etc.)? ______

Psychological event ______

Physical event ______

Both psychological and physical ______

Nothing ______

Don't know ______

IV. CONSTIPATION

1. Do you ever suffer from constipation?

   1 = yes, 0 = no ______

2. (If yes) about how many days were you constipated over the past 2 weeks?

   No. days ______

3. Is this typical of your IBS over its lifetime course?

   1 = yes, 0 = no ______

4. (If no) how is it different? ______

   ______

5. Different people describe constipation differently. When you are constipated what do you mean? ______

   ______

   Go for 1 day with no bowel movement 1 = yes, 0 = no ______

   Go for 2 days with no bowel movement 1 = yes, 0 = no ______

   Go for 3 or more days with no bowel movement 1 = yes, 0 = no ______

   Do you have very hard bowel movements? 1 = yes, 0 = no ______

6. Do you ever have the sense after a bowel movement, that you were unable to pass all of the fecal matter or that you did not really finish the emptying?

   1 = yes, 0 = no ______

7. (If yes) how often does this happen?

   How often ______

8. About what percentage of time does this happen?

   % time ______

9. Do you ever have to strain, or try to force the feces out, in order to have a bowel movement?

   1 = yes, 0 = no ______

10. (If yes) about what percentage of time does this happen?

% time ______

11. Do you take anything (such as laxatives, bulk agents, fiber, etc.) or do anything to counteract constipation?

1 = yes, 0 = no ______

12. (If yes) what do you do and how often? ______________________________

____

How often ______________________________________

13. Are there any things regularly associated with constipation? (Certain foods, eating too much, abdominal pain or tenderness or bloating, stress, etc.).

1 = yes, 0 = no ______

14. (If yes) describe ______________________________________

15. Do you ever have times when you feel as if you should have a bowel movement and sit on the toilet for awhile but nothing happens?

1 = yes, 0 = no ______

16. (If yes) elaborate ______________________________________

____

V. BLOATING

1. Do you ever have feelings of being bloated, or excessively/uncomfortably full, or that your abdomen is enlarged or protruding?

1 = yes, 0 = no ______

2. (If yes) over the last 2 weeks, how many days were you bloated? ______

3. Now, ever since you have had IBS, about what percentage of time has bloating been a problem?

% time ______

4. How severe is the bloating as its worst?

Mild ______

Moderate ______

Severe ______

Debilitating ______

5. Does the bloating ever cause you to forgo activities?

1 = yes, 0 = no ______

6. (If yes) what? ______________________________________

7. Is bloating associated with particular events? 1 = yes, 0 = no ______

Psychological event ______

Physical event ______

Both psychological and physical ______

Nothing ______

Don't know ______

8. *Borborygmi* (How about gurgling noises? Can you hear them?)

1 = yes, 0 = no ______

9. As part of your bloating, do you ever notice audible sounds from your abdomen?

1 = yes, 0 = no ______

10. Do you notice them at other times? 1 = yes, 0 = no ______

Elaborate. ______________________________

____

11. Can other people hear these bowel sounds (borborygmi)?

1 = yes, 0 = no ______

12. Have you felt embarrassed because of these bowel sounds occurring when you were with others?

1 = yes, 0 = no ______

13. Or avoided activities because of them? 1 = yes, 0 = no ______

Elaborate. ______________________________

____

14. How intense of a problem are borborygmi?

Mild ______

Moderate ______

Severe ______

Debilitating ______

15. About how often do you have audible bowel sounds?

How often? ______

VI. FLATULENCE

1. Do you ever pass gas as a part of your IBS? This is called flatulence.

1 = yes, 0 = no ______

2. (If yes) over the last 2 weeks, on about how many days were you flatulent?

No. days ______

3. As a general part of your IBS, what percent of time is flatulence a problem?

% time ______

4. How severe is your problem with flatulence?

Mild ______

Moderate ______

Severe ______

Debilitating ______

5. What factors are associated with an increase in flatulence? (Certain foods, stress, etc.)

Elaborate. ______________________________

____

6. Have you ever had an accident and soiled your underwear when passing gas?

1 = yes, 0 = no ______

Elaborate. ______________________________

____

7. Have you ever been embarrassed because of flatulence?

1 = yes, 0 = no ______

8. Do you avoid any activities because of potential flatulence?

1 = yes, 0 = no ______

Elaborate. ______________________________

____

VII. BELCHING

1. Do you ever belch or burp as part of your IBS?

1 = yes, 0 = no ______

2. (If yes) over the last 2 weeks, on about how many days was belching noticeable?

No. days ______

3. As a general part of your IBS, what percent of time is belching a problem?

% time ______

4. How severe is your problem with belching?

Mild ______

Moderate ______

Severe ______

Debilitating ______

5. What factors are associated with an increase in belching? ______

______

______

6. Have you ever been embarrassed because of belching?

1 = yes, 0 = no ______

Elaborate. ______

______

7. Do you avoid activities because of potential belching?

1 = yes, 0 = no ______

Elaborate. ______

______

VIII. NAUSEA AND VOMITING

1. Do you ever experience nausea (feeling sick and as if you might vomit or throw up)?

1 = yes, 0 = no ______

2. (If yes) is nausea a part of your IBS?

1 = yes, 0 = no ______

3. (If yes to 2) over the last 2 weeks, on about how many days was nausea present?

No. days ______

4. As a general part of your IBS, what percent of time is nausea a problem?

% of time ______

5. How severe is your problem with nausea?

Mild ______

Moderate ______

Severe ______

Debilitating ______

6. Is your nausea associated with any particular foods, beverages, or activities?

1 = yes, 0 = no ______

Elaborate. ______________________________

____

7. Do you ever vomit when you feel nauseous?

1 = yes, 0 = no ______

8. About how many times have you vomited in the last year?

No. times ______

9. In general, how severe is your problem with vomiting?

Mild ______

Moderate ______

Severe ______

Debilitating ______

IX. OTHER SYMPTOMS

1. Do you frequently have a low-grade or higher fever?

1 = yes, 0 = no ______

How often? ______

2. Do you frequently feel very tired and lethargic because of IBS, even when you have not been exercising?

1 = yes, 0 = no ______

How often? ______

3. Have you gained or lost weight, without dieting, over the past year?

1 = yes, 0 = no ______

How many lbs.? ______

4. Have you ever had dark, somewhat tarry-looking stools?

1 = yes, 0 = no ______

5. Have you ever noticed bright red blood in the toilet or on toilet paper after wiping yourself?

1 = yes, 0 = no ______

6. (If yes) do you know the cause? ______________________

Psychological event ______

Physical event ______

Both psychological and physical ______

Nothing ______

Don't know ______

X. OTHER—INTERFERENCE WITH LIFE

1. Have any of your IBS symptoms ever caused you to miss work or school?

1 = yes, 0 = no ______

2. About how many days over the last year?

Days/last year ______

Last 2 years? ______

3. Have any of your IBS symptoms ever interfered in your social or family life?

1 = yes, 0 = no ______

Avoid activities ______

Alter schedules ______

Avoid foods, etc. ______

Elaborate ______________________________________

____

4. How would your life be different without IBS? Elaborate. ______________

____

5. Overall degree of interference (Interviewer Rating)

1. None–very mild ______

2. Mild–noticeable ______

3. Moderate ______

4. Severe ______

5. Debilitating ______

Part 2—Psychosocial Factors in IBS

Reinforcing Factors

(1) Does your GI problem frequently prevent you from engaging in certain activities?

1 = yes, 0 = no ______

Using the following scale to answer the next 3 questions: (Give client Card #1)

1 = don't know
2 = know, but don't comment
3 = express concern, offer no help
4 = express concern, offer help
5 = don't express concern, don't offer help

(2) How do members of your family respond to your problems? ______

(3) How do coworkers respond? ______

(4) How do close friends respond? ______

(5) Would your life be significantly different if you never had this GI problem?

1 = yes, 0 = no ______

Family History of Gastrointestinal Disorders

Use the following code for this section: (Give client Card #2)

1 = IBS or IBS-like symptoms
2 = Ileitis/Crohn's Disease
3 = Ulcerative colitis
4 = Gall bladder disease
5 = Ulcers (gastric or intestinal)
6 = Cancer (stomach/esophagus)
7 = Cancer (intestinal tract)
8 = Don't know
9 = Does not apply

Relative	Type of problem
Mother	
Father	
Brother 1	
Brother 2	
Brother 3	
Sister 1	
Sister 2	

Sister 3	
Maternal grandmother	
Maternal grandfather	
Paternal grandmother	
Paternal grandfather	
Maternal aunt 1	
Maternal aunt 2	
Paternal aunt 1	
Paternal aunt 2	
Maternal uncle 1	
Maternal uncle 2	
Paternal uncle 1	
Paternal uncle 2	
Son 1	
Son 2	
Son 3	
Daughter 1	
Daughter 2	
Daughter 3	

Relations with Others

I am going to read you a series of situations. I want you to rate how accurately each statement describes you. Use the following scale: *1 = not very descriptive of you* ranging to *5 = very descriptive of you.* (Give client Card #3).

(1) Do you find it difficult to make decisions? ______

(2) Can you be openly critical of others' ideas, opinions, or behavior? ______

(3) Do you often avoid people or situations for fear of embarrassment? ______

(4) Do you usually have confidence in your own judgment? ______

(5) Are you prone to "fly off the handle?" ______

(6) Do you generally express what you feel? ______

(7) Are you able to ask your friends for small favors or help? ______

(8) Are you able to refuse requests made by a friend if you do not wish to do what the person is asking? ______

(9) Do you say "I'm sorry" a good deal of the time when you do not really mean it? ______

(10) Do you usually keep your opinions to yourself? ______

(11) Considering the above items, what overall rating would you give yourself regarding your ability to comfortably perform these various items? (*Scale: 1 = very comfortable* to *5 = not very comfortable*) ______

Marital or Significant Other Problems

(1) How long have you been married (or been seeing __) No. years ______

(2) I'm going to read a list of problems to you. I want you to rate each for the extent to which you judge it to be a problem and if a problem, how long the problem has existed. Use a 5-point scale for the ratings where: *1 = the item is not a problem* and *5 = the item is a significant problem.* (Give client Card #4)

Problem	Severity Rating	How Long Existed?
Money		
Communication		
In-laws		
Sex		
Religion		
Recreation		
Household duties and responsibilities		
Friends		
Alcohol and drugs		
Children		
Jealousy		
Others (please list)		

(3) In what areas are you and your spouse/significant other most compatible?

____

____

(4) In what areas are you most incompatible? ______________________________

____

(5) Give examples of things that your spouse (significant other) does that you like most.

____

____

(6) Give examples of things that your spouse (significant other) does that you dislike most.

____

____

(7) Overall, how would you rate your marriage or relationship?

1 = very good and 5 = very bad ______

Child-rearing or Parenting

(1) Please give me the first name and age of each of your children.

Name	Age

(Interviewer indicate total number of children) ______

(2) Do you feel that any of your children have special problems or are difficult to manage?

1 = yes, 0 = no ______

(3) If yes, which one(s) and why? ______________________

____

____

____

(4) For this child (or these children) please give your rating of the extent of the problem for each item below, on the same scale we used earlier (*1 = not a problem* and *5 = a significant problem*); also, indicate the duration of the problem. (Refer again to Card #4).

	Rating	How Long?
Temper tantrums	______	______
Bed wetting (after toilet trained)	______	______
Talking back	______	______
Discipline	______	______
School work	______	______
Not minding	______	______
Others (please list)		
______________	______	______
______________	______	______

(5) What do you like most about this child (or these children)?

____

(6) What do you like least about this child (or these children)?

____

____

(7) Overall, how would you rate your capabilities as a parent?

1 = very capable and 5 = very incapable ______

(8) Overall, how would you rate your relationship with your children?

1 = very good and 5 = very bad ______

Inquire if client works full-time, part-time, or is a student. If the client works, continue with the following section; if a student, either full or part-time, proceed to School and School-Related Problems, page 46.

Work and Work-Related Problems

(1) Do you have a job at present? 1 = yes, 0 = no ______

(2) What are your main responsibilities at your job? ______________

____

(3) How long have you worked at this job? No. years ______

(4) I'm going to describe to you some situations or matters that are related to work. I want you to rate the extent to which you consider each to be a problem for you and if a problem, how long the problem has been going on. Use scale where *1 = not a problem* and *5 = a significant problem*. (Again refer to scale on Card #4.)

	Rating	How Long?
Relationship with your boss	______	______
Relationship with coworkers	______	______
Pace and schedule at work	______	______
Feelings of pressure or too much to do	______	______

(5) What about your job do you like most? ______________________________

____

(6) What about your job do you dislike most? ______________________________

____

(7) Overall, rate how satisfied you are with your job on the scale where *1 = very satisfied* and *5 = very dissatisfied.*

(8) Would your job history be different if you did not have a GI problem?

1 = yes, 0 = no ______

How so? ____

(9) How many days of work did you miss this past year because of GI problems?

No. days ______

(10) How often did you leave work early this past year because of GI problems?

No. days ______

(11) How often did you arrive late at work this past year because of GI problems?

No. days ______

School and School-Related Problems (use if a full or part-time student)

(1) Are you enrolled in school at present? 1 = yes, 0 = no ______

(2) Part-time: 1 = yes, 0 = no ______

No. Credits ______

(3) Full-time: 1 = yes, 0 = no ______

No. Credits ______

(4) What are your main responsibilities at school? ______________________________

____

(5) How long have you been enrolled in school? No. years ______

(6) I'm going to describe to you some situations or matters that are related to school. I want you to rate the extent to which you consider each to be a problem for you and if a problem, how long the problem has been going on. Use scale where *1 = not a problem* and *5 = a significant problem.* (Again, refer to scale on Card #4.)

	Rating	How Long?
Relationship with your supervisor	______	______
Relationship with other students	______	______
Pace and schedule at school	______	______
Feelings of pressure or too much to do	______	______

(7) What about school do you like most? ________________________

(8) What about school do you dislike most? ________________________

(9) Overall, rate how satisfied you are with school on the scale where *1 = very satisfied* and *5 = very dissatisfied.* ______

(10) Would your educational history be different if you did not have a GI problem?

1 = yes, 0 = no ______

How? ____

(11) How many days of school did you miss this past year because of GI problems?

No. days ______

(12) How often did you leave school early this past year because of GI problems?

No. days ______

(13) How often did you arrive late at school this past year because of GI problems?

No. days ______

Maladaptive Cognitions

(1) Do you feel that you spend a great deal of time worrying?

1 = yes, 0 = no ______

(2) Can you stop the worrying if you want to?

1 = yes, 0 = no ______

(3) Do you feel tense or anxious most of the time?

1 = yes, 0 = no ______

(4) Do you feel depressed much of the time?

1 = yes, 0 = no ______

(5) Do you feel angry most of the time?

1 = yes, 0 = no ______

(6) If yes to any of these questions, what do you feel is causing you to feel this way?

____

____

Daily Schedule of Activities

(1) How effective are you at accomplishing things that you want to do?

(Scale *1 = very effective* and *5 = not very effective*) ______

(2) How pressured do you feel to accomplish things?

(Scale *1 = very unpressured* and *5 = very pressured*) ______

(3) If you had a choice, would you try to accomplish more or less during a typical week?

(Scale *1 = more* and *0 = less*) ______

(4) Do you frequently set "hard to meet" deadlines for accomplishing various things?

(Scale *1 = rarely/not at all* and *5 = very frequently*) ______

(5) Do you find that you regularly take on more than you can accomplish?

(Scale *1 = rarely/not at all* and *5 = very frequently*) ______

(6) Interviewer makes a determination of the extent of involvement of over-scheduling, etc.

(Scale *1 = not a problem* and *5 = significant problem*) ______

Part 3—Brief Mental Status Examination

(Optional if Structured Psychiatric Evaluation to be conducted)

These next few questions are somewhat different from the previous questions.

(1) What is today's date?

1 = correct response
0 = incorrect response ______

(2) What is the day of the week?

1 = correct response
0 = incorrect response ______

(3) Do you remember my name?

1 = correct response
0 = incorrect response ______

(4) I am going to say some numbers; listen carefully, then repeat them back to me. (Interviewer gives digits approximately one/second; do not repeat digits.)

(a) 5-8-2

1 = correct response
0 = incorrect response ______

(b) 6-9-4

1 = correct response
0 = incorrect response ______

(c) 6-4-3-9

1 = correct response
0 = incorrect response ______

(d) 7-2-8-6

1 = correct response
0 = incorrect response ______

(e) 4-2-7-3-1

1 = correct response
0 = incorrect response ______

(f) 7-5-8-3-6

1 = correct response
0 = incorrect response ______

(5) Who is the President of the U.S.?

1 = correct response
0 = incorrect response ______

(6) Who is the Governor of New York?

1 = correct response
0 = incorrect response ______

(7) Have you ever had any strange experiences?

1 = yes, 0 = no ______

(8) Have you ever heard things other people could not hear or heard things when no one was there?

1 = yes, 0 = no ______

(9) Have you ever seen things that other people could not see?

1 = yes, 0 = no ______

(10) Do you believe you have special powers?

1 = yes, 0 = no ______

(11) Have you ever felt or thought people were out to get you?

1 = yes, 0 = no ______

Mental History

(1) Have you ever received any psychiatric or psychological treatment for mental or emotional problems?

1 = yes, 0 = no ______

(2) If yes to #1, obtain brief details including current treatment status.

____

____

____

(3) Have you ever had any major illness or operations?

1 = yes, 0 = no ______

(4) If yes to #3, obtain details. ______________________________

____

____

(5) Have you ever been very depressed?

1 = yes, 0 = no ______

(6) If yes to #5, are you depressed now?

1 = yes, 0 = no ______

(7) If yes to #6, check for details (especially suicidal ideation). ______________

____

____

(7) Have you ever been really "speeded up," had a great deal of energy, and didn't need sleep?

1 = yes, 0 = no ______

(9) Have you ever had a problem with alcohol?

1 = yes, 0 = no ______

(10) Have you ever had a problem with drugs?

1 = yes, 0 = no ______

Are there any things we have not covered that you feel are important to your GI symptoms?

EXHIBIT 3.1
IBS HISTORY—CARD #1

1 = don't know
2 = know, but don't comment
3 = express concern, offer no help
4 = express concern, offer help
5 = don't express concern, offer help

EXHIBIT 3.2
IBS HISTORY—CARD #2

1 = IBS or IBS-like symptoms
2 = ileitis/Crohn's Disease
3 = ulcerative colitis
4 = gall bladder disease
5 = ulcers (gastric or intestinal)
6 = cancer (stomach/esophagus)
7 = cancer (intestinal tract)
8 = "don't know"
9 = does not apply

EXHIBIT 3.3
IBS HISTORY—CARD #3

1	2	3	4	5
Not very descriptive of me				Very descriptive of me

EXHIBIT 3.4
IBS HISTORY—CARD #4

1	2	3	4	5
Item is not a problem				Item is a significant problem

4

THE GI SYMPTOM DIARY: HOW TO TELL IF THE PATIENT IS IMPROVING

After taking a detailed history from the potential IBS patient to confirm the diagnosis, the next step in the assessment procedures is to have the patient begin to keep a daily diary in which levels of GI symptoms are recorded. Although one can gain some sense of how the patient's IBS symptoms fluctuate over time from the history, the best way to determine this is with a prospectively gathered symptom diary. I recommend gathering at least two weeks' worth of diaries before starting treatment. Two weeks of self-monitoring is also the baseline minimum, in my opinion, for research studies. Four weeks of diaries is probably better for research purposes and leads to averages that are more stable. However, it is probably unrealistic to put off clinical treatment for four weeks.

A sample GI symptom diary page that allows for gathering data for one week is presented in Exhibit 4.1. I ask patients to make a single rating per day of how distressing and interfering seven GI symptoms are for that day, using a 0–4 rating scale (see Exhibit 4.1). I have never tested multiple daily ratings versus the single daily rating. However, I know from research on chronic headaches (Hermann, Peters, & Blanchard, 1995) conducted with hand-held computers with an internal clock to record when headache pain ratings were actually done that (a) some patients miss some ratings during the day and (b) the single best time interval (the one most likely to be recorded at the specified time) across mealtimes and bedtime is the

EXHIBIT 4.1
GI SYMPTOM DIARY

Name: ______________________ Week of ______________________

Using the following rating scale, please identify how much of a problem each of the listed symptoms caused you over the day as well as any medication you took for the problem.

RATING SCALE: 0 = not a problem
1 = mildly distressing and interfering
2 = moderately distressing and interfering
3 = severely distressing and interfering
4 = debilitating

Symptoms	Sunday	Monday	Tuesday	Wednesday	Thursday	Friday	Saturday
abdominal pain							
abdominal tenderness							
constipation							
diarrhea (rating)							
diarrhea (# of times)							
bloating/"fullness"							
nausea							
flatulence							
belching							
Did abdominal problems cause you to avoid certain foods or beverages? (Y or N)							
Did abdominal problems cause you to avoid certain activities? (Y or N)							
What medications did you take? (list dose)							

bedtime rating. In addition to recording GI symptom levels, I ask for medications taken and activities avoided.

Clinical Hint

I believe that once per day ratings are adequate to capture the level of symptoms and interference. I recommend that patients make the rating in the evening before bedtime. I believe better compliance is obtained with this instruction with this sampling time. The patient should be told that the rating should reflect his or her whole day.

Clinical Hint

It can be very helpful to have the patient make some notation about events occurring in his or her life that coincide with increased symptom ratings (stressful events, eating certain foods, onset of other episodic illnesses, etc.). This gives the therapist a better understanding of the patient and also prepares the patient for some of the detailed monitoring needed in cognitive–behavioral therapy and cognitive therapy treatments.

Clinical Hint

I advise having the patient keep the GI symptom diary throughout treatment and for a week or two after treatment is terminated. Being able to show the patient that the average level of symptoms has changed can be helpful. Unfortunately, some patients define themselves as improved only when they are essentially symptom free.

For research purposes, we have typically used a 2-week recording period as the posttreatment or follow-up data collection interval. As Table 2.3 has shown, the average degree of symptom reduction for a period of extended symptom monitoring is about 5%. However, an average of 15% of the patients who only monitor GI symptoms for two to three months do show a clinically significant reduction in the principal IBS symptoms of abdominal pain and diarrhea and/or constipation.

WHY USE A GI SYMPTOM DIARY?

There are reasons for and against using a GI symptom diary. On the positive side, a daily diary is more accurate than the patient's global self-report and has come to be seen by some (Blanchard & Schwarz, 1988) as the "gold standard" in IBS research. This is especially the case at the conclusion of treatment when the patient might feel pressure to claim more improvement than there actually was just to please the therapist. Research from our center (Meissner, Blanchard, & Malamood, 1997) shows that the degree of improvement as measured by the diary correlates only moderately with a global self-report rating ($r = .45$, $p < .01$).

A second benefit from the diary is that many symptoms of IBS are not readily amenable to objective verification. For example, abdominal pain is entirely subjective. Diarrhea or constipation as aspects of toileting are, essentially, private events.

A difficulty with IBS is that there are no agreed upon biological markers for the disorder. Undoubtedly, most IBS sufferers have a disorder of lower bowel motility. To the best of my knowledge, there is no universally agreed upon measure of this. At a 1992 conference on IBS sponsored by the National Institute of Diabetes, Digestive, and Kidney Diseases (NIDDK, 1992), several investigators presented their data on the way to measure disordered bowel motility, but there was no consensus among them. Thus, given the absence of a biological marker, I must rely on the patient's report of symptoms to detect the disorder and to discern whether it has abated with treatment. (See chapter 11 for a summary on another biological marker, altered rectal pain sensitivity.)

REDUCTION OF THE GI SYMPTOM DIARY FOR RESEARCH

Although the GI symptom diary does a very good job of capturing most of the troubling symptoms the IBS patient presents with, data derived from it are a problem in research because of the "multiple comparison problem." Each of the GI symptoms measured with the diary is a problem of some magnitude for the IBS patient. He or she would like complete relief and, barring that, at least a noticeable reduction. From the patient's point of view, analyzing the relative degree of change for each symptom makes sense: The patient would probably like to know, for example, whether abdominal pain and/or diarrhea and/or bloating are likely to be reduced by a particular treatment.

However, from the statistical point of view, performing multiple statistical analyses (i.e., analyzing each symptom separately) on the data from a set of patients leads to the possibility of capitalizing on chance rather than finding true differences. That is, if one performed 20 analyses on the data from a set of patients, by chance alone 1 out of 20 analyses should be significant at the .05 level. There are, however, statistical corrections for performing multiple analyses on the data from a single set of patients, the so-called Bonferoni correction being a popular one.

To avoid this problem in the Albany IBS studies, we developed a composite measure, Composite Primary Symptom Reduction (CPSR) score, which was used for the principal analysis in all treatment trials. In this way, we could perform a single analysis on a set of patients to test treatment efficacy. (We also typically reported the values for individual GI symptoms, but the primary conclusions were drawn from the CPSR score analysis.)

The CPSR score is calculated in the following way. For the three primary symptoms of IBS (abdominal pain or tenderness, diarrhea, and constipation), we first calculate a symptom reduction score. For diarrhea, the formula would be as follows:

diarrhea reduction score

$$= 100 \times \frac{\text{baseline diarrhea score} - \text{posttreatment diarrhea score}}{\text{baseline diarrhea score}}$$

where the baseline diarrhea score equals the sum of all daily diarrhea ratings for 2 weeks (or the average diarrhea rating for 2 weeks), and the posttreatment diarrhea score equals the sum of all daily diarrhea ratings for 2 weeks after treatment (or the average diarrhea rating for 2 weeks).

This score has the property that if the symptom has disappeared by the end of treatment, the value will be 100, representing 100% improvement. Thus, positive scores represent improvement, and negative scores represent a worsening in condition.

The CPSR score is then the average of the symptom reduction scores for the three primary symptoms:

$$\text{CPSR} = \frac{\begin{matrix}\text{pain and tenderness} \\ \text{reduction score}\end{matrix} + \begin{matrix}\text{diarrhea} \\ \text{reduction score}\end{matrix} + \begin{matrix}\text{constipation} \\ \text{reduction score}\end{matrix}}{\text{2 or 3 (depending on appropriate number of symptoms)}}$$

The divisor is 2 or 3, depending on the patient's symptom picture. If the patient suffers only from pain and diarrhea, but never constipation, then the divisor would be 2; if the patient suffers from all three symptoms, then the divisor is 3.

Clinical Hint

Although this description of the CPSR score is a bit tedious, I believe it is important for the clinician to grasp what it represents, because all of the results from the Albany studies are presented in terms of it. A good way to think about an individual CPSR score is as the average percent reduction in primary GI symptoms from before to after treatment.

This CPSR score makes the assumption that improvement in one symptom, such as diarrhea, is equivalent to improvement in another symptom such as abdominal pain. For research purposes, this seems a reasonable assumption when averaging across 10 to 30 cases. It might not be as good an assumption with the individual clinical case. In the latter instance, one might want to consider using the symptom reduction scores for the symptoms that are most distressing to the individual patient. In the chapters on treatment (15–19), I present both CPSR scores and average symptom reduction values from before to after treatment to help the clinician to know what can be expected in the individual cases.

One last point on CPSR scores: we have made the assumption (Blanchard & Schwarz, 1988) that a CPSR score of 50 or greater represents clinically meaningful improvement. Others (Lynch & Zamble, 1989; van Dulmen, Fennis, & Bleijenberg, 1996) have adopted this level as well.

5

PSYCHOLOGICAL DISTRESS IN IRRITABLE BOWEL SYNDROME

It has long been recognized that individuals with IBS who seek treatment are somewhat psychologically distressed. This does not mean that all IBS patients are psychologically distressed: One can readily find IBS patients whose psychological test scores are well within the range of the general population. In fact, in this chapter, I present norms for IBS patients on some well-recognized measures of psychological distress, which show that a distinct proportion of patients have scores in the normal range. However, the average scores across a group of IBS patients will probably be in the distressed range.

In this chapter, I have summarized the literature on psychological testing with IBS patients. Table 5.1 summarizes studies published between 1971 and 1982; Table 5.2 summarizes more recent studies published between 1986 and 1995. Table 5.3 summarizes group mean psychological test scores from the Albany studies. In Table 5.4, I present a comparison of Albany test scores for IBS patients to those of other chronic pain populations with which we work, namely patients with tension-type and migraine headaches. The remaining tables present norms for psychological tests administered to large numbers of IBS patients. In chapter 6, I present information on the effects of psychological treatment of IBS on psychological test scores, summarizing both what is available from reports by other investigators and from our own Albany studies (Table 6.2).

TABLE 5.1
Psychological Assessment of IBS Patients, 1971–1982

Authors and patient type	Sample characteristics: *n*	Mean age	% female	IBS criteria	Psychological measures used and mean scores								
Hislop, 1971 (UK)				symptoms and diagnostic evaluation	Interview/patient self-report of symptoms (% of sample)								
					Fatigue	Depression	Insomnia	Weeping	Anorexia	Suicidal			
IBS	67	N/R	70		89.5%	73.1%	80.6%	62.7%	89.6%	22.4%			
control	67	N/R	70		16.4%	17.9%	26.8%	11.9%	19.4%	3.0%			
Esler & Goulston, 1973 (US)				symptoms and diagnostic evaluation	EPI		IPAT						
					Neuroticism (N)	Extraversion (Ex.)	Anxiety (Anx.)						
IBS-diarrhea	16	40	63		15.6	8.5	7.8						
IBS-pain predominant	15	41	87		11.5	8.7	6.1						
Ulcerative colitis	16	35	50		8.4	10.8	5.6						
general medical	40	36	50		11.1	11.1	5.9						
Palmer et al., 1974 (UK)				symptoms and diagnostic evaluation	EPI			MHQ					
					N	Ex	Lie	Anx.	Phob.	Obs.	Som.	Dep.	Hyst.
IBS	41	N/R	61		12.0	10.7	4.0	6.9	5.0	7.7	6.3	5.1	4.4
neurotic	25	N/R			15.9	10.4	2.9	—	—	—	—	—	—
control	2000	N/R			9.1	12.1	2.3	4.3	3.4	6.7	4.5	3.6	3.3

Latimer et al., 1981 (US)				clinical criteria	EPI			BDI	STAI	
					N	Ex	Lie		State	Trait
IBS	16	45	56		15.7^{a}	$10.4^{a,b}$	4.1^{a}	16.4^{a}	47.3^{a}	47.9^{a}
neurotic	8	N/R	25		13.9^{a}	7.4^{a}	$1.6^{a,b}$	13.0^{a}	44.4^{a}	46.4^{a}
control	17	N/R	59		6.5^{b}	12.7^{b}	2.5^{b}	2.8^{b}	32.9^{b}	30.8^{b}
Welch et al., 1985 (NZ)				Drossman, 1977	Hopkins Symptom Checklist					
					Somatic distress	General distress	Performance difficulty			
IBS reporters	26	36	77		18.1^{a}	35.9	12.7			
IBS nonreporters	41	30	51		18.8^{a}	36.1	14.7			
control	60	35	55		15.8^{b}	33.2	12.3			
Welgan et al., 1985 (UK)				clinical criteria	MMPI (*t*-scores)					
					Hypochon. [1]	Depression [2]	Hysteria [3]	Mania [9]		
IBS	12	37	100		65.8	60.6	67.5	55.8		
control	10	23	100		52.7	50.5	56.8	60.5		
Wise et al., 1982 (US)				clinical criteria	SCL-90			Rotter's Locus of Control		
IBS	20	55	70		IBS significantly higher than normals on all scales except phobic anxiety and paranoia			IBS more external than normals.		
control										

Note. Group means that share a superscript letter are not statistically different. EPI = Eysenck Personality Inventory; STAI = State–Trait Anxiety Inventory; IPAT = Institute for Personality and Ability Testing; MHQ = Middlesex Hospital Questionnaire; BDI = Beck Depression Inventory; N = neuroticism; Ex = extraversion; Anx. = anxiety; Phob. = phobia; Obs. = obsessional; Som. = somatization; Dep. = depression; Hys. = Hysteria.

TABLE 5.2
Psychological Assessment of IBS Patients, 1986–1995

Authors and patient type	Sample characteristics: *n*	Sample characteristics: Mean age	Sample characteristics: % female	IBS criteria	Psychological measures used and mean scores				
Toner et al., 1990 (Canada)				clinical	BDI				
IBS	21	39	86		14.0[a]				
Depressed outpatients	21	37	43		13.1[a]				
Control	19	33	68		3.0[b]				
Talley et al., 1990 (US)				Manning	MMPI median scores				
					Hypochondria	Depression	Hysteria		
IBS	67	53	67		62[a]	57[a]	62[a]		
Organic GI disease	64	58	53		61[a]	55[a]	61[a]		
Control	128	49	41		52[b]	49[b]	53[b]		
Corney & Stanton, 1990 (UK)	42	33	74	clinical	GHQ 0–4: 17	5–12: 17	13+: 8		
Arapakis et al., 1986 (Greece)				clinical	States of Anxiety & Depression				
					Depression	Anxiety	Dominance	Extrapun.	Intropun.
IBS	38	47	61		2.8[a]	6.1[a]	32.2[a]	29.6[a]	21.5[b]
Ulcerative colitis	37	44	46		2.7[a]	4.7[a]	25.6[b]	28.0[a,b]	26.4[a]
Medical control	43	46	51		0.5[b]	1.0[b]	34.4[a]	27.5[b]	18.6[c]

Thornton et al., 1990 (UK)				Manning	STAI		HADS	Illness Behavior				
					State	Trait	Anxiety	Depression				
	25	40	76		36.1	40.4	$n = 4$	$n = 0$				
Walker, Roy-Byrne, Katon, Li, et al., 1990 (US)				Manning		SCL-90						
					BDI	Somat.	Depression	Anxiety	Hostility	GSI		
IBS	28	37	79		7.4	59.6[a]	61.2	58.1[a]	56.3	60.4[a]		
IBD	19	35	53		4.1	52.0[b]	55.8	48.9[b]	49.4	51.4[b]		
Gomborone et al., 1995 (UK)				Manning		Illness Attitude Scale						
					BDI	Effect of Symptom	Worry About Illness	Death Phobia	Hypochondria Beliefs	Disease Phobia		
IBS	40	36	70		9.3[a]	7.0[a]	6.9[a]	4.7	4.4[a]	3.7[a]		
Organic GI disease (IBD)	35	31	63		4.6[b]	4.8[b]	4.8[b]	2.0	.9[b]	1.0[b]		
Healthy control participants	40	34	73		2.6[b]	2.3[c]	3.9[b]	1.9	.4[b]	0.6[b]		
Depressed outpatients	37	37	68		17.0[c]	6.7[a]	5.4[a]	3.8	1.1[b]	1.8[b]		
Schwarz et al., 1993 (US)				clinical		STAI		Rathus	MMPI			
					BDI	State	Trait	Assert.	Hypochon.	Dep.	Hyst.	Psych.
IBS	121	43	69		11.3[a]	50.7[a]	47.2[a]	−2.6[a]	68.4[a]	70.1[a]	65.8[a]	66.7[a]
Organic GI disease (IBD)	46	42	63		9.1[a]	43.2[b]	41.6[b]	5.4[a,b]	68.2[a]	68.8[a]	65.0[a]	60.7[b]
control	45	37	76		5.1[b]	39.6[b]	36.0[c]	15.2[b]	52.8[b]	56.8[b]	58.6[b]	57.0[b]

Note. Column means that share superscripts do not differ at the .05 level. BDI = Beck Depresson Inventory; GHQ = General Health Questionnaire; STAI = State–Trait Anxiety Inventory; HADS = Hospital Anxiety and Depression Scale; SCL-90 = Symptom Checklist–90; GSI = Global Severity Index of SCL-90; Rathus Assert. = Rathus Assertiveness Scale; Extrapun. = extrapunitiveness; Intropun. = intropunitiveness.

TABLE 5.3
Summary of Psychological Test Results From the Albany Studies

Authors	Sample characteristics			IBS criteria	Psychological measures used and mean scores								
	n	Mean age	% female										
Neff & Blanchard, 1987				clinical	BDI	STAI State	STAI Trait	STAS State	STAS Trait	Life Events Total-12	Life Events #Event	Rathus Assert.	MHS
	19	41	68		13.6	40.1	48.4	19.7	30.4	197	6.9	−1.1	64.6
Blanchard, Schwarz, et al., 1992				clinical	BDI	STAI-State	STAI-Trait						
Study 1	30	42	77		13.7	45.0	48.2						
Study 2	92	43	66	clinical	10.9	51.5	46.9						
Greene & Blanchard, 1994				clinical	BDI	STAI-State	STAI-Trait	ATQ-N	DAS				
	20	38	75		11.2	40.1	47.0	43.7	125.5				
Payne & Blanchard, 1995				Rome	BDI	STAI-State	STAI-Trait	ATQ-N	DAS	Hassles Freq.	Hassles Intensity		
	34	40	85		12.5	44.3	48.4	52.1	124	17.4	1.9		
Vollmer & Blanchard, 1998				Rome	BDI	STAI-State	STAI-Trait	ATQ-P	ATQ-N	DAS	PSWQ		
·	32	43	78		11.4	55.7	57.6	68.5	54.5	187	39.7		

Note. BDI = Beck Depression Inventory; STAI = State–Trait Anxiety Inventory; STAS = State–Trait Anger Scale; Life Events = Social Readjustment Rating Scale; Rathus Assert. = Rathus Assertiveness Scale; MHS = Marital Happiness Scale; ATQ-N = Automatic Thoughts Questionnaire-Negative; ATQ-P = Automatic Thoughts Questionnaire-Positive; DAS = Dysfunctional Attitude Scale; Hassles = Hassles Scale; PSWQ = Pennsylvania State Worry Questionnaire.

TABLE 5.4
Demographic Characteristics and Psychological Test Scores of Four Samples

	Samples			
Characteristics	IBS	Tension headache	Migraine headache	Control participants
Age, X	41.9	40.3	38.4	41.7
Range	21–76	18–68	19–68	21–68
Sex: women/men	40/15	52/16	49/19	46/17
Percent female	72.7%	76.5%	72.1%	73.0%
Marital status: married/single	33/22	49/19	53/15	43/20
	Sample Means			
Measures	IBS	Tension headache	Migraine headache	Control participants
BDI	13.4[a]	9.6[b]	7.6[b]	4.3[c]
STAI-State	41.9[a]	37.9[a,b]	34.3[b,c]	31.0[c]
STAI-Trait	47.7[a]	44.1[a]	40.0[b]	34.6[c]
PSC	46.2[a]	39.2[a]	25.2[b]	9.1[c]
LES (12 months)	224.8[a]	170.9[a,b]	147.4[b]	166.1[b]
MMPI scales				
F	58.2[a]	54.5[b]	54.6[c]	51.9[b]
1	69.5[a]	65.1[a]	59.5[b]	47.9[c]
2	70.8[a]	67.3[a]	59.3[b]	51.5[c]
3	66.9[a]	66.7[a]	61.8[b]	54.4[c]
4	62.9[a]	59.9[a,b]	54.9[b,c]	51.6[c]
6	69.5[a]	65.1[a]	59.5[b]	47.9[c]
7	65.6[a]	61.4[a]	54.5[b]	50.3[b]
8	63.6[a]	60.1[a]	54.3[b]	51.8[b]
9	59.0[a]	58.2[a]	56.3[a,b]	52.1[b]

Note. From "Psychological Changes Associated With Self-Regulatory Treatments of Irritable Bowel Syndrome," by E. B. Blanchard, C. Radnitz, S. P. Schwarz, D. F. Neff, and M. A. Gerardi, 1987, *Biofeedback and Self-Regulation, 12,* pp. 31–38. Copyright 1987 by Plenum Publishing Co. Adapted by permission. Means that share a superscript are not significantly different at the .05 level according to Tukey HSD analytic comparisons. BDI = Beck Depression Inventory; LES = Life Event Score Social Readjustment Rating Scale; STAI = State–Trait Anxiety Inventory; PSC = Psychosomatic Symptom Checklist.

An examination of Tables 5.1 and 5.2 shows clearly that IBS patients, regardless of how they were diagnosed, report more psychological distress across a variety of measures than do comparison groups with organic GI disease (e.g., Esler & Goulston, 1973; Schwarz et al., 1993; Talley et al., 1990; Walker, Roy-Byrne, Katon, Li, et al., 1990) or healthy control participants (Gomborone, Dewsnap, Libby, & Farthing, 1995; Latimer et al., 1981; Talley et al., 1990; Toner et al., 1990). In some instances the differences are not statistically significant, but they seem invariably to be at least arithmetically higher.

An exception to this conclusion was found by Latimer et al. (1981), who compared IBS patients to psychoneurotics (probably a group comprised of those with anxiety and mood disorders). In these comparisons, there were no significant differences on the Eysenck Personality Inventory (EPI; Eysenck & Eysenck, 1968) dimensions of neuroticism or extraversion. Similar results were found by Gomborone et al. (1995), who compared IBS patients (n = 40) to three groups: those with organic GI disease, that is, IBD (n = 35), outpatients with major depression (n = 37), and healthy control participants (n = 40). The depressed outpatients (X = 17.0) had higher Beck Depression Inventory (BDI; Beck, Ward, Mendelson, Mock, & Erbaugh, 1961) scores than did the patients with IBS (X = 9.3), who in turn had higher scores than did those with organic GI disease (X = 4.6) or the healthy control participants (X = 2.6). On subscales of Kellner's (1981) Illness Attitude Scale, the IBS group and the depressed outpatients endorsed more worry about illness, death phobia, and greater effects of the symptoms than did the other two groups. However, those with IBS scored higher than even the psychiatric control participants on hypochondriacal beliefs and disease phobia. In contrast, Toner et al. (1990) found no difference in depression as measured by the BDI between depressed outpatients in a psychiatric clinic and IBS patients.

Turning to the group mean psychological test scores from the Albany studies (see chapter 16 for a full description of these studies), Table 5.3 shows that BDI mean scores ranged from 10.9 to 13.7, all within the range normally seen as at least noticeably, if mildly, depressed. The scores on the State–Trait Anxiety Inventory (STAI; Spielberger, Gorsuch, & Lushene, 1970) varied widely for both state anxiety (how anxious the patient is at the current point in time), from 40.1 to 55.7, and on trait anxiety (how anxious the patient is in general), from 46.9 to 57.6. It is obvious from Table 5.3 that we have used various psychological tests over the years.

COMPARISON OF IBS PATIENTS TO OTHER POPULATIONS WITH CHRONIC PAIN

Because we had routinely studied another population with chronic pain in Albany, we (Blanchard, Radnitz, et al., 1986) compared the psychological test scores of a group of IBS patients to age- and gender-matched samples (72% to 76% were women) of tension-type headache patients and migraine headache patients as well as a set of nonpatient control participants. Demographic characteristics and the mean psychological test scores are presented in Table 5.4.

Table 5.4 shows that IBS patients were more depressed according to the BDI than were the headache groups, who were more depressed than the nonpatient control participants. On all of the other comparisons (which were conducted very conservatively using Tukey's Honestly Significant Difference Test), the IBS patients showed more distress than did those with migraine. For the most part, the three patient groups were more distressed than were the control participants. What was especially surprising was that the IBS patients also reported more life events over the preceding 12 months than did the migraine patients and control participants.

For the most part, the IBS patients did not score statistically higher than the tension-type headache patients on measures, even though they were arithmetically higher. It is well recognized that tension-type headache patients are the most distressed group among chronic headache patients (Blanchard & Andrasik, 1985). This latter finding was attributed to a construct of "pain density," that is, having to deal with a pain problem almost every day. IBS patients are certainly similar on that dimension to tension-type headache patients.

PSYCHOLOGICAL TEST NORMS

Because we have collected certain psychological tests across many IBS patients over the years, I am in the fortunate position of being able to provide norms for many of these tests. Depending on the instrument, I have from 190 to 350 cases. For the larger sets, I have provided separate norms for men and women (see Tables 5.5–5.12). Reanalysis of our data showed that female IBS patients as a group were slightly (but significantly) more distressed on several measures. When the sample size dropped below 200, I combined the data for men and women on the Minnesota Multiphasic Personality Inventory (MMPI).

As was noted earlier, although the mean scores for various samples of IBS patients are often in the range labeled distressed or depressed, reference

TABLE 5.5
Beck Depression Inventory Norms for IBS Patients (by Gender)

Score	Cumulative percentage	
	Women (n = 269)	Men (n = 82)
0–3	10.1	17.1
4–6	22.4	30.5
7–9	43.5	57.3
10–12	51.1	70.7
13–15	70.9	80.5
16–18	77.6	91.5
19–21	86.9	92.7
22–24	92.0	96.3
25–27	95.8	98.8
28–30	97.5	100.0
31–33	98.3	—
34–36	99.2	—
37+	100.0	—
Median	10	9

TABLE 5.6
State–Trait Anxiety Inventory State Anxiety Norms for IBS Patients (by Gender)

Score	Cumulative percentage	
	Women (n = 238)	Men (n = 83)
20–25	1.3	6.0
26–30	6.3	10.8
31–35	15.1	20.5
36–40	26.1	36.1
41–45	43.3	53.0
46–50	56.7	63.9
51–55	71.0	75.9
56–60	82.4	86.7
61–65	89.5	89.2
66–70	93.3	95.2
71–75	97.1	97.6
76–80	100.0	100.0
Median	48	45

TABLE 5.7
State–Trait Anxiety Inventory Trait Anxiety Norms for IBS Patients (by Gender)

Score	Cumulative percentage	
	Women (n = 236)	Men (n = 83)
20–25	0.8	1.2
26–30	5.5	8.4
31–35	8.9	14.5
36–40	20.8	36.1
41–45	36.4	54.2
46–50	59.3	69.9
51–55	77.1	83.1
56–60	91.5	94.0
61–65	94.1	96.4
66–70	97.5	100.0
71–75	99.2	—
76–80	100.0	—
Median	48	45

TABLE 5.8
Social Readjustment Rating Scale Norms (12 months) for IBS Patients (by Gender)

Score	Cumulative percentage	
	Women (n = 127)	Men (n = 51)
0–50	6.3	13.7
51–100	16.5	25.5
101–150	24.4	37.3
151–200	35.4	41.2
201–250	50.4	52.9
251–300	57.5	62.7
301–350	71.7	70.6
351–400	80.3	78.4
401–450	85.8	84.3
451–500	90.6	90.2
501–550	91.3	92.2
551+	100.0	100.0
Median	247	238

TABLE 5.9
Psychosomatic Symptom Checklist Norms for IBS Patients (by Gender)

Score	Cumulative percentage	
	Women (n = 166)	Men (n = 63)
0–10	2.4	12.7
11–20	16.9	30.2
21–30	33.7	47.6
31–40	51.2	68.3
41–50	64.5	87.3
51–60	75.3	90.5
61–70	83.7	95.2
71–80	88.0	100.0
81–90	92.8	—
91–100	97.0	—
101+	100.0	—
Median	40	32

TABLE 5.10
Hamilton Rating Scale for Depression Norms for IBS Patients (by Gender)

Score	Cumulative percentage	
	Women (n = 158)	Men (n = 51)
0–2	9.5	11.8
3–5	20.9	25.5
6–8	34.2	33.3
9–11	53.8	62.7
12–14	70.3	70.6
15–17	81.6	76.5
18–20	91.1	86.3
21–23	93.0	98.0
24–26	97.5	100.0
27–29	98.7	—
30+	100.0	—
Median	11	10

TABLE 5.11
Hamilton Anxiety Rating Scale Norms for IBS Patients (by Gender)

Score	Cumulative percentage	
	Women (n = 158)	Men (n = 51)
0–2	0	0
3–5	4.4	2.0
6–8	11.4	11.8
9–11	26.6	37.3
12–14	37.3	49.0
15–17	57.6	64.7
18–20	72.8	78.4
21–23	81.6	84.3
24–26	89.9	92.2
27–29	94.3	92.2
30+	100.0	100.0
Median	16	15

TABLE 5.12
MMPI Norms for IBS Patients

t score	Cumulative percentages									
	F	K	1 (Hy)	2 (D)	3 (Hs)	4 (Pd)	6 (Pa)	7 (Pt)	8 (Sc)	9 (Ma)
<40	1.1	1.6	0	0	0	3.6	1.6	0	0	4.1
40–45	1.6	14.7	1.0	3.1	1.0	6.2	4.7	1.0	1.0	21.2
46–50	23.7	31.6	2.6	5.7	5.2	15.0	18.7	4.7	7.3	36.8
51–55	51.6	52.1	6.2	13.5	11.4	26.9	28.0	15.5	24.9	53.9
56–60	70.0	69.5	20.2	26.9	28.0	43.0	48.7	33.2	50.8	70.5
61–65	83.2	87.9	42.5	41.5	46.6	58.0	71.5	49.2	65.3	84.5
66–70	94.7	97.9	59.6	52.8	65.3	72.0	86.0	67.9	76.2	93.3
71–75	96.3	99.5	73.6	63.7	86.5	84.5	91.2	79.3	86.0	97.4
76–80	98.9	100.0	88.6	80.8	96.4	90.7	93.8	88.1	91.7	98.4
81–90	100.0	—	98.4	92.7	99.0	98.4	99.5	97.4	95.3	100.0
90+	—	—	100.0	100.0	100.0	100.0	100.0	100.0	100.0	—
n	190	190	193	193	193	193	193	193	193	193
Median	55.0	55.0	68.0	69.0	66.0	62.0	61.0	66.0	60.0	54.0

to the tables will show that a sizable proportion of treatment-seeking IBS patients are not especially distressed psychometrically. For example, on the BDI (Table 5.5), about 23% of women and 30% of men had scores of 6 or less. Likewise, on the MMPI Depression scale, almost 27% had T scores of 60 or below.

Clinical Hint

Although separate norms exist for most of these measures, I believe that it is useful for the therapist working with an individual IBS patient to know how that patient compares to other IBS patients. Hence the test norms.

It thus does seem clear from the literature review and from our psychological test data norms that IBS patients, on average, have noticeable, but generally mild, levels of psychological distress across a variety of dimensions. In the next chapter, I examine what happens to these psychometric levels of distress with treatment.

6

WHICH COMES FIRST: PATIENTHOOD OR NEUROSIS? STUDIES OF IBS PATIENTS AND IBS NONPATIENTS

As was repeatedly shown in chapter 5, IBS patients as a group showed increased levels of psychological distress across a variety of measures in almost every study presented. The individual psychological test norms from the Albany studies, however, make it clear that some IBS patients are well within the normal range on many standard measures of psychological distress. It is also the case, as is shown by the epidemiological studies reviewed in chapter 2, especially the Olmsted County study (Talley et al., 1991), that many individuals who meet the symptomatic criteria for IBS never seek treatment for their GI symptoms. This leads one to wonder whether everyone with the symptoms of IBS is psychologically distressed (or to use an older term, neurotic), or whether only those individuals who are psychologically distressed (neurotic) and who suffer from IBS symptoms eventually seek medical care for IBS.

Another way of viewing this issue is in terms of at least three hypotheses: (1) living with IBS symptoms over the years leads to psychological distress (the "somatopsychic hypothesis"); (2) psychologically distressed individuals (neurotics) who develop GI symptoms are likely to seek help for IBS (the "psychosomatic hypotheses"); or (3) some other variable (e.g., abnormal illness behavior) present in individuals who become patients leads to both the psychological distress and the IBS symptoms (the "third variable hypothesis").

A research team at the University of North Carolina (UNC) at Chapel Hill, led by Sandler and Drossman, first began addressing this issue by administering a questionnaire on bowel habit patterns to a large group ($N = 566$) of individuals undergoing routine health screening (Sandler, Drossman, Nathan, & McKee, 1984). The questionnaire allowed the researchers to determine whether the participants (students entering UNC, entering medical students, and new employees of the hosptial) met the clinical criteria for IBS (Exhibit 1.1). The team found that 86 (15.2%) of the sample met symptomatic criteria for IBS. The most important finding, however, was that 53 of these individuals (62% of those who endorsed the symptom criteria) had never sought medical care for their GI symptoms. (Throughout this book I refer to individuals who meet the symptomatic criteria for IBS and have sought medical or psychological treatment for it as *IBS patients*; I refer to those who meet the symptomatic criteria for IBS but have not sought treatment as *IBS nonpatients*.) In the Sandler et al. (1984) study, IBS patients were more likely than nonpatients to complain of abdominal pain (48% vs. 15%, $p = .005$) and less likely to complain of constipation (6% vs. 28%, $p = .01$). The IBS patients were also significantly older (mean age 23.6 vs. 21.2, $p < .05$).

The first study in which the psychological characteristics of IBS patients and IBS nonpatients were compared was conducted in New Zealand by Welch, Hillman, and Pomare (1985). They compared 26 consecutive outpatients with IBS at a gastroenterology clinic to a group of 41 blood donors who met symptomatic Manning criteria for IBS and to a group of 60 control participants from the same blood donor pool. All participants completed the Hopkins Symptom Checklist (Derogatis, Lipman, Rickels, Uhlenhuth, & Covi, 1974), a predecessor of the Symptom Checklist–90 (SCL-90; Derogatis et al., 1973). It was scored for three factors: General Feelings of Distress (primarily anxiety and depression), Somatic Distress (primarily somatization), and Performance Difficulty (primarily obsessive–compulsive disorder). As Table 6.1 shows, *IBS nonpatients scored consistently higher than the IBS patients*, but none of the comparisons were significant. Only on the measure of somatization did the two patient groups score significantly higher than did the healthy control participants.

In 1988, two studies on this topic appeared in the same issue of *Gastroenterology*. In the stronger of the two studies (Drossman, McKee, et al., 1988), the authors compared IBS patients (72) to IBS nonpatients (82), who were identified initially from a screening questionnaire given to students and new hospital employees. They were subsequently given a thorough gastroenterological examination to confirm the IBS diagnosis. None of the latter had sought medical attention for GI problems. A group without GI complaints from the same pool was included. The IBS patients were much more likely to complain of abdominal pain (94% vs. 56%, $p < .001$) and diarrhea (49% vs. 29%, $p < .01$) than were the IBS nonpatients.

The main psychological comparison involved the MMPI (also the MPQ; McGill Pain Questionnaire, Melzack, 1975). Values for the clinical scales that yielded differences appear in Table 6.1, along with another interesting way of presenting the MMPI data: the percent of samples with T scores greater than 70, indicating clinically significant evaluation. The results from this primarily female, Caucasian, college-educated population clearly showed that the IBS patients were significantly more distressed than IBS nonpatients on measures of depression (MMPI scale 2), somatization (MMPI scales 1 and 3), and anxiety (MMPI scale 7). They also complained of more severe pain (MPQ total score) and more days with pain (8.2 vs. 3.0 days per 2 weeks).

In the other article (Whitehead, Bosmajian, Zonderman, Costa, & Schuster, 1988), results from a study with patients from a university medical center GI clinic were reported. The patients had either IBS (based on Manning criteria); functional bowel disorder (FBD), a condition similar to IBS in which patients meet clinical criteria for IBS but not the Manning criteria; or lactose malabsorption (LMA), a condition with abdominal pain and altered bowel habit, which is confirmed by a hydrogen breath test following ingestion of a standard dose of lactose. They were compared to 149 middle-aged, middle-class, Caucasian women recruited through church groups and charities. The IBS and FBD nonpatients were diagnosed by questionnaire; the LMA nonpatients were confirmed by hydrogen breath test. Only community sample members who had not sought treatment for GI problems over the past six months were used.

Analyses showed significantly higher scores for the patient groups combined than for the diagnosed nonpatients (excluding control participants) on all scales of the Hopkins Symptom Checklist. No specific comparisons of IBS patients to IBS nonpatients were reported. Furthermore, on the Depression, Hostility, and Psychoticism subscales, there were significant differences among diagnostic groups, collapsed across patient versus nonpatient status, with those individuals with FBD scoring higher than those with IBS or LMA, who did not differ. There were no interactions.

Thus, despite the noticeable arithmetic differences in all subtest scores between IBS patients and IBS nonpatients (the former score two to three times higher than the latter), these differences were not significant (possibly a function of relatively small subsample size.) The authors made the point that individuals with FBD are the more psychologically distressed among nonpatients and patients. Although the means are in the appropriate direction, none of the specific statistical comparisons to confirm this idea are presented. The only between-group comparison reported was between both sets of FBD subjects (patients and nonpatients) combined versus the control participants. These were different for anxiety, hostility, and somatization.

A recent study addressing this topic was reported by Whitehead, Bur-

TABLE 6.1
Psychological Test Score Comparison of IBS Patients and IBS Nonpatients

Authors and patient groups	*n*	Age	% female	IBS criteria	Source of IBS nonpatients	Comparisons						
Welch et al., 1985				Manning	blood donors undergoing screening	Hopkins Symptom Checklist						
						general distress anx. & D	somatic distress	performance diff. (OCD)				
IBS patients	26	36	77			35.9	18.1[a]	12.7				
IBS nonpatients	41	30	51			36.1	18.8[a]	14.7				
Control	60	35	55			33.2	15.8[b]	12.3				
Drossman et al., 1988				Manning, physical exam	students and hospital employees who were screened and then examined	MMPI (% with *t* score > 70)						
						HY	D	HS	Psychas.	Sc.	MPQ total Sc.	Pain days
IBS patients	72	30	86			33[a]	21[a]	20[a]	23[a]	25[a]	9.1[a]	8.2[a]
IBS nonpatients	82	26	94			5[b]	7[b]	9[b]	9[b]	17[b]	5.6[b]	3.0[b]
control	84	28	88			0[b]	4[b]	2[b]	2[b]	4[c]	3.2[c]	1.1[b]
						Mean *t* scores (extrapolated)						
						62[a]	59[a]	61[a]	62[a]			
						56[b]	55[b]	58[a,b]	60[a,b]			
						52[b]	51[b]	55[b]	55[b]			

Whitehead et al., 1988			all female	IBS: Manning FBD: clinical LMA: H_2 breath test	middle-class women from church groups or charities	Hopkins Symptom Checklist						
						Somat.[a]	Depr.[a,b]	Anx.[a]	OCD[a]	Host.[a,b]	Psych.[a,b]	GSI[a]
IBS patients	10	41, 47[d]				1.34	1.15	0.95	1.32	1.05	0.32	1.01
IBS nonpatients	16					0.34	0.56	0.46	0.55	0.30	0.17	0.41
FBD patients	12					1.27	1.85	1.03	1.08	1.25	0.78	1.08
FBD nonpatients	26					0.73	0.94	0.67	0.92	0.71	0.35	0.69
LMA patients	23					1.22	1.21	0.87	1.00	0.65	0.27	0.87
LMA nonpatients	28					0.55	0.59	0.38	0.73	0.36	0.13	0.46
control	46					0.43	0.64	0.36	0.67	0.31	0.25	0.45
Whitehead et al., 1996				Manning; LMA: H_2 breath test	college students in psychology class			SF-36 (Quality of Life)				
						NEO Neurot.	SCL-90 GSI	Phys. Func.	Pain	Gen'l. Hlth.	Vital.	Soc. Func.
IBS patients	84	24	49			97.2[a]	62.6[a]	91[a]	52[a]	62[a]	46[a]	78[a]
IBS nonpatients	165	23	55			97.9[a]	61.3[a]	92[a]	56[b]	71[b]	52[b]	84[b]
control	122	21	43			78.9[b]	48.8[b]	97[b]	66[c]	86[c]	66[c]	93[c]
Gick & Thompson, 1997				Rome, by questionnaire	psychology class	STAI-Trait						
IBS patients	44	—	71			42.6[a]						
IBS nonpatients	52	—	58			42.1[a]						
control	41	—	68			36.0[b]						
Jarrett et al., 1998				Rome	paid volunteers	SCL-90						
IBS patients	32	34.9	100			0.54[a]						
IBS nonpatients	29	30.7	100			0.63[a]						
control	34	32.6	100			0.28[b]						

Note. MPQ = McGill Pain Questionnaire; FBD = functional bowel disorder; LMA = lactose malabsorption; SCL-90 = symptom checklist–90; GSI = Global Severity Index; D = depression; HS = hysteria; HY = hypochondriasis; Psychas. = psychasthenia, Sc. = schizophrenia; STAI = State–Trait Anxiety Inventory; NEO = Neuroticism–Extroversion–Openness Inventory. For Whitehead et al. (1988), superscripts denote: [a]Significant difference for patients versus nonpatients; [b]significant difference among diagnostic groups; [c]between-group comparisons; [d]N/R by group: 41 = average for patients, 47 = average for nonpatients. For between-group comparisons, means that share a superscript do not differ.

nett, Cook, and Taub (1996). They sought to replicate or disconfirm Drossman et al.'s (1988) positive results by using relatively large samples from a young adult population (college students at the University of Alabama at Birmingham). More than 2,400 students were screened in psychology classes with a questionnaire. This resulted in identifying 84 students who met Manning criteria for IBS who had seen a physician in the past year for GI symptoms, 165 who met Manning criteria for IBS but had not seen a physician over the past year, and 122 nonsymptomatic control participants. Those with LMA were excluded by hydrogen breath test. (Interestingly, this worked out to 10.4% of the students being diagnosed with IBS.)

Participants completed the NEO Personality Inventory (Costa & McCrea, 1985), which was scored for neuroticism; the SCL-90-R (Derogatis, 1994), scored for the Global Symptom Index (GSI), an overall index of psychological distress; and the SF-36 Health Survey (Ware, 1993), a commonly used measure of quality of life along nine dimensions. The patients did not differ on the three measures, but both groups were significantly higher than the control participants on all measures. However, on numerous aspects of quality of life (such as pain, general health, vitality, and social functioning), the IBS patients were more impaired (or functioning less well) than were the IBS nonpatients (see Table 6.1).

Another recent study on this topic was conducted by Gick and Thompson (1997) in Canada. They had 905 college students answer a questionnaire about bowel symptoms and the seeking of medical care for these symptoms. Using Rome criteria, 66 (7.3%) were identified as IBS patients (they acknowledged seeking medical care for their GI symptoms, mostly from primary care physicians), whereas 284 (31.4%) were identified as IBS nonpatients based on the questionnaire response. Portions of these two groups, selected to be approximate gender matches, and a group of non-GI disorder control participants were administered the trait anxiety scale of the Strait–Trait Anxiety Inventory (STAI; Spielberger et al., 1970). Mean scores for the three samples were as follows: IBS patients, 42.6; IBS nonpatients, 42.1; and control participants, 36.0. The two IBS groups did not differ but were more trait anxious than were the control participants ($p < .003$).

Finally, in a recent study of female volunteers who monitored stress and GI symptoms, Jarrett et al. (1998) compared 32 women who met Rome criteria for IBS and had sought medical care for GI symptoms to 29 women who also met Rome criteria for IBS but had not sought medical care and to 34 women without noticeable GI distress. The two IBS groups were more likely to meet criteria for one or more *DSM–III–R* (American Psychiatric Association, 1987) Axis I disorders than were control participants (67%, IBS patients; 59%, IBS nonpatients; 35%, control participants) but did not differ. Moreover, the two IBS groups did not differ on any scale of the SCL-90, but scored higher than the control participants in most cases. Thus, again there were no differences between these two IBS populations.

CONCLUSIONS

In five of the six studies described, no difference in measures of psychological distress between IBS patients and IBS nonpatients were found. Only Drossman et al. (1988) found differences on the MMPI scales usually associated with neuroticism and somatization (Hypochondriasis, Depression, Hysteria, and Psychasthenia). In four studies showing no differences, the SCL-90 or the Hopkins Symptom Checklist was used; the STAI trait anxiety scale was used in the other. Thus, a measurement instrument difference may account for the conflicting results. The failure of the early Whitehead et al. (1988) study to show differences between patients and nonpatients could also be due to relatively small sample sizes (only 10 IBS patients and 16 IBS nonpatients) or to use of an older and exclusively female population. However, both of these concerns were addressed in the later Whitehead et al. (1996) study.

Another study of similar design, recently conducted in the United Kingdom, is that of Heaton et al. (1992). Unfortunately, no psychological data were reported. They collected data on a representative sample of 1,058 women and 838 men in the Bristol area, representing 72.2% of those approached. They ranged in age from 25 to 69. Using a questionnaire to identify IBS based on Manning criteria, they found that 13% of women and 5% of men had three or more symptoms, thus reasonably meeting the Manning criteria for IBS. Only about half of those meeting diagnostic criteria had consulted a physician, and the likelihood of seeing a doctor was directly proportional to the number of symptoms. Among men with three or more symptoms, abdominal pain was the most likely cause of seeking medical attention.

So, researchers are left with a lack of consensus on this issue. Unfortunately, I have nothing to contribute directly from my work because I have always dealt with IBS patients. It does seem clear from the data summarized in chapter 5 and in this chapter that IBS patients will usually present with some degree of psychological distress. In the next section, I address the issue of what happens to this psychological distress when the IBS is treated psychologically.

EFFECTS OF PSYCHOLOGICAL TREATMENTS ON PSYCHOLOGICAL DISTRESS

Given the results summarized in chapter 5 that show a noticeable level of psychological distress in IBS patients, regardless of how they are diagnosed and regardless of what psychological test is used to measure psychological distress, a question of some clinical importance becomes apparent: What are the effects of psychological treatments on such psychological distress? Jumping ahead (because I have not yet discussed psychological treatments of IBS), Table 6.2 summarizes the effects of various psychological treatments we have evaluated in Albany over the past 15 years on psychological measures, not on GI symptoms. I included the Beck Depression Inventory (BDI) and the STAI in all of the studies. In two studies focusing on cognitive therapy exclusively (Greene & Blanchard, 1994; Payne & Blanchard, 1995), I also included two standard cognitive measures, the Dysfunctional Attitude Scale (Weissman & Beck, 1978) and the Automatic Thoughts Questionnaire-Negative (Hollon & Kendall, 1980), as process measures.

As can be seen in Table 6.2, in five out of six studies, the primary treatment, either CBT or a purely cognitive therapy, led to a significant reduction in depressive symptoms as measured by the BDI. In all of these instances, patients as a group went from scoring on average in the mildly depressed range (12 to 13) to the normal range (about 7). The attention-placebo condition described in Blanchard, Schwarz, et al. (1992) also led to significant reduction in depressive symptoms.

In four out of six comparisons, active treatment led to a significant reduction in trait anxiety, and in two of six comparisons, treatment led to a reduction in state anxiety, as measured by the STAI. Finally, in two instances, cognitive therapy led to the expected changes in dysfunctional attitudes and automatic negative thoughts. For the most part, symptom monitoring led to small nonsignificant reductions in psychological distress measures. An exception was evident in Blanchard, Schwarz, et al. (1992), who found a significant reduction in trait anxiety in Study 1 and in state anxiety in Study 2. The psychological control conditions, designed to be psychologically engaging but otherwise inert, led to significant reductions in depression in both Study 1 and Study 2 and to changes in state and trait anxiety in the larger study (Study 2). Clearly these treatments were not inert!

Clinical Hint

The main conclusion drawn from this work is that taking part in systematic cognitive therapy or CBT has positive side effects for the IBS patient: Depression and, to a lesser extent, anxiety, are significantly reduced as a result of treatment.

TABLE 6.2
Change in Psychological Test Scores as a Result of IBS Treatment in the Albany Studies

Authors	Treatment conditions	*n*	BDI		STAI-State		STAI-Trait		ATQ-N		DAS	
			Pre-	Post-	Pre-	Post-	Pre-	Post-	Pre-	Post-	Pre-	Post-
Neff & Blanchard, 1987	CBT	10	13.4	7.6*	41.4	36.5	48.4	40.4**				
	SM	9	15.2	13.6	39.4	43.8	53.0	50.0	—	—	—	—
Blanchard, Schwarz, et al., 1992												
Study 1	CBT	10	14.0	8.4*	44.4	33.3*	46.4	37.9***				
	Attention–Placebo	10	15.0	7.9*	43.2	36.3	44.9	40.8				
	SM	10	12.2	11.7	47.5	42.2	53.3	48.5*	—	—	—	—
Study 2	CBT	31	11.1	6.6***	52.4	35.9***	48.1	43.8*				
	Attention–Placebo	30	11.1	6.7***	50.5	36.2***	45.3	39.6***				
	SM	31	10.6	10.5	51.6	44.5**	47.3	46.5	—	—	—	—
Greene & Blanchard, 1994	Cog. Ther.	10	10.6	5.1*	41.1	38.4	49.9	43.7	45.3	37.5*	126	111′
	SM	10	11.8	9.5	39.1	38.5	44.1	42.5	42.1	44.9	125	132
Payne & Blanchard, 1995	Cog. Ther.	12	14.6	8.3**	49.1	43.8	53.0	44.9***	57.3	42.4***	135	120*
	Psycho-Ed.	12	11.2	10.8	41.5	41.6	46.8	47.2	48.7	51.0	109	100
	SM	10	11.7	11.3	41.8	40.9	45.1	46.2	49.9	51.0	129	132
Vollmer & Blanchard, 1998	Cog Ther.	12	9.8	8.0	50.9	47.1	54.0	50.1				
	SM	9	17.5	14.5	69.2	64.7	64.9	67.0	—	—	—	—
Galovski & Blanchard, 1999	Hypnotherapy	9	13.6	10.0	40.4	34.0*	46.9	39.7**	—	—	—	—

Note. ′$p < .10$; *$p < .05$; **$p < .01$; ***$p < .001$; BDI = Beck Depression Inventory; STAI = State–Trait Anxiety Inventory; ATQ-N = Automatic Thoughts Questionnaire–Negative; DAS = Dysfunctional Attitude Scale; CBT = Cognitive–Behavioral Therapy; SM = Symptom Monitoring; Cog. Ther. = Cognitive Therapy; Psycho-Ed. = Psychoeducational Support Groups.

OTHER RESEARCH ON PSYCHOLOGICAL CHANGES ACCOMPANYING PSYCHOLOGICAL TREATMENT

In addition to the results from the Albany studies summarized in Table 6.2, there are scattered reports in the literature from other centers that describe changes in psychological measures accompanying treatment. That treatment literature is reviewed in depth in chapter 15. Results on psychological changes are summarized here in Table 6.3. As the table shows, there have been significant reductions in various standard measures of anxiety resulting from a variety of psychological treatments. For example, in their controlled evaluation of brief dynamic psychotherapy, Guthrie, Creed, Dawson, and Tomenson (1991) found significantly greater reductions in Hamilton Rating Scale for Depression (Hamilton, 1960) scores for the treated group than in their waiting list control group. They also found a similar advantage on the Clinical Anxiety Scale (CAS; Snaith, Baugh, Clayden, Hussain, & Sipple, 1982).

There are consistent advantages of various CBT treatments versus control conditions for reducing trait anxiety (Bennett & Wilkinson, 1985; Lynch & Zamble, 1989) and depression as measured by the BDI (Lynch & Zamble, 1989; Toner et al., 1998). Interestingly, van Dulmen et al. (1996), using CBT in groups, found no significant change in an index of overall psychological distress derived from the SCL-90. Treatments seem much more likely to reduce depression and trait anxiety than overall psychological distress. It is interesting that for Toner et al. (1998) only the measure of depression, the BDI, showed a significant differential advantage for her CBT group treatment in comparison to the other conditions. This differential advantage was not present for the GI symptoms.

DOES BEING IN TREATMENT OR BEING SUCCESSFUL IN TREATMENT CAUSE POSITIVE PSYCHOLOGICAL EFFECTS?

This long rhetorical question frames an important issue for the psychological side effects of treatment for IBS. It could be that the experience of being in treatment, with the concomitant regular monitoring of GI symptoms, regular interaction with a warm, supportive therapist, and skills learned in treatment, lead to some alleviation of anxiety, depression, and general psychological distress. In similar research involving the treatment of patients with chronic headache with relaxation, biofeedback, and cognitive therapy, we (Blanchard, Andrasik, et al., 1986) found that both those individuals whose headaches were reduced significantly (successes) and those whose headaches were reduced only slightly or not at all were significantly less depressed and less anxious after treatment, whereas those who merely monitored headaches did not change.

TABLE 6.3
Change in Psychological Test Scores as a Result of Various Psychological Treatments

Authors	Treatment condition	n	Results
Bennett & Wilkinson, 1985	CBT drugs	12 12	Significantly greater change in STAI-Trait for CBT in comparison to drug treatment.
Lynch & Zamble, 1989	CBT SM	10 11	Significantly greater change in BDI for CBT in comparison to SM: within-group change, including treated control participants for BDI (10.5–4.2***), STAI-Trait (44.4–37.5**), PSC (47.8–30.9***).
Toner et al., 1998	CBT Psycho-Ed SM-routine medical tx.	N/R	Significantly greater change in BDI for CBT in comparison to other two conditions. Within-group change in BDI: CBT ($t = 2.24$; $p = .026$); SG ($t = 1.81$; $p = .073$); SM-Med ($t = -2.85$; $p = .01$)
van Dulmen et al., 1996	CBT SM	27 20	No significant difference in change in two conditions on SCL-90 and total score.
Guthrie et al., 1991	Psychotherapy SM	46 43	Significantly greater change in HRSD and CAS for psychotherapy in comparison to SM. Within-group change for HRSD, 13.5–4.0***; CAS, 6.3–3.8**.

Note. ** $p < .01$; *** $p < .001$; CBT = Cognitive–Behavioral Therapy; SM = Symptom Monitoring; Psycho-Ed = Psychoeducational Support Group; STAI = State–Trait Anxiety Inventory; BDI = Beck Depression Inventory; PSC = Psychosomatic Symptom Checklist; SCL-90 = Symptom Checklist-90; HRSD = Hamilton Rating Scale for Depression; CAS = Clinical Anxiety Scale.

Alternatively, it could be that psychological improvement accompanies improvement in IBS symptoms and that the psychological changes frequently seen in the entire sample (see Table 6.2), reflect noticeable improvement in the psychological measure only by those IBS patients who are treatment successes. Thus, the average score for the group shows change but is misleading (as group means sometimes can be), because not everyone showed the psychological improvement.

We (Blanchard, Radnitz, Schwarz, Neff, & Gerardi, 1987) have addressed this issue in a reanalysis of the data from several studies. We obtained pretreatment and posttreatment psychological test data for 41 IBS patients, diagnosed by clinical criteria. Treatment was a combination of relaxation training, biofeedback, and, in some cases, cognitive therapy delivered by advanced doctoral students and/or doctoral-level therapists. Treatment was for 12 sessions over an 8-week interval. Nine patients merely monitored GI symptoms for the 8 weeks and were then retested.

The GI symptom data were gathered using the GI symptom diary described in chapter 4. Success or failure in terms of IBS symptom relief was determined by the CPSR; a value of 50 (an average reduction in GI symptoms of 50% or greater) was used to separate successes from failures. The average CPSR score for the 20 successes was 0.70. Seven of the 12 failures were unchanged or worse.

The psychological tests included in this analysis were the BDI, the STAI (scored for both state and trait anxiety), and the Psychosomatic Symptom Checklist (Attanasio et al., 1984). The data were subjected to a Groups × Pre–Post MANOVA, which showed a significant pre–post main effect (p = .01) and a trend for a Group × Pre–Post interaction (p = .10). The scores for each group on each test were subjected to a correlated t test. Data from both administrations of these tests are presented in Table 6.4.

Several points emerge from Table 6.4. First, for each of the four psychological tests, those IBS patients whose GI symptoms were successfully reduced showed significant (p = .009 or better) reductions in psychological distress. Certainly, noticeable psychological improvement accompanies physical improvement.

These psychological changes are clinically meaningful. For example, on the BDI, the successfully treated patients' scores were reduced on average from 14.3 to 7.1, that is, from clearly within the clinically meaningful but mildly depressed range (score above 9 to 10) to within the normal, nondepressed range. A similar large change was seen for state anxiety. A second point to notice is that the failures did show a significant decrease on trait anxiety (p = .027). Thus, being in treatment does make some difference—but not nearly as much as being successful with treatment. Last, those patients who monitored GI symptoms did not change; in fact,

TABLE 6.4
Psychological Test Scores for All Participants at Pre- and Posttreatment

Psychological test	*n*	Pretreatment X	Posttreatment X	Within-group change *t*	*p*
Beck Depression Inventory					
success	18	14.3	7.1	2.93	.009
failure	12	13.6	12.8	0.38	ns
symptom monitoring	9	14.3	13.2	0.97	ns
State–Trait Anxiety Inventory (state)					
success	18	41.7	31.3	2.92	.009
failure	11	48.3	49.2	−0.16	ns
symptom monitoring	9	42.8	48.7	−1.96	.086
State–Trait Anxiety Inventory (trait)					
success	17	45.4	38.7	3.24	.005
failure	10	52.9	46.6	2.64	.027
symptom monitoring	9	53.8	51.6	1.40	ns
Psychosomatic Symptom Checklist—Total Score					
success	20	47.1	26.8	3.03	.007
failure	12	45.5	39.3	1.28	ns
symptom monitoring	8	49.8	50.0	−0.04	ns

Note. From "Psychological Changes Associated with Self-Regulatory Treatments of Irritable Bowel Syndrome," by E. B. Blanchard, C. Radnitz, S. P. Schwarz, D. F. Neff, and M. A. Gerardi, 1987, *Biofeedback and Self-Regulation, 12*, pp. 31–38. Copyright 1987 by Plenum Publishing Co. Adapted by permission.

there was a trend ($p = .086$) for these patients to deteriorate on state anxiety.

To see whether the psychological changes were related to GI symptom changes in a dose–response relation, we calculated correlations between CPSR scores and changes in psychological test; only the correlation between change in state anxiety and GI symptom change score approached significance ($r[29] = 0.277$, $p = .07$).

Clinical Hint

An obvious implication of these results is that the IBS patients who respond successfully to your psychological treatment are likely to feel twice blessed: Not only are their GI symptoms reduced, but also their psychological state is likely to improve to a noticeable degree. In fact, the improvement may be great enough that you do not have to provide additional treatment for their comorbid mood or anxiety disorder. Failures, however, will not show much collateral improvement except possibly in state anxiety. This could make it difficult to hold the patient in another round of treatment if the first 8 to 12 visits have not brought relief.

CONCLUSIONS

There is still no clear answer to the question that opened this chapter. For the somatopsychic hypothesis, my work (Blanchard et al., 1987) is supportive in that relief of GI symptoms is accompanied by significant reduction in psychological distress. This improvement was not found in those who went through treatment but did not experience substantial GI symptom reduction. On the other hand, Whitehead et al. (1988) found that individuals who had suffered for years with the GI symptoms resulting from LMA did not become noticeably psychologically distressed.

Of the five comparisons of IBS patients and nonpatients, only Drossman et al.'s (1988) shows consistent support for the psychosomatic hypothesis—that IBS patients are more psychologically distressed than are IBS nonpatients. Whitehead et al. (1996) found a poorer quality of life among IBS patients but not more classic psychological distress. Whitehead et al. (1988) found that patienthood, per se, regardless of the diagnosis, was regularly accompanied by more psychological distress, but this was not specific to IBS. From a box score perspective, the weight of evidence does not support the idea that IBS patients are significantly more distressed than are IBS nonpatients: Four of five studies do not support it.

My own view, unsubstantiated by my own research, is that the third variable hypothesis is probably correct. That is, some characteristic leads to both the psychological distress and to help-seeking for the GI symptoms. Thus, my answer to the opening question is that neither comes first, but both are the result of a yet-to-be-identified third variable.

Clinical Hint

This chapter is, in part, an academic research exercise. I feel certain that the mental health practitioner who ventures into the GI disorder business will overwhelmingly encounter IBS patients, individuals with the symptoms of IBS who are also psychologically distressed. I recommend assessing for this distress and taking it into account in your treatment planning. I also believe this distress will be alleviated in tandem with the relief from the GI symptoms.

7

PSYCHIATRIC STUDIES OF PATIENTS WITH IRRITABLE BOWEL SYNDROME

The work I reviewed in chapter 5 took a dimensional approach to measuring or assessing the extent of psychological distress or deviance found among IBS patients. For example, one could ask what the average degree of depression was, as measured by the Beck Depression Inventory (BDI), among IBS patients who sought psychological treatment in Albany. As Table 5.3 showed, the average BDI score was 11.9.

An alternative approach to measuring the extent of psychological distress or deviance is the categorical approach of *psychiatric diagnosis*, whereby one determines what fraction of an IBS population meets the criteria for major depressive disorder or any mood disorder. This approach has almost as long and rich a history as that of the dimensional approach of psychological tests. In this chapter I summarize the literature on psychiatric diagnosis of IBS patients. Included are data from more than 200 IBS patients assessed with structured psychiatric interviews in Albany. I also discuss the implications of these findings for the psychologist and other nonphysician caregivers.

EARLY PSYCHIATRIC DIAGNOSTIC STUDIES

I have restricted this literature review primarily to studies in which recognized structured diagnostic interviews and objective diagnostic criteria were used. This effectively rules out any study using the second edition of the *Diagnostic and Statistical Manual of Mental Disorders* (*DSM–II*; American Psychiatric Association, 1968) or earlier criteria. It should be noted that Hislop (1971) and Esler and Goulston (1973), who used clinical interviews and *DSM–II* criteria, did report large proportions of IBS patients as having diagnosable psychopathology. Table 7.1 summarizes early studies of psychiatric disorders in IBS patients, which includes three studies in which structured psychiatric interviews, before they became the standard for research in the field, and the well-established diagnostic criteria of Feighner et al. (1972) were used.

Several points need to be made about these early studies. First, the percentage of IBS patients with some psychiatric diagnosis varied from 100% (Latimer et al., 1981) to 53% (Young, Alpers, Norland, & Woodruff, 1976), but in all instances more than half of the sample had a diagnosable condition. This latter point needs to be qualified by the high percentage (25% to 32%) of patients with an undiagnosed psychiatric disorder. The criteria published in Feighner et al. (1972) preceded those of the *DSM–III* and its successors; therefore, Feighner et al. pioneered the use of explicit inclusion and exclusion criteria. They also included only a limited set of disorders for which they felt good interrater agreement could be obtained. Thus, to account for everyone who was believed to have a psychiatric disorder but for whom a specific diagnosis could not be made, they included undiagnosed psychiatric disorder as a residual category. The category is somewhat analogous to the *DSM* diagnosis of NOS (not otherwise specified) found at the end of the entry for each disorder.

The common diagnoses were primary affective disorder, depressed type, which maps onto major depressive disorder; anxiety neurosis, which maps onto panic disorder (PD) or generalized anxiety disorder (GAD); and hysteria, which maps roughly onto Briquet's syndrome or somatization disorder (see Table 7.2). An interesting exception to those diagnoses is represented by a study by Wender and Kalm (1983), who found that 27% of those with IBS met the criteria for attention deficit hyperactivity disorder.

More recent research, in which criteria were based on the third revised edition of the *DSM* (*DSM–III–R*; American Psychiatric Association (1987), is summarized in Tables 7.3 and 7.4. Table 7.3 provides methodological details, including descriptions of the groups, instruments, and criteria. Table 7.4 shows the percentage of samples with various Axis I disorders.

Table 7.3 illustrates several interesting points. First, the proportion of IBS samples with no diagnosable psychiatric disorder was highly variable, ranging from a low of 6% (Lydiard, 1992; Walker, Roy-Byrne, & Katon, 1990) to about 66% (Blewett et al., 1996; Thornton, McIntyre, Murray-Lyon, & Gruzelier, 1990). Both of these latter two studies are from the United Kingdom. My own published report (Blanchard, Scharff, Schwarz,

TABLE 7.1
Summary of Early Psychiatric Studies of IBS Patients (Demographics)

Authors and patient groups	*n*	Age	% female	IBS criteria	Patient source	Psychiatric diagnosis: criteria	Psychiatric diagnosis: method	% excluded
Liss, Alpers, & Woodruff, 1973	25	46	68	clinical + physical exam & tests	university medical school GI clinic	Feighner	structured interview	8%
Young et al., 1976				clinical	consecutive new cases of IBS in private primary care practice	Feighner	structured interview	17%
IBS	29	49	79					
GI illness & other (*n* = 10)	33	48	48					
MacDonald & Bouchier, 1980				clinical	consecutive general medical outpatient clinic	ICD-9	clinical interview + GHQ	6%
IBS	32	N/R	N/R					
organic illness (*n* = 10)	35							
Latimer et al., 1981	16	N/R	56	clinical		Feighner	clinical interview	
Wender & Kalm, 1983	22	28	77	clinical	university medical school GI clinic	DSM–III	SADS–L	
Ford et al., 1987				clinical	outpatients referred to GI specialist	RDC	PSE	
Functional	48	37	65					
IBS (*n* = 36)								
Dyspepsia (*n* = 12)								
Organic	16	39	50					

Note. ICD-9 = International Classification of Diseases, 9th Edition; GHQ = General Health Questionnaire; SADS–L = Schizophrenia and Affective Disorders Schedule–Lifetime version; RDC = Research Diagnostic Criteria; PSE = Present State Examination.

TABLE 7.2
Summary of Early Psychiatric Studies of IBS Patients (Disorders Diagnosed)

	Number and percent of IBS patients diagnosed with specified disorders															
Authors and patient groups	no dis.	maj. dep.	other mood	anx., neur.	GAD	soc. phob.	PTSD	other anx.	somat. disorder	subs. abuse	ADHD	pers. dis.	Current caseness	psychotic disorder	eat. dis.	other
Liss, Alpers, & Woodruff, 1973	8	8	—	24[1]	—	—	—	—	28							32[2]
Young et al., 1976																
IBS	28	17	—	4[1]					17	4						31[2]
GI illness & other (n = 10)	82	6	—	3[1]					3	3						3[2]
MacDonald & Bouchier, 1980																
IBS	47	13	12[3]	19[1]					3	3						3[4]
organic illness (n = 10)	80	—	6[3]	14[1]												
Latimer et al., 1981	0	31		19[1]					13							25[2]
Wender & Kalm, 1983	27	23	27	—	14	—	—	—	—	—	27	15				0
Ford et al., 1987																
Functional	46	15		29[1]									42			20[2]
IBS (n = 36)																
Dyspepsia (n = 12)																
Organic	87	6		6									6			

Note. [1]Anxiety neurosis: a combination of PD and GAD. [2]Undiagnosed psychiatric disorder. [3]Depressive neurosis, probably dysthymia. [4]Bereavement.

Suls, & Barlow, 1990) yielded results at about the midpoint, with 44% free of any Axis I diagnosis.

The comparable values of no diagnosable Axis I disorder for comparison groups of patients with IBD are 75% (Blanchard et al., 1990), 81% (Walker, Roy-Byrne, & Katon, 1990), and 35% (Walker, Gelfand, Gelfand, & Katon, 1995), or for groups with any organic disorder, 87% had no diagnosable Axis I disorder (Ford, Miller, Eastwood, & Eastwood, 1987). IBD makes a good comparison condition because it represents a chronic illness with flares and remissions, and patients suffer from abdominal pain and diarrhea frequently. (See chapter 12 for more detail on IBD.)

The psychiatric disorders typically found in IBS are primarily mood, anxiety, and somatoform disorders. Whereas Walker et al. (1990) and Lydiard (1992) have tended to find the most common comorbid disorders to be mood disorders, especially major depression, in the Albany samples we have tended to find more anxiety disorders, especially GAD. Panic disorder (PD) is also commonly found, as are many other anxiety disorders. Both Walker et al. and Lydiard reported high levels of somatization disorder; Walker et al. also found a relatively high level of alcohol abuse or dependence.

There may be a tendency to find the kind of comorbidity one seeks. In a recent study from South Carolina, Irwin et al. (1996) found that 36% of their IBS sample met criteria for posttraumatic stress disorder (PTSD). In this study, special attention had been paid to trauma history, and two members of the research team specialized in trauma and PTSD.

An alternative approach to this comorbidity question was taken by several other researchers. For example, instead of seeking to identify what diagnoses might be present in a set of IBS patients, Tollefson, Tollefson, Pederson, Luxenberg, and Dunsmore (1991) and Lydiard (1992) have examined carefully diagnosed psychiatric samples for the presence of IBS. Tollefson et al. found that 37% of participants with GAD also met criteria for IBS and that 29% met criteria for major depression. Lydiard (1992) found that 41% of patients with panic disorder (*DSM–III–R*) met the criteria for IBS. Noyes, Cook, Garvey, and Summers (1990) found that 17% of their patients with panic disorder met criteria for IBS.

Continuing along this line, Masand et al. (1995) compared 56 patients seeking outpatient care for major depression to 40 patients seeking outpatient medical care. Among those with major depression, 15 (27%) met Rome criteria for IBS, as compared to only one (2.5%) of the control participants. Another 9 (16%) met part of the Rome criteria. In the United Kingdom, Dewsnap, Gomborone, Libby, and Farthing (1996) studied 87 inpatients with affective diagnoses. The sample (56% women) had diagnoses of either major depression (90%) or an anxiety state based on the International Classification of Diseases (9th ed., ICD-9), and 41.9% met Manning criteria for IBS. Almost all (93.5%) claimed the IBS antedated

TABLE 7.3
Summary of Psychiatric Studies of IBS Patients Based on the *DSM–III–R* (Demographics)

Authors and patient groups	*n*	Age	% female	IBS criteria	Patient source	Psychiatric diagnosis criteria	Psychiatric diagnosis method
Blanchard et al., 1990				clinical	seeking psychological treatment	DSM–III–R	ADIS
IBS	68	43	74				
IBD	44	43	64				
control	38	38	66				
Walker, Roy-Byrne, &				Manning	university medical school GI clinic + private practice	DSM–III–R	DIS–III–A
Katon, 1990	28	37	79				
IBS	19	35	53				
IBD							
Tollefson et al., 1991				clinical	outpatient psychiatry clinic	DSM–III–R	SCID
GAD	33	N/R	N/R				
major depression	34	N/R	N/R				
control	28	N/R	N/R				
Walker et al., 1995				Rome	GI specialty clinic consecutive	DSM–III–R	DIS
IBS	71	52	85				
IBD	40	41	73				
Lydiard, 1992				Manning	university medical school GI clinic	DSM–III–R	N/R
IBS	35	N/R	N/R				
Panic disorder	68	N/R	N/R				

Fossey & Lydiard, 1990				N/R	university medical school GI clinic	DSM–III–R	Structured Interview
IBS	30	N/R	N/R				
Thornton et al., 1990				Manning	university GI clinic	N/R	HADS
IBS	25	40	76				
Blewett et al., 1996				Manning	GI specialty clinic	N/R	CIDI
IBS	63	35	68				
Sullivan et al., 1995				Manning	university GI clinic depressed, 1st time at clinic	N/R	CIDI + HADS
IBS	70	N/R	N/R				
major depression	60	N/R	N/R				
control	46	N/R	N/R				
Irwin et al., 1996				Rome	university GI clinic	DSM–III–R	SCID
IBS	50	44.1	80				
Jarrett et al., 1998				Rome	volunteers	DSM–III–R	DIS
IBS patients	32	34.9	100				
IBS nonpatients	29	30.7	100				
control	34	32.6	100				

Note. ADIS = Anxiety Disorders Interview Schedule; DIS = Diagnostic Interview Schedule; SCID = Structured Clinical Interview for DSM–III–R; HADS = Hospital Anxiety and Depression Scale; CIDI = Composite International Diagnostic Interview.

TABLE 7.4
Summary of Psychiatric Studies of IBS Patients Based on the *DSM–III–R* (Disorders Diagnosed)

Authors and patient groups	Percent of IBS patients diagnosed with specified disorders													
	no. dis.	maj. dep.	other mood	panic dis.	GAD	soc. phob.	PTSD	other anx.	somat. dis.	subs. abuse	ADHD	pers. dis.	psychotic disorder	eat. dis.	% refused
Blanchard et al., 1990															
IBS	44	6	6	3	21	7	4	4	1	1	—		1		
IBD	75	—	2	7	7	—	—	9	—	—	—		—		
control	82	—	—	5	3	3	—	3	—	5	—		—		
Walker, Roy-Byrne, & Katon, 1990															
IBS	7	61	—	29	54	11	—	29	32	32*					25
IBD	81	16	—	0	11	0	—	11	0	16					
Tollefson et al., 1991	Researchers looked for frequency of IBS among psychiatric diagnostic groups														
GAD	12/33 = 37%														
major depression	10/34 = 29%														
control	3/28 = 11%														
Walker et al., 1995															
IBS	6	76*	39	41	58*	—	—	41*	48*	25				10	9
IBD	35	45	23	25	35	—	—	23	3	23				18	20
Lydiard, 1992															
IBS	6	46	29	31	34	29	—	9	26	—					N/R
Panic Disorder	41% of PD patients met criteria for IBS														

Fossey & Lydiard, 1990															
IBS	17	63	20	23	13	—	—	7	30	10	7	—			N/R
Thornton et al., 1990	16% prior mood disorders														
IBS	16% current anxiety disorder														
Blewett et al., 1996															17
IBS	67	17	5	16	5										
Sullivan et al., 1995															
IBS	67%	53% had HADS score in morbid range (100)													
major depression	0														
control	N/R														
1st-degree relatives															
IBS (280)	67.1[a]	6.7[a]		1.4						0.7	0.7				
mood disorder (279)	58.7[a]	6.4[a]		1.4						1.8	0.7				
control (224)	83.0[b]	2.3[b]		1.4						0.5	0				
Irwin et al., 1996	46	32		18	4	10	36			4					
Trauma + PTSD (18)	28[a]	44[a]		22	—	22	100[a]			11					
No Trauma, No PTSD (28)	75[b]	14[b]		18	—	0	0[b]			0					
Jarrett et al., 1998															
IBS patients	33[a]	44	22	19	31[a]				3	9[a]					
IBS nonpatients	41[a]	37	30	19	19[a,b]				4	33[b]					
control	65[b]	24	9	12	6[b]				0	15[a,b]					

Note. HADS = Hospital Anxiety and Depression Scale. *Significant difference in percent of IBS sample and percent of IBD sample with this diagnosis; [a,b]Groups that share a superscript do not have significantly different percentages of participants who meet this diagnosis.

the onset of their psychiatric problems. Slightly less than half (42%) of those meeting criteria for IBS had sought medical care for it.

Part of the difficulty with the data contained in Tables 7.2 and 7.4 is that the IBS samples were of modest size (mostly 20–30 participants, with a few in the 60–70 range). A second obvious difficulty is the use of differing psychiatric diagnostic criteria and diagnostic instruments. With regard to criteria, because the Research Diagnostic Criteria (RDC) and the *DSM–III* are both hierarchical in terms of diagnostic rules (the presence of major depression mitigated against diagnosing any anxiety disorder or somatoform disorder), the true picture of the extent of comorbid diagnoses is obscured. With the advent of the *DSM–III–R* and the *DSM–IV* (American Psychiatric Association, 1994), more comorbidity can be legitimately coded, and more anxiety disorder diagnoses emerge.

Yet a different approach to the issue of the degree of psychiatric comorbidity among IBS sufferers was taken by two groups of researchers (Lydiard et al., 1994; Walker, Katon, Jemelka, & Roy-Byrne, 1992), who presented a reanalysis of data from a large mental health epidemiologic study, the NIMH Epidemiologic Catchment Area (ECA) study (Robins & Regier, 1991). In brief, in the ECA study, trained lay interviewers interviewed approximately 3,500 community-dwelling adults in five different communities (New Haven, CT; Baltimore, MD; St. Louis, MO; Durham, NC; and Los Angeles, CA) with the NIMH Diagnostic Interview Schedule (DIS; Robins, Helzer, Croughan, & Ratcliff, 1981). It was constructed so that reliable and valid *DSM–III* diagnoses could be made.

Included in the interviews were data for a number of physical symptoms (as part of the assessment for somatization disorder). From these physical symptom data (presence of abdominal pain, diarrhea, constipation, and stomach bloating, which were not medically explained), the researchers deduced a diagnoses of probable IBS. It is clear that no exclusionary examinations were done and that there were only limited symptom descriptions. Nevertheless, these two reports represent a clever use of a large existing data set.

Walker et al. (1992) examined data from all five sites (*N* = 18,571), using as a diagnosis for probable IBS any combination of two of the following: abdominal pain, diarrhea, and/or constipation, which were either medically unexplained or not caused by medical illness. A total of 412 cases of probable IBS (with no other pain problem) were identified and compared to 1,572 cases with no GI symptoms. In all instances, women outnumbered men among those with probable IBS (353 women to 59 men). Among the total samples, probable IBS cases compared to non-IBS cases showed higher rates of major depression (13.4% vs. 3.8%), Panic Disorder (PD, 5.2% vs. 1.0%), and agoraphobia (17.8% vs. 5.1%). (I should note that current diagnostic practices would label those with agoraphobia as having PD with agoraphobic avoidance and those with PD as having PD with mild or no avoidance.)

Lydiard et al. (1994) took a more conservative approach. First, data from one site (New Haven) was eliminated because of questions about the assessment of the somatic symptoms (leaving a total *N* of 13,537). Second, only GI symptoms that were rated as medically unexplained were counted. Using this procedure, they found a lifetime prevalence of probable IBS of only 0.8% when IBS was defined by the presence of abdominal pain, diarrhea, constipation, and bloating, all of which were medically unexplained. (This prevalence rate is extremely low in comparison to the 11% to 17% values presented in chapter 2.) They also compared the prevalence of IBS among four mutually exclusive groups as follows: 7.2% among those with PD only (*DSM–III–R*; $n = 194$); 2.1% among those with phobia or OCD only ($n = 2{,}438$); 1.3% among those with any other psychiatric disorder ($n = 1{,}932$); and 0.7% among those with no psychiatric disorder ($n = 8{,}973$). It is thus clear that there was a high association of IBS with PD, even when this much more conservative approach was applied to the data.

Interestingly, two additional studies have focused on what happens to IBS if the psychiatric disorder is treated. Lydiard, Laraia, Howell, and Ballenger (1986) reported on the drug treatment of five people who met the *DSM–III* criteria for PD who also had clear cases of IBS. The pharmacological treatment regiments were highly varied and included benzodiazepines and high-potency benzodiazepines (alprazolam), as well as tricyclic antidepressants. In all five cases, successful treatment of the PD was accompanied by major relief of IBS symptoms.

In another study, Noyes et al. (1990) treated 30 patients who had been diagnosed with PD via the *DSM–III* and the Structured Clinical Interview for the *DSM–III* (SCID; Spitzer & Williams, 1982). The patients were treated in a double-blind trial with diazepam, alprazolam, or placebo for 8 weeks. Five (16.7%) of the PD patients met Manning criteria for IBS. In all instances, the onset of the IBS coincided with the onset of PD. All of the patients with PD and IBS responded to the PD treatment. Average change in scores on the Hamilton Rating Scale for Depression (Hamilton, 1959) was from 18.4 to 5.8 ($p < .001$) for the treatment successes (primarily for those with PD without IBS). Their scores on a digestive symptom inventory fell from 11.2 to 5.2 ($p < .001$).

Clinical Hint

These results from drug treatments of individuals with a primary diagnosis of an anxiety disorder (usually PD) seem to show that alleviating the anxiety disorder is accompanied by major improvement in IBS symptoms. The results raise the interesting question of what would happen to psychiatric comorbidity if the IBS was successfully treated with a psychological therapy. Although data described in chapter 6 speak to the point (Blanchard et al., 1987), I have no direct answer, nor does anyone else! A question for future research studies is what happens to categorical comorbid diagnoses when IBS is treated successfully by psychological means.

PSYCHIATRIC DIAGNOSES AMONG PATIENTS IN THE ALBANY STUDY

We have data on 250 IBS patients who underwent structured psychiatric interviews, administered by highly trained interviewers. About three quarters of the interviewers used the Anxiety Disorders Interview Schedule–Revised (ADIS–R; DiNardo & Barlow, 1988), whereas other interviewers used the SCID. In all instances I have presented the primary psychiatric diagnosis, based on clinical severity. In Table 7.5 the data are summarized separately for male and female IBS patients. A third column presents the data for the entire sample.

One of the first things that stands out in Table 7.5 is the lack of gender difference in diagnosable mental disorders. We found that a nonsignificantly higher percentage of male (69.4%) than female (64.4%) IBS

TABLE 7.5
Primary Psychiatric Diagnoses (Axis I) for IBS Patients in Albany Studies

Diagnosis	% Women (n = 188)	% Men (n = 62)	Total (N = 250)
Age	43.0	40.5	42.8
No mental disorder	35.6	30.6	34.4
Major depression	3.2	3.2	3.2
Dysthymia	3.7	9.7	6.4
Bipolar I	0.5	—	0.4
Mood disorder NOS	—	1.6	0.4
Any mood disorder	*7.4*	*14.5*	*10.4*
GAD	26.6	25.8	26.4
PD	2.7	1.6	2.4
Panic with agoraphobia	5.9	1.6	4.8
Agoraphobia without panic	2.7	3.2	2.8
Social phobia	8.0	14.5	9.6
Specific phobia	4.3	1.6	3.6
PTSD	3.7	—	2.8
Any anxiety disorder	*53.9*	*48.3*	*52.4*
Somatization disorder	0.5	3.2	0.4
Hypochondriasis	0.5	—	0.4
Bulimia	0.5	—	0.4
Alcohol abuse	—	1.6	0.4
Schizophreniform psychosis (past)	—	1.6	0.4

patients met criteria for one or more Axis I disorders (X^2[*df* 1, *N* = 250] .52, n.s.). This contrasts with the finding reported in chapter 5 that women tend to score higher than men on dimensional measures of anxiety and depression.

The most common broad category of psychiatric disorders includes anxiety disorders, encompassing 52.4% of the sample, followed by mood disorders (10.4%). What is especially striking is the prevalence of GAD: 26.4% of the total sample met the criteria for this disorder as a primary psychiatric diagnosis. Moreover, the rate was essentially the same for men and women. The second most common Axis I diagnosis is social phobia. We found surprisingly little major depression or dysthymia, especially in light of the research summarized in Tables 7.2 and 7.4.

One needs to keep in mind when examining these data that they come from a treatment-seeking sample of IBS patients; these patients were volunteering for psychological treatments. I know that some IBS patients referred to me never follow through, but I do not know much else about them. Thus, there are biases in these data, but I cannot determine the nature of the biases. In any event, it is a large sample and thus should help anyone in the field gain a sense of what psychiatric comorbidity may accompany the IBS patients who are referred to you.

8

IRRITABLE BOWEL SYNDROME AND STRESS: WHICH COMES FIRST?

If you ask IBS patients whether stress (not defined) plays a role in their GI symptoms, the overwhelming majority will answer, "yes!" If you become a bit more precise and ask whether stress *causes* their IBS symptoms, a large majority will continue to answer affirmatively. (For a data-based affirmative answer, see Drossman et al., 1982.) Their answers agree with conventional clinical wisdom (Whitehead, 1994) that IBS is a stress-related disorder, or a good example of a psychosomatic disorder wherein psychological factors (mainly psychological stress or conflicts) lead to, or cause, the somatic symptoms one finds in IBS. In this chapter I want to examine the evidence on this topic including a relatively unique study from our center. As usual, I will summarize the pertinent data from the English language literature and then present comparable data from our Albany studies.

It seems to me that there are two possible extreme cases. Either stress (psychological stress) leads to, or causes, IBS symptoms (or more precisely, an increase in psychological stress will, in the vulnerable IBS patient, be followed by an increase in GI symptoms). Or, alternatively, it could be that having to live with the periodic pain, discomfort, and inconvenience of IBS symptoms (such as never being too far away from a toilet) is a major source of stress to IBS patients. This implies a somatopsychic disorder in which a flare or increase in IBS symptoms is a major source of psychological distress and hence a life stressor that may set the stage for more stressful events in the patients' lives.

MEASUREMENT OF PSYCHOLOGICAL STRESS

The study of psychological or psychosocial stressors has taken several directions. Early on, following the pioneering work of Holmes and Rahe (1967), investigators have used various surveys of the occurrence of major life events or life changes to see if one group, say those with current IBS, had had more life events occur in the preceding year than comparison groups such as those with organic GI diseases or control participants. Holmes and Rahe also included weights, related to the relative stressfulness of each event, for each event in their scale, the Social Readjustment Rating Scale (SRRS). For example, death of a spouse was top weighted at 100. A more precise score was obtained by adding the weighted value of the events that had occurred in the preceding year.

Following Lazarus's (1966) pioneering ideas that the importance of the individual's appraisal (or interpretation) of events determines their impact on the individual or their stressfulness, and that events could thus be positive (marriage) or negative (death of a child), Sarason, Johnson, and Siegel (1978) put forth a modification to Holmes and Rahe's approach (the Life Experiences Survey; LES). In their work, the valence of the event was taken into account, and the valence itself could vary from person to person. Thus, the 91 events in the LES were each graded from 0 to −3 or from 0 to +3.

The next major step was the realization that it was not only the major life events that were stressful for individuals but also the frequent minor annoyances of everyday life (hassles) could be contributing to how stressed an individual felt. Counteracting these negative minor events were minor positive events (uplifts). Thus, Kanner, Coyne, Schaefer, and Lazarus (1981) published their daily hassles and uplifts scale, which contained 117 minor stressors or hassles and 135 positive events or uplifts. The occurrence of each hassle (minor negative event) over the past month was first noted. Then the severity of each event that occurred for the patient was noted on a 1 to 3 scale (somewhat severe to extremely severe).

The most recent entry into this field is the Daily Stress Inventory (DSI) of Brantley and Jones (1989), a weekly form on which patients note the occurrence of 57 stressful events for each day and rate the impact of those events on a 1 (occurred but was not stressful) to 7 (caused me to panic) scale. It then yields several scores: number of events each day, total intensity of events each day, and an average intensity per event. Weekly averages are also calculated.

THE RELATION OF IBS TO MAJOR LIFE EVENTS

Table 8.1 summarizes studies that have presented data on the level of major life events in patients with IBS. Both studies in which IBS patients were compared to other groups and studies of IBS patients alone are included. Table 8.1 shows little in the way of consistent results. For example, in two studies, IBS patients endorsed more stressful events (or stressful negative events) than did either patients with IBD (Mendeloff, Monk, Siegel, & Lilienfeld, 1970) or patients with organic GI diseases (Craig & Brown, 1984). However, two other studies, one using the Life Events and Difficulties (LED) Interview (Ford et al., 1987), and one using the SRRS (Schwarz et al., 1993), showed no significant differences. Blanchard, Radnitz, et al.'s (1986) comparisons of IBS patients to age- and gender-matched migraine headache patients showed more stressful life events for the IBS patients but no difference between IBS and tension headache patients (see Table 5.4).

Comparisons of IBS patients to nonill control participants show more uniformity; four studies show greater number of stressful life events or weighted life event scores than for control participants (Blanchard, Radnitz, et al., 1986; Drossman et al., 1988; Mendeloff et al., 1970; Whitehead, Crowell, Robinson, Heller, & Schuster, 1992); only two more recent studies did not (Levy, Cain, Jarrett, & Heitkemper, 1997; Schwarz et al., 1993).

When IBS patients were compared to IBS nonpatients, Drossman et al. (1988) found more negative life events and greater weighted scores for the IBS nonpatients, whereas Levy et al. (1997) found no significant differences. Whitehead et al. (1992) found no differences between IBS patients and FBD patients (who met the clinical but not Manning criteria for IBS). Finally, Bennett et al. (1998) found among patients with functional GI disorders (includes IBS, functional dyspepsia, and other disorders) a significant relation between number of functional GI symptoms and number of chronic stressors undergone (for an average of 3.9 years).

Firm conclusions are difficult to draw from this literature; the weight of evidence does seem to show more recent major life stressors for IBS patients than for nonill control participants but few other consistent effects. I should note that the two separate studies from Albany (Blanchard, Radnitz, et al., 1986; Schwarz et al., 1993) add to the confusion. In the earlier study (n = 55) we found higher scores on the SRRS for IBS patients than nonill control participants (n = 63). In the later study, we found no difference on the SRRS for IBS patients (n = 121) compared to nonill control participants (n = 45).

THE RELATION OF IBS TO MINOR LIFE STRESSES

Studies of minor life stressors (hassles) in the lives of IBS patients are summarized in Table 8.2. The list is noticeably shorter (and more re-

TABLE 8.1
Summary of Research on IBS and Major Life Stresses

Authors and patient groups	*n*	Age	% female	IBS criteria	Stress measure	Time interval	Results
Mendeloff et al., 1970				clinical	early death of parents, inconsistent work history or education, multiple marriages, recent death of someone close	lifetime	IBS > UC on previous illnesses (especially for women). IBS > UC on average stress index (men 4.85 vs. 4.19; population, 4.55/women 2.18 vs. 1.60; population, 2.07). IBS > UC on precipitating (recent) factors (women 1.79 vs. men 1.42; population, 1.42)
IBS	102	43	64				
IBD (UC only)	158	N/R	57				
Nonill (control)	753	N/R	N/R				
Blanchard, Radnitz, et al., 1986				clinical	SRRS	1 yr	
IBS	55	42	73				225[a]
Tension headache	68	40	76				171[a,b]
Migraine headache	68	38	72				147[b]
Nonill (control)	63	42	73				166[b]
Schwarz et al., 1993				clinical	SRRS	1 yr	
IBS	121	43	69				276 (no significant differences)
IBD	46	42	63				269
Nonill (control)	45	36	76				299
Ford et al., 1987				Manning	LED Interview	6 mos	anxiety-provoking episode (only) present in 17/48 (35%) of functional and 2/16 (12.5%) of organic, n.s.
Functional GI	48	37	66				
IBS 75%							
Dyspepsia 25%							
Organic GI	16	39	50				

Craig & Brown, 1984				N/R	LED Interview	9 mos	% severe event		% goal frustration event	
Organic GI	56	38	48				23%[b]		9%[c]	
Nonill (control)	135	N/R	N/R				15%[c]		54%[a]	
Functional GI	79	35	73				57%[a]		24%[b]	
IBS	21								14%	
Dyspepsia	14								29%	
Drossman et al., 1988				Manning	LES	6 mos	positive events score	positive events # events	negative events score	negative events # events
IBS patients	72	30	86				3.2[a]	1.7[a]	1.7[a]	1.6[a]
IBS nonpatients	82	26	94				5.7[b]	2.8[b]	5.6[c]	2.9[b]
Nonill (control)	84	28	88				6.2[b]	2.9[b]	3.7[b]	2.3[a,b]
Whitehead et al., 1992				Manning	Paykel et al. (1971) Life Events Scale	5 in 12 mos	# stress events		stress score weights	
IBS	39	28	100				5.4[a]		9.6[a]	
FBD*	108	26	100				4.8[a,b]		8.4[a,b]	
Control participants	232	26	100				4.3[b]		7.2[b]	
Levy et al., 1997		33		Rome	LES	6 mos	+ events score	+ events # events	− events score	− events # events
IBS patients	26		100				13.9	6.6	11.2	5.1
IBS nonpatients	23		100				15.5	7.4	11.7	5.4
Control participants	26		100				12.2	6.0	10.2	4.9
							all between-group comparisons n.s.			
Bennett et al., 1998				Rome	LED Interview	6 mos	Significant regression coefficient between # of functional GI symptoms and # of chronic stressors. 95% of sample exposed to current stressor average # of stressors −2.4; average duration 3.9 years.			
Total	188	44	72							
IBS	122									
Functional dyspepsia	117									
Other FBD	21									

Note: Results column means that share a superscript do not differ. *Participants diagnosed with clinical IBS criteria. IBD = Inflammatory Bowel Disease; UC = ulcerative colitis; SRRS = Social Readjustment Rating Scale; LED = Life Events and Difficulties Interview; LES = Life Events Survey.

TABLE 8.2
Summary of Research on IBS and Minor Life Stresses (Hassles)

Authors and patient groups	*n*	Age	% female	IBS criteria	Stress measure	Time interval	Results
Payne & Blanchard, 1995	34	40	85	Rome	Hassles Scale	past month	Hassles frequency, 17.4; Intensity, 1.9
Dancey et al., 1995	30	N/R	100	N/R	Hassles Scale	1/wk for 5 wks	Average hassles, 35.5
Dancey et al., 1998	31	N/R	74	N/R	Hassles Scale	1/day for 28 days	Average scores, N/R

cent). There are no comparisons of IBS patients to other groups. Payne and Blanchard (1995) reported an average hassle frequency of 17.4, with an intensity of 1.9 in their sample of 34. Dancey, Whitehouse, Painter, and Backhouse (1995) reported an average hassles frequency of 35.5 (no intensity score given) over a 5-week period. Thus, little can be said about this.

There is, however, an interesting finding in this area if one jumps ahead to treatment (see chapter 16). Twelve of the thirty-four patients in the Payne and Blanchard (1995) study received cognitive therapy and as a group significantly improved (i.e., CPSR scores of 0.5 or greater in 75% of those treated; see chapter 4). Hassles scales scores collected *after treatment* on these 12 patients showed no change in frequency of hassles (pretreatment score, 20.1; posttreatment score, 17.3) *but did show a significant decrease in the intensity ratings* (pretreatment intensity, 2.0; posttreatment intensity 1.6, $t(11) = 2.81$, $p = .017$). The two other groups did not change. The data from the symptom-monitoring control participants ($n = 10$) provide evidence of the relative stability of hassles (pretreatment score, 16.3; posttreatment score, 15.4; pretreatment intensity, 1.7; posttreatment intensity, 1.8).

Clinical Hint

It appears that some forms of treatment, especially cognitive therapy, equip recipients with the ability to better withstand the minor stresses of everyday life. Although they continue to experience these minor stressors or hassles, patients are less distressed by these stressors after treatment.

PROSPECTIVE STUDIES OF IBS SYMPTOMS AND STRESS

Given the lack of consistency in the findings on whether IBS patients have suffered more recent (six months plus) or lifetime life stressors, and given the strong opinion of patients who claim that stress causes their IBS symptoms, researchers have recently turned to a different kind of study—the prospective examination of the link between life stress and GI symptoms. In essence, these studies have asked, do life stressors occurring in the current time period, n, lead to an increase in GI symptoms in the next time period, $n + 1$. Such a finding would be consistent with causality. Table 8.3 summarizes the prospective studies. The results in Table 8.3 are very complicated, even after having been simplified for the table. This stems in part from the complex statistics used to analyze time series data.

There are two chief conclusions supported by these studies. One, most studies show significant concurrent relations between stress and GI symptoms, whether the time interval is three months (Whitehead et al., 1992),

TABLE 8.3
Prospective Studies of IBS Symptoms and Stress

Authors and patient groups	*n*	Age	% female	IBS criteria	IBS measure	Stress measure	Time interval	Results
Whitehead et al., 1992				Rome	frequency of IBS symptoms and total score	LED (frequency × intensity) for 3 months	5 every 3 months	1. Stress for period *n* did not predict GI symptoms for period *n* + *1* among IBS or FBD patients for any period. 2. There were stronger concurrent relations (GI symptoms and stress for period *n*) for IBS than for FBD patients or control participants for the first 2 intervals but not the second 2 intervals. 3. Averaged across all intervals, IBS patients showed fewer significant correlations between specific GI symptoms and stress (2) than did FBD patients (6).
IBS	39	28	100					
FBD	108	26	100					
Control participants	232	26	100					
Dancey et al., 1995				N/R	daily ratings of 7 GI symptoms	Hassles Scale (53 items)	5 wks	1. Hassles scores significantly correlated with total GI symptoms scores (week *n*), averaged across all systems (*R* = .47). 2. Hassles scores (week *n*) significantly correlated with week *n* − *1* total GI symptom scores averaged across participants (*R* = .54). 3. Hassles score (week *n*) correlation with GI symptoms in week *n* + *1* was lower than (1) or (2) and n.s.
IBS	30	45	100					
Levy et al., 1997		33		Rome	daily ratings of 5 GI symptoms	Daily question "How stressful was your day today?"	2 menstrual cycles ~32 days	1. Mean daily stress scores were higher for two IBS groups. 2. Same-day stress ratings and GI symptom scores were significantly correlated for both IBS groups (patients = .08; nonpatients = .16), but they were not greater than correlation for nonpatients. 3. Day *n* − *1* stress ratings were not correlated for any group with day *n* GI symptom scores. 4. Average of *n* and *n* − *1* stress ratings correlated significantly for both IBS groups (patients = .10; nonpatients = .20) and greater than rating for control participants.
IBS patients	26		100					
IBS nonpatients	23		100					
Control participants	26		100					

								5. 10/26 IBS patients had significant correlations ($n - 1$ and n) of stress and with n GI symptoms. 13/23 of IBS nonpatients had significant correlations. There were very few $n - 1$ stress and n GI correlations (4/26 IBS patients; 5/23 IBS nonpatients).
Dancey et al., 1998 IBS	30	N/R	74	N/R	daily ratings of 7 GI symptoms	Hassles Scale (117 items)	28 days	1. For 23%, GI symptoms on day n predicted GI symptoms on day $n + 1$. For 53%, hassles on day n predicted hassles on day $n + 1$. 2. For 14 (47%) there was a significant same-day correlation of GI symptoms and daily hassles. 3. For 13 (43%) hassles on days $n - 4$, $n - 3$, $n - 2$, and $n - 1$ correlated significantly with GI symptoms on day n, accounting for 35% of variance, but significant correlations for hassles on day $n - 1$ and GI symptoms were found for only 5 cases day n.
Suls et al., 1994 IBS	44	43	75	clinical	daily ratings of pain, constipation, and diarrhea	Bothersome Events (85 items)	3 wks	1. Week 1 stress correlated significantly (R = .33) with Week 1 GI symptoms; Week 2 stress correlated significantly (R = .44) with Week 2 Gi symptoms. 2. Week 1 GI symptoms accounted for the most variance (R^2 = .46) in Week 2 GI symptoms; Week 2 GI symptoms accounted for most of the variance (R^2 = 46) in Week 3 GI symptoms. 3. Week n and $n - 1$ stress did not predict week n GI symptoms. 4. Day $n - 1$ stress did not account for day n GI symptoms; low level (R < .10) for concurrent correlations. 5. Day $n - 1$ GI symptoms predicted day n GI symptoms (R^2 = .19). 6. Only 8/44 (18%) of individuals showed significant concurrent correlations of stress and GI symptoms (6 positive, 2 negative).

Note. LED = Life Events and Difficulties; FBD = Functional Bowel Disorder.

one week averages (Dancey et al., 1995; Suls, Wan, & Blanchard, 1994), or daily ratings (Dancey, Taghavi, & Fox, 1998; Levy et al., 1997; but not Suls et al., 1994). Two, no study shows support for a causative model, that is, stress at time n predicting GI symptoms at time $n + 1$. Levy et al. (1997), however, found that significant relations for stress at times n and $n + 1$ combined predicted GI symptoms at time $n + 1$, but stress at n alone did not.

When examining individual patient data using time series analyses, Levy et al. (1997) found that 38% of IBS patients and 57% of IBS nonpatients had significant relations between stress on days n and $n + 1$ combined and GI symptoms on day $n + 1$. Dancey et al. (1998), using an undiagnosed sample who were part of a support group, found that 43% had significant correlations from stress on days $n - 4$, $n - 3$, $n - 2$, and $n - 1$ with GI symptoms on day n; only 16% had a significant relation between day $n - 1$ stress and day n GI symptoms. As Suls et al. (1994) had pointed out, however, Dancey et al. failed to control for the autocorrelations of stress on day n with stress on day $n + 1$ or GI symptoms on day n with GI symptoms on day $n + 1$, (56% of participants showed the stress autocorrelation, and 23% showed the GI symptom autocorrelation). Suls et al. (1994) showed that 46% of variance in GI symptoms at week $n + 1$ was accounted for by GI symptoms at week n; that is, last week's GI symptoms predict this week's GI symptoms. Another difficulty with the Dancey et al. (1998) study was the failure to correct for the possible statistical artifact of multiple analyses on small samples. Despite the methodological problems, the Dancey et al. study does suggest that if one views stress cumulatively over up to 4 days, then this cumulative stress does seem to predict subsequent GI symptoms.

In my opinion, the most methodologically rigorous study on this topic was completed by Suls and Wan at our center (Suls et al., 1994). As they pointed out, to examine the causal hypothesis, one needs to control for the correlations from time n to time $n + 1$ for the GI symptoms (these account for 46% of variance [$r = .68$] on a week-by-week basis and 19% of variance [$r = .45$] on a day-by-day basis). When that was done, most of the correlations between stress and concurrent or subsequent GI symptoms was accounted for, leaving only 1% to 2% of new variance. They examined weekly averages and daily data for stress and individual GI symptoms and a GI symptom composite while controlling for gender, psychiatric status, and IBS subtype. No study has yet refuted their conclusions on the lack of relationship between yesterday's stress and today's GI symptoms (the causal model).

A point that has not been carefully examined is the somatopsychic hypothesis that suggests that a flare up of IBS symptoms is a very stressful experience. All studies to date have omitted GI symptom increases or flares as a possible life stressor. Yet, we know well from patients' reports that such flare ups are a major cause of concern and stress in the patient's life, and that worry and anticipation of GI symptoms are major problems for patients.

CONCLUSIONS

IBS patients as a whole may have stressful lives. It is not yet clear whether they experience more stressful life events than others. It seems that IBS nonpatients may have even more stressful lives than IBS patients. Although the bulk of the evidence supports a concurrent relation between change in stress and change in GI symptoms, the evidence is very weak on a causal relationship between a change in stress and a subsequent (next day or next week) change in GI symptoms. There are, however, some proportion of individuals (up to 43% in Dancey et al., 1998) who do show such a relation if the period for considering stress is left variable (from one to four preceding days). This is obviously a topic needing further research on a relatively large and well-characterized population.

9

IRRITABLE BOWEL SYNDROME AND EARLY ABUSE

In 1990, Drossman and his colleagues at the University of North Carolina at Chapel Hill published an article in the prestigious journal, *Annals of Internal Medicine*, that purported to show that female patients with functional GI disorders (including IBS) reported significantly higher levels of early sexual and physical abuse than did comparable female patients with a variety of organic GI disorders (Drossman, Leserman, et al., 1990). I was very skeptical of the report and remember dismissing it to myself as some sort of sampling fluke or aberration. Later research by others, a replication by Drossman's group, and work from our center (after I overcame my skepticism) convinced me that I was initially wrong. There are now at least seven published reports supporting Drossman, Leserman, et al.'s (1990) early observation. This research is summarized in Table 9.1.

In the initial study on this topic, Drossman, Leserman, et al. (1990) gave the questions described in Table 9.1 to 75 patients (37.5%) with functional GI disorders and 125 patients with a variety of organic GI diseases who were consecutive female attendees at a medical school GI clinic. His primary comparisons were between those with functional GI disorders versus those with organic GI diseases. In every comparison, there was a numerically greater history of various forms of sexual abuse among those with functional GI disorders than among those with organic GI diseases, with 53% of the functional cases reporting some history of sexual abuse

TABLE 9.1
Summary of Research on Sexual Abuse and IBS

Sample characteristics and abuse questions	Drossman, Leserman, et al., 1990			Talley et al., 1994				Talley, Fett, & Zinsmeister, 1995				
	functional	organic	IBS	child	adult	IBS	non-IBS	child	adult	functional	organic	IBS
Sample size	75	131	38	919		130	789			440	557	203
Percent female	100%	100%	100%	50%		68.5	50			67.5	48.5	N/R
Mean age	43.5			39.5		39.6	39.5			54.6	58.7	N/R
IBS diagnostic criteria	Rome					Rome				Manning	Manning	
Source of IBS patients	University clinic GI patients			Olmsted County survey				University clinic GI outpatients				
Sexual Abuse during childhood (< 14 years) has anyone ever:												
1. Exposed the sex organs of their body to you?	39%	23%	N/R	8.7	9.3	—	—	3.7	3.3	—	—	
2. Threatened to have sex with you?	40%	23%	N/R	4.4	9.6	—	—	1.7	3.7	—	—	
3. Touched the sex organs of your body?	37%	27%	N/R	9.0	11.2	—	—	3.9	3.4	—	—	
4. Made you touch the sex organs of their body?	18%	15%	N/R	5.0	5.0	—	—	1.6	2.0	—	—	
5. Tried forcefully or succeeded to have sex when you didn't want this?	31%	8%		4.2	9.9	—	—	1.4	4.1	—	—	
Total Sexual Abuse	53%	37%	50%	—	—	43.1	19.4*	—	—	—	—	
Physical Abuse When you were a chlid (< 14), did an older person hit, kick, or beat you? (1 = never, 2 = seldom, 3 = occasionally, 4 = often)	13%	2%*	N/R	1.5	1.1	6.2	1.7	0.3	0.2			
Total Sexual and Physical Abuse	N/R	N/R	N/R	18.0	16.8	50.0	23.3*	6.9	6.0	13.4	8.8	12.8
Child and adult combined								18.7		22.1	16.2	21.7
Emotional or verbal abuse (often)	N/R	N/R	N/R	4.1	3.6	23.1	8.2*	2.6	1.3	2.5	3.4	

Sample characteristics and abuse questions	Walker, Katon, et al., 1993		Leserman et al., 1996	Delvaux et al., 1997				Dill et al., 1997	
	IBS	IBD		IBS	organic	opthal.	control	child	adult
Sample size Percent female Mean age IBS diagnostic criteria	28 79 37.1 clinical	19 53 35.3	239 100% 39.4 Rome	196 81% 41 Rome	135 45% 42	200 55% 44	172 53% 40	77 79% 54 Manning	
Source of IBS patients	University clinic GI patients			Clinic				Private practice GI patients	
Sexual Abuse during childhood (< 14 years) has anyone ever:			no difference in functional vs. organic GI disorder						
1. Exposed the sex organs of their body to you?	—	—	—					17	14
2. Threatened to have sex with you?	—	—	—	2%	1%	5%	1%	13	18
3. Touched the sex organs of your body?	—	—	—	11%	5%	3%	5%	15	21
4. Made you touch the sex organs of their body?	—	—	—					10	15
5. Tried forcefully or succeeded to have sex when you didn't want this?	—	—	—	9%	5%	2%	1%	4	14
Total Sexual Abuse	54%	5*	55.2	31.6[a]%	14.1[b]%	12.5%	7.6[a,b]%	42%	
Physical Abuse When you were a chlid (< 14), did an older person hit, kick, or beat you? (1 = never, 2 = seldom, 3 = occasionally, 4 = often)	—	—	48.5	—	—	—	—	N/R	N/R
Total Sexual and Physical Abuse	—	—	66.5	—	—	—	—	—	—
Child and adult combined								—	—
Emotional or verbal abuse (often)	—	—	—	—	—	—	—	—	—

Note. *Significant row difference at .05 or better within a study. Row entries that share a superscript are different at the .05 level. IBD = inflammatory bowel disease. Opthal. = Opthalmologic patients.

versus 37% of those with organic GI diseases. Interestingly, however, only the history of physical abuse was significantly different between the two sets of gastroenterology patients. Among those patients with functional GI disorders were 38 patients with IBS (as diagnosed by Rome criteria) and 19 IBS patients (50%) with a history of sexual or physical abuse.

Early replications of Drossman, Leserman, et al.'s findings appeared within four years. Walker, Katon, Roy-Byrne, Jemelka, and Russo (1993) found a significantly greater frequency of history of sexual abuse among IBS patients (54%) than among patients with IBD (5%). Talley, Fett, Zinsmeister, and Melton (1994) were able to use their Olmsted County survey data (see chapter 2) taken from 919 adults ages 30 to 49. The sample included 130 cases of IBS (68.5% female). They found a significantly greater history of sexual abuse among those with IBS (43.1%) than among the others (19.4%). They also found a greater report of all abuse (sexual and physical) among IBS patients (50.0%) versus those without IBS (23.3%).

Later replications have not been as positive. Talley, Fett, and Zinsmeister (1995) found no significant differences on total physical and sexual abuse among those with functional GI disorders (22.1% positive for abuse) versus organic GI disorders (16.2%) among 997 outpatients seeking gastroenterological services at the Mayo Clinic. Of the 203 people with IBS, 12.8% reported a history of sexual and physical abuse. A replication from Drossman's group (Leserman, Drossman, et al., 1996) failed to find any significant differences between functional versus organic GI patients (n = 239, all female) on sexual or physical abuse. The overall average values were high: 55.2% with a history of sexual abuse, 48.5% with a history of physical abuse, and 66.5% with some form of abuse in their history.

In an attempted replication from France, Delvaux, Denis, Allemand, et al. (1997) found significantly greater history of sexual abuse among IBS patients (31.6%) versus control participants (7.6%); there was also a higher rate of reported abuse among those with organic GI disease (14.1%) compared to the control participants. *The two GI groups were not significantly different.* Two other studies not summarized in Table 9.1 (Feliti, 1991; Longstreth & Wolde-Tsadik, 1993) generally confirm the finding. The latter study, with HMO patients, revealed more frequent reports of a history of physical abuse among IBS patients (about 22%) than among patients without IBS (12.3%). All of the sexual abuse items showed histories of higher frequencies among those with severe IBS (average 22%) than among those with less severe IBS (10%), who showed greater frequency of abuse than did the population without IBS (5%).

Finally, Dill, Sibcy, Dill, and Brende (1997) studied 77 consecutive outpatients with a diagnosis of IBS from a solo gastroenterologist practice, using Drossman, Leserman, et al.'s (1990) questionnaire. Twelve failed to complete the questionnaire, some of whom admitted distress from the abuse questions (and thus were probably positive for past abuse). A total of 42% admitted to childhood or adult sexual abuse, about half with threat of force.

In another related study, Whitehead, Crowell, Davidoff, Palsson, and Schuster (1997) examined rectal distension pain threshold in four groups of women: IBS patients with a history of sexual abuse (n = 17), comparable IBS patients without a history of abuse (n = 15), women without IBS but with a history of sexual abuse (n = 13), and women without IBS and no history of abuse (n = 14). (See chapter 11 for a full description of the procedure and research on this aspect of IBS.)

The average distension volume at which women first reported pain showed the usual main effect of IBS (patients with IBS report pain at significantly lower volume than women without IBS). Among abused women, there were no differences attributable to IBS status. Abuse history had no effect on pain threshold, especially among IBS patients. The authors concluded that history of sexual abuse did not account for the altered rectal distension pain sensitivity frequently reported by IBS patients (see chapter 11).

The GI community has accepted as fact that there is a high incidence of early sexual abuse and other abuse in the histories of IBS patients and other patients with functional GI disorders. One would have to agree that values ranging from 20% to 66.5% are surprising and high. As to whether there is a greater history of abuse among those with functional GI disorders versus organic GI diseases, the picture is mixed. Careful reading shows that in four studies (Delvaux et al., 1997; Drossman, Leserman, et al., 1990; Leserman et al., 1996; Talley, Fett, & Zinsmeister, 1995) there was no significant difference in history of sexual abuse between those with functional GI disorders versus organic GI disease. The study by Walker, Katon, et al. (1993) is the exception. When IBS patients are compared to patients without GI disorders or IBD, differences do emerge. It is also the case, as was pointed out in a review by Drossman, Talley, Leserman, Olden, and Barreiro (1995), that the history of abuse among those with IBS seems greater the more severe the disorder, with cases presenting at tertiary care centers averaging about 50% with a positive abuse history.

THE ALBANY STUDY OF EARLY ABUSE AND IBS

In 1993 we (Payne, Blanchard, Vollmer, & Brown, 1993) conducted a study on this topic that I was never able to publish. Using Drossman, Leserman, et al.'s (1990) questions on sexual and physical abuse occurring before age 14 (childhood) or from age 14 onward (adolescent and adult), we compared the responses of 34 IBS patients, 35 psychiatric outpatients presenting at an anxiety disorders clinic, and 27 students free from GI disorders. A copy of the form we used appears in Exhibit 9.1. The re-

EXHIBIT 9.1
IBS Abuse Questionnaire

	During Childhood	During Adulthood
	Yes/No	Yes/No
Sexual Abuse During your childhood (< 14 years) or adulthood, has anyone ever . . .		
A. Exposed the sex organs of their body to you?		
B. Threatened to have sex with you?		
C. Touched the sex organs of your body?		
D. Made you touch the sex organs of their body?		
E. Tried forcefully or succeeded to have sex when you didn't want this?		
F. If yes to any item A through E, have you discussed these experiences with anyone else?		
TOTAL SEXUAL ABUSE		
Physical Abuse		
When you were a child (now that you are an adult), did an older person (does any other adult) . . .		
hit, kick, or beat you? (1 = never, 2 = seldom, 3 = occasionally, 4 = often)		
TOTAL SEXUAL AND PHYSICAL ABUSE		
Have you discussed these experiences with anyone else?		

Rating: Patients are considered to be sexually abused if they answer yes to any questions about sexual abuse except for Category A during adulthood and they are considered to be physically abused if they answer "often" (Response 4) to the question about physical abuse.

sults on the abuse questions for the three populations are presented in Table 9.2.

Three points emerged from our results. First, the patients with IBS reported numerically higher levels of all categories of childhood sexual and physical abuse than did the psychiatric patients who, in turn, reported higher levels than the nonpatients: total childhood sexual abuse was 47.1%, IBS patients; 31.4%, psychiatric patients; and 29.6%, nonpatients. However, only for the question about exposure of sex organs were the levels

TABLE 9.2
Summary of the Albany Study of Childhood Sexual and Physical Abuse and IBS

	Child (< 14)			Adult (14+)		
Sample characteristics and abuse questions	IBS	psychiatric	control	IBS	psychiatric	control
Sample size	34	35	27			
Percent female	85%	51%	59%			
Mean age	40	36	22			
IBS diagnostic criteria	Rome					
Psychiatric diagnostic tool	ADIS	ADIS	—			
Source of IBS patients	Seeking outpatient psychiatric treatment					
Sexual Abuse during childhood (< 14 years) has anyone ever:						
1. Exposed the sex organs of their body to you? (b)	41.2	22.9	18.5	14.7	5.7	14.8
2. Threatened to have sex with you? (a,c)	26.5	14.3	3.7	17.6	11.4	–0–
3. Touched the sex organs of your body? (a,c,d)	29.4	22.9	7.4	14.7	14.3	3.7
4. Made you touch the sex organs of their body? (a,c,d)	20.6	14.3	11.1	17.6	2.9	–0–
5. Tried forcefully or succeeded to have sex when you didn't want this?	17.6	5.7	–0–	14.7	14.3	3.7
Total Sexual Abuse	47.1	31.4	29.6	17.6	17.1	18.5
Physical Abuse When you were a child (< 14), did an older person hit, kick, or beat you? (1 = never, 2 = seldom, 3 = occasionally, 4 = often)	17.6[c]	14.3	7.4	11.8	14.3	–0–
Total Sexual and Physical Abuse	55.9	31.7	33.3	26.5	20.0	18.5
Percent w/Axis I Diagnosis	91%	94%	—			
Hamilton Anxiety Score	16.2	16.3	—			
Hamilton Depression Score	13.5	14.8	—			
Total Abuse: Child, Adolescent, and Adult	62.9	52.9	44.4			

Note. [a]Significant patients vs. control (child). [b]Significant IBS vs. psychiatric (child). [c]Significant patients vs. control (adult). [d]Significant IBS vs. psychiatric (adult).

of those with IBS significantly greater ($p < .05$) than those of patients with psychiatric disorders. The more common pattern was for the IBS patients and psychiatric patients not to differ on frequency of history of abuse but to report greater frequencies than do nonpatients. The lack of statistically significant differences may be a function of statistical power; that is, the sample sizes were too small to detect a difference.

Second, as adolescents and adults, there were few differences among the three groups except that the two groups of patients had suffered more physical abuse (11.6%) than had the nonpatients (0.0%). Third, overall levels of a history of abuse in childhood, adolescence, or adulthood were very high: 62.9% of those with IBS had a positive history of abuse, 52.9% of psychiatric patients had a history, and 44.4% of the young nonpatient group had a history. (We were very surprised by the level of past abuse in my control group.)

Two other points warrant attention. One, 91% of my IBS patients had a current or past Axis I psychiatric diagnoses. Thus, both patient groups could be seen as psychiatric patients. In fact, scores on the Hamilton Anxiety and Hamilton Depression scales were very similar. Two, among the IBS patients, those with histories of abuse had significantly higher scores on measures of anxiety and depression than did those with no history of abuse. For example, those with a history of abuse scored 15.9 on the Beck Depression Inventory (BDI); those without a history scored 8.9. Thus, we generally confirmed the findings of others about the high level of history of abuse among IBS patients. Moreover, those IBS patients with such a history were likely to be currently more anxious and more depressed.

COMMENTARY

The following statement may sound trite and overly simplistic to many, but I can find no better way to say it: *Early sexual or physical abuse is bad for you*. The results from IBS patients just summarized are but one more example of the long-term ill effects of early abuse. I know that individuals who are suffering from borderline personality disorder and dissociative identity disorder are highly likely to have a history of childhood abuse. From the work on IBS, I now know another consequence of childhood abuse.

Drossman, Talley, et al. (1995) have offered a conceptual model linking childhood abuse and adult IBS and other functional GI disorders. Figure 9.1 is my adaptation of their model. IBS sufferers start with a physiological predisposition to manifest GI symptoms, especially when psychologically distressed. Then the distressing trauma of abuse is added. This leads to the manifestation of GI symptoms, especially complaints of abdominal pain as an example of illness behavior. These somatic symptoms

Physiological predisposition to manifest GI symptoms, especially when psychologically distressed.
+
Early abuse leading to acute and/or chronic psychological arousal and distress.
↓
GI Symptoms and Illness Behavior (complaining of symptoms)
(Reinforcement of Illness Behavior + Continued Psychological Distress)
↓
Symptom Amplification + Health Care Seeking
↓
Becoming an IBS Patient

Figure 9.1. Possible pathways between early abuse and adult IBS.

are reinforced by attention and nurturance in the face of possible continued psychological distress. There then follows a process of symptom amplification and health care seeking leading the individual to become an IBS patient.

I know that many individuals with IBS symptoms never become IBS patients (see chapter 6). Instead, they live with their symptoms. For them (the IBS nonpatients), the symptom amplification and health care seeking do not take place. It would be of interest to learn whether IBS nonpatients have a high frequency of abuse in their histories. I do not know this yet.

Several points need to be clarified. First, not everyone who is sexually or physically abused as a child or adolescent develops IBS. The abuse can lead to many other disorders, especially psychiatric disorders. (The latter finding could account for some of the high levels of psychiatric comorbidity found in IBS patient populations; see chapter 7). Second, not all adult IBS patients give a history of early sexual or physical abuse. From 35% to 80% of IBS patients do not report abuse as a child or adolescent. Thus, I have several possibilities: The clearest is that there are many pathways, other than early abuse, to develop IBS. Alternatively, those IBS patients who deny early abuse may be mistaken and not able to remember the earlier trauma. Related to this point are the data from Longstreth and Wolde-Tsadik (1993) and those of Drossman, Talley, et al. (1995), which show progressively higher levels of abuse history in cases of less severe IBS (10%), more severe IBS (22%), and IBS in tertiary referral centers (30 to 50%).

Clinical Hints

The first question that comes to mind for many clinicians, when they become aware of the IBS–abuse linkage, is whether one should screen for early or later sexual abuse or physical abuse among IBS patients referred to them. (A copy of the Drossman, Leserman, et al., 1990, questionnaire is in Exhibit 9.1.) My answer is probably "no," even though I generally believe more knowledge about a patient and his or her background is generally a good thing.

The reason for this answer is that I am not sure what to do with a positive response from the patient. In my work with IBS patients, I have never focused on their history of abuse. In fact, of the 34 IBS patients described in Table 9.2, only one had a diagnosis of PTSD, although more than 60% had a history of abuse. Instead of focusing on their history, I have focused on how they are dealing with their current lives, thoughts, and symptoms.

There may well be IBS patients who want to deal with abuse issues from their past. It certainly seems a legitimate clinical concern. I, however, have not tended to find that to be the case (but I have not explicitly asked). There are other clinical psychologists working with IBS patients (especially Toner; see chapter 15) who believe that one should be prepared to initiate work on this topic within an overall cognitive–behavioral approach with a feminist perspective.

An argument against my advice not to screen may be made, however, in the case of the refractory patient. Although I have had a fair degree of success with various psychological treatments for IBS, there are patients who do not respond within a time-limited protocol. These refractory cases could arise because of several reasons, including comorbid psychiatric disorders. It is possible that knowledge of a previous abuse history with the refractory patient could give the clinician a different avenue for treatment. It just might be that issues related to the abuse have to be dealt with before progress can be made with the GI symptoms.

10

THE PSYCHOPHYSIOLOGY OF IRRITABLE BOWEL SYNDROME

There is a relatively long history of speculation (e.g., Latimer, 1983) and research that malfunctioning of the autonomic nervous system (ANS) and especially a tendency toward autonomic hyper-reactivity (Almy, Kern, & Tulin, 1949) plays a role in the etiology (and possibly in the maintenance) of IBS. In this chapter I will summarize the empirical research on peripheral psychophysiological research with IBS patients and conclude with a summary of data from a psychophysiological study from Albany. The limited research on the psychophysiological studies of IBS patients involving peripheral ANS measures—primarily measures of the sympathetic nervous system (SNS) response—are summarized in Table 10.1. As the table shows, there are few systematic psychophysiological effects to be found.

For example, whereas Levine, Cain, Jarrett, and Heitkemper (1997) found significant resting baseline differences between the female IBS patients and nonpatient control participants on heart rate (HR) and systolic blood pressure (SBP), with IBS patients rating higher, Fielding (1977) and Fielding and Regan (1984) did not find differences on these measures between IBS patients and matched medical outpatients or between IBS patients and control participants, respectively. In fact, the general research finding has been not to find differences. The significant findings are described in Table 10.2. The few significant differences seem consistent with

TABLE 10.1
Summary of Research on Peripheral Autonomic Nervous System Responses in IBS Patients

Authors and patient groups	Sample characteristics				Responses measured	Experimental conditions	Results			
	n	Age	% female	IBS criteria						
Fielding, 1977				N/R	HR, SBP, DBP, patella tap	baseline measures	HR	SBP	DBP	Sig. greater patella reflex (knee jerk) in IBS (25/33, 76%) in controls (5/33, 15%)
IBS	139	43	66				77	122	75.9	
medical outpatients (age- and sex-matched)	67	N/R	N/R				78	124	78.4	
Fielding & Regan, 1984				clinical	HR, SBP, DBP	baseline, cold pressor (0° C)	Change in measures to cold pressor			
							HR	SBP*	DBP*	
IBS	15	26	73				8.9 bpm	21.9 mm	18.4 mm	
control	10	27	80				4.6 bpm	8.6 mm	8.6 mm	
Thornton et al., 1990				Manning	electrodermal	habituation to 1000 Hz, 70 dB tones	Slow hab.	Fast hab.	or Nonresp.	
IBS	20	40	76				1/20	11/20	6/20	
control	40	40	50				11/40	26/40		
Levine et al., 1997				Manning	SBP, DBP, HR, SCL, skin temperature	BL, Stroop as stress, BL, stress, BL	BL HR	BL SBP		No differences in stress response or recovery between groups on any measure.
IBS patients	26	34	100				65.6[a]	117.6[a]		
IBS nonpatients	21	31	100				64.9[a,b]	114.0[a,b]		
control	22	33	100				59.4[b]	111.0[b]		

Note. *Significant between group difference; [a]Groups which share a superscript are not different. HR = heart rate; SBP = systolic blood pressure; DBP = diagnostic blood pressure; BL = baseline; SCL = skin conductance level.

TABLE 10.2
Summary of Significant Psychophysiological Findings in Studies with IBS Patients

Authors	Significant findings
Keeling & Fielding, 1975	Significantly higher incidence of "cool, clammy hands" in IBS versus control participants (44/50 versus 9/50).
Fielding, 1977	Significantly higher incidence of exaggerated patella reflex ("knee jerk") in IBS versus control participants (25/33 versus 5/33).
Fielding & Regan, 1984	Significantly greater SBP and DBP response to cold pressor (0° C) in IBS versus control participants.
Thornton et al., 1990	Fewer slow habituators with electrodermal response to 70 dB tones in IBS versus control participants (1/20 versus 11/40).
Levine et al., 1997	Higher baseline heart rate and SBP in IBS patients versus control participants. IBS patients had a higher level of urinary norepinephrine than did IBS nonpatients.

Note. SBP = systolic blood pressure; DBP = diastolic blood pressure.

SNS overactivity, which is also consistent with the data from chapter 7 noting a high prevalence of anxiety disorders among IBS patients.

THE ALBANY PSYCHOPHYSIOLOGY AND IBS STUDY

We (Payne, Blanchard, Holt, & Schwarz, 1992) have examined a variety of psychophysiological responses to several laboratory stressors in IBS patients (n = 68), patients with IBD (n = 44), and nonill control participants (n = 38). Some details of the methodology and results are presented to serve as a resource for clinicians and researchers interested in this topic. Characteristics of the samples are given in Table 10.3, and details of the experimental conditions are given in Table 10.4.

As one can see, the two patient samples are fairly well-matched. The experimental conditions were designed to see how physiological responses might change prior to treatment to both stress relief (relaxation, warm hands) and three different stress-inducing conditions (mental arithmetic, negative mental imagery, and cold pressor).

The analysis of the initial basal values revealed no between group differences for electromyogram (EMG) and electrodermal activity (see Table 10.6). The IBS patients had significantly lower heart rates (HR) than did the IBD patients (68.3 vs. 73.0 bpm). This finding is contrary to the idea that IBS patients are anxious and overaroused (in the SNS). As Table

TABLE 10.3
Characteristics of Participants in the Albany Study of Psychophysiology of IBS

Characteristic	Group		
	IBS	IBD	Control participants
Sample size	68	44	38
Mean age (years)	42.5	42.5	37.8
Percent female	73.5%	63.6%	65.8%
Length of illness	12.0	12.3	—
Source of patients	patients seeking psychological treatment	patients seeking psychological treatment	paid volunteers
IBS diagnostic criteria	clinical		

Note. From "Physiological Reactivity to Stressors in Irritable Bowel Syndrome Patients, Inflammatory Bowel Disease Patients, and Nonpatient Controls," by A. Payne, E. B. Blanchard, C. S. Holt, and S. P. Schwarz, 1992, *Behaviour Research and Therapy, 30,* pp. 293–300. Copyright 1992 by Elsevier. Adapted by permission.

10.5 shows, the two patient groups had significantly higher basal finger tip temperatures (IBS patients, 85.8°F; IBD patients, 87.1°F) than the control participants (81.1°F). This finding is contrary to Fielding's (1977) report of IBS patients' having cold clammy hands. It also contradicts Levine et al. (1997), who found no basal difference between female IBS patients and female control participants (but their means were in the same direction [IBS > control participants]).

Other analyses utilizing Groups × Conditions MANOVAs consis-

TABLE 10.4
Experimental Conditions Used and Responses Measured in the Albany Study of the Psychophysiology of IBS

Experimental condition	Duration (min.)
Baseline 1	10
Relaxation (relax your body)	3
Warm Hands (warm your hands)	3
Baseline 2	2
Mental Arithmetic (subtract 7s from 100)	2
Baseline 3	5
Negative Imagery (imagine self in stressful situation)	2
Baseline 4	5
Cold Pressor (place hand in ice water, 0° C)	2–7
Baseline 5	5
Heart rate in beats per minute	
Forehead EMG microvolt seconds per minute	
Skin resistance level in ohms	
Fingertip temperature in °F	

Note. EMG = electromyogram.

TABLE 10.5
Heart Rates and Finger Temperatures of All Three Groups for All Conditions in the Albany Study of the Psychophysiology of IBS

	Heart rate (bpm)			Finger tip temperature (°F)		
Condition	IBS	IBD	control	IBS	IBD	control
Baseline 1	68.3	73.0	72.1	85.8	87.1	81.1
Relaxation	68.4	72.7	72.1	85.6	87.1	81.2
Warm Hands	69.6	73.1	72.9	85.4	87.0	80.4
Baseline 2	69.1	73.6	72.3	85.3	87.0	80.3
Mental Arithmetic	75.6	81.4	80.9	85.3	86.5	80.0
Baseline 3	69.5	73.6	72.1	85.2	86.7	80.0
Negative Image	71.1	75.6	73.5	85.0	86.2	79.7
Baseline 4	68.0	72.3	71.6	84.7	86.1	79.1
Cold Pressor	76.2	77.0	78.2	83.9	85.6	78.8
Baseline 5	67.3	71.5	70.9	82.8	84.8	77.5

Note. From "Physiological Reactivity to Stressors in Irritable Bowel Syndrome Patients, Inflammatory Bowel Disease Patients, and Nonpatient Controls," by A. Payne, E. B. Blanchard, C. S. Holt, and S. P. Schwarz, 1992, *Behaviour Research and Therapy, 30,* pp. 293–300. Copyright 1992 by Elsevier. Adapted by permission.

tently showed condition or stressor main effects ($p < .001$ for all responses but finger tip temperature) but no differential responding (see Tables 10.5 and 10.6). Analyses of stress response scores or reactivity scores (obtained from the difference between the value for a stressor and the preceding baseline (for HR to cold pressor, this was 76.2 − 68.0 = 8.2 bpm) showed no between-group differences (see Table 10.5). Thus, the IBS patients, despite being thought of as neurotic (Latimer, 1983) and thus chronically

TABLE 10.6
Forehead EMG and Electrodermal Activity of All Three Groups for All Conditions in the Albany Study of the Psychophysiology of IBS

	Forehead EMG (μV–sec/min)			Skin resistance level (k ohms)		
Condition	IBS	IBD	control	IBS	IBD	control
Baseline 1	37.0	39.5	41.1	16.8	18.5	13.0
Relaxation	34.3	36.2	36.3	16.2	17.7	15.6
Warm Hands	34.7	35.7	36.8	16.0	17.5	16.0
Baseline 2	35.3	37.0	37.7	15.9	17.2	15.2
Mental Arithmetic	42.2	45.4	46.6	13.2	12.7	12.2
Baseline 3	34.6	36.2	37.9	14.1	13.8	13.0
Negative Image	36.3	38.3	36.7	14.1	14.3	13.2
Baseline 4	35.0	37.1	38.4	14.2	14.7	13.5
Cold Pressor	52.8	46.2	51.3	13.0	13.6	12.2
Baseline 5	35.2	36.7	37.4	13.5	12.8	11.8

Note. From "Physiological Reactivity to Stressors in Irritable Bowel Syndrome Patients, Inflammatory Bowel Disease Patients, and Nonpatient Controls," by A. Payne, E. B. Blanchard, C. S. Holt, and S. P. Schwarz, 1992, *Behaviour Research and Therapy, 30,* pp. 293–300. Copyright 1992 by Elsevier. Adapted by permission.

anxious and aroused, showed no signs of excessive SNS activity to laboratory stressors. Despite the lack of significant differences, these data do provide some normative psychophysiological data for the interested clinician or researcher.

Clinical Hint

These data point away from a basic stress management or relaxation treatment strategy. I was not aware of these results when I was conducting several stress management or CBT trials. Had I known the results of this study, I might not have gone down that particular treatment path.

11

ALTERED PAIN SENSITIVITY AND IRRITABLE BOWEL SYNDROME

A hypothesis that has excited the medical and pharmaceutical communities dealing with IBS over the past decade is that the core problem in IBS is altered pain sensitivity rather than disordered bowel motility. In fact, some pharmaceutical companies have been trying to develop drugs to correct this problem (Whitehead, 1999). According to this hypothesis, patients with IBS are overly sensitive to pain sensations from the abdominal area and label sensations as painful that others might ignore or at least tolerate as being painful. The technical term for this situation is *hyperalgesia.* It is certainly the case that abdominal pain and tenderness is the leading cause for IBS patients to seek medical attention. Moreover, a recent attempt to develop an overall IBS illness severity index (Drossman, Li, Toner, et al., 1995) relied heavily on pain complaints in its weighting.

I should note that I have no formal research experience with altered pain sensitivity; all I know about this topic has come from reading and listening to a presentation by one of the research leaders on the topic, Whitehead (1999). An excellent summary of this research, from which this chapter borrows heavily, can be found in a recent review and critique by Whitehead and Palsson (1998).

Ritchie (1973) was the first to report apparent altered pain sensitivity on the part of 67 IBS patients compared to 16 non-IBS patients. In his procedure, a balloon was inflated in the lower colon, 35 cm from the anus, with a standard volume of air (60 cm^3). Among the IBS patients, 55% reported pain at this inflation volume, whereas only 6% of the non-IBS patients reported pain. Ritchie then introduced the idea of colonic hyperalgesia as a basis for IBS.

Latimer et al. (1979) sought to replicate and extend this finding by comparing the results from 12 patients with IBS, 7 patients who were neurotic, and 18 control participants who were free of psychiatric and GI disorders. Again, a balloon was inserted into the rectosigmoid colon, 15–35 cm from the anus, and it was successively inflated with air in 10 cm^3 increments from 10 cm^3 to 50 cm^3. Contrary to Ritchie's (1973) findings, there were no differences in pain ratings at any volume between the IBS and non-IBS patients; the neurotic patients gave a noticeably higher (X = 3.1) pain rating at the 50 cm^3 volume, whereas the IBS and non-IBS participants gave ratings of about 2.2. At the lowest volume (10 cm^3), about one third of the IBS patients reported pain compared to one sixth of the non-IBS participants. However, at the maximum distention (50 cm^3) only 55% of IBS patients reported pain, compared to 72% of non-IBS participants and 86% of neurotic participants.

Whitehead, Engel, and Schuster (1980) compared 25 IBS patients to 20 control participants, again using a balloon in the rectosigmoid colon that was filled with air in 20 cm^3 steps up to 180 cm^3. At 60 cm^3 there was no report of pain by the control participants, whereas about 8% of the IBS patients reported pain. At maximum inflation, about 25% of non-IBS and 55% of IBS patients reported pain ($p < .05$).

In a later elegant study, Whitehead et al. (1990) compared 16 patients who met the Rome Criteria for IBS to 10 patients with functional bowel disorders (FBD) who met clinical criteria for IBS, 25 patients with lactose malabsorption (LMA), and 18 asymptomatic control participants. Pain tolerance level to balloon distention of the rectosigmoid colon and to the cold pressor test (hand in ice water for up to 4 minutes) were determined. The rectal balloon was inflated in 20 cm^3 steps. A maximum level of colonic distention was set at 200 cm^3; the maximum exposure to the cold pressor was set at four minutes.

The IBS group had a significantly lower pain tolerance level for colonic distention than did the control participants ($p < .05$) with the other two groups in between and not significantly different from either extreme. Mean distention levels were IBS, 120; FBD, 160; LMA, 155; and control participants, 180. Interestingly, 9 of 13 IBS patients had pain tolerance levels below 150 cm^3 compared to 5 of 10 with FBD, 8 of 19 with LMA, and 2 of 12 control participants. There were no significant differences in tolerance level for the cold pressor. However, 6 of 14 (43%) IBS patients were at 150 seconds or less, compared to 4 of 10 with FBD (40%), 13 of 21 (62%) with LMA, and 1 of 12 (8%) control participants. Thus, although there was no significant difference in mean pain tolerance level for the cold pressor between IBS patients and control participants, there was a trend for the IBS patients to be more sensitive to painful stimuli.

In an attempt to develop norms for this procedure and establish whether altered rectal perception was a biological marker in IBS, Mertz, Naliboff, Munakata, Niazi, and Mayer (1995) assessed 100 IBS patients (Rome criteria) and 15 control participants with an air-inflated rectal balloon in pressure increments of 5 mm Hg (rather than volumetric increments). At all pressures tested, the IBS patients gave significantly higher pain ratings than the control participants. The authors also reported that 94% of IBS patients had evidence for altered (lower) perception of aversive rectal sensations that was manifested as lower pain threshold, or increased pain intensity ratings, or altered referents to location of the pain.

THE WHITEHEAD AND PALSSON REVIEW

Whitehead and Palsson (1998) noted that more than 20 studies have been performed on the topic of colonic hyperalgesia and altered rectal pain sensitivity in IBS since Ritchie's (1973) first report of the phenomenon. The overwhelming majority of studies confirm Ritchie's finding that IBS patients, on average, have lower pain thresholds to balloon distention of the rectosigmoid colon. This has led some in the field (Mertz et al., 1995) to view colonic hyperalgesia as the key pathophysiological problem or mechanism in IBS. They further noted that pharmaceutical companies are acting on this belief and have begun to develop drugs to counteract this problem.

Whitehead and Palsson (1998) then noted that whether IBS patients report pain at lower levels of distention than do control participants is highly dependent on the method used to determine pain threshold. In the most common method, the ascending method of limits, the patient is subjected to progressively larger distention volumes, either stepwise or with slow continuous inflation of the balloon (and thus distention), until he or she reports pain or discomfort. With this method, if the patient "feared" noticeable pain or discomfort with the next distention bolus of air or water, because the current level was noticeable, he or she might then report pain at a lower level. This kind of response bias, to avoid real painful stimulation, might be the major difference between IBS patients and control participants.

Because this possible response bias is well-recognized in human pain research, other methods of noxious stimulus presentation have been designed that make the next step less predictable. These techniques, known as the tracking technique and double random staircase, remove the predictability of the next step. Another procedure, from cognitive psychology, involves a signal detection technique (McNicol, 1972).

Whitehead and Palsson (1998) reported that when the highly predictable ascending method of limits is used, 11 of 16 studies showed lower pain thresholds in IBS patients than in control participants, whereas the other 5 showed no difference. Likewise, when the ascending method of limits was used to detect the first report of pain or discomfort, 11 other studies showed lower thresholds for IBS patients than for control participants, whereas 3 did not.

When the less predictable methods of stimulation were used, only 1 of 4 studies showed the IBS patients to be more sensitive than control participants. When the methods were compared in a single study (Naliboff et al., 1997), the ascending method of limits showed the usual lower pain threshold in IBS patients, but the tracking method, *used on the same patients*, showed no difference. Likewise, when the signal detection method was used (Whitehead et al., 1997), no difference was found. Whitehead and Palsson (1998) correctly concluded that the colonic hyperalgesia phenomenon seems very dependent on method of measurement and probably represents more of a response bias on the part of IBS patients (to avoid truly painful stimulation) than a biological difference. Viewing Whitehead et al.'s (1990) own individual case data, one can see that about 40% of IBS patients fit this pattern (IBS and FBD) whereas the other 60% do not. Whitehead and Palsson also noted that of six studies in which researchers have compared pain thresholds from other methods of painful stimulation (cold or electric shock), none has shown a difference between IBS patients and control participants.

Whitehead and Palsson (1998) concluded that "psychological factors influence pain thresholds in patients with irritable bowel syndrome. Two cognitive traits, selective attention to gastrointestinal sensations and disease attribution, may account for increased pain sensitivity" (p. 1263). I find myself in agreement with their scholarly review: It is too early to identify colonic hyperalgesia as the core biological mechanism or basis of IBS. Many psychological factors play a role in the development and maintenance of IBS, and these psychological factors are amenable to psychological treatments.

12

INFLAMMATORY BOWEL DISEASE

As was noted in chapters 1 and 4, IBS is distinct from inflammatory bowel disease (IBD), and IBD is one of the exclusionary criteria used in the clinical criteria for IBS (see chapter 1, Exhibit 1.1). Thus, one might ask, why is there a chapter on IBD in a book devoted to IBS? There are several reasons for its inclusion. The most important reason is practicality: If a clinician is going to assess and treat patients with GI disorders, it will pay for him or her to know something about IBD and to be readily able to make the distinction between IBS and IBD.

Clinical Hint

In my experience, if it becomes known in the community that one treats IBS and other patients with GI disorders, a few patients with IBD will find their way to your door seeking services. I believe it pays to know your limits (see the section of this chapter on psychological treatment of IBD). It is also the case that some patients with IBD do have psychological problems that you can help. The gastroenterologist who refers IBS patients to you may also send the troubled patient with IBD.

I am indebted to Dr. Shirley Schwarz-McMorris and her dissertation for much of this information on IBD.

A second reason for including information on IBD is that patients with IBD are frequently used as a patient comparison group in IBS research. Third, in the heyday of classical psychosomatic theory, authorities such as Alexander (1950) and Engel (1977) described IBD as a prototypical psychosomatic disorder with psychopathology as a primary etiological agent. Alexander (1950) noted a specific unconscious conflict in patients with ulcerative colitis regarding frustration or oral aggressive responses; he also reported that "the integrative capacity of the ego of many patients with ulcerative colitis is relatively weak and that consequently there is a tendency toward projection and psychotic episodes" (p. 124). I subscribe to a somewhat different view.

CLINICAL PRESENTATION

IBD is the term used to encompass two related diseases, ulcerative colitis (UC) and Crohn's Disease (CD). Although they are two distinct and different diseases, they are frequently considered together because they share some of the same symptoms and have a similar clinical course.

Ulcerative Colitis

UC involves inflammation and ulceration of the colonic mucosa, almost always in the rectum and sigmoid colon and possibly extending to the rest of the colon; it rarely involves the small intestine. The principal symptoms are diarrhea, especially the passage of blood and purulent mucus, either alone or accompanied by formed or watery stools, abdominal pain, rectal bleeding, and anorexia leading to subsequent weight loss. Vomiting and fever may also occur, particularly during flares (i.e., periods of exacerbation). The diagnosis is confirmed by proctosigmoidoscopy and barium enema. Stool examinations tend to show large numbers of both white and red blood cells.

Cancer of the colon is a serious complication of UC with the risk for the UC patient being 7 to 11 times greater than that of the general population. In general, 5%–10% of patients with UC for 10 years will develop colon cancer; for patients who have UC for 25 years or more, and for whom the total colon is involved, the risk of colon cancer is approximately 40%.

Crohn's Disease

CD is also known as terminal ileitis or regional enteritis. It involves an inflammatory process that begins under the mucosa and spreads outward, penetrating all layers of the bowel, causing submucosal inflammation and edema. This, in turn, leads to a thickening of the bowel wall, which, along with scarring, may cause bowel obstruction. CD usually affects the lower ileum (small intestine), but it may occur in any part of the GI tract. It may also occur in two or more sites separated by healthy tissue.

The principal symptoms are diarrhea (described as several loose, non-bloody stools per day), abdominal pain, anorexia with weight loss, and fever. The diagnosis is confirmed by radiologic examination and barium enema. Complications of CD include bowel obstructions that may necessitate surgery, development of arthritis, and an increased risk for bowel cancer. McIllmurray and Langman (1975) reported a 20 times greater risk of bowel cancer if CD has been present for 21 years or longer.

Epidemiology

From these symptomatic descriptions, one can see why care must be taken to rule out IBD when diagnosing IBS, because abdominal pain and diarrhea are characteristic of both. The similarities of GI symptoms and chronic course make IBD a reasonable comparison condition for studies of IBS. UC begins before age 20 in about 15% of cases, and its highest incidence occurs in the third and fourth decade. Its prevalence is estimated to be between 36 and 70 per 100,000. CD has an onset in a majority of cases before age 22. Its prevalence is estimated at 20 to 40 per 100,000.

Medical Treatments

Approximately 15%–20% of UC patients eventually require surgery; for CD the figure is higher, in the range of 40% to 50%. Drug treatments tend to be long-term doses of antibacterial agents and steroids, as well as careful monitoring of nutritional status. Thus, IBD is clearly a chronic illness that often requires surgery and can have dire consequences (cancer).

PSYCHOLOGICAL STUDIES OF PATIENTS WITH ULCERATIVE COLITIS AND CROHN'S DISEASE

There are a number of studies summarized in chapters 5 and 6 in which IBD patients were used as a comparison group for a study of IBS patients. As those chapters show, IBD patients as a group tend to be less psychologically distressed across measures and to manifest less diagnosable psychopathology than do IBS patients. For example, in one study from my center (Schwarz, Blanchard, Berreman, et al., 1993), in which we compared 46 IBD patients to 45 IBS patients and 45 nonpatient control participants, there were differences between IBD and IBS on the Beck Depression Inventory (BDI) (9.1 vs. 11.3, respectively), State–Trait Anxiety Inventory (STAI) state (43.2 vs. 50.7, respectively); STAI trait (41.6 vs. 47.2, respectively); as well as on scale 6 (Psychasthenia) of the MMPI (60.7 vs. 66.7, respectively). I should note that the two groups did not differ on any other MMPI scale. Other psychological research on IBD (Schwarz & Blanchard, 1990) shows some instances of IBD patients being more distressed than control participants or other medical outpatient control participants, but for the most part they are not different from these comparison groups.

In a second study from my center comparing psychiatric diagnoses based on the Anxiety Disorders Interview Schedule (ADIS; Blanchard et al., 1990), we found that 25% of 44 IBD patients had an Axis I diagnoses as compared to 56% of the 68 IBS patients and 18% of the 38 nonill control participants. Moreover, the IBD group in comparison to IBS had significantly lower Hamilton Anxiety scores (8.8 vs. 15.6, respectively). They did not differ on Hamilton Depression scores. Studies of the prevalance of diagnosable psychiatric pathology tend to show higher levels in CD patients (30% to 60%) than in patients with UC (17% to 30%; summarized in Schwarz & Blanchard, 1990).

PSYCHOLOGICAL TREATMENT OF IBD

As chapter 15 will summarize, there is a growing field of psychological treatments applied to IBS. For IBD, however, there is limited controlled research on psychological treatments. Some of this research is summarized in Schwarz and Blanchard (1990). Two Canadian studies (Joachim, 1983; Milne, Joachim, & Niedhardt, 1986) support the possible role of stress management, especially relaxation training, in the treatment of IBD. Joachim (1983) gave 14 outpatients with IBD four sessions of training in deep abdominal breathing, followed by a 45-minute massage. Patients reported improved discrimination of relaxed versus stressed states, a better sense of control of pain, and improved sleep. In a follow-up study, Milne et al. (1986) randomly assigned 80 IBD patients to either a no-treatment control or to a 6-session series of stress management classes, which included topics such as relaxation, personal planning, and communication skills training. The treated group showed a significant reduction on the Crohn's Disease Activity Index (Best, Becktel, Singleton, & Kern, 1976), whereas the control participants did not change.

Finally, Shaw and Ehrlich (1987) randomized 40 patients with UC to six sessions of relaxation training or to a symptom monitoring control condition for six weeks. The treatment was primarily training in progressive muscle relaxation. The chief dependent variable was measures of abdominal pain. On all measures, including the McGill Pain Questionnaire (MPQ) (Melzack, 1975), the treated patients were improved at posttreatment and at a 6-week follow-up relative to the control participants. The treated participants also reduced antiinflammatory drug use.

The Albany IBD Treatment Study

We (Schwartz & Blanchard, 1991) have completed one small-scale treatment study of IBD patients, using a 12-session multicomponent stress management program similar to the one used for IBS patients and described in chapter 17. Eleven IBD patients (4 UC, 7 CD) received treatment initially on an individual basis. Ten other IBD patients (7 UC, 3 CD) monitored symptoms for eight weeks, were then reassessed, and subsequently treated. They constituted the control group of which 8 were then treated.

In terms of the many possible GI symptoms in the treated group, 65% of reported (and rated) GI symptoms were reduced, whereas 35% were unchanged or worse. For the control group, 61% of symptoms were reduced whereas 39% were unchanged or worse. When the control participants were treated, there were positive changes, compared to initial pretreatment level, in 82% of symptoms.

Post hoc analyses, taking into account the confound of more CD cases in those who initially monitored symptoms and then were treated, seemed to show that CD patients respond initially to treatment with symptom reduction, which dissipated to a degree over the 3-month follow-up. However, 8 of 9 UC patients showed increases in symptoms after treatment in comparison to all 7 of 7 UC patients showing a decrease in symptoms during symptom monitoring. The only UC symptom to respond to treatment was abdominal pain, a finding consistent with that of Shaw and Ehrlich (1987).

Leaving the GI symptoms, we found significant reductions in BDI and STAI scores, as well as reports of improved coping with stress following treatment. For the most part, patients with CD were more psychologically distressed than those with UC, with significant pretreatment differences on the BDI (10.6 vs. 6.6, respectively), STAI state (49.0 vs. 39.7, respectively), and STAI trait (46.9 vs. 37.4, respectively). The patients with UC were more likely to show noticeable improvement with treatment on the psychological tests.

My overall conclusion is that patients with UC do not respond well in terms of reduction of GI symptoms to a multicomponent stress management program, but patients with CD do show some GI symptom improvement. Conversely, with treatment, UC patients are more likely to show improved *psychological* status than are CD patients.

Clinical Hint

This hint is based on one small study conducted in my center. I do not believe that stress management programs are very helpful for patients with UC. Those with CD (who are likely to be more distressed) may show some benefit. Based on my work, I recommend against treating the IBD population with the cognitive–behavioral procedures described in chapter 17. My opinion could be changed with data from a larger study.

13

RECURRENT ABDOMINAL PAIN IN CHILDREN: A PRECURSOR OF IRRITABLE BOWEL SYNDROME?

All of our research on IBS has been done with adults, defined as those 18 years of age or older. An examination of the many tables in the preceding chapters summarizing psychosocial research on IBS will reveal a lower age limit of 17 or 18 in almost all studies. Thus, IBS is not a diagnosis usually associated with children and younger adolescents; however, there is nothing in any of the formal definitions or diagnostic criteria (see chapter 2) of IBS that precludes one from diagnosing it in adolescents. There is a disorder of childhood and adolescence, however, that bears some resemblance to IBS, namely, Recurrent Abdominal Pain (RAP). At the onset of this discussion, however, let me make it clear that RAP is a descriptive term, not the label for a disease or even a disorder. The most common definition of RAP is that put forth by Apley and Naish (1958): at least three episodes of pain occurring within three months that are severe enough to affect the child's activities. One ordinarily excludes from the category of RAP children for whom an organic explanation of the pain complaints can be found. Thus, it is a functional disorder.

I am indebted to Dr. Lisa Scharff and her dissertation (Scharff, 1995) for much of this information on RAP.

NATURAL HISTORY OF RAP

The prevalence of RAP seems relatively high; in fact, it is probably the most common recurrent pain problem of childhood and adolescence. In one of the oldest and largest studies, Apley and Naish (1958) surveyed 1,000 children from primary and secondary schools and found that 10.8% met diagnostic criteria for RAP. Faull and Nicol (1986) conducted an epidemiological study in a town in the north of England, using Apley and Naish's criteria, and found a prevalence rate of 24.5% among 439 5- and 6-year-olds.

Although cases of RAP have been reported in children as young as 3 and as old as 18, the peak age appears to be 11–12 years of age (Stickler & Murphy, 1979). With regard to gender effects, Faull and Nicol (1986) found equivalent prevalence in 5- and 6-year-olds. However, Apley and Naish (1958) and Stickler and Murphy (1979) reported a noticeably higher prevalence among girls than boys of adolescent age, mirroring the findings with adults for IBS.

In addition to the unpleasant experience of pain, RAP in many children has major effects on their lives. In particular, sufferers frequently miss several days of school per year (Bury, 1987; Robinson, Alverez, & Dodge, 1990) in addition to necessitating many visits to physicians and hospitals. McGrath (1990) estimated that at least 25% of pediatric emergency room visits for abdominal pain are due to RAP.

LONG-TERM STUDIES

The key issue for this chapter is what happens over time to children with RAP: Does it remit spontaneously or with minimal treatment (thorough diagnostic assessment to rule out organic causes and then reassurance and support of the parents and child patient)? Or does the patient go on to a career as a chronic GI patient with a diagnosis of IBS? The results of several long-term follow-up studies of children with RAP are summarized in Table 13.1.

Table 13.1 shows that one can see that follow-ups have ranged from 8 to 28 years in the older studies and for 5 years in the recent prospective study by Walker, Guite, Duke, Barnard, and Greene (1998). The percent of cases with notable continuing abdominal pain ranged from 24% (Stickler & Murphy, 1979) to 53% (Christensen & Mortensen, 1975). The latter sample may have been the most severe; all probands had been hospitalized.

Of the most relevance to this book, a fairly high percentage of pediatric cases of RAP do warrant a diagnosis of IBS on follow-up. Christensen and Mortensen (1975) reported that 47% of their follow-up cases of RAP warranted a diagnosis of irritable colon. In the most carefully con-

TABLE 13.1
Long-term Follow-up Studies of Children With Recurrent Abdominal Pain

Authors and patient groups	*n*	Age	% female	Source	Length of FU	Results: % rapid remission	% mild, severe pain	% IBS	% anxiety, depression	% organic disease
Apley & Hale, 1973				pediatric hospital clinic						
untreated	30	?	50		8–20 yr	20	40	N/R	43	N/R
treated	30	5–18	50		19–14 yr	47	37	N/R	33	3
Christensen & Mortensen, 1975				pediatric hospital inpatient						
RAP	34	8	59		28 yr	N/R	53	47	N/R	12
control	45	8	144			N/R	29	N/R	N/R	N/R
Stickler & Murphy, 1979				Mayo Clinic						
RAP	161	10	62		about 8 yr	57 (76% total)	24	N/R	18	2
Walker et al., 1998				university pediatric clinic						
RAP male	25	11	0		5 yr	N/R	36	32	N/R	N/R
RAP female	51	11	100			N/R	49	35	N/R	N/R
control male	26	11	0			N/R	15	31	N/R	N/R
control female	23	11	100			N/R	26	0	N/R	N/R

Note. For all four studies, RAP was diagnosed with Apley & Naish (1958) criteria. FU = follow up.

ducted study to date (in terms of applying diagnostic criteria for IBS at the follow-up), Walker et al. (1998) applied conservative Manning criteria (pain plus three or more symptoms) to RAP children and found that 35% of girls and 32% of boys met the criteria for IBS at a 5-year follow-up. The value for girls with RAP was statistically greater than that found for the female control participants but not for the boys.

Two other points emerge from these studies: Conservative treatment (reassurance and support; Apley & Hale, 1973) did not lead to a better long-term outcome, but it did lead to more rapid elimination of symptoms. Christensen and Mortensen (1975) examined the children of their RAP probands and control participants and found that 19.1% of the children of RAP probands had noticeable abdominal pain as opposed to 12.1% of the children of the control probands. The difference is not significant.

RAP is a prevalent pain disorder of childhood and adolescence with females outnumbering males from puberty onward. Although it remits in a majority of cases, a sizable minority of adults who had RAP as a child continue to have notable abdominal pain as an adult and about one third of children with RAP will meet criteria for IBS as adults.

TREATMENT

The standard medical treatment for RAP is that recommended by Apley and Naish (1958):

1. Perform a careful and thorough medical workup to identify or rule out organic causes of the pain complaints.
2. Reassure the parents and the child that there is no organic or structural reason for the pain.
3. Provide support for the parent and the child as they deal with the functional problem.

As is shown in Table 13.1, this approach is effective on a relatively immediate basis in about half of cases (47% in Apley & Hale, 1973; 57% in Stickler & Murphy, 1979) and in about 75% of cases over time (Stickler & Murphy, 1979).

Cognitive–Behavioral Treatment

Over the last 10 years there have been several small-scale studies utilizing a variety of CBT procedures in a rationally constructed treatment package for RAP in children. For example, Sanders, Rebgetz, Morrison, et al. (1989) randomly assigned 8 children with RAP (mean age 9; 6 girls, 2 boys) to a symptom monitoring control condition, whereas 8 others (mean age 9; 6 girls, 2 boys) received a combination CBT procedures. These included self-monitoring of pain, operant behavioral training of the parents (with attention to differentially reinforcing behavior in the child other than pain behaviors), and distraction techniques. In addition, the child was taught a combination of relaxation training, imagery as a pain control strategy, and self-control techniques such as self-instruction in coping statements. Treatment was for 8 visits over 8 weeks with both parent and child attending.

Results showed significantly greater reductions in pain reports by the child proband and the parent for the treated participants versus control participants. At posttreatment, 6 of 8 (75%) treated children were pain-free; at a 3-month follow-up this increased to 7 of 8 (87.5%) versus 37.5% for the control participants.

In a similar study, Finney, Lemanek, Cataldo, Katz, and Fuqua (1989) treated 16 children with RAP (average age 11 years 3 months; 6 boys, 10 girls) with a CBT program utilizing self-monitoring of pain, teaching parents to limit attention to pain complaining, relaxation training, and dietary fiber supplementation. Patients were seen in a pediatric clinic for 2 to 6 visits. In 13 of 16 cases, pain problems were seen as improved or resolved (81%). In addition, health care utilization was reduced significantly.

In replication of their earlier work, Sanders, Shepherd, Cleghorn, and Woolford (1994) compared their earlier CBT package to standard pediatric care, equated for number of visits in a study of 44 children with RAP. The latter emphasized reassurance that the child's pain was real but that no serious organic disease was present. Importantly, patients were reassessed at 6- and 12-month follow-ups. Results showed a significant advantage for CBT over standard pediatric care at posttreatment. Average pain reduction was reported as 80% for the CBT condition compared to 40% for standard pediatric care, according to patients' diaries. Results held up well at the 6- and 12-month follow-ups with further improvement in both conditions. At 6 months, 66.7% of children in the CBT condition were pain free, compared to 27.8% in standard pediatric care.

THE ALBANY STUDY OF CBT FOR RECURRENT ABDOMINAL PAIN

We (Scharff & Blanchard, 1996) have completed one small-scale study of RAP patients in which we sought to determine the relative contributions of the two chief components in CBT treatment packages for RAP, utilizing single-subject experiments with crossovers. It seems obvious that there are two broad approaches that have been used by behaviorists in the treatment of RAP. One approach focuses on the child patient with RAP and involves relaxation training and other stress management and cognitive techniques (e.g., examining and altering self-talk). This part of the treatment is designed to help the child better cope with periodic pain and discomfort. The second approach focuses on the parents and applies operant learning technology to teach the parent how to reinforce, with parental attention and nurturance, non-pain-complaining behaviors by withdrawing reinforcement for pain complaining and other sick-role behaviors. It is based, in part, on Fordyce's (1974) classic work on treating chronic pain.

The study population consisted of 10 children (6 girls and 4 boys) between the ages of 8 and 13, diagnosed and referred by a pediatric gastroenterologist. Duration of illness varied from 3 months to 7 years (mean = 30 months). Children were randomly assigned to one of two treatments: parent training or stress management. Treatment consisted of 4 one-hour sessions over 4 to 6 weeks. After the completion of treatment, children and parents monitored pain for two weeks. If pain had not remitted completely, the patient was crossed over to the other treatment (this occurred with 9 of 10 participants).

The parent training took place without the child's presence and consisted of educating the parents about RAP and psychosomatic symptoms as well as behavior modification techniques based on Patterson's (1976) book, *Living With Children*. Emphasis was placed on parents' ignoring mild pain behaviors and encouraging other active behaviors in their child. Parents were instructed to place their child in a quiet, dark room with no distractions when he or she complained of abdominal pain. School attendance was required unless the child manifested symptoms of illness such as vomiting or fever. Parents were helped to develop an individualized behavior modification program for their child.

The stress management training focused on the child. A parent was encouraged to accompany the child to sessions and to aid the child in completing homework and relaxation practice. Children were taught progressive relaxation and deep breathing exercises. They were also taught distraction techniques to deal with acute pain as well as the use of positive imagery. They were also taught to use positive coping self-statements in the manner of Meichenbaum (1977).

Measures and Results

Parents were asked to note the occurrence of any pain behaviors during each half of the day. The child made pain thermometer ratings once per day on a 0 to 4 scale ("no pain" to "very bad pain"). Both RAP patients and parents kept pain records for 6 weeks before treatment and throughout treatments and for 2 weeks after the last treatment and again for 2 weeks at a 3-month follow-up.

There were significant reductions in both children's pain thermometer ratings (from 1.2 to 0.2, $p < .001$) and parents' ratings of frequency of pain behavior intervals (from 40% to 8%, $p < .001$) from the second baseline to the end of the second treatment. Results were maintained at the follow-up. There was a trend ($p = .06$) for children's pain ratings to decrease more (66.8%) when the stress management was the first treatment than when the parent training (24.0%) was first. Overall, the average degree of improvement in the children's ratings was 86% and 82% according to parents' ratings of frequency of pain behaviors. The individual percent reduction scores for each child, along with basic demographics and order of treatment are shown in Table 13.2.

On an individual case basis, 2 children who received the stress management first showed great improvement (100% and 88%, respectively). Moreover, 2 children who showed almost no change when the parent training was first (17.1% and −31.7%, respectively) were markedly improved after the stress management (100% and 91%, respectively). Overall, all 10 children were improved 62% or greater, with 9 of 10 showing a 75% reduction in children's pain diary ratings. From the parents' diaries of pain-complaining behaviors, all children were 61% improved or greater with 6 of 10 showing 75% reductions or greater.

Clinical Hint

Our very limited data show a slight advantage for the stress management training. I would certainly recommend using it first. The parent training may be helpful if there is not almost complete remission with stress management. (It did help 60% of children to improve from an average of about a 50% reduction in pain ratings to about 85% reduction.)

There was little change in anxiety or depression ratings for the sample; however, the pretreatment depression scores (Child Depression Inventory; Kovacs, 1980) was 5.6, and the trait anxiety score (State–Trait Anxiety Inventory for children; Spielberger, 1973) was 33.6. The depression scores are on the low side compared to other reports on children with RAP, whereas the trait anxiety score is slightly higher (Walker, Garber, & Greene, 1993).

SPECULATION

Although it seems clear that about one third of children with RAP will go on to manifest IBS as adults, there are two interesting issues yet to be settled. The first is a prevention or early intervention issue. If we successfully treat children with RAP, will that prevent them from having IBS as adults? We already know that a majority of children with RAP respond fairly promptly to "reassurance and support." Do these reassurance responders later reappear as adults with IBS, or is it primarily the child with RAP

TABLE 13.2
Summary of Results from the Albany Study of CBT for RAP

Patient #	Age	Sex	Axis I Dx	Illness duration (months)	Protocol	Posttreatment 1		Posttreatment 2	
						Change child	Scores parent	Change child	Scores parent
1	12	F	sub-GAD	12	SM-PT	47.8	−16.7	86.8	61.1
2	10	F	sub-phobia	84	PT-SM	17.1	0.0	100.0	100.0
3	13	F	over-anxious	24	SM-PT	51.1	34.3	89.9	100.0
4	8	F	none	3	PT-SM	62.2	45.8	83.9	75.2
5	9	F	none	36	SM-PT	88.2	84.2	100.0	100.0
6	12	M	none	48	SM-PT	46.8	−1.5	74.7	72.8
7	12	M	none	24	PT-SM	33.3	70.0	83.0	90.0
8	11	M	over-anxious	4	SM only	100.0	100.0	N/A	N/A
9	10	M	over-anxious	60	PT-SM	−31.7	−11.1	91.1	66.7
10	12	F	sub-GAD	6	PT-SM	38.8	40.7	62.0	71.3

Note. GAD = generalized anxiety disorder; over-anxious = over-anxious disorder; SM = stress management (child); PT = parent training.

who continues to manifest GI symptoms who evolves into an adult with IBS? Thus, it would be of interest to treat some of the refractory RAP cases (they are the ones who are usually referred) with CBT and then follow up the successes (expected to be a high percentage) into adulthood to see whether IBS is prevented in comparison to refractory RAP cases who receive standard medical care.

The second issue is, what is it about suffering from RAP as a child that predisposes the adult to develop IBS? It could be that the child with RAP is overly sensitive to abdominal pain and continues with this GI tract sensitivity as an adult. Or it could be that RAP develops in children who are more anxious than the average child and that the anxious child grows up to become an anxious adult who is more prone to develop IBS. Another alternative is that the child's early learning about GI symptoms, the sick role, and health care seeking predisposes him or her to be sensitive to GI symptoms and seek health care (and nurturing) as an adult. Prospective studies such as the one by Walker et al. (1998) are needed to follow the child with RAP well into adulthood. We also need large-scale CBT treatment trials of children with RAP who are then followed up for 6 to 10 years.

One last bit of speculation involves the findings of chapter 9 that a large percentage of adult IBS patients report a history of abuse during childhood. Could it be the case that children with RAP have a history of earlier abuse or are victims of concurrent abuse? Or could it be that the children with RAP who evolve into adult IBS patients are the same adult IBS patients who acknowledge a history of abuse in childhood? To the best of my knowledge, the field does not know the answers to my questions. Long-term follow-up of the pediatric RAP cases with a thorough and ongoing assessment of psychological state (anxiety, depression, and somatization) and of trauma experiences and abuse might help us understand the speculation illustrated in Figure 9.1.

II

TREATMENT

Whereas the first part of this book dealt with assessment and descriptive aspects of IBS, this second part is concerned primarily with treatment and treatment-related issues such as long-term follow-up (Chapter 21) and prediction of outcome (Chapter 20). I have arranged this material into a traditional dichotomy of assessment and treatment for ease of presentation. In point of fact, I believe that assessment should be an integral part of treatment and that one should assess the patient in an ongoing fashion throughout treatment.

Because this book was written from the perspective of the psychologist (as a nonmedical therapist), there is little attention paid to two of the three broad approaches to treating IBS, namely pharmacological approaches and dietary approaches (the third being psychological approaches). I do not prescribe drugs, nor do I prescribe dietary alterations. My students and I have engaged in a number of different psychological therapies with IBS patients. How to conduct those forms of therapy and what the results of those efforts are is the major focus of this section of the book. I also attempt to give adequate coverage of the work of others around the world who have applied psychological treatments to patients with IBS (Chapter 15).

14

DRUG AND DIETARY TREATMENTS FOR IRRITABLE BOWEL SYNDROME

As the title of this book indicates, and as was mentioned in the introduction to the treatment section of this book, the focus of treatment is psychological. (This does not mean that only psychologists can apply these treatments; any mental health professional could apply them. Moreover, nurses and primary care physicians could also readily apply these treatments if the economics of reimbursement would permit the investment of time.) In this chapter I provide a brief overview of nonpsychological treatments for IBS. It is certainly not comprehensive. One needs to seek out medical or gastroenterological texts for comprehensive coverage.

DROSSMAN AND THOMPSON'S GRADUATED TREATMENT APPROACH

Two of the leading physicians in the area of IBS, Drossman and Thompson, published an article on IBS in 1992, from which I draw heavily here. They divided the IBS patient population into three groups, based on the severity and impact of IBS on the patient's life, and they provided treatment recommendations for each segment of the population (see chapter 2).

Patients With Mild IBS

Patients with mild IBS are estimated to constitute about 70% of those with IBS who seek medical attention for the disorder. They are seen as generally not having much in the way of psychological or psychiatric comorbidity and as having an episodic disorder that does not interfere greatly in their lives. For these patients, Drossman and Thompson (1992) recommended (a) education, (b) reassurance that they do not have a serious or life-threatening disease, and (c) possible dietary interventions to detect food sensitivities and/or adding fiber and bulking agents such as psyllium (e.g., Metamucil). They did not see this segment of the IBS population as needing psychological help.

Patients With Moderate IBS

Patients with moderate IBS are estimated to constitute 25% of those with IBS who seek medical attention. They are more likely to have their lives disrupted by IBS and to have psychological and psychiatric comorbidity. These patients are more likely to find their way to the specialist, the gastroenterologist, whereas those with mild IBS probably stay with the primary care physician.

Drossman and Thompson (1992) made general, but cautious, pharmacotherapy recommendations for patients with mild or moderate IBS and made different recommendations for when diarrhea, constipation, or pain is predominant. They also recommended referring patients in these groups for various psychological treatments. (Patients with moderate to severe IBS are probably more likely candidates to be referred to a psychologist or other mental health practitioner.)

Patients With Severe IBS

Patients with severe IBS constitute 5% of those seeking treatment. They tend to be refractory to most treatments and to have a noticeable level of psychological and psychiatric comorbidity. They are also likely to be seriously concerned about having some life-threatening GI disease that was overlooked previously. According to Drossman and Thompson (1992), these patients will probably not readily take a referral to a mental health professional. They suggest treating these patients like patients with other chronic pain problems, using a multidisciplinary approach that includes antidepressants and physician-based behavioral techniques.

Clinical Hint

If Drossman and Thompson (1992) are correct about the percentages of IBS patients who fall into their categories, there is a sizable population whom they see as benefiting from referral to a psychologist. This would mean establishing contacts with gastroenterologists for referrals rather than primary care physicians. However, the primary care physician could just as well be trained to identify and refer those patients with moderate to severe IBS.

One should also keep in mind that Drossman and Thompson's (1992) subdivision and categorization are conceptual rather than empirically based. Nevertheless, the paper does give guidance as to which IBS patients one is likely to see as a mental health professional.

DRUG TREATMENTS FOR IBS

In 1988 Klein published a summary and critique of the published literature on drug treatment for patients with IBS. He identified 43 double-blind, randomized, placebo–controlled trials, which he further analyzed. In addition, he noted 50 other resources that had not met his inclusion criteria. Among these trials, there were 12 evalutating antispasmodics (most of which were anticholinergic agents), 3 evaluating anticholinergic/barbiturate combinations, 5 evaluating tricyclic antidepressants, 6 using bulking agents as the active drug, 3 using dopamine antagonists, 4 with tranquilizers, 3 with the opioid *loperamide* as antidiarrheal agent, and 2 evaluating peppermint oil (carminatives).

His conclusion was a stinging indictment of the drug treatment literature: "It is concluded that not a single study offers convincing evidence that any therapy is effective in treatment of the IBS symptom complex" (Klein, 1988, p. 232). Much of his conclusion was based on what he saw as methodological flaws in all of the trials he reviewed. He also noted a sizable placebo response ranging from 20% to 70%. To the best of my knowledge, no review has refuted Klein's conclusion. Despite this state of affairs, drugs continue to be prescribed for IBS and are a part of the graduated treatment approach of Drossman and Thompson (1992).

I have deliberately not undertaken a comprehensive review of the recent literature on the drug treatment of IBS because it did not fit the scope or focus of this book. However, I hope someone will in the near future. From my limited reading of the literature, I am most impressed by a study of desipramine (Pamelor; Greenbaum, Mayle, Vanegeren, et al., 1987). Of 41 patients who started the trial, 29 completed a double-blind crossover trial involving desipramine, atropine as an active placebo with known side effects, and inert placebo, administered for six weeks.

Results showed a significant advantage for desipramine over placebo for episodes of diarrhea, abdominal pain ratings, and total psychological symptoms on the Brief Psychiatric Rating Scale (Overall & Gorham, 1962). For the diarrhea-predominant subgroup (n = 19), these same effects were observed, as well as a significant advantage for desipramine over placebo on patients' ratings of diarrhea. Comparisons of desipramine to the active placebo were significant (favoring desipramine) for pain rating reduction, patients' ratings of constipation, and Hamilton Rating Scale for Depression (HRSD) scores (desipramine scores were reduced from 26, indicating moderate depression, to less than 19, still noticeably depressed). Three of the 12 dropouts had adverse reactions to desipramine.

DIETARY INTERVENTIONS

The primary dietary intervention used with IBS is the addition of dietary fiber, either a natural product like wheat bran, or a product such as psyllium (Metamucil). Mueller-Lissner published a meta-analytic review of the wheat bran literature in 1988. His dependent variables of interest were weight of stool and GI transit time. Included in the 20 studies in his report were 4 on patients with IBS and 5 on constipated patients (with cause of constipation not specified). Patients with IBS had responses to bran similar to those of control participants—significantly increased stool weight and decreased GI transit time—when taking bran as a supplement to their regular diet. Although patients with constipation showed appropriate changes on the bran supplement, their values for stool weight and transit time approached the range of values for control participants only without the bran supplement. It thus may be that wheat bran or psyllium can be useful for the IBS patient with the constipation predominant.

15

PSYCHOLOGICAL TREATMENT OF IRRITABLE BOWEL SYNDROME

In this chapter I present an overview of the research from around the world on the psychological treatment of IBS. The review is limited to reports of randomized controlled trials (RCTs) that have been published in English. I have omitted my Albany studies from this overview; they are summarized in chapter 16. Details of how to conduct the various treatments are contained in chapters 17 to 19. Research on possible prediction of treatment outcome is summarized in chapter 20. Finally, available knowledge on long-term follow-up (defined as greater than 6 months posttreatment) is summarized in chapter 21.

There are at least four (and possibly six) distinctly different psychological treatments that have been evaluated in RCTs as treatments for IBS: brief psychodynamic psychotherapy, hypnotherapy, biofeedback, and various combinations of CBT. Two of the components or techniques frequently included in CBT, relaxation training and cognitive therapy alone, have also been evaluated as individual treatments in RCTs.

Methodological details of treatment studies, including descriptions of samples, control conditions, and drop-out rates, are summarized in Table 15.1. Table 15.2 summarizes information on treatment outcome—information that is difficult to summarize, because each investigator has used his or her own outcome measures, which are not necessarily comparable.

TABLE 15.1
Methodological Details of Controlled Studies of Psychological Treatment of IBS

Authors	Conditions	*n*	Age	% female	IBS criteria	# sessions/ duration	Drop-out	# therapists	Ratings			Other measures
									symptom diary	physician global	patient global	
Svedlund et al., 1983	psychotherapy + medical	50	33	70	clinical	10/3 mos	8	N/R	no	yes	yes	global ratings of anxiety/ depression
	medical	51	35	69			—					
Guthrie et al., 1991	psychotherapy + home relaxation	53	49	85	clinical	7/3 mos	7	1	yes	yes	yes	HSRD
	wait list	49	46	65*		3 brief visits	6					clinical anxiety
Whorwell et al., 1984	hypnotherapy + home autohypnosis	15	24–53	87	clinical	7/3 mos	0	1	yes	yes	yes	rating of well-being
	placebo + support psychotherapy	15				7/3 mos	0	1				
Whorwell et al., 1987	hypnotherapy	50	23–65	88	clinical	10/3 mos	0	1	yes	?	yes	rating of well-being

Harvey et al., 1989	individual hypnotherapy group hypnotherapy	16 17	19–62	82	clinical	5/3 mos	3	2	yes	—	—	—
Houghton et al., 1996	hypnotherapy wait list	25 25	22–55 21–58	84 92	Rome	12/3 mos	0	N/R	?	?	yes	quality of life rating
Bennett & Wilkinson, 1985	CBT medical (3 drugs)	12 12	37	70	clinical new diag.	8/8 wks 2 visits	2 2	1 —	yes yes	no no	yes yes	STAI
Lynch & Zamble, 1989	CBT wait list	11 10	36 43	64 70	clinical	8 (2-hr)/8 wks	6	1	yes	no	no	psychological tests
Shaw et al., 1991	stress management drug (Colpermin)	18 17	50 44	61 71	clinical	6/6 mos	0	?	no	no	yes	none
Corney et al., 1991	CBT medical	22 20	32 40	73 75	clinical	6–16/3 mos	0	?	no	—	yes	clinical rating
van Dulmen et al., 1996	CBT group wait list	27 20	44 48	59 40	clinical	8 (2-hr)/3 mos	2	1	yes	no	yes	SCL-90
Toner et al., 1998	CBT group group psychoeducation medical	101 total ?	18–65	?	Rome	12/3 mos 12/3 mos	?	?	yes	?	?	BDI

Note. *Two conditions were significantly different. ? = Information is unclear on this point. HSRD = Hamilton Rating Scale for Depression; CBT = Cognitive Behavioral Therapy; BDI = Beck Depression Inventory; STAI = State–Trait Anxiety Inventory; SCL-90 = Symposium Checklist–90.

TABLE 15.2
Outcome Results of Controlled Studies of Psychological Treatment of IBS

Authors	Conditions	% improved on symptoms: total sample	pain	diarrhea	constipation	bloating	Differential effects
Svedlund et al., 1983	psychotherapy	N/R	50	36	36	N/R	Psychotherapy patients had significantly greater reduction in pain at post-treatment and follow-up and rated selves as better able to cope.
	medical	N/R	18	16	16	N/R	
Guthrie et al., 1991	psychotherapy	67	70	86	—	43	Psychotherapy patients had significantly greater reduction in anxiety and depression. Global ratings (including physician) for female patients showed greater change on all GI symptoms combined.
	wait list	23	18	50	—	17	
Whorwell et al., 1984	hypnotherapy	100	85	94	—	79	Hypnotherapy patients had significantly greater change in pain, bowel habit disturbance, bloating, and well-being.
	psychological support	N/R	14	8	—	13	
Whorwell et al., 1987	hypnotherapy	84	69	73	—	80	No differential effects were tested.
Harvey et al., 1989	individual hypotherapy	50	—	—	—	—	No differential effects; both forms of hypnotherapy worked.
	group hypnotherapy	70	—	—	—	—	

Houghton et al., 1996	hypnotherapy wait list	N/R	80	—	—	50	Hypnotherapy patients had superior improvement on pain, bloating, bowel dissatisfaction, and quality of life.
Bennett & Wilkinson, 1985	CBT drugs	N/R N/R	N/R *	N/R *	— —	N/R *	CBT patients improved significantly more on the STAI (trait) than did those on drug treatment.
Lynch & Zamble, 1989	CBT wait list	64 0	38 24	58 27	41 40	26 25	CBT patients improved more on abdominal pain and discomfort, constipation, and STAI (trait).
Shaw et al., 1991	stress management drugs	50 12	33 22	67 0	— —	— —	Stress management rated greater global improvement than drug treatment.
Corney et al., 1991	CBT medical	59 30	30 23	39 −39	27 34	— —	CBT patients avoided foods and tasks significantly less than did medical patients.
van Dulmen et al., 1996	CBT group wait list	44 11	— —	— —	— —	— —	CBT patients improved more than wait-list patients on GI symptom composites from diaries.
Toner et al., 1998	CBT group group psychoeducation medical	N/R	* N/R N/R	* N/R N/R	* N/R N/R	* N/R N/R	CBT patients showed more improvement on the BDI and on bloating than did medical patients.

Note. *SR = significant reduction. STAI = State–Trait Anxiety Inventory; BDI = Beck Depression Inventory.

(To brag a bit, all of the Albany studies used the same measures and are thus directly comparable within the set.)

BRIEF PSYCHODYNAMIC PSYCHOTHERAPY

Brief psychodynamic psychotherapy may seem to be a contradiction in terms, but it is accurate. The treatments have been delivered over a 3-month span and consisted of 10 visits in one instance and only 7 in the other. This is not the time span nor the number of therapy sessions one normally associates with psychodynamic psychotherapy. The therapy is psychodynamic to the extent that it seeks insight (Svedlund, Sjodin, Ottosson, & Dotevall, 1983) and exploration of "patients' feelings about their illness" (Guthrie et al., 1991). It certainly appears to focus on a relatively surface level rather than attempting to uncover deep, unconscious material.

There are two RCTs evaluating brief psychodynamic psychotherapy as treatment for IBS. Svedlund et al.'s (1983) is the oldest RCT evaluating any psychological treatment for IBS, and in many ways is one of the best: It was a large study (50 participants in the treatment condition and 51 in the control condition) with a 12-month follow-up. Patients in both conditions "received conventional medical care including bulk-forming agents, and when appropriate, anticholinergic drugs, antacids, and minor tranquilizers." Individuals were assessed using structured interviews by blinded assessors at pretreatment, 3 months after treatment began (posttreatment), and at a 12-month follow-up.

The psychotherapy was described as "aimed at modifying maladaptive behaviors and finding new solutions to problems. The focus was on means of coping with stress and emotions and on teaching about relations between stressful life events and abdominal symptoms. All psychotherapeutic measures were tailored to suit individuals and took the patients' tolerance of anxiety into account" (p. 589).

This sounds at first glance very much like a description of a cognitive–behavioral approach to a patient problem or disorder. At a later point the more psychodynamic aspects of the treatment become clearer. The authors go on to say, "the psychotherapy was dynamically oriented and mainly supportive, and flexible enough to be adapted according to degree of patient's insight. The therapeutic goals therefore could vary from pointing out connections between symptoms and stressors to handling of more specific conflicts of great importance to the patient. The principles were to work on a conscious level to consider the patients' own concept of their disorder which could be modified by therapy" (p. 591).

As Table 15.2 shows, outcome was assessed primarily by independent physician evaluators, rating six different clusters of symptoms, and secondarily by patient global ratings at the posttreatment and follow-up point. No patient diary was used. The physician ratings showed significantly greater improvement for the psychotherapy condition in comparison to routine medical care for abdominal pain and total somatic symptoms at posttreatment and for these two plus bowel dysfunction at the 12-month follow-up (all $p < .001$). On all of the mental health symptoms (anxiety, depression, etc.) there were comparable improvements at end of treatment for both conditions; these were maintained at the one-year follow-up. The authors noted that 18 eligible patients declined to enter the study and that 7 patients in the psychotherapy condition terminated treatment early (after one to five visits). To the authors' credit, the latter were reevaluated at posttreatment and follow-up.

The second RCT, by Guthrie et al. (1991) in the U.K., was also a large-scale trial with a 12-month posttreatment follow-up. All participants had failed to respond appreciably to standard medical care, a combination of bulking agents and antispasmodic medication, over at least the past 6 months. All eligible cases were approached about the study. As in the Svedlund et al. (1983) study, conventional medical care continued for both conditions. Individuals were assessed by their gastroenterologist (who was blind to treatment condition) with ratings of GI symptoms, by patient diary ratings of the same symptoms, and by ratings of how much the GI symptoms interfered in their lives. A psychiatrist completed Hamilton Rating Scale for Depression and Clinical Anxiety Scale ratings for participants. Fifty-three patients were randomized to treatment and 49 to the control condition. Treatment consisted of one long initial interview (2 to 4 hours), "during which bowel and psychiatric symptoms were assessed and the patients' feelings about their illness and any emotional problems were explored." There were six additional interviews over the next 3 months. *Patients were given a relaxation tape to use at home on a regular basis*. The latter represents a noticeable departure from the procedures of Svedlund et al. (1983). The control group members saw the psychiatrist for three brief visits to discuss GI symptom diary ratings.

According to the primary therapist, Elspeth Guthrie (Guthrie et al., 1999), the treatment can be seen as having three parts. At the initial visit (which can last 2 to 4 hours), there is a prolonged conversation with the patient about his or her GI symptoms, feelings about these symptoms, and how these feelings affect relationships. Guthrie noted that there is usually a great deal of emotion expressed in the descriptive phase, as it may be the first time the patient has ever talked to anyone about the GI symptoms and his or her feelings. There is a strong effort to understand and use the patient's language and to understand surface-level images and interpretations of the patient.

At later sessions in the middle part of therapy, there is an attempt to convert the patient to having a positive attitude, rather than the typical negative, defeatist attitude one can find in chronic IBS patients about the disorder. There is also an emphasis on change in beliefs and attitudes using small steps. The therapist is expected to develop an interpersonal formulation of the patient's problems, but this is not given to the patient. The final part of the therapy is the concluding visit, which has a review of progress and emphasizes the patient's gains and need for continued progress. According to Guthrie et al. (1999), the use of relaxation has been discontinued. There are thus about 10 hours of patient–therapist contact over 12 weeks.

Seven patients dropped out of the psychotherapy condition compared to six in the control group. After the 3-month reevaluation (posttreatment), 33 of the control patients received treatment, whereas the 10 who were improved from symptom monitoring alone were merely followed. Gastroenterologists' ratings showed significantly greater improvement for abdominal pain and diarrhea for the treatment group versus control participants at end of treatment. The patient's ratings showed the same significant differences plus greater improvement in bloating. The treated group also showed greater changes on ratings of depression and anxiety than did the control participants.

The one-year follow-up data, based on global patient ratings (no gastroenterologist ratings and no patient diaries), revealed that, for those who were treated initially, 32 of 47 (68%) patients rated themselves as better or much better, including 28 of 33 (85%) who were improved at posttreatment. Among the treated patients, 21 of 33 (64%) rated themselves as better or much better at follow-up. Interestingly, only 4 of the 10 (40%) of the patients who were spontaneously improved at posttreatment remained improved at the follow-up. There was also a significant reduction in outpatient GI clinic visits from a year before the trial (median = 4) to the year following treatment (median = 1; $p < .001$).

Conclusion

Although it is not possible to compare the content of the two treatments directly, they do seem roughly equivalent. Importantly, they both show significantly greater improvement for the treated cases in abdominal pain at posttreatment than in the control condition, and greater improvement in bowel functioning at posttreatment (Guthrie et al., 1991) or follow-up (Svedlund et al., 1983) than for the control participants. There was also greater reduction in anxiety and depression at posttreatment (Guthrie et al.) or follow-up (Svedlund et al.) than among the control participants. Thus, they are yielding comparable improved results across a spectrum of symptoms, and the improvements appear to hold up over time. The replicability across different research groups is also a notable plus. The within-study replication in Guthrie et al., that is, the treatment of the unimproved symptom monitoring controls, is a decided plus, especially the find-ing of comparable long-term improvement rates (68% for those treated initially vs. 64% for those treated later). (I understand that Guthrie and Creed are completing a new RCT comparing the psychotherapy to a selective seratonin re-uptake inhibitor (SSRI) antidepressant; results are not yet available.)

Although one would have preferred a more substantial form of assessment than patient global reports at the follow-up point in Guthrie et al. (1991), the results are encouraging. A decided plus in Guthrie et al.'s results are data on frequency (or percent of sample) who were improved in addition to group mean scores. The frequency data give the clinician a better idea of how likely his or her patients are to respond favorably to such a treatment.

HYPNOTHERAPY

In 1984 a British physician, Peter Whorwell, reported on the successful treatment of relatively refractory cases of IBS using hypnotherapy (Whorwell, Prior, & Faragher, 1984). The details of the hypnotherapy protocol are contained in chapter 19. Briefly, it consisted of initial hypnotic induction using an arm levitation procedure. Hypnotherapy was aimed at general relaxation and gaining control of intestinal motility with some attention to ego strengthening. Patients also received an audiotape for autohypnosis to be practiced daily.

Hypnotherapy treatment was for seven 30-minute sessions of decreasing frequency over 3 months. There was a control condition in which patients received a medication placebo plus supportive psychotherapy (discussion of GI symptoms and exploration of possible contributions of emotional problems and stressful life events) with the same frequency as active treatment (seven 30-minute sessions) delivered by the same therapist. Evaluations were performed by an independent assessor based on daily diary ratings of patients. These ratings were of abdominal pain, bloating, dysfunctional bowel habit, and general improvement and well-being.

Results showed significantly ($p < .001$) greater reductions on all four measures for patients receiving hypnotherapy than for those in the control condition at the 3-month point. The control group showed significant ($p < .05$), but modest, improvement on abdominal pain, bloating, and general sense of well-being. All 15 patients in the hypnotherapy condition were either symptom free or suffering from only mild symptoms by the end of treatment. *These were very strong results in terms of both the generality of results (100% of the sample of very refractory IBS patients improved) and the comparison condition, which controlled for therapist contact and was itself somewhat active.*

Extension

In the next report by Whorwell's group, Whorwell, Prior, and Colgan (1987) reported data from a total of 50 IBS patients treated with hypnotherapy. These 50 included the original 15 from the 1984 report plus 35 more cases of refractory IBS. Evaluations were by the same gastroenterologist and from daily patient symptom diaries. Interestingly, the treatment was now described as "10 weekly sessions of hypnotherapy," rather than the 7 sessions reported in 1984. The hypnotherapy treatment protocol appeared to remain the same.

For the 38 cases described as classical IBS, 36 (95%) responded with elimination of symptoms or no more than mild symptoms. For 5 classical cases with high scores on the General Health Questionnaire (GHQ; Goldberg, 1972; indicative of psychiatric disturbance), only 3 (60%) responded. Finally, of 7 atypical IBS cases (primarily intractable abdominal pain with little altered bowel habit or bloating), only 3 (43%) responded. Thus, overall, there were positive results in 42 of 50 cases (84%).

They also reported on an 18-month follow-up of the original 15 cases from Whorwell et al. (1984). Two had suffered relapses at 12 to 14 months but were treated again with a single session of hypnotherapy that led to alleviation of the returned symptoms. Although uncontrolled, the high rate of success in this study, as measured independently of the treating therapist, and the identification of factors that predict lack of success, are very impressive.

Replication

In the last trial by this group (Houghton, Heyman, & Whorwell, 1996), data from 25 new cases of refractory IBS treated by hypnotherapy were compared to data from 25 additional cases of refractory IBS who were on a waiting list for hypnotherapy. Thus, it was not strictly an RCT because there was no random assignment. However, the samples are comparable in that both are refractory and have been referred for hypnotherapy.

Evaluation was by means of questionnaires filled out by patients who rated GI symptoms as well as quality of life for the previous 3 months. The hypnotherapy was described as the same as used previously by Whorwell et al. (1984, 1987). However, it is now described as twelve 30-minute sessions rather than 7 (1984) or 10 (1987). Results showed equivalent GI symptom ratings for the two groups before treatment. After treatment, the hypnotherapy group gave significantly ($p < .001$) lower ratings for abdominal pain and bowel habit dysfunction than did the control participants. There were also significant ($p < .05$) advantages for hypnotherapy over the control condition for bloating and sense of incomplete evacuation. Treated cases also reported significantly better quality of life than control participants on psychic well-being, mood, physical well-being, and attitude toward work ($p < .001$). Of patients who were working, those treated with hypnotherapy took off fewer work days because of IBS (32% vs. 79% [$p = .02$] took at least one day off); mean days work missed for control participants was 17 days vs. 2 days for those receiving hypnotherapy, $p = .015$. *Interestingly, among IBS patients who were on disability because of their IBS, 3 of 4 patients treated with hypnotherapy returned to work, whereas none of the 6 in the control condition returned to work.*

Again, there was a significant advantage in GI symptom reduction for IBS patients treated with hypnotherapy in comparison to those on a waiting list. Moreover, quality of life was improved and time lost from work was noticeably reduced. The study suffers from several methodological problems such as nonrandom assignment to condition and use of global retrospective ratings of symptoms. Moreover, the treatment is much more intensive (12 vs. 7 sessions), and the overall results are not as strong in terms of residual symptoms at the end of treatment. Nevertheless, the results for hypnotherapy did continue to replicate, and very important quality of life and health care utilization benefits were documented.

It seems fairly clear that gut-directed hypnotherapy, specifically as administered by Whorwell, is a reasonably effective treatment for relatively refractory IBS. Although there is only one RCT among his studies (Whorwell et al., 1984), it showed very strong advantages in comparison to a strong comparison condition. Moreover, the results held up well for the most part to 18 months posttreatment. Later studies showed less dramatic results and began to define the boundary conditions for whom the treatment is helpful and for whom it is not (see chapter 20). Houghton et al. (1996) also produced valuable data on the impact of hypnotherapy for IBS on quality of life and work time lost to illness. These wider impacts are impressive.

Hypnotherapy and Rectal Sensitivity

An interesting study of Whorwell's hypnotherapy for IBS was published in 1990 by Prior, Colgan, and Whorwell. They sought to learn whether hypnotherapy would affect rectal sensitivity (see chapter 11). Rectal sensitivity was determined by anorectal manometry before and after treatment for 15 IBS patients who underwent hypnotherapy for their refractory IBS and 15 comparable IBS patients who did not receive treatment but were retested after a similar interval (about 3 months). Data on posttreatment responses were obtained twice, initially while patients were not in a hypnotic state and later, at the same measurement session, while they were hypnotized. Thirteen of the 15 (86.7%) treated patients rated their GI symptoms as improved, with a change in GI symptom score from 23.5 (out of a maximum of 30) to 9.6. Only the 13 who improved were retested.

The diarrhea-predominant subset of IBS patients at posttreatment showed significant increases in volumes needed to elicit sensations of gas and urgency (to defecate). Under hypnosis at posttreatment, all of the improvements in rectal tolerance, including the volume to produce pain and discomfort, improved significantly and approached normal control values. The constipation-predominant IBS patients had higher values on all parameters; no changes were significant. The IBS control group showed no significant test–retest changes on any parameter. The results seem to show that at least for diarrhea-predominant IBS patients, hypnotherapy tends to lead to a normalization of rectal sensitivity values.

Independent Replication

One of the important factors in establishing the value and utility of a treatment is the replicability of results, especially by an independent research team. Harvey, Hinton, Gunary, and Barry (1989) conducted an RCT comparing individualized hypnotherapy for IBS to hypnotherapy in small groups of 5 to 7. Refractory IBS patients and two different hypnotherapists were used.

The authors stated that the hypnotherapy was similar to that described by Whorwell et al. (1984). Participants received four 40-minute sessions (at weeks 0, 1, 3, and 7) and were asked to practice autohypnosis for two 10-minute periods daily. Evaluation was on the basis of daily patient symptom diaries in which were rated abdominal pain and bloating (combined), ease of bowel actions, and general sense of well-being.

There were no differences between the two treatment conditions: For individual hypnotherapy, 5 of 16 (31.3%) patients were symptom free at the 3-month follow-up, 3 had fewer symptoms (18.8%), and 8 (50%) showed no improvement. For the group treatment, 6 of 17 (35.3%) were symptom free, 6 of 17 (35.3%) were improved, and 5 (29.4%) were unchanged. Overall, 20 of 33 (60.6%) participants were improved or symptom free, based on patient diaries, 3 months posttreatment. Patients with high GHQ scores tended not to do well. Although these results are not as strong as those of Whorwell et al. (1984), and they were not compared to a symptom monitoring or routine medical care control condition, they certainly strengthen the case for hypnotherapy as a treatment for IBS.

The Albany Replication

We (Galovski & Blanchard, 1999) have completed an independent replication of Whorwell's hypnotherapy, using materials supplied by him. Six matched pairs of IBS patients, meeting Rome criteria, were compared in a series of multiple baseline across-subjects experiments. Evaluation was by means of daily GI symptom diaries. Twelve weekly sessions, replicating

Whorwell's latest treatment program (Houghton et al., 1996), were used as was a tape for daily home practice of autohypnosis.

A comparison of Composite Primary Symptom Reduction (CPSR) scores (see chapter 16) for those who received initial treatment versus an extended symptom-monitoring baseline revealed significantly (p = .016) greater improvement in this diary-based composite GI symptom score for immediate treatment (mean CPSR = 0.52) than for the symptom monitoring (mean CPSR = −.32). When results after treatment for all 11 patients were examined, 6 (55%) met criteria for improvement (at least a 50% reduction in primary GI symptoms), 2 (18%) were somewhat improved, and 3 (27%) were unimproved. For individual GI symptoms, there were significant reductions for diary ratings of abdominal pain, constipation, and flatulence. There were also significant reductions in state and trait anxiety as measured by the State–Trait Anxiety Inventory (STAI). A 2-month follow-up revealed good maintenance of improvements in abdominal pain, flatulence, and state and trait anxiety. Interestingly, improvement was not related to degree of hypnotic susceptibility as measured by the Stanford Hypnotic Susceptibility Scale, Form A (Weitzenhoffer & Hilgard, 1959). Although these results are not as strong as those of Whorwell, they are comparable to those of Harvey et al. (1989). As such, they provide an additional replication of the utility of hypnotherapy for IBS.

Conclusion

With the continued success demonstrated by Whorwell's group across several studies, and two independent replications, one must conclude that hypnotherapy is a very viable treatment for IBS. It has yet to be subjected to the large-scale evaluations one finds with brief psychodynamic psychotherapy. However, finding significant positive results from small studies is, in a statistical sense, stronger support for the efficacy, because significance was found with a sample of 11 (Galovski & Blanchard, 1999) in contrast to a sample of 100. It is also reassuring that no subjects have been noted who could not be hypnotized sufficiently for the treatment to be viable.

COGNITIVE AND BEHAVIORAL TREATMENTS

In this section I review studies in which various treatment techniques or procedures that are usually considered behavioral or cognitive were used. The unifying principle is that they represent a direct attempt to change the patient's behaviors and/or thoughts (cognitions) with the patient's cooperation. They are thus seen as focused in the present and on the conscious level, as opposed to an unconscious level and on historical antecedents.

Included in the set of techniques and procedures are forms of relaxation training, the pairing of relaxation with guided and directed imagery as in systematic desensitization training, assertiveness and social skills training through role-playing, and prescribing graduated homework exercises designed to help the patient have new experiences with usually avoided situations. In the more cognitive realm there may be direct attempts to change internal dialogue (self-talk) by helping the patient to become aware of thoughts in difficult or stressful situations and then directly altering the messages or thoughts. There is help for the patient to identify and correct self-defeating and illogical thought patterns or schemas. In addition, various forms of biofeedback to help the patient to learn directly to control musculoskeletal and autonomic responses have been used as has direct education about bowel functioning and normality.

These techniques and procedures have usually been used in combinations, known as treatment packages. The combinations are usually described as cognitive–behavioral therapy (CBT). In some instances, individual cognitive or behavioral elements or techniques have been evaluated. My own work at Albany has all been within this tradition or framework with the exception of Galovski and Blanchard's (1999) replication of Whorwell's hypnotherapy. My research is summarized in chapter 16. To avoid repetition, it will only be mentioned in passing and will not be summarized in Tables 15.1 and 15.2.

In the first RCT to evaluate CBT, Bennett and Wilkinson (1985) recruited 33 newly diagnosed IBS patients who had not responded to reassurance and simple symptomatic medical treatment to begin a 6-week waiting period with one week's worth of daily diary ratings of bowel symptoms at the beginning and end of the period. Five patients dropped out. The remaining 28 were randomly assigned to one of two treatment regimens over the next 8 weeks: medical care combining an antidepressant or anxiolytic, a smooth muscle relaxant, and a bulking agent or to a combination of education, progressive muscle relaxation (PMR), and cognitive therapy to change self-talk (Meichenbaum, 1977). Participants completed another week's worth of diaries after treatment. Two patients dropped out from each condition.

Results showed no significant changes during the 6-week baseline. There was significant improvement by both groups on abdominal pain, abdominal discomfort, frequency of bowel movements, and frequency of abnormal bowel movements (term not defined) after treatment. Only on the STAI (trait anxiety) scale was there differential change, with the CBT group improving significantly ($p < .01$), whereas the medical care group did not. Partial data (14 of 24 treatment completers) from patient partners revealed significant reductions of the partner's ratings of patient complaints of pain.

This first CBT trial showed no advantage for CBT versus medication in patients' diary ratings of GI symptoms but did show differential improvement in psychological state for the CBT group. Importantly, the psychological treatment did as well as then state-of-the-art combination drug therapy in relieving GI symptoms. These results were not nearly as impressive as those of Svedlund et al. (1983) with psychodynamic psychotherapy or of Whorwell et al. (1984) with hypnotherapy, either in terms of differential treatment effects or in terms of follow-up maintenance of the treatment effects. Moreover, the populations were different: Both Svedlund et al. and Whorwell et al. targeted chronic, refractory IBS patients as opposed to the relatively new cases used by Bennett and Wilkinson (1985).

The next RCT was the first Albany study (Neff & Blanchard, 1987; see chapter 16). For this chapter's chronology, the next RCT was that of Lynch and Zamble (1989). They used a combination of PMR and other briefer forms of relaxation, Meichenbaum's (1985) stress inoculation therapy, and cognitive therapy modeled on the work of Burns (1980) to teach participants to identify stressful situations and cognitive reactions to them and later to control stress-producing cognitions. Finally, assertiveness training modeled after the work of Lange and Jakubowski (1976) was added. Treatment was for eight 2-hour individual sessions over 8 weeks. The comparison group monitored GI symptoms for two 4-week periods separated by a 2-month wait. The waiting list group was then crossed over and given treatment. All cases were followed up with another set of measures after 3 months.

Results showed significantly greater improvement on a composite of all GI symptoms from the diary for CBT versus control ($p < .05$) and on individual symptoms of abdominal discomfort and constipation (but not pain or diarrhea). There was also greater improvement for CBT versus wait list on the Beck Depression Inventory (BDI) ($p < .05$) and the Queen's Stress Inventory (Malton, 1982; $p < .05$). When all treated patients were examined, there was significant improvement in abdominal pain and discomfort, constipation, diarrhea, and bloating, as well as on scores for the BDI, STAI (Trait), Psychosomatic Symptom Checklist, and Queen's Stress Inventory. All of these improvements were maintained at the 3-month follow-up. Eleven of the 21 treated patients (52%) were clinically improved (at least a 50% reduction in primary GI symptoms).

These results were much stronger than Bennett and Wilkinson's (1985) and also more thoroughly documented, including the 3-month follow-up data. The comparison condition was probably weaker in that a new robust medical regimen was not introduced. The authors noted the comparability of their results to those of Neff and Blanchard (1987), both in terms of portion of the sample improved and the improvement in psychological state.

Lynch and Zamble (1987) also reported success with 5 of 6 IBS patients given their CBT combination treatment in an earlier, uncontrolled

A–B design. Degree of reduction in pain was 36% and bloating was 76%. There were also improvements in BDI scores for 5 of 6 participants.

Two additional RCTs of CBT appeared in 1991: that of Shaw et al. (1991) and that of Corney, Stanton, Newell, Clare, and Fairclough (1991). Shaw et al. (1991) randomized 18 IBS patients to a stress management program consisting of education about IBS and discussions of the relation between abdominal symptoms and personal stress and tension. Patients also received individual sessions of relaxation training that emphasized breathing exercises. The program was spread over 6 months. Participants received a median of 6 individual sessions, with 16 of 18 receiving 4 or more treatments. Seventeen other patients were randomized to receive the antispasmodic drug, Colpermin. Measurement was by means of a locally designed questionnaire on which patients rated any change in IBS symptoms. This was completed again at a 12-month post-entry follow-up.

On all four global ratings, those patients receiving the stress management reported more improvement than those receiving the medication ($p < .05$ or better). The variables rated (and percent improved in stress management) were (1) frequency of attacks of symptoms (67%), (2) severity of attacks (67%), overall benefit (a little help or considerable benefit; 72%), and future confidence (67%). Thirteen of the stress management participants rated one IBS symptom as most improved: 3/9 (33%) abdominal pain, 5/5 (100%) bloating or flatulence, and 4/6 (67%) diarrhea. Although no data were presented from the 12-month follow-up, the authors reported, "at the final review, 12 months after commencement of trial, with very few exceptions, the earlier changes in frequency and severity of symptoms were maintained" (p. 40).

Although the simplicity of the treatment, the controlled comparison to a drug, and the 12-month follow-up are very positive features of this study, relying entirely on patient global retrospective reports seriously detracts from its value. The absence of patient diary data and the relative absence of analysis of individual GI symptom data also limit its value.

In the second RCT, Corney et al. (1991) randomly assigned 22 IBS patients to a combination of cognitive and behavioral treatments including education about bowel functioning, some elicitation, discussion and correction of mistaken ideas, graduated reengagement in avoided activities after role-playing with the therapist, bowel habit retraining, and pain management modeled after the operant work of Fordyce (1976). In the latter, one seeks to reinforce performance and nonpain behavior while extinguishing pain-related behaviors and pain-related avoidance. Patients were seen for 6 to 15 one-hour sessions and booster visits every 3 months. One CBT patient dropped out.

Twenty other patients were randomized to medical care that included education and reassurance plus the physician's choice of antispasmodics, bulking agents, and dietary advice (similar to Bennett & Wilkinson, 1985).

They were seen one to four times over the course of the study. Dependent measures included patient global visual analog scale ratings of abdominal pain, diarrhea, and constipation over the last 7 days at the beginning and after 4 months and 9 months. Patients also completed the GHQ, a well-known measure of psychiatric "caseness" and the Clinical Interview Schedule (CIS; Goldberg, Cooper, Eastwood, Kedward, & Shepherd, 1970) and rated levels of avoidance of specific activities.

Results showed significant improvement at 4 and 9 months in both groups for stomach pain, constipation, irritability, and headache with no significant differential effect. Diarrhea showed a trend (p = .06) for improvement. All of the other pain scores showed similar significant improvement. On the avoidance behaviors, the CBT group improved significantly more than did the medical care control group and showed a trend (p = .07) to have a greater reduction in mental health symptoms as noted by the CIS. Finally, the authors noted a significant correlation between decrease in psychiatric symptoms and decrease in abdominal pain ($r = +.37$) and in diarrhea ($r = +.29$).

This study yielded results very similar to those of Bennett and Wilkinson (1985): The CBT and optimal medical care groups both improved significantly on IBS symptoms and general mental health; however, in this study there were no differential effects, despite a sample size almost double that of Bennett and Wilkinson's (1985). The only differential advantage was found in reduction in avoidance behaviors by the CBT condition. This is consistent with the specific focus on this problem in this condition. However, the pain management focus in CBT did not lead to differential pain reduction. Thus, when careful measurement is done, as in Corney et al. (1991) in contrast to Shaw et al. (1991), and an array of IBS medications is permitted, as in Corney et al. (1991) in contrast to the single medication in Shaw et al. (1991), the CBT condition does not surpass the drug treatment. However, it is the case that Shaw et al.'s treatment was noticeably simpler than Corney et al.'s.

Group Studies

The latest phase in the development of CBT as a psychological treatment for IBS has been the evaluation of a CBT package administered in a small group format. In many ways this is a logical step given the pressures in health care for cost containment; if efficacy can be maintained while the cost per patient is being reduced by spreading therapist time or costs across several patients, then this is a logical step. I should note that in the Albany studies, I went down this path with a quasi-controlled trial (Blanchard & Schwarz, 1987) of my initial CBT protocol and later with a direct comparison of individual versus group cognitive therapy (Vollmer & Blanchard, 1998; see chapter 16).

In the first of these evaluations of group CBT, van Dulmen et al. (1996) working in the Netherlands, assigned 27 IBS patients to a group treatment consisting of eight 2-hour sessions over 3 months, led by two therapists. Content included education about bowel functioning and the interrelations of cognitions, behavior, emotions, and abdominal complaints. Patients were taught to determine antecedent and consequent thoughts, feelings, and behaviors around stressful events and how to directly change cognitions during homework trials. They were encouraged to try out new behaviors. Participants were taught PMR, and later how to apply it, and coping imagery, to deal with stressors and abdominal pain. The protocol emphasized group sharing of experiences and support.

The comparison group consisted of 20 IBS patients who were assessed and then waited 3 months for treatment. Those who had completed the wait-list period were then added to treatment groups.

Thus, it seems that patients were not truly randomly assigned. Instead, sequential cases were assigned to immediate treatment to fill a group, then the next few patients were assigned to the wait-list condition. It is also not clear whether those patients in the wait-list condition were double counted, first as a wait-list subject and then as a treatment subject.

Dependent variables included a daily symptom diary of abdominal pain intensity and duration as well as of activity avoidance due to GI symptoms. Other GI symptoms noted were flatulence, belching, nausea, heartburn, borbyrygmi, and degree of diarrhea. The diary was completed four times per day. Patients also made global GI symptom ratings and completed the Symptom Checklist–90 (SCL–90) as a measure of overall psychological distress.

Initial results showed significantly greater ($p < .05$ or better) reduction in abdominal pain intensity and pain duration for the CBT group ($n = 24$) than for the wait-list group ($n = 18$) and significantly ($p = .003$) greater reduction of avoidance behaviors caused by GI symptoms. There was a trend ($p = .09$) for the CBT group to reduce other GI symptoms (in a combined composite) more than the wait-list group. Forty-four percent of the CBT group showed clinically significant improvement (at least a 50% reduction in abdominal pain intensity and duration), whereas only 11% of the control participants showed this ($p = .02$). There were no significant between- or within-group effects on the SCL–90.

To their great credit, van Dulmen et al. (1996) attempted to follow up all of their treated patients (45) for up to 48 months posttreatment. They obtained questionnaire data for 32 patients (71%) and abdominal pain diary data for 27 patients (60%). Average length of follow-up was 27 months. Five patients had received other treatment during the follow-up interval. At the follow-up point, patients reported significantly less pain intensity and duration and less avoidance than at pretreatment. There was also a trend ($p = .09$) for other GI symptoms combined to have improved.

There was no change in the SCL–90 scores, and 37% met the 50% reduction criteria of clinically improved.

This study showed clearly that CBT in a group format was superior to a wait-list condition in reducing abdominal pain intensity and duration in the short term and that these treatment results held up well over a two-plus year average follow-up. Other GI symptoms were somewhat less improved. Overall psychological state did not change.

In the second study, Toner et al. (1998) described a rationale and composition of CBT for IBS in great detail, but they presented limited data on the patient population and even more limited data on the outcome. In design, this was an excellent study, comparing CBT groups (12 weekly 90-minute sessions) to groups receiving psychoeducational therapy, which met for the same times as the CBT groups, and to a set of patients who received routine medical care. Patients completed the BDI and a GI symptom diary.

The CBT group condition also included two individual therapy sessions; the initial one preceded the group and was devoted to education about bowel function and the cognitive–behavioral model of how cognitions and beliefs can play a role in IBS and to explain the treatment. The second individual session came at midtreatment (after Session 6) and was designed to clarify issues regarding the group and review individual progress.

Cognitive and behavioral techniques used included pain management; introduction to the gate control theory of pain (Melzack & Wall, 1965); work on bowel-related anxiety and avoidance through graduated performance tasks and feedback; and work on anger, lack of assertiveness, and shame through trying directly to correct dysfunctional beliefs and attitudes, challenge negative schema and fallacies, and improve self-efficacy.

Very limited results were reported. The CBT group showed significantly greater reductions in BDI scores than the other two groups (p = .001; mean scores not given). The medical care group became more depressed (p = .01), whereas the psychoeducation control group showed a trend (p = .07) for lower scores. There were no differential effects on any GI symptoms, abdominal pain and tenderness, diarrhea, or constipation. The reason given was floor effects, that is, low pretreatment levels of these symptoms. (One thus wonders how severely symptomatic these patients were.) There was a differential effect on bloating (p = .024), with the CBT group showing a significant decrease.

The authors reported significant within-group changes for the CBT condition for abdominal pain (p = .001), diarrhea (p = .048), and constipation (p = .017). The psychoeducational group showed a trend (p = .08) for a reduction in abdominal pain and tenderness (p = .10), whereas the routine medical care group did not change. Given the highly variable number of cases in each of the within-group analyses (from 13 to 20 in CBT, from 15 to 27 in psychoeducational condition, and from 9 to 13 in routine medical care), it appears that many patients lacked many symptoms. The total cases of patients with abdominal pain appears to be 60, leading one to wonder about the diagnoses in 40% of the sample.

These results are not impressive, given the ostensible sample sizes of 30 to 35 per condition. At best, they seem to show that the CBT condition is a good treatment for depression, and possibly bloating, in IBS patients. The failure to find a differential advantage for group CBT over routine medical care for the primary symptoms of IBS is problematic. We are left with a study for which we know more detail about CBT than in any other study, but with very weak evidence of the treatment's efficacy.

BIOFEEDBACK

Biofeedback has been defined as "a process in which a person learns to reliably influence physiological responses of two kinds: either responses which are not ordinarily under voluntary control or responses which ordinarily are easily regulated but for which regulation has broken down due to trauma or disease" (Blanchard & Epstein, 1978, p. 2) It consists of three steps: the detection and amplification of biological signals, the conversion of the amplified signal into easy-to-process information, and feeding back this information to the subject on a relatively immediate basis (Blanchard & Epstein, 1978, p. 3). Biofeedback is thus construed in this book as a subset of behavioral techniques for which the goal is to change behavior or responses directly at the physiological level. Biofeedback has been used in two ways in treating IBS: either directly to modify a gut-related biological response or indirectly as part of an arousal reduction or stress management treatment program.

Direct Modification of Gut-Related Biological Responses

The literature in this area is meager, perhaps attesting to the general lack of success in this area. There is only one true RCT, a small (n = 4 per condition) one by Whitehead (1985) and another controlled trial using single-subject experimental analysis (Radnitz & Blanchard, 1988).

Bowel Sound Biofeedback

Furman (1973) first described biofeedback of bowel sounds as a treatment for 5 patients complaining of diarrhea and abdominal pain (thus, probably meeting the criteria for diarrhea-predominant IBS). The bell of an electronic stethoscope was placed on the abdomen, about 2 to 3 inches below the umbilicus. The patient was then instructed alternately to increase and then decrease bowel sounds. The therapist verbally reinforced the patient for successful changes in the level of bowel sounds.

Furman reported that patients became asymptomatic once they gained control of their bowel sounds. He reported continued success in the use of the treatment (Furman, personal communication, October 25, 1985). Two attempted replications (O'Connell & Russ, 1978; Weinstock, 1976) were not successful. Weinstock (1976) reported treating 12 patients with chronic "functional colitis" (probably IBS) with bowel sound biofeedback. Three patients dropped out. He stated, "Response to treatment was at best sporadic." The nine remaining patients were then crossed over to systematic charting of episodes of bowel discomfort, frontal EMG biofeedback sessions three times per week as a relaxation strategy, and regular practice of relaxation using an audiotape. Weinstock concluded, "The response to treatment was uniformly positive."

The one experimentally controlled trial of bowel sound biofeedback was conducted in Albany. Radnitz and Blanchard (1988) screened 15 IBS patients to find 8 who were truly diarrhea-predominant based on diary records and for whom diarrhea was the primary symptom. Of the 8, two eventually declined the treatment, leaving 3 pairs who were treated in a multiple-baseline, across subjects design with baselines of 2 and 8 weeks. One subject in the short baseline dropped out in treatment. Treatment consisted of 10 twice-weekly sessions over a 5- to 6-week interval. The sessions consisted of two 3-minute self-control trials (no feedback available) of increasing and then decreasing bowel sounds and followed by eight 4-min trials for which increasing level of bowel sounds (4 min) and then decreasing level of bowel sounds (4 min) was alternated. An electronic stethoscope was used in the manner originally described by Furman (1973). After the stethoscope bell was in place, it was held there by a heavy towel draped over the lower abdomen. Thus, the patient needed to be in a semirecumbent position, preferably in a recliner. Patients were given inexpensive acoustic stethoscopes to use for daily home practice.

Evaluation was by means of the Albany GI symptom diary (see chapter 4) that patients completed on a daily basis. Visual inspection showed an advantage of treatment over symptom monitoring. Three of five patients had CPSR scores of 50 or greater at posttreatment; a fourth subject met this level in follow-up. The fifth treatment completer did not improve.

By recording the bowel sound signal on a strip chart (Grass Polygraph), it was possible to quantify the level of sound control. Two of the three clinical successes had statistical control of bowel sounds (activity higher on increase vs. decrease trials), whereas the third success showed a trend. There was also evidence of learning across trials and of a dose–response relation between symptom reduction and increased control of bowel sounds.

The results held up, based on 2-week GI symptom diary recordings at 6 months for all four who were initially successful. At one- and two-year follow-ups, there was continued success for 4 cases at one year and for the 3 who reported at two years (Radnitz & Blanchard, 1989). Although these results were not at the 100% level in all cases as reported by Furman (1973, 1985), they certainly seem worthwhile and worthy of further exploration. It is not known whether the technique would work with patients with alternating diarrhea and constipation.

In an unpublished dissertation, Bergeron (1983) used bowel sound biofeedback along with frontal EMG and thermal biofeedback for hand-warming as relaxation strategies, combined with systematic desensitization (Wolpe, 1958) as one condition in a study comparing biofeedback-based treatments to relaxation-based treatments and to assertiveness training and cognitive stress reduction. For the most part, the three conditions did not show differential improvement. The biofeedback group did show significant within-group improvement on abdominal pain, bowel functioning, and overall IBS severity ratings, as well as on state and trait anxiety. Independent evaluations by gastroenterologists noted that 6 of 12 (50%) of patients were notably improved. It is hard to attribute any of the positive results to the bowel sound biofeedback, because it was, at best, a minor part of the total treatment regimen.

Biofeedback of Colon Motility

Bueno-Miranda, Cerulli, and Schuster (1976) reported on 21 patients with IBS treated with a single 2-hour session in which they provided feedback to the patient of colonic motility from a balloon inserted into the rectosigmoid junction and then inflated in a stepwise fashion to elicit motility. Fourteen of 21 patients learned to reduce colonic motility and to increase the volume of distension required to provoke a threshold rectosigmoid spasm. No clinical data were obtained.

Whitehead (1985) in Read (1985) reported on a small RCT comparing biofeedback of colon motility ($n = 4$) to stress management ($n = 4$) in IBS patients. Patients kept symptom diaries for one month of baseline and during the 4 months of treatment. The biofeedback sessions, administered every 2 weeks for a total of 8, consisted of insertion of the balloon into the rectosigmoid junction and then the standard stepwise inflation of 20 ml of air every 2 minutes to a total volume of 200 ml. The patient was shown the polygraph tracing and asked to try to relax and prevent the occurrence of colonic contractions. Two or three inflation trials were run per session in addition to a no-feedback measurement trial (same stepwise inflation) at the beginning of the session. Patients were asked to practice at home daily what they had done in the laboratory to inhibit colonic contractions. (If nothing else, this procedure should desensitize the patient to the colonic motility study and the stepwise inflation procedure since he or she received 25 to 30 trials during the course of treatment.)

In the stress management condition, patients were seen on the same schedule and taught PMR. They then went through a standard systematic desensitization in imagination program (Wolpe, 1958) to pair relaxation with visualization of situations that elicited IBS symptoms. Results showed substantial reduction in abdominal pain ratings in the stress management group (about 50%) with no change in the biofeedback group. When 2 of the 4 who initially received biofeedback were crossed over to the stress management condition, they also experienced pain reduction. The biofeedback treatment did lead to a reduction in measured bowel motility whereas the stress management condition did not. It was clear that the more global stress management condition had better effects on IBS symptoms, especially abdominal pain, than the biofeedback of colonic motility. Moreover, Whitehead noted that the stress management condition was better tolerated by patients than the biofeedback condition, which necessitated the many colonic motility studies.

Conclusions

Although Whitehead (1985) clearly showed that, with the repeated trials of biofeedback of colon motility, patients could demonstrate feedback-assisted control of colonic motility, this situation did not lead to symptomatic improvement. Given the invasiveness and stress of the procedure, it seems clear that it was not a practical or useful treatment. We owe a debt to Whitehead and his patients for demonstrating this.

Bowel sound biofeedback is another matter, however. Furman (1973) reported strong positive results with diarrhea-predominant IBS. In Albany (Radnitz & Blanchard, 1988, 1989), we replicated these results and demonstrated stability of improvement with diary-based follow-ups of one and two years, again using diarrhea-predominant IBS cases. Weinstock (1976), however, reported poor acceptance and failure of the procedures in his 12 cases. I do not know, however, what Weinstock's patients were like. He may not have restricted his study to diarrhea-predominant cases. Bergeron's (1983) treatment condition is too confounded to help resolve this issue. I am cautiously optimistic about this procedure and would recommend further study. A small RCT would be advisable. Also, one might try the procedure across a variety of IBS subtypes to learn whether it is specific for diarrhea-predominant IBS.

Biofeedback-Based Relaxation and Stress Management

The second way in which biofeedback has been used in the treatment of IBS is as part of a relaxation and/or stress management program. Two forms of biofeedback, frontal EMG biofeedback and thermal biofeedback, have been widely used to assist a variety of patients in learning relaxation and thus to accrue the benefits of a relaxed state. In frontal EMG biofeedback, sensors are placed on the forehead with the active electrodes above each eye and a ground in between. With this wide horizontal placement, signals from muscles all over the head and neck are detected. Frontal EMG biofeedback training has been touted as a strategy for generalized relaxation (Budzynski, 1973; Schwartz, 1987). In thermal biofeedback, a temperature sensor is attached to a fingertip, and the patient is asked to warm the hands volitionally. Regular practice of this procedure has beneficial effects on migraine headaches (Blanchard, 1992) and Raynaud's disease (Freedman, 1993). It is also seen as a way to reduce peripheral SNS activity (Schwartz, 1987). Thus, it is touted as a technique complementary to EMG biofeedback, because the latter targets the musculoskeletal system, whereas thermal biofeedback targets the ANS.

In another unpublished dissertation, Giles (1978) targeted 40 subjects with GI complaints from a college student health service; 23 probably had IBS. The four conditions were (1) relaxation-based stress management for which PMR and other forms of relaxation were taught; (2) biofeedback-based relaxation using EMG biofeedback, thermal biofeedback, and relaxation tapes; (3) a combination of both, achieved by doubling the length of the session; and (4) a wait-list symptom monitoring control. Ten patients were assigned to each condition and received 8 weekly treatment sessions.

Although participants ostensibly kept a symptom diary, no useful information was obtained from it because of compliance problems. Ratings of three items from the Hopkins Symptom Checklist—loose bowel movements, nausea, and constipation—were analyzed for possible pre–post changes. There were no differential effects (including all treated subjects vs. no treatment) for nausea or constipation. For the loose bowel movements rating (related to diarrhea), all treated groups improved significantly ($p < .01$) more than the control participants. There was a weak trend ($p < .125$) for the biofeedback condition to be superior to the other two treatments for improvement. Half of the sample was lost at the follow-up, leading to no differences among groups.

As described earlier, Bergeron (1983) compared (a) a biofeedback-based condition, comprised of EMG biofeedback, thermal biofeedback, and one session of bowel sound biofeedback along with systematic desensitization, (b) a relaxation-based condition that also included systematic desensitization, and (c) a condition emphasizing assertiveness training and cognitive stress reduction. All three treated groups had approximately 50% of their participants rated as improved at a posttreatment assessment by blinded gastroenterologists. At follow-up, there were no relapses in the biofeedback condition but a high relapse rate (4 of 6) in the assertiveness training condition. Interestingly, those in the relaxation-based conditions continued to improve, going from 54% (7 of 13) improved at posttest to

77% (10 of 13) improved at the follow-up. Other patient ratings of GI symptoms showed no differential treatment effect.

These two unpublished RCTs show some advantage for biofeedback-based relaxation and stress management conditions, especially in comparison to no treatment (Giles, 1978). However, they do not show a notable advantage over nonbiofeedback-based relaxation training.

The Albany Studies

Four of the Albany studies, which are described in detail in chapter 16, utilized thermal biofeedback to assist patients in achieving a very deep state of relaxation. It was introduced after patients had been taught PMR; patients were told it would help them become very deeply relaxed. It was a part of five sessions. Patients were given an alcohol-in-glass thermometer to use for home practice.

In those four studies (Blanchard & Schwarz, 1988; Blanchard, Schwarz, et al., 1992, Study 1 and 2; Neff & Blanchard, 1987), we routinely had 50 to 60% of the participants in the CBT condition, which included the thermal biofeedback, achieve a clinically significant reduction in GI symptoms as measured by daily symptom diary. It is not clear what role the thermal biofeedback played in the total treatment and whether it was a necessary component. No studies were done to isolate its contribution. In hindsight, I do not believe the thermal biofeedback was a necessary part of the treatment. That remains to be tested.

CONCLUSION

It seems clear that there is strong empirical support from the studies summarized in this chapter, for brief psychodynamic psychotherapy and hypnotherapy. The evidence in support of various CBT treatments is less impressive but much more widespread. Combining these results with those from Albany to be summarized in the next chapters, I can support CBT as a third viable treatment alternative for IBS. Biofeedback of bowel sounds for diarrhea-predominant IBS patients is intriguing and awaits further study, especially with larger samples.

16

THE ALBANY IBS TREATMENT STUDIES

In the preceding chapter I referred several times to one or more of the Albany Studies. In this chapter, I present a summary of the 10 separate IBS treatment studies that have been done over the last 15 years. Most of the studies represented doctoral dissertations or master's theses. However, they were all performed in the same setting, using the same dependent variables, and essentially the same diagnostic and selection procedures. For these reasons they are comparable-across studies.[1]

Demographic characteristics of the subsamples in each study are contained in Table 16.1. In Table 16.2 are the average Composite Primary Symptom Reduction scores (CPSR, see Chapter 4) for each subgroup as well as the percent of the sample who reached our criteria for being called clinically improved (CPSR score of 0.50 or greater, an average reduction in the primary GI symptoms of abdominal pain and tenderness, diarrhea and constipation of 50% or greater, Blanchard & Schwarz, 1988). In Table 16.3 are the within-group statistical analyses for each GI symptom for each

[1]I am proud of this series of studies. Much of the credit for them goes to the dedicated doctoral students who performed them and who are acknowledged in the Preface. With the exception of Whorwell's work on hypnotherapy, summarized in Chapter 15, ours is the only lab which has stayed with this treatment problem over the years. I believe the series represents persistence in trying to find a psychological approach that would *reliably* help patients, study after study, even when the therapist changed. That consistency and reliability are what we need to be able to claim.

TABLE 16.1
Demographic Characteristics and Treatment Parameters for Albany Treatment Studies of IBS

Authors	Conditions	N	Age	% Women	Years w/IBS	% with Axis I	No. Therapists	No. Sessions/ No. Weeks
Neff & Blanchard (1987)	*Study 1*							
	CBT	4	34.5	50	11.3	—	1	12/8
	Study 2							
	CBT	10	40.8	50	5.3	—	1	12/8
	SM	9	42.1	78	6.1	—		—
Blanchard & Schwarz (1987)	Group CBT	14	38.4	79	6.3	—	2	12/8
Blanchard, Schwarz, et al. (1992)	*Study 1*							
	CBT	10	43.3	90	18.4	—	1	12/8
	Attention–Placebo	10	43.3	60	13.7	—	1	12/8
	SM	10	41.0	80	16.8	—	—	—
	Study 2							
	CBT	31	43.9	68	12.6	51	8	12/8
	Attention–Placebo	30	43.9	67	13.4	50	8	12/8
	SM	31	42.3	65	15.9	58	8	—
Radnitz & Blanchard (1988)	Bowel Sound Biofeedback	5	31.3	60	9.7	—	1	10/15
Blanchard et al. (1993)	Relaxation Training	8	39	75	15.0	50	3	10/8
	SM	8	42	75	11.0	63	—	—
Greene & Blanchard (1990)	CT	10	38.0	70	15.1	90	1	10/1
	SM	10	38.3	80	14.1	90	—	—
Payne & Blanchard (1995)	CT	12	39.7	83	18.1	83	1	10/8
	Support Group	12	44.0	92	15.9	92	1	8/8
	SM	10	35.9	80	13.8	80	—	—
Vollmer & Blanchard (1998)	Individual CT	11	40.6	73	13.8	82	1	10/10
	Group CT	11	42.5	82	8.0	82	1	10/10
	SM	10	47.7	80	17.9	90	—	—
Galovski & Blanchard (1999)	HPT	6	38.7	83	5.1	50	1	12/12
	SM-then HPT	6	39.0	83	6.8	50	1	—

Note. CBT = Cognitive–Behavioral Therapy (see Chapter 17), CT = Cognitive Therapy (see Chapter 18), SM = Symptom Monitoring, HPT = Hypnotherapy (see Chapter 19).

condition. There are some logical groupings of these studies. The discussion of the studies follows these groupings.

COGNITIVE AND BEHAVIORAL TREATMENT PACKAGE

Our initial research with IBS evaluated a multicomponent cognitive and behavioral treatment package (Neff & Blanchard, 1987), that was inspired by Latimer's (1983) cognitive–behavioral formulation of IBS. Treatment was for 12 individual sessions, spread over 8 weeks: twice per week for 4 weeks, followed by once per week. The components were:

1. Education about IBS and normal bowel functioning.
2. Progressive muscle relaxation (PMR), beginning with 16 muscle groups, reducing to 8 muscle groups, then to 4 muscle groups and eventually to relaxation-by-recall. Finally, cue controlled relaxation was taught as an active coping strategy for stressful events. Regular home practice, assisted by an audio tape, was stressed.
3. Thermal biofeedback for hand warming was introduced for 4 sessions as an additional relaxation strategy.
4. Cognitive therapy, primarily modeled after the work of Meichenbaum (1977) and Holroyd, Andrasik, and Westbrook (1977), was introduced at Session 2 and was a part of each visit. The focus was on helping individuals identify personally stressful situations, especially those related to GI symptoms, then analyze antecedents and consequences, especially "self-talk"; and finally begin to deal more effectively with the stresses. See Chapter 17 for the complete treatment manual.

In a pilot study with 4 cases (2 men, 2 women), two individuals (1 man, 1 woman) had very good results reducing symptoms by over 80 percent, one man was slightly improved on pain and diarrhea, and one woman was slightly worse with no change in constipation and an increase in diary measured pain (interestingly, she claimed to be 50% improved on a global measure).

The primary study we conducted was a RCT with 10 patients assigned to the CBT package and 10 assigned to a symptom monitoring, wait list control condition for 12 weeks (2 weeks pretreatment baseline, 8 weeks of treatment, 2 weeks posttreatment baseline). One control dropped out after one week of monitoring and was not replaced. Seven of the controls were crossed over and later given the same treatment. The therapist was a single advanced doctoral student in clinical psychology.

Results showed a significantly (p = .034) greater reduction in symptoms for the CBT condition (CPSR score of 50.4) than the symptom mon-

TABLE 16.2
Average CPSR Scores and Fraction of Sample Improved for All Conditions in Albany Treatment Studies of IBS

Authors	Conditions	N	Drop-outs	CPSR Score	% Sample Improved
Neff & Blanchard (1987)	*Study 1*		0		
	CBT	4		NR	50%
	Study 2		0		
	CBT	10	1	50.4	60%
	SM	9	—	15.4	11%
	Treatment SM (CBT)	7		NR	43%
Blanchard & Schwarz (1987)	CBT-Group	14	1	47.5	64%
Blanchard, Schwarz, et al. (1992)	*Study 1*				
	CBT	10	0	45.2	60%
	Attention–Placebo	10	0	38.0	50%
	SM	10	0	9.5	20%
	Study 2				52%
	CBT	31	7	32.4	47%
	Attention–Placebo	30	8	30.2	32%
	SM	31	8	6.4	40%
	Treatment SM (CBT)	30	2	—	

Radnitz & Blanchard (1988)	Bowel Sound Biofeedback	5	1	41.6	60%
Blanchard et al. (1993)	Relaxation	8	6	51.6	50%
	SM	8	1	−1.4	0
Greene & Blanchard (1994)	CT	10	2	66.0	80%
	SM	10	0	2.0	10%
	Treatment SM CT	6	0	64.0	66%
Payne & Blanchard (1995)	CT	12	1	67	75%
	Support Group	12	0	31	25%
	SM	10	0	10	10%
Vollmer & Blanchard (1998)	Individual CT	11	1	46	55%
	Group CT	11	1	52	64%
	SM	10	0	−4	10%
Galovski & Blanchard (1999)	HPT	6	1	55	60%
	SM	6	1	−32	0
	Treatment SM HPT	6	—	47	50%

Note. CPSR = Composite Primary Symptom Reduction; CBT = Cognitive–Behavioral Therapy (see Chapter 17); CT = Cognitive Therapy (see Chapter 18), SM = Symptom Monitoring, HPT = Hypnotherapy (see Chapter 19).

TABLE 16.3
Summary of Within Group Analyses of Individual GI Symptoms for Albany Treatment Studies of IBS

Authors	Conditions	N	Abdom. Pain & Tenderness		Diarrhea		Constipation		Bloating		Flatulence		Belching	
			t	p	t	p	t	p	t	p	t	p	t	p
Neff & Blanchard (1987)	*Study 2*													
	CBT	10	2.13	ns	3.35	**	1.41	ns	N/R		2.75	*	1.99	ns
	SM	9	1.23	ns	1.87		−.32	ns	N/R		ns		ns	
	Combined CBT + Treated SM	17	N/R	*	N/R	*	N/R	*	N/R			*		ns
Blanchard & Schwarz (1987)	CBT-Group	14	2.28	*	2.84	*		ns	N/R			ns		ns
Blanchard, Schwarz, et al. (1992)	*Study 1*													
	CBT	10	2.20	*	2.28	*	1.99	*	N/R		1.63	ns	3.03	**
	Attention–Placebo	10	2.22	*	−.41	ns	2.95	**	N/R		2.03	*	2.24	*
	SM	10	0.42	ns	−.89	ns	.38	ns	N/R		−.89	ns	.98	ns
	Study 2													
	CBT	31	2.18	*	2.95	**	2.62	*	2.65	*	3.68	**	1.42	ns
	Attention–Placebo	30	3.50	**	2.11	*	1.29		2.30	*	3.64	*	2.91	**
	SM	31	−.13	ns	.20	ns	.99	ns	.44	ns	3.21	**	.99	ns
	Tx. SM (CBT)	28	2.13	*	1.03	ns	2.10	ns *	3.25	**	4.15	*	2.10	*

Radnitz & Blanchard (1988)	Bowel Sound Biofeedback	5	N/R		N/R		N/R		N/R		N/R		N/R	
Blanchard et al. (1993)	Relaxation	8	2.44	*	.86	ns	2.06	a	N/R		1.67	ns	1.32	ns
	SM	8	.68	ns	.36	ns	.88	ns	N/R		1.56	ns	1.53	
Greene & Blanchard (1994)	CT	10	3.0	*	5.89	***	4.09	**	3.03	*	3.16	*	2.83	*
	SM	10	−.42	ns	1.43	ns	.40	ns	1.26	ns	1.18	ns	1.46	ns
	Tx. SM (CT)		2.44	*	2.14	a	2.44	*	7.69	***	2.74	*	1.69	ns
Payne & Blanchard (1995)	CT	12	4.63	***	7.01	***	2.78	*	3.20	**	2.04	a	2.13	a
	Support Group	12	.84	ns	1.51	ns	.86	ns	.64	ns	.49	ns	.62	ns
	SM	10	−.19	ns	1.78	ns	1.54	ns	1.89	a	2.04	a	−1.15	ns
Vollmer & Blanchard (1998)	Individual CT	11	2.28	*	3.21	**	1.19	ns	2.40	*	2.90	*	3.27	**
	Group CT	11	2.74	*	2.77	*	2.72	*	2.00	a	1.46	ns	7.47	*
	SM	10	1.28	ns	.30	ns	.49	ns	1.46	ns	2.22	*	1.29	ns
Galovski & Blanchard (1999)	HPT	6	N/R											
	SM	6	N/R											
	Combined HPT + Tx. SM	11	3.07	**	.98	ns	2.93	*	1.99	a	3.44	**	1.55	ns

Note. CBT = Cognitive–Behavioral Therapy (see Chapter 17), CT = Cognitive Therapy (see Chapter 18), SM = Symptom Monitoring, HPT = Hypnotherapy (see Chapter 19). [a]$p < .10$; *$p < .05$; **$p < .01$; ***$p < .001$; ns = non-significant; N/R = not reported.

itoring control (CPSR score of 15.4). Moreover, 6 of 10 in the CBT condition were improved compared to 1 of 9 in the symptom monitoring condition (p = .04, Fisher's exact probability test). Three of the seven (43%) controls experienced clinically significant improvement when crossed over to treatment. For the combined treated sample (n = 17), there was significant (p < .05) reductions in abdominal pain and tenderness, diarrhea, flatulence, belching and nausea.

These patients were followed up at one year, two years and four years posttreatment (see Chapter 21). For the most part, improvement as documented by symptom diary held up well over time.

Adaptation to Small Group Format

The next study (Blanchard & Schwarz, 1987) was a quasiexperimental design. Sixteen IBS patients (5 men, 11 women) monitored GI symptoms for 12 weeks. They were then given the same 12-session treatment in small groups of 3 to 6. The therapists were a PhD-level psychologist and a RN in her first year of doctoral training in clinical psychology. Thermal biofeedback was used in 6 of the 12 sessions.

Changes to the individual format included time spent on group introductions and group cohesion building at the first session. The cognitive therapy component was modified in that there was time to deal with only a single stressful event per patient at each session. Support and suggestions for coping strategies were solicited from other group members.

In my opinion, the cognitive therapy component was not as fully implemented in the group adaptation as it had been in the individual therapy sessions. However, the group support (especially getting to know some others who had suffered for years with the same problems) and vicarious learning (listening to how someone else was going to deal with a stressful situation) seemed to compensate for the lack of individual attention.

Clinical Hint

Two male patients declined treatment after the 12 weeks of symptom monitoring when they learned that treatment was to be in small, mixed gender groups. We suspect this was due to potential embarrassment over discussing bowel symptoms in mixed company. It might be better to have an all male group for such hesitant patients, preferably led by a male therapist. One other patient dropped out after 4 visits.

Results showed only one change with the prolonged symptom monitoring baseline, a significant (p < .05) *increase* in diarrhea ratings. After treatment, 9 of 14 patients (64.3%) showed CPSR scores of 50% or greater, indicating clinically significant improvement. The average CPSR score for the 14 patients was 47.5. There were significant ($p < .05$) within-group improvement effects for abdominal pain and diarrhea at end of treatment, and on constipation and flatulence by a 6-week follow-up.

The results seems to clearly support using this CBT package with small groups as well as individuals. Moreover, the results replicated across different experienced therapists.

Comparison to an Attention–Placebo Control

The next step in our research was to compare the CBT package to an attention placebo control condition and to a symptom monitoring, wait list control condition. Klein (1988) had already reported a relatively large placebo effect in drug treatments of IBS. Thus, it made sense to try to evaluate this potential effect in the psychological treatments. In essence, we were asking, "Are there specific effects of symptom relief among the components of the CBT treatment for IBS, or is it the case (the alternative hypotheses) that all of the symptom relief arises from the patient's expectations of benefits and symptom relief and from the regular interaction with a warm, supportive therapist delivering a treatment with a plausible rationale?"

In designing an attention–placebo condition, several factors came into play: (1) it had to have the same amount of contact, frequency of sessions and duration of sessions, as the CBT condition; (2) it had to have multiple components; and (3) it needed to be plausible to patients. We put together two elements: (1) a pseudomeditation condition which Holroyd and colleagues (Holroyd, Andrasik, and Noble, 1980) had developed and used successfully with tension-type headache patients and (2) EEG biofeedback for alpha suppression which Plotkin and Rice (1981) and Rice, Blanchard, and Purcell (1993) had shown was very psychologically engaging and believable. At the same time, we wanted procedures that were not clear relaxation strategies since relaxation was a primary component of the CBT package.

In the pseudomeditation procedure, patients sat erect and were repeatedly told not to relax. In the first portion, labeled "body awareness training," patients were asked to mentally scan the body in a systematic fashion, but not to relax the area being attended to. In the second part, called "cognitive control training," patients were asked to create vivid mental images of everyday activities. The two were then combined to form the meditation training. Patients were asked to practice the procedures on their own at home for about 20 minutes per day. They were reminded to guard against becoming relaxed or drowsy during the practice.

The alpha suppression biofeedback was chosen for several reasons: (1)

it provided a "biofeedback" element to the condition with all of the lay mystique that might entail; (2) it was a response for which subjects do not ordinarily have much naïve awareness (unlike forehead muscle or finger tip temperature) and for which changes are not readily detectable without monitoring equipment; and (3) suppression of alpha in the EEG is fairly easy for most people to learn (by focusing attention) and is *not* associated with a relaxed state.

We used a Bio-Feedback System, Inc., Model AT-2 EEG trainer with Model DQ-1 digital quantifier. EEG was recorded from an electrode over the occipital lobe (O_2) and over the mastoid with the forehead as a ground. Recording sites were cleaned with acetone and then electrodes with EEG paste were attached. The equipment was set to provide a digital display of electrical activity within the alpha (8–13 Hz) band, integrated over 2 minutes. During the feedback portion of the session, *veridical* auditory feedback of alpha level was available to the patients who were instructed to try to *reduce* the feedback tone. The feedback trial, itself, was 20 min.

In addition to the auditory feedback from the device, patients were given periodic (once per 2 min) verbal feedback which was designed to show success at the task. Patients were read their actual scores from the first 2 min. Thereafter, they were given verbal feedback that showed a 2% accumulating decrease for each 2-min trial. Patients were thus led to believe they were succeeding at the task at a convincing rate.

Patients from both the CBT condition and attention–placebo condition were given questionnaires to assess treatment credibility and expectations at the initial and final session. There were also process manipulation checks on the CBT: relaxation ratings in session as well as changes in temperature and diary recordings of home practice of relaxation and home thermal biofeedback. For the attention–placebo condition, they made ratings in session of depth of concentration and home diary ratings of practice. For the EEG biofeedback, values for EEG were recorded to see if, in fact, it was being suppressed.

Study 1

Thirty individuals with IBS (7 men, 23 women) of average age 42 began and finished the study; there were no dropouts. They were randomly assigned to one of three conditions: (1) the CBT package described earlier in this chapter; (2) the attention–placebo condition combining pseudomeditation and EEG alpha suppression biofeedback; (3) symptom monitoring, wait-list control. The single therapist was an advanced doctoral student in clinical psychology with much experience in the treatment procedures. The treatment credibility and expectancy scores for the two treatment conditions were high initially (8.5 for CBT, 7.9 for attention–placebo) on a 0–9 scale and at the conclusion; they did not differ in either instance.

Results showed CPSR scores of 45.2, 38.0 and 9.5, for the CBT, attention–placebo, and symptom monitoring control conditions, respectively. Despite the sizeable differences among groups, they were not significantly different on this composite measure. Six (of 10) patients in the CBT condition were clinically improved as were 5 (of 10) patients in the attention–placebo condition and 2 (of 10) in the symptom monitoring condition.

There were significant ($p < .05$) within-group changes on abdominal pain and tenderness, constipation, and belching for both treated groups, and for diarrhea for the CBT condition; the symptom monitoring group did not change significantly on any measure. There were also significant reductions on the Beck Depression Inventory (BDI) for both treated groups and on state and trait anxiety for the CBT condition.

Comment

While the results for the CBT condition replicated fairly well our previous research (see Table 16.2) with a CPSR score of 45.2 and 60% of the sample reaching the criteria for clinically significant improvement, both control groups performed better than expected, especially the symptom monitoring controls. Thus, we failed, with an $n = 10$ per cell, to show an effect of CBT over the control condition which was very credible and psychologically engaging. We were encouraged enough, however, to try a larger scale study.

Study 2

The second study was supported by a grant from the National Institute of Diabetes, Digestive, and Kidney Diseases (NIDDK), DK-38614. There were a few minor changes from Study 1: (1) the initial baseline of GI symptom monitoring was lengthened to 4 weeks; (2) all patients were evaluated by one of two academic gastroenterologists; and (3) bloating was added to the list of GI symptoms being monitored. Its initial omission was an oversight, especially since it is one of the primary reasons (after pain) that IBS patients seek help. A major change was the use of multiple therapists. A total of 8 different doctoral students in clinical psychology treated patients in this study. Their experience ranged from several years to a few months. They all underwent training in the treatment procedures over several months. However, the level of basic clinical experience varied greatly among the therapists.

A total of 115 IBS patients began treatment. Twenty-three (20%) dropped out in treatment, a noticeably higher rate than we had seen previously. They did not differ from those who completed on any dimension we assessed. Among the 92 who completed, 31 (34%) were men, a higher percentage than usual. Patients were matched into triads based on sex, age and primary GI symptoms, and randomly assigned to conditions. Dropouts were replaced with the goal of completing 30 patients per condition.

The mean CPSR scores for the three conditions were 32.4, 30.2, and 6.4, for CBT, attention–placebo, and symptom monitoring, respectively. There were no significant differences among the 3 groups. Sixteen of those in the CBT condition reached our criteria for clinically improved, as did 14 of those in the attention–placebo condition and 10 in the symptom-monitoring condition. Among the 30 patients from the symptom-monitoring control condition who were crossed over to receive the CBT treatment, 12 reached the criteria for clinically significant improvement.

Thus, the results on the average composite score were noticeably poorer than we had seen in the past (see Table 16.2 for comparisons). This arose in part because of a high percentage (9/31, 29%) of patients from the CBT condition who were worse at end of treatment. Another factor in the results were the much more positive results for those in the symptom monitoring condition, almost a third (10/31, 32%) met our criteria for clinical improvement by the end of the 10 weeks of monitoring. This was offset in part by 13 (42%) who were worse at the posttreatment point.

With regards to individual GI symptoms, there were significant within-group reductions for all 7 symptoms in the attention placebo condition and for 6 of 7 in CBT (the symptom of belching was not significantly reduced). For symptom monitoring there was a significant reduction in bloating and in flatulence, but not in any primary symptom. When the controls were crossed over to CBT, there were significant reductions in abdominal pain and tenderness, constipation, bloating, belching, flatulence, and nausea.

Again, both treated groups showed significant reductions in BDI scores as well as state and trait anxiety. The CBT treated controls showed similar effects.

All of the manipulation checks were positive; initial expectations were again high (7.7 for CBT, 8.0 for attention–placebo, out of 9). Interestingly, the attention–placebo group showed higher hand temperatures at Session 12 than did those in the CBT condition who had been receiving explicit training in thermal biofeedback for hand warming.

Two-month and six-month follow-ups showed generally good maintenance of symptom reduction in patients from both conditions. The diary ratings for all symptoms except diarrhea were significantly lower at 6-month follow-up than at pretreatment.

Comment

Clearly, these were very disappointing results for the CBT treatment. Overall results were poorer than in earlier trials and CBT was not different from either control condition.

Three things seemed to have happened: (1) the CBT treatment did not work as well. This may have been a function of using less experienced therapists. Results from the one male therapist, who was one of the inexperienced ones, were noticeably poorer. Moreover, almost one-third of patients were worse after treatment. (2) Many patients in the attention–placebo condition acknowledged using the "meditational procedures" to relax or calm themselves or as a way of distracting attention in stressful situations. It thus appears that patients found a way to make the "inactive" treatment active for them. (3) Those in symptom monitoring did far better than usual with almost a third reaching the criteria for clinically improved.

Comment

At this point we were faced with a problem. We had a treatment which failed its *big* test, but which seemed helpful to many. Our task became one of trying to understand the failure, and also to understand how the placebo treatment led to symptom abatement. A grant application to examine these points was not funded. We subsequently set about breaking down the CBT treatment to see which components might be responsible for improvement and to see if we could obtain more consistently positive results.

Relaxation Training Alone

Our first step in breaking down the CBT package was to examine training in PMR alone as a treatment for IBS (Blanchard, Greene, Scharff, & Schwarz-McMorris, 1993). Twenty-three IBS patients started the study; 16 (8 in active treatment and 8 in symptom monitoring control) completed it. The 7 dropouts (6 from treatment, 1 from the control condition) did not differ from those who completed the study on demographic variables. The total sample was 78% women; 61% met criteria for at least one Axis I diagnosis.

The patients in the relaxation condition received 10 treatment sessions, twice per week for the first 2 weeks, then once per week for the next 6 weeks. After a brief introduction the relaxation regimen began with a lengthy 16-muscle group relaxation regimen (it is described in detail in Chapter 17), which included many suggestions of relaxation, warmth, and heaviness interspersed with the tension release exercises. An audio tape to guide home practice was given each of the participants. They were asked to practice for 20–25 minutes once per day. Relaxing imagery and deep diaphragmatic breathing were added to this induction.

The relaxation regimen was next reduced to 8-muscle groups and then to 4. There followed training in a passive form of relaxation known as relaxation-by-recall in which the patient passively relaxes the muscle groups by matching the memory of what the relaxed state felt like rather than actively tensing and relaxing muscle groups. A second audiotape to guide the relaxation-by-recall was also provided for home practice. Finally, the patients were taught cue-controlled relaxation in which the exhalation of a deep diaphragmatic breath is paired with subvocalizing the word "relax." Patients were asked to use this 10 to 20 times per day as a way of counteracting feelings of tension or stress.

The controls continued to monitor GI symptoms in the daily diary. They were seen at 4 weeks to maintain contact. Patients monitored GI symptoms for 4 weeks prior to treatment randomization and for 4 more weeks after completion.

A comparison of average CPSR scores revealed a significant advantage for the relaxation training over symptom monitoring, 51.6 versus −1.4 ($t[14] = 2.18$, $p = .05$). Four of the eight participants in relaxation met our criteria for improvement versus only one of those in symptom monitoring ($p = .10$). The patients receiving relaxation showed a significant pre–post reduction in abdominal pain and tenderness and nausea, with a trend ($p = .10$) for constipation. There was also a significant reduction in nausea for the controls.

Comment

The overall results from this small study show that for those who completed treatment, average reduction in primary IBS symptoms is roughly comparable to what we have seen for the full CBT package, the same was true for the fraction of the sample who are clinically improved.

However, this positive evaluation must be tempered by the very large dropout rate. We lost 43% of those who started the relaxation condition. This is almost double our worst previous dropout rate. The therapists in this study were all advanced doctoral students with two or three years experience in treating IBS patients and in using the relaxation training procedures.

Clinical Hint

We believe the relaxation training, which is fairly protocol driven, does not engage the IBS patients enough to hold him or her in treatment. That is, there is no planned discussion of IBS symptoms and the difficulties they cause the patient nor any discussion of the stresses in the patient's life. Such elements may be crucial to keeping the patient in treatment.

It might well be the case that systematic relaxation training in the context of supportive psychotherapy would be a very effective treatment for IBS. We have not tested this. However, the work of Shaw et al. (1991)

appears to be somewhat like that and to have been generally effective (see Chapter 15).

Cognitive Therapy Alone

The next step in the dismantling process was to examine the effects of the cognitive therapy alone on IBS. I was blessed by having three successive doctoral students (Barbara Greene, Annette Payne, and Alisa Vollmer) who were experienced with IBS and who had become well versed in cognitive approaches to therapy during their doctoral training. Their dissertation studies, described in this section, represent an original RCT evaluating cognitive therapy alone as a treatment for IBS and two independent replications, all based in the same setting with the same treatment protocol.

Initial Trial (Greene & Blanchard, 1994)

The initial study compared cognitive therapy to a symptom-monitoring control condition in a RCT involving 20 IBS patients. The total sample was 75% women, of average age 38.2 years, who had suffered from IBS for an average of 14.4 years.

The cognitive therapy regimen (for more details see Chapter 18) consisted of 10 individual one-hour sessions, twice per week for the first 2 weeks, then once per week for the next 6 weeks. Treatment started with a clear rationale for the treatment approach, describing IBS as an autonomic-nervous-system-mediated reaction to stress; the reaction was described as having three related components: cognitions, behaviors, and physiological responses. *Cognitions were emphasized as the determining factors in IBS symptomatology*.

The therapy was an amalgamation of elements from the work of Meichenbaum (1985), Beck (1976), and Persons (1989). The intervention was structured and directive, yet it required the patient's active collaboration. Therapy focused on increasing the patient's awareness of the association among stressors, thoughts, and IBS symptoms. Next, was emphasized training patients to identify and then modify their appraisals and interpretations of threatening stimuli. Intervention encompassed the use of both verbal and behavioral techniques to identify and modify underlying psychological mechanisms, fundamental beliefs, and assumptions.

Self-recording of automatic thoughts was emphasized. Patients were provided monitoring forms and asked to monitor daily, throughout treatment, automatic thoughts as they occurred across daily situations that they found to be stressful. The therapist focused on the cognitive responses generated on the patient's monitoring sheets and, working collaboratively with the patient, identified control themes, or "working hypotheses," concerning the patient's underlying psychological mechanisms.

Therapeutic work was directed at activating three change mechanisms:

1. "Rational self-analysis," or self-understanding (in which the patient explores idiosyncratic beliefs and fears, their connection to the cognitive, behavioral, and affective components of their IBS, and in which they reach an understanding of their fundamental maladaptive orientation to self and world).
2. The second part of the therapeutic change mechanisms was "decentering," in which the patient gains distance from self by identifying his or her self-talk and labeling this as self-talk, thereby explicitly "owning" automatic thoughts.
3. Lastly, one begins to involve experiential disconfirmation (admittedly focused) in which patients are led to challenge their maladaptive beliefs through strategically planned behavioral experiments and deliberately acting differently so as to experience the self in different ways.

Clinical Hint

Some patients balk at step 1. They may claim to live a stress-free life and to find no connection between IBS symptoms and environmental events and their thoughts. The first step is to push the patient gently to reexamine his or her life. If that fails, one can ask the patient to adopt a working hypothesis that there may be a connection. They are then asked to go along with the recording and analysis, even if "they know" it does not apply to them personally.

If the latter fails, then this may not be an approach which will work for this patient. We find this in about 10% of cases, mostly men.

Compliance was generally good. Two patients dropped out of this condition (2/12 = 17%). All ten symptom-monitoring controls completed that condition. Six were subsequently treated with the cognitive therapy.

Results

For the cognitive therapy condition, we found the strongest results we had ever had: the average CPSR was 0.66 as compared to 0.02 for the symptom-monitoring control group; moreover, 8 of 10 (80%) of those in the cognitive therapy condition met our criteria for being clinically improved (versus 1 of 10 for the controls), and the two other treated patients had CPSR scores of 0.48 and 0.42, respectively. The difference in CPSR scores was highly significant ($t(18) = 3.51$, $p = .005$). Six of the controls were subsequently treated (the others declined). The CPSR score, relative to pretreatment, for these six was 0.64 with 4 of 6 (67%) meeting our criteria for being clinically improved.

We had added bloating to the list of GI symptoms monitored in the GI Symptom Diary. It and every other symptom showed a significant within-group change ($p < .02$ or better) whereas, none of the changes in the controls were significant.

The cognitive therapy group showed significant reductions in depression (BDI) (10.6 to 5.1), but not in state or trait anxiety. The controls did not change. Two measures of the cognitive processes targeted in the therapy, the Automatic Thoughts Questionnaire (ATQ); (Hollon & Kendall, 1980) and Dysfunctional Attitudes Scale (DAS); (Weissman & Beck, 1978) also showed significant decreases for the cognitive therapy group, but not for the controls. Finally, a measure derived from patients' homework sheets of positive and negative self-talk showed the expected changes with negative talk decreasing from 0.80 to 0.11, whereas positive talk increased from 0.03 to 0.85 by the end of treatment.

A 3-month follow-up of 9 of 10 patients initially treated with cognitive therapy revealed a CPSR score relative to pretreatment of 0.59, and 7 of 9 (77%) of cases still met criteria for clinical improvement.

Comment

As noted above, these were the strongest results, in terms of average change in primary GI symptoms (CPSR score) and in terms of the fraction of the sample who were improved (80%), that we had ever seen. Moreover, the results held up over short term follow-up, and they replicated when 6 of the 10 controls were treated. To say the least, we were pleased but also wary since we had previously seen positive results which would not replicate. Finally, these results were accomplished in a somewhat troubled sample, in that 9 of 10 patients in each condition met the criteria for at least one Axis I disorder, a factor associated with poorer outcome in our earlier work (see Chapter 20 on prediction of outcome).

Payne and Blanchard (1995)

The next two steps were obvious: (1) to see if the very positive results from cognitive therapy could be replicated with a new set of patients and, more importantly, with a *new therapist* (it could be that success was due to the unique skills and personality of Barbara Greene); and (2) to test the treatment against a credible attention–placebo condition so as to control for patient expectations of benefit as the primary active ingredient. With these ideas in mind, the next study was one comparing individual cognitive therapy, following the treatment manual developed for Greene and Blanchard (1994), to (1) a psychoeducational support group and to (2) a symptom-monitoring, wait-list control group.

Since our earlier experience with an attention–placebo control had revealed it was a relatively active treatment (yielding results in terms of GI symptom relief comparable to our CBT treatment), which patients turned to clinical advantage by using it in stressful situations for relaxation and/or distraction, we obviously needed something different. Moreover, since patients were given a certain amount of educative information about IBS in the cognitive therapy condition and we needed something which would be credible to patients, we developed a psychoeducation support group. Self-help psychoeducation support groups are a widespread phenomenon in the United States at present, thus it seemed prudent to capitalize on the widespread nature of this phenomenon. (The treatment manual for this condition is in Appendix A.)

There was one noticeable change in subject selection for this study: we began using the Rome criteria for selection of IBS cases rather than the clinical criteria (see Chapter 1). The same GI Symptom Diary was used (continuing to include bloating). The same battery of psychological tests was administered (Beck Depression Inventory, State–Trait Anxiety Inventory, Automatic Thoughts Questionnaire, and Dysfunctional Attitude Scale); we added the Hassles Scale (DeLongis, Folkman, & Lazarus, 1988), a measure of the occurrence and severity of daily stressors, to see if there was possible differential change in daily stressors that might account for improvement.

Very importantly, we added a measure of patient expectancy, given at the beginning and end of treatment. It was adapted from earlier work on headache and hypertension (Blanchard & Andrasik, 1985; Blanchard, Martin, & Dubbert, 1988). The questions and scores of the two treatment groups, both at pretreatment and posttreatment, are presented in Table 16.4.

Thirty-four IBS patients (5 men, 29 women) of average age 40, who had been suffering from IBS for about 16 years, were randomized to the three conditions: 12 to cognitive therapy, 12 to the support groups, and 10 to symptom monitoring. One patient dropped out from the cognitive therapy condition and was replaced. Twenty-nine (85%) met criteria for at least one Axis I disorder. The latter were equally distributed across the three conditions.

Both treatments lasted for 8 weeks. In the cognitive therapy, patients were seen for two 60-min individual sessions each week for the first two weeks, followed by 6 weekly 60-min sessions. The total amount of therapy time was held constant by having the support groups meet for 75 min, once per week for 8 weeks for a total of 600 min.

The cognitive therapy condition was the same as used in Greene and Blanchard (1994) and followed the treatment manual developed for that condition.

TABLE 16.4
Pretreatment and Posttreatment Expectancies and Treatment Credibility Ratings for Cognitive Therapy and Support Group Conditions

Pretreatment* Expectancies	Group CT	Means SG	Univariate F	p
1. How logical is treatment?	8.00	8.00	0.00	1.00
2. How confident are you that treatment will reduce GI symptoms?	5.75	6.67	1.28	.27
3. Would you recommend this treatment to a friend?	7.25	6.92	.19	.67
4. How important is it that this treatment be available for others?	7.67	8.25	1.10	.31
5. How successful would this treatment be for others?	7.00	7.00	0.00	1.00
6. What do you think your level of mastery will be?	6.58	7.42	1.70	.21

Posttreatment Expectancies	Group CT	Means SG	Univariate F	p
1. How logical is treatment?	7.83	7.92	.20	.89
2. How confident are you that treatment will reduce GI symptoms?	6.75	7.17	.06	.81
3. Would you recommend this treatment to a friend?	8.08	8.08	.01	.94
4. How important is it that this treatment be available for others?	8.42	8.25	.24	.63
5. What do you think your level of mastery will be?	6.50	7.17	.71	.41
6. What is your total level of success?	6.46	5.45	1.76	.20

Note. CT = Cognitive Treatment, SG = Support Group. Range of Measure 0 (not at all) to 9 (very likely). Adapted from Table 2 of "A controlled comparison of cognitive therapy and self-help support groups in the treatment of irritable bowel syndrome," by A. Payne and E. B. Blanchard, 1995, *Journal of Consulting and Clinical Psychology, 63,* 779–786. *Pretreatment expectancies were measured at the conclusion of the first session. Thus, patients had heard a full explanation for the treatment and its rationale before answering the questions.

Self-Help Support Group

Groups in this condition were made up of 3 to 5 members and were designed to focus specifically on IBS and those issues related to the development and maintenance of IBS such as stress and diet. The weekly group sessions focused on specific topics introduced by the therapist as well as an open group discussion about each group member's experiences or reactions to the topic of discussion. Each week, the group session consisted of two parts. The first part included information about a topic (i.e., specific aspect of IBS) for that week. Within this portion, patients were encouraged to provide examples from their own experiences to enhance the group's understanding of the given topic. The therapist facilitated discussion and answered questions as they arose. However, the therapist provided very little didactic information and no prescriptions or advice for change. The purpose of the group was for the members to help each other understand different aspects of IBS. Members were informed that the topics were more relevant for some than others and that each member might find some issues more salient than others. In addition, it was the responsibility of each member to participate and take from the discussion the information that was most relevant for him or her.

In addition to the informational part of the group, each group member was asked to participate and to support each other. Discussion centered on how each topic related to the members specifically and each member provided personal examples. The goal of the second part of the group was for each member to recognize the similarities and differences among the group members' experiences with IBS. In the process of sharing experiences, it became apparent that each member was not the only individual who suffered with these types of problems and issues. Thus, in the group format, the members spent much of each session learning from each other and providing support.

In sum, the group attempted to gather as much information about IBS as possible from both the therapist and each other to further understand the development and maintenance of IBS. The therapist explicitly refrained from giving specific advice on how to view or cope with various issues which arose, always reflecting such questions back to the group. Through the information provided by the therapist and the experiences shared with each other, the group developed a better understanding of IBS. Armed with information and the support of the group, each member of the group was expected to have increased confidence to face his/her own specific difficulties.

Symptom Monitoring Wait-List Control

Patients continued to monitor their GI symptoms with the GI symptom diaries for the 8 weeks that coincided with the other two treatment conditions. Subjects were contacted at the 4-week point by the therapist to determine whether the subject had any difficulties with the diaries and to set up a post-wait-list assessment. Following 8 weeks of symptoms monitoring, subjects in this condition repeated the assessment procedures including the psychological testing battery. At the completion of the post-wait-list assessment, subjects were offered the support group treatment.

Comment

We introduced a deliberate confound in this study by having the control condition delivered in a group format. We could have changed the cognitive therapy to a small group format but chose not to do so because we wanted to see if the individual cognitive therapy would replicate. Had we changed the cognitive therapy to a small group format, and it had not worked as well as the first trial, we would not have known whether the deficit was due to a change of therapist or a change of format. Thus, to avoid this potential confound, we introduced the confound of delivering the control condition in a small group.

Of course, it would not be possible to have a self-help support group in any format other than as a small group. Thus, to maintain its credibility, it had to be delivered in a small group format.

Results

For the most part, the positive results from the individual cognitive therapy were replicated. The mean pre–post CPSR scores for the three conditions, cognitive therapy, self-help support group, and symptom monitoring, were 0.67, 0.31, and 0.10, respectively. The cognitive therapy was statistically superior to both controls which did not differ. The mean CPSR score (.67) thus replicates that of Greene and Blanchard (0.66). In terms of frequency of meeting the criteria for clinically meaningful improvement, 9 of 12 (75%) of those in cognitive therapy met the criteria (and two others had scores of 0.40 and 0.43), respectively. This distribution also essentially replicates the results of Greene and Blanchard (80%). Three participants from the support groups (25%) also met the criteria for clinically meaningful improvement whereas one of the symptom monitoring controls (10%) met the criteria.

Clinical Hint

The three successes from the support group each came from a different support group. Thus, they were not clustered in any one specific group. As an indication of the psychological "engagedness" of the support groups, in two groups, participants exchanged addresses and phone numbers at the end of the formal group program so that they could arrange to continue to meet.

At a three-month follow-up, 10 of the 12 patients (83%) in the cognitive therapy condition continued to meet the criteria for clinically meaningful improvement, whereas 2 of 11 (18%) of those from the support group did. One successful patient from cognitive therapy had a complete relapse. The CPSR scores relative to pretreatment were 0.66 for cognitive therapy and 0.28 for the support group.

In terms of individual GI symptoms, the cognitive therapy condition led to a significant decrease in abdominal pain and tenderness, diarrhea, bloating, and nausea and belching. The changes for the cognitive therapy group were significantly greater than those for either control group for abdominal pain and tenderness, diarrhea, bloating, and nausea.

On the psychological tests, those in the cognitive therapy condition showed significant reductions on depression and trait anxiety, and on the ATQ, while the other two groups did not change. For example, on the BDI, those in cognitive therapy showed a change from a pretreatment average of 14.6 (mildly, but noticeably, depressed) to 8.3 at posttest and 5.3 at follow-up (well within the normal range).

On the Hassles Scale, there was no change in number of hassles (minor negative life events) from before to after treatment. On the average intensity rating, however, those in cognitive therapy showed a significant decrease (pre-2.0, post-1.6) whereas the other two groups did not change. This seems to mean that the patients continued to be confronted by the same frequency of minor daily stresses. Those who had had cognitive therapy were, however, less bothered by these hassles after treatment, probably indicating that they were coping with events more readily. The other two conditions did not change.

Consistent with other reports on delayed effects in cognitive therapy, two measures which had not shown a significant decrease from pretreatment to posttreatment, the DAS and State Anxiety, were significantly lower than pretreatment at the follow-up point.

Comment

To say the least, we were pleased that the basic results from individual cognitive therapy for IBS replicated with a new therapist and a new cohort of patients, both in terms of average percent reduction in primary GI symptoms and in terms of the fraction of sample who were clinically improved. It was also good to be able to demonstrate a significant advantage over a credible control condition. Although there have been studies showing psychological treatment was superior to a placebo treatment (Whorwell et al., 1984), no treatment credibility or expectancies were reported for that study. In our current instance, we have documented that the support group was equally credible, as shown in Table 16.4.

We were also able to document that measures of the cognitive constructs we believed that we were targeting changed significantly with the cognitive therapy. The actual dose–response relations between cognitive change and GI symptom change, while positive, did not reach conventional levels of significance.

Issues which remained were whether the cognitive therapy would work in small groups, how long the results would hold up, and what was the relation between cognitive change and GI symptom change. We sought to address the first issue in the next study.

Vollmer and Blanchard (1998)

In the next study, we sought to address the issue of whether the cognitive therapy would work in small groups, in comparison to individual one-on-one sessions, and whether the individual cognitive therapy could be replicated one more time with yet another therapist and another cohort of IBS patients.

There were slight changes in treatment format for this study. Both treatments were given in once-per-week sessions over 10 weeks: the individual therapy sessions were 60 min whereas, for the group therapy, they were 90 min.

Other than spending some time on building group cohesiveness, treatment was very similar in the two conditions. As in Blanchard and Schwarz (1987), one cannot devote as much individual time to a patient in the group setting as in the individual therapy. Thus, there was always work with each patient in each session about some issue. Participants were encouraged to learn from each other and to try to apply the behavioral, and then cognitive, analysis which was taught to their responses in the session.

Rome criteria were used for subject selection. We omitted the cognitive measures, keeping the initial treatment credibility measure and adding a measure of group cohesiveness. Although we attempted to collect measures of psychological distress, compliance was poor so that we do not have meaningful data in this domain.

We recruited 34 IBS patients (7 men, 27 women) of average age 43.6 years who had had IBS for over 13 years. There were 2 dropouts, one from each treatment condition. The remaining 32 patients were randomly assigned to individual cognitive therapy (n = 11), group cognitive therapy (n = 11), or symptom monitoring, wait list control (n = 10).

Results

The average CPSR scores for the two treatment groups were 0.46 and 0.52, for individual and group treatment respectively; they did not differ and were significantly (p = .01) greater than the score for the symptom monitoring controls (CPSR score = −.04). The average score for the individual cognitive therapy was noticeably lower than what we found in the first two trials (0.66 and 0.67, respectively).

Six of 11 participants (55%) in individual cognitive therapy met our criteria for clinically meaningful improvement (also lower [but not significantly] than the 80% and 75% seen in earlier studies) while 4 participants were essentially unchanged and one was worse. For the group cognitive therapy condition, seven of 11 participants (64%) met the criteria for improvement, two were somewhat improved, one patient was noticeably worse, and one was essentially unchanged. Thus, the group version of cognitive therapy was slightly (but not significantly) better than the individually administered version.

For individual GI symptoms, both treatments led to significant decreases in abdominal pain and tenderness, diarrhea, bloating, and belching. Individual therapy led to improvement in flatulence whereas group treatment led to improvement in constipation.

Patient global ratings of improvement in all GI symptoms were 52.0 and 53.0 (on a 0–100 scale), respectively for individual and group versions of cognitive therapy. Overall well-being ratings were 61.0 and 77.8 (on a 0–100 scale), respectively for individual and group versions of cognitive therapy. Thus, on these global measures, patients seemed to indicate a good outcome.

Three month follow-up GI symptom diary data on 6 patients from each treatment revealed good maintenance of treatment effects: those in individual cognitive therapy stayed the same, CPSR score of 0.56; for the group cognitive therapy, the follow-up CPSR score was 0.64, which approaches previous strong values.

Patient expectations were equally high for both treatment conditions at the beginning and end of treatment. Although group cohesion increased from the beginning to end of treatment, the change was not significant, reflecting a relatively high starting level.

Comment

As mentioned above, the results for the individual cognitive therapy condition in this study, while positive, were not as strong as those seen in Greene and Blanchard (1994) or Payne and Blanchard (1995). The same treatment manual and procedures were used. The patient populations were very similar in terms of age, gender distribution, and length of illness. All three therapists were advanced doctoral students, in their fourth year of study, who had gone through the same training program.

The variation could reflect differences in therapist skill. More likely, it represents part of the natural variation in outcome one might expect to see from successive samples of 10 to 12 randomly selected IBS patients. Thus, Greene and Blanchard's 80% improved may represent an upper limit while Vollmer and Blanchard's 55% improved may represent the lower limit of what one could expect from this treatment program with an experienced therapist. Only further research with additional therapists and larger samples will tell.

Clearly, the cognitive therapy can be adapted to a small group format. In fact, the overall results from this format were slightly more positive than for the individual format.

Bowel Sound Biofeedback

As mentioned in Chapter 15, we (Radnitz & Blanchard, 1988) have conducted one small scale study of Furman's (1973) bowel sound biofeedback treatment for patients with diarrhea-predominant IBS. Fifteen patients with IBS were screened; 7 were not eligible because of having constipation problems in addition to diarrhea; 2 eligible patients declined the treatment leaving 6 patients, 3 men and 3 women of average age 31 years who had had IBS for an average of almost 10 years.

The six patients were treated in 3 multiple baselines across-subject experiments (Hersen & Barlow, 1976) in which one patient monitored symptoms for 2 weeks with the standard GI Symptom Diary and then began twice per week treatment sessions for 5 weeks (for a total of 10 treatment sessions), whereas the other patient of the pair monitored symptoms for 5 weeks before beginning treatment. One patient dropped out of treatment because of schedule difficulties. Patients then monitored symptoms for two weeks posttreatment and at follow-up points.

At the first session, a treatment rationale was given: it stated in essence that by learning to control bowel sounds through both increasing and decreasing the level of sounds (activity), they could learn to regulate bowel activity and thus obtain symptom relief.

In the session, the patient was in a separate room from the therapist, but in voice contact by intercom. The were semirecumbent in a recliner. They were asked to place the bell of an electronic stethoscope on the abdomen, below the umbilicus, at the area they were most likely to experience the greatest pain or spasms. The stethoscope head was then held in place by a heavy towel on the abdomen. (In this way there was a constant level of pressure of the stethoscope bell against the skin. This also freed the hands so that the patient did not need to attend to keeping the stethoscope in place.)

For our purposes, the signal from the electronic stethoscope was split, going both to a speaker in the patient room (thus, providing immediate auditory feedback) and to a polygraph for recording. The recording was initially processed by a wide band AC preamplifier and that signal was sent to a cumulative integrator to provide a permanent record of level of activity.

The 10 sessions were identical in that for each session, the patient spent the first 6 minutes in a baseline condition, listening to bowel sounds. Then the sound was turned off and the patient had two 3-minute self-control trials for which he was supposed first to increase and then to decrease bowel sound activity. Which came first depended on the patient's baseline level of activity (e.g., if baseline bowel sounds occurred only sporadically in baseline, the initial instruction would be to increase activity followed by decrease, or vice versa).

Next, the sound was turned back on and eight 4-min phases, alternating between increases (4 min) and decreases (4 min), were conducted. During a phase, the patient was to increase (or decrease) bowel sound activity for the entire phase, using whatever means seemed to work. The sounds were amplified and fed back to the patient. During this procedure, verbal positive reinforcement (e.g., "you are doing better," "that is the right direction") was given to the patient as he succeeded in changing the sound level in the desired direction.

Patients were loaned regular stethoscopes to use for home practice. They were asked to try increasing and decreasing bowel sounds for four phases of 4 min each, alternating increases and decreases.

Patients rated how logical therapy was at the end of the first visit on the same 0–9 scale shown in Table 16.4. Average rating was either 7 or 8 (mean 7.5).

Results

By quantifying the degree of bowel sound activity, it was possible to test whether there was statistically reliable control. For two patients, there was statistically significant ($p < .05$) control with increase trials showing more activity than decrease trials. One other patient showed a trend. One patient showed no control and one reverse control.

Using the diarrhea improvement score (see Chapter 4), three of five patients met our 50% reduction criteria at end of treatment (scores of 94, 54, and 100% reduction) while a fourth patient was a success (100% reduction) at the one-month follow-up (the other three continued to meet the criteria for success at that point). One patient was a clear failure at posttreatment and at every follow-up point.

Follow-ups at 3 and 6 months revealed continued high levels of symptom reduction for the four successes (scores of 94, 82, 100, and 100%). There was a modest dose–response relation between degree of control of bowel sounds exhibited and degree of diarrhea relief. The patient with no control of bowel sounds showed no relief of diarrhea (and even a worsening during follow-up).

Comment

This was a small scale study, but the results are intriguing. In terms of percentage of the sample who benefited, the results show 60 to 80%. This is as good as we have seen in other treatments. There are problems, of course: the subject selectivity is one, and the very small sample is another.

Others have not replicated Furman's (1973) very positive results (e.g., Weinstock, 1976), but Furman (personal communication, 1985) reported continued success with it. What is obviously needed is a larger scale, more tightly controlled, trial. We in Albany have been remiss in not undertaking such a trial ourselves.

Hypnotherapy

Our most recent study was a small scale attempt to replicate Whorwell's success with hypnotherapy (Galovski & Blanchard, 1999). We had two purposes in this study: (1) to see if Whorwell's hypnotherapy for IBS would be acceptable to, and efficacious with, an American population; (2) to see if GI symptom reduction was related to initial degree of hypnotic susceptibility.

As with the bowel sound biofeedback, we used a multiple baseline across subjects design on six pairs of patients, with baseline symptom monitoring lengths of two weeks or six weeks.

Twelve patients with IBS, diagnosed by Rome criteria, were matched into pairs on the basis of gender, age, presence or absence of a comorbid Axis I condition, and degree of hypnotic susceptibility. We used the Stanford Hypnotic Susceptibility Scale, Form A (Weitzenhoffer & Hilgard, 1959) to test susceptibility. Scores ranged from 2 (not very susceptible) to 12 (very susceptible) with an average of 7.6. The sample was comprised of 2 men and 10 women of average age 39. Eight of 12 (67%) met criteria for a current or past Axis I psychiatric disorder.

The therapist was a doctoral student in clinical psychology with experience in clinical hypnosis and certification by the *American Guild of Hypnotherapy*. Treatment was for 12 weekly sessions of 30 to 60 min duration, following Whorwell's most recent protocol (see Chapter 19).

In answer to our first question, all 12 eligible IBS patients accepted admission to the treatment program based on hypnotherapy. All sessions began with a review of the symptoms and discussion of progress and questions. The initial hypnotic induction utilized an eye fixation technique followed by progressive relaxation. Sessions 1 and 2 involved guided imagery and utilized metaphoric ego-strengthening to help deepen the hypnotic trance. There were few gut-directed suggestions in these sessions.

Sessions 3–12 followed the same format except that the imagery became much more gut-directed. Such imagery consisted of smoothly flowing rivers and waterfalls which were likened to gut motility. The patient was asked to place his/her hands on the abdomen in a warming exercise intended to generate heat and soothing feelings to the gut. Posthypnotically, the hands placed on the abdomen acted as a cue for relaxation and improved gut motility. Treatments were individualized to reflect the particular patient's symptoms. Patients were given tapes of sessions and asked to practice auto-hypnosis daily.

One patient discontinued treatment, appropriately, when the basis of her pain complaints was discovered by her neurologist to be due to a pinched nerve. A second subject was excluded from the analyses when it was discovered that she had no altered bowel habit symptoms (diarrhea or constipation) throughout baseline and treatment.

Results

The graphical analyses of the single subject experiments were inconclusive with some suggestions of an advantage of treatment over symptom monitoring for abdominal pain and tenderness and for bloating.

We also conducted between-group comparisons of treatment versus symptom monitoring using CPSR scores from the end of treatment for the short baseline group and end of symptom monitoring for the long baseline group. This comparison revealed an advantage for treatment (CPSR = 0.55) over symptom monitoring (CPSR = −0.32), $p = .016$.

When the data from all treated subjects was considered, the average CPSR score was 0.49. Six of 11 (54.5%) patients met our criteria for being called clinically improved while 2 others were moderately improved (CPSR scores of 0.42 and 0.49), respectively. The other 3 were unimproved or slightly worse. At a 2-month follow-up, diary data from 9 cases yielded an average CPSR score, relative to initial baseline, of 0.54, with only 4 of 9 (44%) still at the 50% reduction in primary symptom level. Three others had CPSR scores of 0.40 to 0.49.

For individual GI symptoms, there were significant reductions in abdominal pain and tenderness, constipation, and flatulence (p's $< .02$) and trends (p's $< .10$) for bloating and nausea. Psychological test scores did not change significantly; however, four patients did show appreciable decreases in BDI scores. At the 2-month follow-up, six of nine patients gave global ratings indicating substantial overall change in IBS and substantial improvement in overall well-being.

Clinical Hint

There was no relation of hypnotic susceptibility to clinical improvement. This means one could apply this treatment to any willing patient.

Comment

This small scale study yielded generally positive results for hypnotherapy, showing good acceptance of the treatment modality and generally positive results. Six of eleven patients were clinically improved. While this is not as strong a result as Whorwell has reported, it is on par with the Harvey et al. (1989) replication. It certainly warrants additional research and perhaps comparison with other psychological treatments.

CONCLUSIONS

So there you have our 15 years of research on the treatment of IBS (Neff & Blanchard, 1987, was conducted in 1984). Across the 10 separate studies, cognitive therapy seems to be the most promising treatment, having yielded the most consistently positive results. It is the treatment we are currently exploring.

The CBT combination did not yield consistently positive results, especially when administered by less well trained therapists. It is my suspicion that one needs at least an advanced doctoral student with a good conceptual background in cognitive therapy and a good level of prior general clinical experience to make it work.

In the next three chapters, we provide detailed treatment manuals for the CBT treatment, the cognitive therapy, and hypnotherapy. Following these are summary chapters on long-term follow-up and prediction of treatment outcome.

17

THE ALBANY COGNITIVE–BEHAVIORAL TREATMENT MANUAL

INTRODUCTION

In this chapter I lay out the detailed session-by-session CBT program we used at Albany for our first four outcome studies. The results of those studies are summarized in Chapter 16. As I mentioned earlier, we have moved away from this treatment program and are not actively using it at this point. Instead, we have gone on to evaluate components of the combined CBT program as monotherapies.

Clinical Hint

Our experience with this program leads me to three early conclusions about it:

1. It is a relatively effective therapy program for IBS when the therapist is relatively knowledgeable and experienced with cognitive and behavioral techniques. Thus, advanced doctoral students in their third or fourth year of course work and

---

I would like to acknowledge the initial development work on this protocol by Dr. Debra Neff.

practicum have used it successfully as have doctoral level therapists. In fact, this treatment manual assumes a good working knowledge of cognitive therapy techniques and a reasonable level of basic clinical experience and skills.

2. A corollary of (1) is that it is probably unwise to use relatively inexperienced therapists or therapists who are not comfortable with a cognitive–behavioral approach to clinical problems. This treatment cannot be delivered by rote: clinical skill and judgment are needed.
3. This treatment program can be effective in small groups. I would recommend having two therapists if the group has four or more members. (This may reflect my own insecurity with groups, however.)

There are four parts to this CBT program:

1. Education about normal bowel functioning and about how widespread a problem IBS is.
2. Relaxation training, i.e., progressive muscle relaxation (PMR), designed to reduce tonic levels of arousal and anxiety and to provide a portable coping strategy to assist in dealing with stressful daily events.
3. Thermal biofeedback designed to help patients achieve a deeper level of relaxation, with a more autonomic nervous system focus than usually found with PMR, and to give the patient a sense of mastery over some aspect of his or her body.
4. Cognitive therapy which is designed to help patients identify stresses in their lives and their cognitive reactions (self-talk) to stressors and to GI symptoms, to help patients see the connection between cognitive stress reactions and onset of GI symptoms (and vice versa), and to develop improved coping strategies including correction of self-talk and correction of faulty mental schema or logical fallacies, in Beck et al.'s (1980) sense.

Clinical Hint

IBS patients often present as somewhat depressed and with a mindset that they have little control of their bowels, that they are passive "victims" of their body (see Chapters 5 and 7). Learning the hand warming response shows patients they can gain control of a normally involuntary response; it then becomes easier (possibly through a self-efficacy mechanism) for them to believe they can gain control of GI functioning and GI symptoms.

This program was delivered as 12 sessions over 8 weeks, twice a week for the first 4 weeks then once per week for the next 4 weeks. An outline of the treatment program is given in Table 17.1.

There is nothing magical about the number of visits or spacing of visits. This was a regimen that seemed logical to us. Clearly, it is more intensive in the first month and less so in the second month. One of the reasons for compressing the actual treatment sessions into 2 months was to limit the patient's active involvement from pretreatment baseline through posttreatment baseline to 3 months.

Thus, this program assumes the therapist has already had an extensive initial assessment visit (history and diagnosis of IBS, diagnosis of Axis I disorders, psychological testing) and started the patient on a GI Symptom Diary. Medical confirmation of the IBS can be obtained during the pretreatment GI symptom monitoring phase. As noted earlier (Chapter 4), we recommend a 2 week baseline of GI symptom monitoring before beginning treatment.

The relaxation regimen described as part of the CBT treatment package was evaluated as a separate monotherapy by Blanchard et al. (1993). Details and results are contained in Chapter 16.

Treatment Session 1

Materials needed

IBS educational booklet (see Appendix C)
Cognitive monitoring sheets (see Table 17.2)
IBS symptom diary

1. Discuss the appointment schedule with patient. There will be 12 treatment sessions spread over 8 weeks; sessions will be held twice a week for the first 4 weeks, then once a week for 4 weeks. Each session will last approximately 45 to 60 minutes. The posttreatment evaluation will take place 2 weeks after the last treatment session and will last about an hour and a half. Discuss and resolve any conflicts with treatment schedule.
2. Remind the patient of the importance of keeping the daily *IBS symptom diary* throughout treatment and for the follow-up evaluations.
3. Provide educational information to the patient and give him or her the *IBS information booklet* (see Appendix C) to take home and read. Remind the patient to jot down any questions he or she may have and ask them at the next session. The purpose of this component is to:
   a. correct any misconceptions patients may have about normal gastrointestinal functioning;
   b. reduce anxiety these possible misconceptions may have raised;
   c. provide conceptualizations of IBS on which treatment is based (i.e., treatment rationale).

   Possible script:

   > There is no single definition of what normal gastrointestinal functioning is; rather, there is a range of functioning within which most people fall. While it is not uncommon for healthy individuals to experience occasional pain, discomfort, diarrhea, or constipation, individuals with IBS experience greater frequency and intensity of these symptoms. A diagnosis of IBS is made when these symptoms are present and no physical explanation can be found (i.e., all diagnostic tests are negative). Thus, IBS can be viewed on a continuum of gastrointestinal functioning from normal to full-blown IBS.

To explain how gastrointestinal symptoms occur, disturbances in colonic motility are most often implicated.

Possible script:

> Because there are a number of different patterns of IBS, (you can discuss individual patient's pattern here), researchers have found that there are disturbances in colonic motility of the lower gastrointestinal tract. Diarrhea is associated with increased motility, and constipation with decreased motility. Motility refers to the contractions of the smooth muscle of the gastrointestinal tract as food particles are moved through and digestion is taking place. Motility is under the control of the autonomic nervous system (ANS). Other effects of ANS arousal can be muscles tensing, blood vessels constricting, and heart rate increasing. (See if the patient has experienced any of these.) ANS arousal can be the result of stress. Everyone is under stress in varying degrees, and the effect of this stress on the body also differs from one individual to another.

4. Provide a treatment rationale.

Possible script:

> This treatment program is designed to teach you skills to deal more effectively with the stress you encounter in everyday living situations. You will be taught to physically relax your body through progressive muscle relaxation training. You will also be taught biofeedback to raise your hand temperature as a different means of relaxing. To do this, you will dilate your blood vessels, including the capillaries in your hands. When you increase the blood flow to your hands, your hand temperature will increase. Thus, thermal biofeedback training will aim to produce a deeper relaxation of the ANS. In addition to the relaxation skills, you will also be taught a variety of cognitive coping strategies (see Exhibit 17.7). As a result of the relaxation training you will become more aware of both the tension in your body and the events or situations which contribute to it. Stressful situations may include having a difficult day at work, an argument with your spouse, having your car break down, feeling you don't have enough time to accomplish tasks, and so on. The way you respond to these situations will be explored and alternative responses and reactions that minimize stress will be discussed.

5. Discuss potential treatment outcome with the patient.
   A reduction in gastrointestinal symptoms is expected, to the point where the patient falls in the "normal range of gastrointestinal functioning." This will be defined on an individual basis. The therapist should emphasize that the patient may begin to experience relief from the first week of treatment up to the eighth and beyond, though the average is during the third or fourth week. *Therefore, it is important for the patient not to be discouraged if there is not immediate relief.* This treatment is not like a pill or medicine which may work quickly; instead it is learning a set of skills to make changes over the long haul.
6. Answer any questions.
7. Introduce cognitive monitoring sheets (see example in Table 17.2 at the end of this chapter). They are labeled, "Recording Sheet for the Onset of Gastrointestinal and Other Disorders." For your patient's convenience, you will probably want to make this form to fit an 8½ by 11 inch piece of paper. Explain the categories (situation, physical sensations experienced, thoughts, and behavior or outcome). Instruct the patient to take a few minutes to record this information for at least two or three situations in the coming week when he or she experiences an onset of gastrointestinal distress or an increase in general distress. Give the patient several sheets to take home and complete.
8. Make an appointment for session 2 with at least one day between appointments 1 and 2. Record on appointment card and in the appointment schedule book.

Treatment Session 2

Materials needed

IBS Symptom diary
Patient relaxation practice records (see Table 17.2)
Audiotape of 16-muscle group relaxation (see Exhibit 17.1 for script)

1. Check symptom diary, and cognitive monitoring sheets and encourage their continued use. Also encourage patients to bring all completed forms to the next treatment session. If patient has nothing on cognitive monitoring sheet, troubleshoot to see if the patient understands the task.
2. Introduce relaxation training with 16 muscle groups. Have patient recline comfortably in the chair while explaining the relaxation procedures. Begin by briefly reviewing rationale for relaxation discussed in the first session (i.e., reduce overall level of tension in the body which will hopefully result in more regular muscle contractions of the gastrointestinal tract that will, in turn, reduce symptomatology).

   Possible script:

   > Relaxation training consists of the systematic tensing and relaxing of the major muscle groups of the body. During the tension–release cycle, it is important to pay attention to the sensations experienced. Tensing the muscles first will serve to exaggerate the "releasing" of the tension, therefore emphasizing this response. After going through this series of tension–release cycles, you should feel quite relaxed.
   >
   > Learning to relax is a learned skill, like learning to ride a bicycle. With regular practice you become better at it. It is recommended that you practice at least once a day for 20 to 25 minutes, twice if you can. If you cannot, or *will not*, practice regularly, then you probably will not receive the major benefits of the training.

3. Next, show the patient the muscle groups that will be involved and demonstrate how each will be tensed; the reason for this is that the patient's eyes will be closed during relaxation training.
   1. Holding your *right arm* out over your lap, make a fist, and tense the lower right arm muscles.
   2. Holding your *left* arm out over your lap, make a fist, and tense the lower left arm muscles.

3. Bring *both* arms out over your lap, make two fists, tensing both hands simultaneously.
4. Bring your *right hand* up to your shoulder, and tense the muscles in your *right upper arm.*
5. Bring your left hand up to your shoulder, and tense the muscles in your left *upper arm.*
6. Bring *both hands* up to your shoulders, and tense the muscles in *both upper* arms simultaneously.
7. Tense the muscles in your *right lower leg* or calf, by pointing your right foot and toes toward the wall.
8. Tense the muscles in your *left lower leg* or calf, by pointing your left foot and toes toward the wall.
9. Tense the muscles in *both lower legs* by pointing both feet and all toes toward the wall.
10. Tense the muscles of *both upper legs* or thighs by either straightening your knees to tighten these muscles or by pressing your thighs together.
11. Tense the muscles in your *abdomen* by drawing them in tightly toward your backbone.
12. Tense the muscles in the *chest* by taking a deep breath and deliberately holding it for 7–10 seconds while attending to the tension building up in your chest, and then exhale.
13. Tense the muscles in your *shoulders* by hunching them upwards towards your ears.
14. Tense the muscles in the *back of your neck* by pressing your head backward against the chair or bed.
15. Tense the muscles of your *lips* by pressing them together tightly without clamping your jaw or biting down.
16. Tense the muscles around your *eyes* by closing them tightly, squeezing the lids together.
17. Tense the muscles in your *lower forehead* by frowning, trying to bring your eyebrows downward.
18. Tense the muscles in your *upper forehead* by arching your eyebrows upward.

Clinical Hint

Be sure to check if the patient has any musculoskeletal pain problem (prior injuries, etc.) which would be aggravated by tensing certain muscles. If there is, omit that muscle group. Tell the patient to ignore that instruction on the relaxation tape when practicing at home.

Tell the patient that you will want him or her to have the *eyes closed during the entire training.* After the patient understands what the sequence will be, have him or her remove eyeglasses and loosen any tight, restrictive clothing.

---

4. To ensure that the patient knows how to fully relax muscles, you should demonstrate the relaxation using the right lower arm. Ask the patient to tense the right hand and lower arm, to attend to the sensations of tension in that arm, and then to relax it. Most patients will not relax the whole arm from the shoulder down, Next, ask the patient to try again and *really let go completely* so that the whole arm from the shoulder all the way down can become limp. You can "catch" the arm to show what you mean. Repeat until the arm becomes fairly relaxed with your catching it.

   Next, tell the patient that you will be instructing him or her to tense the muscle groups which you have demonstrated, that you will be asking that he pay attention to the sensations, and you will be giving various other suggestions.
5. An option we have frequently incorporated into the full 16 muscle group relaxation induction is to incorporate a relaxing imaginal scene after the deepening exercise. It can be helpful for IBS patients who tend to be worriers and who have trouble becoming relaxed because they cannot "shut off their minds." It can later be useful as a form of relaxing, or anti-stress, imagery to use as a coping strategy. The relaxing imagery script is described in Exhibit 17.2. (You should discuss this briefly with the patient to be certain he or she does not have some idiosyncratic aversion to the beach and sunbathing. If so, find another calming scene with the patient.)
6. Now, go through the muscle relaxation exercise (the scripts for 16 muscle group relaxation, relaxing or anti stress imagery, 8 muscle group relaxation, 4 muscle group relaxation, and 4 muscle group relaxation-by-recall are in Exhibits 17.1 through 17.5). Have the client tense each muscle group for 5–10 seconds, while attending to the sensations of tension in that group and area of the body, and then to compare the relaxation sensations when relaxing that muscle group. Between each muscle group, allow about 20 seconds with perhaps a comment "just continue to relax" or one of the other suggestions from the script. There is no special magic to the particular wording of the relaxation suggestions, but try to use something approximating this content.

   The tension–relaxation exercises should take about

20–25 minutes; then proceed with the deepening exercise, attention to breathing, pleasant imagery, and alerting by counting as outlined in the script.

7. Have the client remain sitting up after alerting, drop the footrest so the client is sitting upright; and return eyeglasses. Inquire if the client became relaxed, ask him or her to rate the depth of relaxation achieved on a scale from 0 to 10 where 10 is maximum depth of relaxation, then ask if there were any particular signs of residual tension, and finally ask if there were any other noticeable sensations or things which should be discussed.
8. Give the client the 16-muscle group relaxation tape; check to make sure the client has a cassette tape player. Explain how to complete the *relaxation practice records*. Practice should be at least once per day, with twice being better at this learning stage.
9. Make an appointment for session 3 for the following week, give the client an appointment card, and schedule a room in the appointment book.

Clinical Hint

Occasionally, patients will obtain only a moderate sense of relaxation from this induction. Reassure them by reminding them it will take practice.

We have also seen occasional examples of relaxation-induced anxiety or panic (1 patient in 100). If you have taken a psychiatric history, you will know if there is a history or current problem with Panic Disorder. If your patient is positive for Panic Disorder, discuss the fact that there may be some "strange" sensations as he or she becomes relaxed. If the client becomes alarmed, he or she should let you know immediately before the panic attack becomes full blown.

Treatment Session 3

Materials needed

IBS diary
Relaxation practice records
Cognitive monitoring sheets (Table 17.2)

1. Inquire as to success of relaxation practice at home and discuss any difficulties; collect completed IBS symptom diaries.
2. Explain that you will be adding discrimination training to today's session. The importance of this is to learn to distinguish between varying degrees of tension that may be experienced. For the two muscle groups (abdomen and forehead) the patient will be asked to tense these muscles fully, then relax them (go through the usual 20–30 second interval between tension–release exercises with pause or additional suggestions. Next, have the patient tense the muscles only half the level they used the first time, then relax, etc. Last, have the patient tense the muscles only half as much as before (one-quarter of the full tension level) and then relax. Again, follow the relax instruction with the usual 20–30 second interval with pause or additional suggestions.
3. Go through the 16-muscle group relaxation exercise as outlined in the script for session 2, including discrimination training, deepening by counting, attention to breathing, relaxing imagery, and alerting by counting.
4. After alerting by counting, again assess client's sensations and feelings and depth of relaxation, then explore any difficulties. Remind the client to continue to practice and to continue to fill out the IBS diary.
5. Go over the cognitive monitoring sheets (onset of GI and other distress). Try to see if there are patterns. Ask the patient for their insights from the monitoring as to what distressing things are happening and how they react to them. Also, discuss how GI symptom flare-ups are stressors. Remind the patient that the treatment will begin to focus more on this topic next time.
6. Make an appointment for session 4 for later this week and give the client an appointment card.

Treatment Session 4

Materials needed

IBS diary
Relaxation practice sheets
Cognitive monitoring sheets (Table 17.2)
Cognitive coping strategies (Exhibit 17.7)

1. Check self-monitoring sheets and relaxation home practice recordings.
2. Introduce relaxation training with 8 muscle groups. Explain that an important long-range goal is for the client to be able to become deeply relaxed in a very brief period of time in as many different situations as possible. Reducing the number of muscle groups to 8 is one step in that direction. Explain and demonstrate the 8 groups as follows:
   a. *Both arms together*: Create tension in both arms by tensing lower and upper arms and clenching both fists simultaneously.
   b. *Both legs together*: Tense both feet in the manner that you learned previously while also tensing the thighs by pressing them together.
   c. *Abdomen*: remains the same.
   d. *Chest by deep breathing*: remains the same.
   e. *Shoulders*: remains the same.
   f. *Back of the neck*: remains the same.
   g. *Eyes and mouth together*: remains the same.
   h. *Forehead*: remains the same.
3. Go through the exercise using the script for 8 muscle group relaxation (see Exhibit 17.3).
4. After alerting and responding to questions or concerns, discuss situations recorded on the *cognitive monitoring sheets*. Patients should have recorded situations where GI distress was problematic. Both these recordings and the increased feelings of relaxation resulting from practicing their relaxation exercises should have allowed patients to become more aware of when they experience increases in tension. Depending on the situation, patients can then use cognitive strategies to reduce stress.

   These stress reduction strategies may include:

   1. *Changing cognitive appraisal of the situation* (i.e., reevaluating how much responsibility they have at home or

work in terms of getting things done, thinking of alternate explanations for the behavior of people with whom they interact).

2. *Planning to avoid stressful situations* (i.e., first becoming aware of situations they are exposed to that result in GI distress, then thinking of ways to circumvent it, such as coming in earlier to work to plan the day, taking a few short breaks during the work day rather than one long break, or taking the phone off the hook when they do not want to be disturbed).
3. *Thinking of alternative behaviors* (because they cannot avoid the situation, they can become aware of the physical manifestations of their tension and practice relaxation skills while saying to themselves, "Is it worth it for me to get upset and end up with a stomach ache when my boss/spouse/coworker won't. . . .").
4. *Recognizing the need to practice relaxation* (by becoming more aware of how stress affects them physically, they can use cueing strategies more frequently and will be more motivated to practice when they see the positive results of their efforts).

Give the patient a copy of the *cognitive coping skills* (Exhibit 17.7) to take home as a reminder of the suggested strategies (see sheet at end of this chapter). Respond to any questions or concerns; then make an appointment for the following week for session 5.

Treatment Session 5

Materials needed

IBS diary
Relaxation practice sheet
Cognitive monitoring sheets (Table 17.2)
4-Muscle Group Relaxation-by-Recall Tape (Exhibit 17.5)

1. Check relaxation practice progress and self-monitoring sheets.
2. Inform the patient that in this session you are reducing, still further, the number of muscle groups they will use to relax. You will go through 2 relaxation exercises, the first with 4 muscle groups being tensed then released, the second with the same muscle groups, but without tensing them. Explain that reducing the muscle groups will further decrease the time spent getting relaxed and allow the patient to spend more time in a relaxed state. The goal of relaxation training is for the patient to become relaxed as quickly and easily as possible.
3. Demonstrate the 4 muscle groups:
   a. both arms together
   b. abdomen
   c. neck and shoulders
   d. eyes, forehead, and face.
4. Go through abbreviated exercise using the script, doing 4 tension–release cycles of the specified muscle groups and then alerting by counting from 5 to 1.
5. Introduce relaxation by recall, learning to relax without first tensing the muscles. Explain that this is the final change to the exercise. The patient will attend to the sensations of tightness or tension that are present in the muscle, then will relax the muscle by mentally recalling the sensations of relaxation and releasing the tension.
6. Before beginning the exercise, tell the patient that after each muscle group you will ask them to raise a finger if the muscle was not completely relaxed. If the patient is not relaxed he or she should again focus on relaxation by recall. If this is not successful, go through a tension–release cycle for that muscle group.
7. Go through relaxation-by-recall exercise using the 4 muscle groups, deepening by counting, attention to breathing, pleasant imagery, and alerting by counting.

8. Review cognitive coping strategies and applications.
9. Give the client a copy of the 4-muscle group relaxation-by-recall tape and suggest practicing twice a day; switching back to the 16-muscle group tape may help initially while learning the shorter relaxation method; make an appointment for session 6 for later in the week.

Treatment Session 6

Materials needed

IBS diary
Relaxation practice sheets
Cognitive monitoring sheets (Table 17.2)

1. Check success of home practice with 4 muscle groups.
2. Repeat relaxation-by-recall exercise as done at end of session 5; while patient is in the focus on breathing portion of the session, obtain a rating of the depth of relaxation using the *relaxation rating scale* and record your ratings.
3. Introduce "cue-controlled" relaxation. This involves having the patient consciously focus on breathing, taking a deep breath, holding it for a few seconds, then letting it out, pairing each exhalation with mentally saying "relax." Remind patients of how during the relaxation exercise emphasis was placed on their breathing, associating it with being relaxed. "Cueing" can be done anytime, anywhere (with eyes opened or closed). It is an effective strategy that can be done quickly and frequently to produce automatic, on-the-spot relaxation. It is useful to help keep a check on tension rather than waiting until tension levels build up and then trying to reduce them. It is not always feasible to find a quiet, dark room and 15 minutes to go through a complete relaxation exercise; Cueing is a very portable, flexible method for dealing with tension.
4. Discuss with the patient that this is the last formal relaxation training session. Up to this point they have been taught a number of different relaxation skills. For the next 5 sessions they will have the opportunity to continue practicing these skills and identifying what works best for them. It is important to emphasize that it is still early in treatment, and if there has not been an effect on the GI tract, that is O.K. They should not be discouraged but continue to practice faithfully.
5. The next 5 sessions will be spent on biofeedback training. A part of each session (about 15 minutes) will be spent discussing coping strategies as in previous sessions. Patients should be encouraged to bring up any issues they feel are relevant to responses to stress, especially in the integration of physical and cognitive responses.

6. Spend the remainder of the session on the cognitive monitoring sheets and the cognitive coping strategies and applications. Refer back to material from session 4.
7. Make an appointment for session 7 for the following week.

Treatment Session 7

Materials needed

IBS diaries
Biofeedback practice sheets
Autogenic phrases sheet (Exhibit 17.6)
Home thermometer

1. Check diaries and relaxation practice.
2. Introduce thermal biofeedback training. First, review the rationale: hand temperature is under the control of the autonomic nervous system (ANS) that dilates blood vessels when relaxed and contracts them when tense. Colonic motility is also under the control of the ANS. Therefore, patients can achieve a deeper relaxation by learning to raise hand temperature, which concurrently allows colonic motility to become more regulated.
3. Possible script for describing the biofeedback:

   The main idea involved is to help you to learn to control certain physiological responses. In this particular case, we want you to learn how to warm your fingers and hands using purely mental means.

   There are three basic parts to biofeedback:

   1. We need an electronic sensor to detect very small changes in fingertip temperature, changes so small that you ordinarily can't detect them. This little sensor detects the temperature changes (show sensor to patient).
   2. We need to convert these small changes to a signal you can easily process. We do this electronically also.
   3. We feed this information ("biofeedback") back to you. For this purpose we use this electronic meter. Thus, as the temperature goes up, the pen on the meter will move to the right.

   There are two important parts of learning to control a response:

   1. You can use the biofeedback situation as a laboratory in which you can discover what strategies or tactics or maneuvers work for you. Thus, we encourage you to experiment, to try ideas or images which you think might work for you.
   2. It is very important to *allow the response to occur*, to be somewhat *passive*. If you try to force it, to make your hands warmer, typically they will become cooler. So re-

member to relax and let your hands become warm. Remember what you are thinking, feeling, and doing when your temperature is rising. Later recreate these thoughts, feelings, and actions so that you can become able to raise the temperature of your hands at will.

At today's session, I am going to be in the room with you during the actual biofeedback phase reading you a list of what we call *autogenic phrases* (see Exhibit 17.6). These phrases are designed to help you achieve an overall physiological state of relaxation and are designed to specifically help you warm your hands. Many clients use methods other than autogenic phrases to try to increase their hand temperature. For instance, some people imagine their hands over a fire, or imagine blood flowing to their fingertips. For today, let's try the autogenic phrases and see how they work.

4. Hook up the patient to the thermistor, start baseline monitoring, then review and practice relaxation-by-recall.
5. Biofeedback training begins with the therapist leaving the room, marking the temperature tape for baseline, and also recording the patient's name, the date, session number, and room temperature on the tape. Continue as follows:
    1. *4 minutes baseline* (BL). Instruct the patient to sit quietly with his eyes closed.
    2. *4 minutes self-control* (SC1). Instruct the patient to try to raise hand temperature by purely mental means, without receiving any biofeedback.
    3. *20 minutes biofeedback* (BF). Instruct the patient to use the feedback meter to try to raise hand temperature. (Turn on the meter so patient can view it; readjust periodically to center needle, always informing the patient via intercom that you are recentering.)
    4. *4 minutes self-control #2* (SC2). Instruct the patient to continue to try to raise hand temperature, or if they have reached 96 degrees, to try to maintain their increase. (Turn off the meter so the patient is no longer receiving biofeedback.) If you are pressed for time, you can omit this phase.
6. For this first session of biofeedback during the first ten minutes of biofeedback training, go in the room with the patient and read the autogenic phrases, one about every 30 seconds; ask the patient to repeat the phrases mentally, and then try to have them experience the phase described (see attached list for autogenic phrases after this session). When

finished reading, the therapist should leave the room, instructing the patient to use this or any other strategies that come to mind to warm hands.

7. After the session ask the patient to describe the experience. Try to minimize any frustration that may have been experienced in not raising hand temperature, while praising success. Emphasize that this is a training experience where the patient will learn not only to raise hand temperature but also to prevent it from decreasing. If any decreases did occur, it was most likely due to anxiety over the newness of this task and the stress of trying to perform well.
8. Give the patient the home practice thermometer and instruct him or her to practice at least once a day. Ask that the starting and finishing temperatures be recorded on the biofeedback diary sheets and give several copies to take home. Starting temperature should be recorded after the thermometer is on the finger for a few minutes. Tape, if used to anchor the thermometer, should not cover the fingernail to avoid restricting circulation. Velcro is also a good way to secure the thermometer to the fingertip.
9. Make appointment for later in the week for session 8.

Treatment Session 8

Materials needed

IBS diary
Biofeedback practice sheets
Cognitive monitoring sheets (Table 17.2)

1. Check treatment and diary progress.
2. Attach the sensor and instruct the patient to sit back quietly, then leave the room and turn on the temperature monitor. Be sure to record the patient's name, the date, session number, and room temperature on the temperature print-out tape.
3. Review and practice relaxation-by-recall.
4. Go through biofeedback training (4 min BL, 4 min SC1, 20 min BF, and 4 min SC2 as outlined in session 7); the therapist should not be in the room with the patient during BF after session 7.
5. Assess for difficulties in raising hand temperature, being sure to praise *any success*; it's important that the patient not become discouraged at this early stage of training.
6. Review coping strategies, especially the application of relaxation to stressful situations.
7. Make appointment for session 9 for one week from today (treatment now goes to once per week).

Treatment Sessions 9, 10, and 11

Materials needed

IBS diary
Biofeedback practice sheets
Cognitive monitoring sheets (Table 17.2)

1. Check treatment and diary progress.
2. Attach the sensor, instruct the patient to sit back quietly, leave the room and turn on the temperature monitor. Be sure to record the patient's name, the date, session number, and room temperature on the temperature print-out tape.
3. Review and practice relaxation-by-recall. While patient is attending to his or her breathing, obtain a rating of depth of relaxation as obtained in sessions 3 and 6 and record on form.
4. Go through biofeedback training (4 min BL, 4 min SC1, 20 min BF, and 4 min SC2 as outlined in session 7); therapist should not be in the room with the patient after session 7 during BF.
5. Assess for difficulties in raising hand temperature, being sure to praise *any success*; it's important that the patient not become discouraged at this early stage of training.
6. Review coping strategies, especially the application of relaxation to stressful situations.
7. Make appointment for next session for one week from today (treatment is now once per week).

Treatment Session 12

Materials needed

IBS diaries

1. This session is spent primarily discussing treatment to date. The relative success of treatment should be discussed based on reduction of symptoms recorded on the IBS diaries. Emphasis should be placed on the relatively short time the patient has been in treatment (about 8 weeks). Even if the patient has experienced only minimal relief from treatment, it is very likely he or she will experience more decreases as practice continues in relaxation and cognitive strategies.

   Time should be spent reviewing the strategies and their rationale as outlined in sessions 1 and 4. How the patient has incorporated them should be highlighted. Particular emphasis should be placed on their continued use once treatment has ended.

   Finally, it should be pointed out that it is very likely the patient will experience some GI distress in the future, as part of what might be considered normal bowel functioning. However, the intensity and frequency should be much less than what was experienced at start of treatment. The patient should be instructed that while some distress is normal, care should be taken to continue practicing relaxation regularly. Distress could be interpreted as the body's way of warning that a physical reaction is occurring to stress, and that the patient should slow down and pay attention. As a result of treatment, the patient has the ability and control to reduce the level of physical tension.
2. Conduct a relaxation-by-recall session followed by an abbreviated biofeedback session (4 min BL, 4 min SC1, 10 min BF, as outlined in session 7). Be sure to record the patient's name, the date, session number, and room temperature on the temperature print-out tape.
3. Calculate a temperature change score by subtracting the lowest score from the highest score recorded during the session and record on the temperature print-out tape, circle it, and label it "temperature change score."
4. It would probably be good to schedule a follow-up visit in 2 to 4 weeks to check on progress. Ask patient to keep a week's worth of GI symptom diaries before that visit.

Clinical Hint

Tell the patient that research has shown that during follow-up, once they have had a successful reduction of GI symptoms, patients usually reintroduce the relaxation and cognitive coping if they have a later flare up or return of symptoms.

TABLE 17.1
Outline of Cognitive–Behavioral Treatment Program for IBS

Week No.	Session No.	Content
1	1	Explanation of treatment and its rationale, provision of educational information, begin cognitive monitoring.
	2	Introduce 16 muscle group relaxation training, check on cognitive monitoring.
2	3	Relaxation training, 16 muscle groups, discrimination training, review cognitive monitoring sheets.
	4	Relaxation training, 8 muscle groups, cognitive coping strategies discussed.
3	5	Relaxation training, 4 muscle groups, relaxation-by-recall introduced, cognitive coping strategies discussed.
	6	Relaxation training, 4 muscle groups, cue-controlled relaxation introduced, cognitive coping strategies discussed.
4	7	Same as session 6.
	8	Thermal biofeedback introduced along with autogenic training.
5	9	Thermal biofeedback, cognitive coping strategies discussed.
6 & 7	10 & 11	Same as session 9.
8	12	Thermal biofeedback, review of all treatment parts, review of progress.

TABLE 17.2
Recording Sheet for the Onset of Gastrointestinal and Other Distress

Date	Stressful Situation (IBS attack, or any other stress)	Physical Symptoms	Thoughts and feelings (before event): depressed, anxious, angry	Thoughts and feelings (during event): depressed, anxious, angry	Behavior	Thoughts and feeling (after event)	Possible positive self-statements

EXHIBIT 17.1
16 Muscle-Group Relaxation Training Tape Script

This is the tape to assist you with home practice of relaxation. You will be going through the same exercises we practiced in the clinic. You should be comfortably seated in a recliner or upholstered chair or lying on a bed. Be sure to remove your glasses if you wear them. Also, loosen any tight or restrictive clothing that you have on . . . .

Now, begin to let yourself relax . . . close your eyes and we will go through the relaxation exercises. I want you to begin by tensing muscles in your right, lower arm and right hand . . . study the tensions in the back of your hand and your right, lower arm . . . study those tensions . . . now relax the muscles. Study the difference between the tension and the relaxation . . . just let yourself become more and more relaxed. If you feel yourself becoming drowsy that will be fine, too. As you think of relaxation, of letting go of your muscles, they will become more loose and heavy and relaxed . . . just let your muscles go as you become more and more deeply relaxed. . . . Next I want you to tense the muscles in your left hand and left, lower arm . . . tense those muscles and study the tensions in the back of your left hand and in your left, lower arm . . . study those tensions . . . and now relax the muscles. . . . Study the difference between the tension and the relaxation . . . (15–20 sec pause) . . . Now this time I want you to tense both hands and both lower arms by making fists and tensing the muscles in both hands and both lower arms. . . . Study those tensions . . . and now relax them. . . . Study the difference between the tension and the relaxation. You are becoming more and more relaxed . . . calm and relaxed . . . as you become more relaxed, you feel yourself settling deep into the chair . . . all your muscles are becoming more and more comfortably relaxed . . . loose . . . and heavy . . . and relaxed. . . . This time I want you to tense the muscles in your right upper arm by bringing your right hand up towards your shoulder and tensing the biceps muscle. . . . Study the tensions there in your right upper arm . . . study those tensions . . . now relax your arm . . . study the difference between the tension and the relaxation . . . (15–20 sec pause). . . . This time I want you to tense the muscles in your left upper arm by bringing the left hand up to your shoulder and tensing the muscles in your left biceps area . . . study those tensions in your left biceps . . . study those tensions . . . and now relax the arm . . . and study the difference between the tension and the relaxation. . . . The relaxation is growing deeper and still deeper . . . you are relaxed, drowsy and relaxed . . . your breathing is regular and relaxed . . . with each breath you take in, the relaxation increases . . . each time you exhale you spread the relaxation throughout your body. . . . This time I want you to tense both upper arms together by bringing both hands up to your shoulders, tense the muscles in both upper arms, both biceps areas . . . study those tensions . . . and now relax the muscles . . . study the difference between the tension and the relaxation. . . . Just continue to let your muscles relax . . . (10 sec pause). . . . Next, I want you to tense the muscles in your right lower leg . . . tense the muscles in your right lower leg, particularly in your calf . . . study the tensions there in your right lower leg . . . study those tensions . . . and now relax the muscles . . . and study the difference between the tension and the relaxation. . . . Note the pleasant feelings of warmth and heaviness that are coming into your body as your muscles relax completely. . . . You will always be clearly aware of what you are doing and what I am saying . . . as you become more deeply relaxed. . . . Next, I want you to tense the muscles in your left lower leg, the left calf area . . . study the tensions in your left lower leg . . . study those tensions . . . and now relax the muscles . . . and study the difference between the tension and the relaxation . . . (10 sec pause) . . . just continue to let your leg relax . . . (10 sec pause). . . . Now, this time I

Exhibit continues

EXHIBIT 17.1 (*Continued*)

want you to tense both lower legs together . . . tense the muscles in both lower legs . . . both calf muscles . . . study those tensions . . . and now relax your legs . . . study the difference between the tension and the relaxation . . . (10 sec pause) . . . just continue to let those muscles relax . . . let them relax. . . . Now the very deep state of relaxation is moving through all the areas of your body . . . you are becoming more and more comfortably relaxed . . . calm and relaxed . . . you can feel the comfortable sensations of relaxation as you go into a deeper . . . deeper . . . state of relaxation. . . . Next, I want you to tense the muscles in your thighs by pressing your legs together from the knees upward . . . press your upper legs against each other . . . study the tensions throughout your thighs . . . study those tensions . . . now relax the muscles . . . study the difference between the tension and the relaxation . . . (10 sec pause) . . . just let those muscles continue to relax . . . (10 sec pause). . . . This time I want you to tense the muscles in the abdominal area by drawing your abdominal muscles in tightly . . . draw them in tightly . . . study the tensions across the entire abdominal region . . . study those tensions . . . and now relax the muscles . . . just let them relax . . . and study the difference between the tension and the relaxation . . . just let yourself become more and more relaxed . . . as you think of relaxation . . . and of letting go of your muscles . . . they will become more loose . . . and heavy . . . and relaxed . . . just let your muscles go as you become more and more deeply relaxed. . . . This time I want you to tense the muscles in your chest by taking a deep breath and holding it . . . hold it . . . hold it . . . now relax . . . and study the difference between the tension and the relaxation . . . the relaxation is going deeper . . . and still deeper . . . you are relaxed . . . your breathing is regular and relaxed . . . and with each breath you take in your relaxation increases . . . each time you exhale . . . you spread the relaxation throughout your body. . . . Next, I want you to tense the muscle in your shoulders and upper back by hunching your shoulders or drawing your shoulders upward towards your ears . . . study those tensions across your upper back . . . study those tensions . . . and now relax your muscles . . . and study the difference . . . between the tension and the relaxation . . . note the pleasant feelings of warmth and heaviness that are coming into your body as your muscles relax completely . . . you will always be clearly aware of what you are doing, and what I am saying, as you become more deeply relaxed. . . . Next, I want you to tense the muscles in the back of your neck by pressing your head backward against the rest or against the bed . . . study the tensions in the back of your neck, across your shoulders and the base of your scalp . . . study those tensions . . . and now relax the muscles . . . and study the difference between the tension and the relaxation . . . (15–20 sec pause). . . . Next, I want you to tense your muscles in the region around your mouth by pressing your lips together tightly . . . press your lips together tightly without biting down and study the tensions in the region around your mouth . . . study those tensions . . . and now relax the muscles . . . and study the difference between the tension and the relaxation . . . and you are becoming more and more relaxed . . . drowsy and relaxed . . . as you become more relaxed . . . you can feel yourself settling deep into the chair . . . all your muscles are becoming more and more comfortably relaxed . . . loose and heavy . . . and relaxed. . . . This time I want you to tense the muscles in the region around your eyes by closing your eyes tightly . . . just close your eyes tightly . . . and study the tensions . . . all around your eyes and upper face . . . study those tensions . . . and now relax the muscles . . . (10 sec pause) . . . just continue to let them relax . . . and study the difference between the tension and the relaxation . . . the very deep state of relaxation is moving through all the areas of your body . . . you are becoming more and more comfortably relaxed . . . drowsy and relaxed . . .

Exhibit continues

EXHIBIT 17.1 (*Continued*)

you can feel the comfortable sensations of relaxation as you go into a deeper and deeper state of relaxation. . . . This time I want you to tense the muscles in your lower forehead by frowning and lowering your eyebrows downward . . . study the tensions there in your lower forehead, the region between your eyes . . . study those tensions . . . and now relax the muscles . . . and study the difference between the tension and the relaxation . . . (15–20 sec pause). . . . This time I want you to tense the muscles in your upper forehead by raising your eyebrows upward and wrinkling your forehead . . . raise them up and wrinkle your forehead and study the tensions in the upper part of your forehead . . . study those tensions . . . and now relax the muscles . . . and study the difference between the tension and the relaxation . . . (20 sec pause). . . . Now I want you to relax all the muscles of your body . . . just let them become more and more relaxed . . . I am going to help you to achieve a deeper state of relaxation by counting from 1 to 5 . . . and as I count you will feel yourself becoming more and more deeply relaxed . . . farther and farther down into a deep restful state . . . of deep relaxation . . . 1 . . . you are going to become more deeply relaxed . . . 2 . . . down . . . down into a very relaxed state . . . 3 . . . 4 . . . more and more relaxed . . . 5 . . . deeply relaxed. . . . Now I want you to remain in your very relaxed state . . . and I want you to begin to attend just to your breathing . . . breath through your nose . . . notice the cool air as you breath in . . . and the warm moist air and you exhale . . . just continue to attend to your breathing . . . and each time you exhale mentally repeat the word RELAX . . . inhale . . . exhale . . . RELAX . . . (about 1 minute pause). . . . Now I'm going to help you return to your normal state of alertfulness. . . . In a little while I will begin counting backwards from 5 to 1 . . . you will gradually become more alert . . . when I reach 2, I want you to open your eyes . . . when I get to 1 you will be entirely aroused up in your normal state of alertfulness . . . READY? . . . 5 . . . 4 . . . you are becoming more and more alert . . . you feel very refreshed . . . 3 . . . 2 . . . now your eyes are open and you are beginning to feel very alert, returning to your normal state of alertfulness . . . 1.

This is the end of your relaxation tape.

EXHIBIT 17.2
Relaxing or Anti-Stress Imagery Tape Script

This can be inserted at the end of any relaxation induction between the deepening instructions and the realerting.

Now try to imagine as clearly and vividly as you can that you are lying on a blanket . . . on a beautiful beach in the summertime . . . the sky is a darkening rich blue . . . and the burnt orange sun is beginning to set over the ocean . . . you are watching the waves as they roll onto the shore . . . and roll back out again . . . in the distance you can hear the cry of the sea birds and the sound of the waves as they roll onto the shore and roll back out again . . . the pleasant saltiness of the sea is in the air . . . you are enveloped by the warmth of the sun from above . . . and the warmth of the sand beneath the blanket . . . let the warmth pour into every muscle of your body . . . you are feeling comfortably warm . . . and very, very relaxed . . . there's a cool breeze and there is nothing for you to do . . . but concentrate on the feelings of pleasant relaxation and warmth . . . just flowing through every muscle of your body . . . just watch and listen to the waves as they roll in and roll out again . . . you feel very pleasant and relaxed . . . (pause 10 seconds)

EXHIBIT 17.3
8 Muscle-Group Relaxation Training Tape Script

This is the new tape for your relaxation practice. It contains only 8 muscle groups. As before, you should be in a relaxed position with your head and neck supported. Loosen any tight or restrictive clothing. Remove your glasses if you wear them.

Now, I want you to begin to let yourself become relaxed. I'm going to start in that I want you to tense both lower arms together . . . flex your arms at the elbow . . . and tense your lower arms . . . concentrate on the tensions in your lower arms . . . study those tensions . . . and now relax your arms . . . and study the difference between the tension . . . and the relaxation . . . and just let yourself become more and more relaxed . . . if you feel yourself becoming drowsy . . . that will be fine too. . . . As you think of relaxation and of letting go of your muscles . . . they will become more loose . . . heavy . . . and relaxed . . . just let your muscles go . . . become more and more deeply relaxed. . . .

Next, I want you to tense the muscles in both of your lower legs . . . tense the muscles in the lower legs . . . in the calf and the instep . . . study those tensions in your lower legs . . . study the tension . . . and now relax the muscles . . . and focus on the difference between the tension . . . and the relaxation . . . you are becoming more and more relaxed . . . calm and relaxed . . . as you become more relaxed . . . you can feel yourself settling deep into the chair . . . all your muscles are becoming more and more comfortably relaxed . . . loose . . . heavy . . . and relaxed. . . .

This time I want you to tense the muscles from the abdominal region by drawing the abdominal muscles in tightly . . . draw them in tightly . . . study the tension across the entire abdominal region . . . study those tensions . . . and now relax the muscles . . . and study the difference between the tension . . . and the relaxation . . . and just continue to let the muscles relax . . . let them relax. . . .

Next, I want you to tense the muscles in your chest by taking a deep breath and holding it . . . hold it . . . hold it . . . and now relax . . . and study the difference between the tension and the relaxation . . . and the relaxation is growing deeper . . . and still deeper . . . you are relaxed . . . drowsy and relaxed . . . and your breathing is regular and relaxed . . . with each breath you take in . . . your relaxation increases . . . each time you exhale . . . you spread the relaxation throughout your body. . . .

Next, I want you to tense your shoulders by drawing your shoulders up toward your ears . . . hunching your shoulders up toward your ears . . . study the tension in your shoulders . . . across your upper back . . . study those tensions . . . and now relax those muscles . . . study the difference between the tension and the relaxation . . . and note the pleasant feelings of warmth and heaviness that are coming into your body as your muscles relax completely . . . you will always be clearly aware of what you are doing and what I am saying . . . as you become more deeply relaxed. . . .

This time I want you to tense the muscles in the back of your neck by pressing your head backwards against the chair . . . press your head back against the chair . . . and study the tension in the back of your neck, upper part of your back, and the base of your scalp . . . study those tensions . . . and now relax the muscles . . . and study the difference between the tension . . . and the relaxation . . . and just continue to let those muscles relax. . . .

Next, I want you to tense the muscles in the region around your eyes by closing your eyes very tightly . . . just close them very tightly . . . study the tension there in the upper part of your face . . . study those tensions . . . and now relax the muscles . . . just let them become smooth and relaxed . . . and study the difference between the tension and the relaxation . . . and now the very deep

Exhibit continues

EXHIBIT 17.3 (*Continued*)

state of relaxation is moving through all of the areas of your body . . . you are becoming more and more comfortably relaxed . . . drowsy and relaxed . . . you can feel the comfortable sensations of relaxation as you go into a deeper . . . and deeper state of relaxation. . . .

Now, I want you to tense the muscles in your forehead by frowning and lowering your eyebrows down . . . sort of frown and knit those eyebrows together . . . and study the tension there in your forehead, particularly the region between your eyes . . . focus on those tensions . . . and now relax those muscles . . . and study the difference between the tension and the relaxation . . . and just let the muscles of your forehead become smooth and relaxed. . . .

Now, I want you to relax all the muscles of your body . . . just let them become more and more relaxed . . . I am going to help you achieve a deeper state of relaxation by counting from 1 to 5 . . . and as I count . . . you will feel yourself becoming more and more deeply relaxed . . . farther and farther down into a deep restful state . . . of deep relaxation . . . 1 . . . you are going to become more deeply relaxed . . . 2 . . . down, down into a very relaxed state . . . 3 . . . 4 . . . more and more relaxed . . . 5 . . . deeply relaxed. . . .

Now, I want you to remain in your very relaxed state and I want you to begin to attend just to your breathing . . . breathe through your nose . . . notice the cool air as you breathe in . . . the warm moist air as you exhale . . . just continue to attend to your breathing . . . now each time you exhale . . . mentally repeat the word RELAX . . . inhale . . . exhale . . . relax . . . inhale . . . exhale . . . relax. . . .

Now, I am going to help you to return to your normal state of alertfulness . . . in a little while as I begin counting backward from 5 to 1 . . . you will gradually become more alert . . . when I reach 2 . . . I want you to open your eyes . . . when I get to 1 . . . you will be entirely roused up . . . in your normal state of alertfulness . . . READY? 5 . . . 4 . . . you are becoming more and more alert . . . you will feel very refreshed . . . 3 . . . 2 . . . now your eyes are open . . . you are beginning to feel very alert . . . returning completely to your normal state . . . and 1. . . .

This is the end of your relaxation tape. . . .

EXHIBIT 17.4
4 Muscle-Group Tape Script

This is the tape for the brief relaxation program. Before you begin, be sure to loosen any tight or restrictive clothing . . . Now close your eyes and take a deep breath . . . breathing with your stomach . . . and let yourself begin to relax. . . .

I want you to start by focusing your attention on both of your arms, tense the muscles in both of your lower arms . . . concentrate on those tensions . . . in both lower arms . . . even the back of your hands . . . study those tensions . . . and now relax your arms . . . study the difference between the tension and the relaxation . . . just continue to let the muscles in your arms relax . . . just let yourself become more and more relaxed . . . and if you begin to feel yourself becoming drowsy that will be fine too . . . as you think of relaxation . . . and of letting go of your muscles . . . they will become more loose and heavy and relaxed . . . just let your muscles go . . . as you become more and more deeply relaxed. . . .

Exhibit continues

EXHIBIT 17.4 (*Continued*)

Next, I want you to tense the muscles in your chest by taking a deep breath and holding it. . . . Hold it . . . study the tensions in your chest and now relax . . . and study the difference between the tension and the relaxation . . . and the relaxation is growing deeper . . . and still deeper . . . you're relaxed . . . drowsy and relaxed . . . your breathing is regular and relaxed . . . and with each breath you take in the relaxation increases . . . and each time you exhale . . . you spread the relaxation throughout your body. . . .

Next, we're going to focus on the muscles of your shoulders, the lower part of the back of your neck by drawing your shoulders up, not so hard that it hurts . . . so you feel the tension there across your shoulders and upper back . . . study those tensions . . . and now relax those muscles . . . just let them relax . . . let them continue to relax . . . and study the difference between the tension and the relaxation . . . in your neck and shoulder muscles . . . note the pleasant feelings of warmth and heaviness . . . that are coming into your body as your muscles relax completely . . . you'll always be clearly aware of what you are doing and what I am saying . . . as you become more deeply relaxed. . . .

This time I want you to close your eyes tightly and tense those muscles all across the upper part of your face . . . just close your eyes very tightly . . . feel the tensions around your eyes, between your eyes and the lower part of your forehead . . . study those tensions and now relax the muscles . . . study the difference between the tension and the relaxation . . . just continue to let those muscles relax . . . feel the muscles of your face . . . smoothing out and relaxing . . . and now the very deep state of relaxation is moving through all of the areas of your body . . . you are becoming more and more comfortably relaxed . . . drowsy and relaxed . . . and you feel the comfortable sensations of relaxation . . . as you go into a deeper and deeper state of relaxation. . . .

Now we are going to go through the deepening of the relaxation . . . I am going to count from 1 to 5 . . . as I count . . . you feel yourself becoming more and more deeply relaxed . . . farther and farther down . . . to a deep restful state . . . of deep relaxation . . . 1 . . . you are going to become more deeply relaxed . . . 2 . . . down . . . down into a very relaxed state . . . 3 . . . 4 . . . more and more relaxed . . . and 5 . . . deeply relaxed. . . .

Now I want you to remain in that very relaxed state for a few moments . . . begin to attend just to your breathing . . . breathe through your nose . . . notice the cool air as you breathe in . . . the warm moist air as you exhale . . . remember to use your stomach muscles as you breathe . . . just continue to attend to your breathing . . . inhale . . . exhale . . . relax . . . each time you exhale repeat the word **RELAX** . . . just relax. . . .

Now, I'm going to help you return to your normal state of alertfulness . . . In a little while I will begin counting backwards from 5 to 1 . . . you will gradually become more alert . . . when I reach 2 I want you to open your eyes . . . when I get to 1 you will be completely roused up in your normal state of alertfulness . . . and feel refreshed . . . 5 . . . 4 . . . you are becoming more and more alert . . . feel very refreshed . . . 3 . . . 2 . . . and now your eyes are open, beginning to feel very alert . . . very refreshed . . . and 1. . . .

That's the end of the tape.

EXHIBIT 17.5
4 Muscle-Groups Relaxation-By-Recall Tape Script

This is the short relaxation tape where you are relaxing by recall rather than by tensing the muscles. Be sure to be in a comfortable, relaxed position, be sure to loosen any tight or restrictive clothing. Now close your eyes and take a deep breath and let yourself begin to relax. Remember with these exercises you are going to remember what it felt like to have your muscles relaxed, you're going to match that memory, relax the muscles by remembering how it felt to have them relaxed.

First, I want you to attend to the muscles in your lower arms, backs of your hands and while they are resting at your side, I want you just to let them become more and more relaxed . . . remember what it felt like . . . after you tensed and released those muscles . . . now just let those muscles become relaxed . . . to match that memory . . . just continue to let the muscles relax . . . and attend to those feelings of relaxation . . . the muscles of your lower arms . . . let all of the tension go . . . let the muscles relax . . . and just let yourself become more and more relaxed . . . if you feel yourself becoming drowsy that will be fine too . . . as you think of relaxation . . . of letting go of your muscles . . . they will become more loose and heavy . . . and relaxed . . . just let your muscles go . . . as you become more and more deeply relaxed. . . .

Next, I want you to focus your attention on your chest . . . take a deep breath . . . hold it . . . study the buildup of tension . . . and now relax . . . and study the difference between the tension and the relaxation . . . just let your breathing be deep and relaxed . . . good diaphragmatic breathing . . . letting your stomach rise and fall as you breathe . . . and the relaxation is growing deeper and still deeper . . . you are relaxed . . . drowsy and relaxed . . . and your breathing is regular and relaxed . . . and with each breath you take in . . . your relaxation increases . . . and each time you exhale . . . you spread the relaxation . . . throughout your body. . . .

Next, I want you to focus on the muscles of your shoulders and upper back, back of your neck and just let those muscles relax . . . remember what it felt like when you tensed them and then let them go . . . I want you to match that pattern now . . . match those feelings of relaxation . . . just let those muscles of your shoulders and upper back and neck relax . . . just continue to let them relax . . . let them drop down and relax . . . just attend to how it feels to have those muscles relaxed . . . note the pleasant feelings of warmth and heaviness . . . that are coming into your body as your muscles relax completely . . . you'll always be clearly aware of what you are doing . . . what I am saying . . . as you become more deeply relaxed. . . .

Next, I want you to relax the muscles in the upper part of your face . . . just relax the muscles around your eyes, and the lower part of your forehead . . . just let those muscles become smooth and relaxed . . . remembering how it felt when they were tensed and then relaxed . . . just match that memory of how those muscles felt . . . when they were relaxed . . . let your muscles become relaxed . . . relaxed as they were after you had tensed them. . . .

Now, the very deep state of relaxation is moving through all of the areas of your body . . . you are becoming more and more comfortably relaxed . . . drowsy and relaxed . . . and you can feel the comfortable sensations of relaxation as you go into a deeper . . . and deeper state of relaxation . . . and now just let all the muscles of your body relax . . . just let the tension drift out of your muscles . . . I want you to attend to letting the muscles go . . . I'm going to count from 1 to 3 . . . and as I count . . . again, you'll feel yourself continuing to become more and more relaxed . . . your breathing will be regular and relaxed . . . 1 . . . you are going to become more deeply relaxed . . . 2 . . . down . . . down into a very

Exhibit continues

EXHIBIT 17.5 (*Continued*)

relaxed state . . . 3 . . . deeply relaxed . . . again, just attend to your breathing . . . notice the warm moist air as you exhale . . . cool air as you breathe in . . . the warm moist air as you exhale . . . remember to breathe with your stomach . . . deep diaphragmatic . . . breaths . . . inhale . . . exhale . . . relax . . . inhale . . . exhale . . . relax. . . . Now, we are going to return to your normal state, I will count backwards from 3 to 1, on 2 you will open your eyes . . . when you get to one you will be roused up in your normal state of alterfulness . . . 3 . . . you are becoming more alert . . . the relaxation is drifting away . . . 2 your eyes are open . . . you are becoming more alert . . . you feel refreshed . . . and 1 . . . back in your normal state of alertfulness . . . but feeling relaxed and refreshed. . . .

This is the end of your relaxation tape.

EXHIBIT 17.6
Autogenic phrases

1. I feel very quiet.
2. I am beginning to feel quite relaxed.
3. My feet feel heavy and relaxed.
4. My ankles, my knees, and my hips feel heavy, relaxed, and comfortable.
5. My solar plexus, and the whole central portion of my body, feel relaxed and quiet.
6. My hands, my arms, and my shoulders, feel heavy, relaxed, and comfortable.
7. My neck, my jaws, and my forehead feel relaxed. They feel comfortable and smooth.
8. My whole body feels quiet, heavy, comfortable, and relaxed.
9. (Now go back through the sequence on your own.)
10. I am quite relaxed.
11. My arms and hands are heavy and warm.
12. I feel quite quiet.
13. My whole body is relaxed and my hands are warm, relaxed and warm.
14. My hands are warm.
15. Warmth is flowing into my hands, they are warm, warm.
16. I can feel the warmth flowing down my arms into my hands.
17. My hands are warm, relaxed and warm.
18. (Now go back through the sequence on your own.)

EXHIBIT 17.7
Cognitive Coping Strategies

1. Before entering the stressful situation:
   a. Plan ahead
   b. Is this a situation that would be better avoided?
2. When in stressful situations:
   a. Try breaking tasks down into smaller parts.
   b. Tell yourself, "I can manage this situation."
   c. Ask the internal questions:
      Is this situation worth developing a stomach problem over?
      How responsible am I for this situation?
      If I'm not responsible and can't change it, can I just accept it?

18

THE ALBANY COGNITIVE THERAPY TREATMENT MANUAL

As was indicated in Chapter 16, a purely cognitive therapy approach to IBS has yielded the most consistently positive results among the various treatment approaches we have used at Albany over the 15 years we have been dealing with IBS sufferers. Three separate, small-scale RCTs, have yielded a statistically significant advantage of individual cognitive therapy over symptom monitoring (Greene & Blanchard, 1994; Payne & Blanchard, 1995; Vollmer & Blanchard, 1998) and one trial showed a significant advantage of individual cognitive therapy over a highly credible control condition, a psychoeducational support group (Payne & Blanchard, 1995).

The detailed session-by-session treatment manual in this chapter is the one used in Vollmer and Blanchard (1998) for cognitive therapy in small groups. My assumption is that a therapist can readily eliminate those portions of the manual that pertain to the group version. It seemed superfluous to provide both a manual for individual treatment and a manual for group treatment.

This chapter is not designed to teach one how to become a cognitive therapist

Much of the work of developing this detailed treatment manual was done by Dr. Barbara Greene as part of her dissertation. It was modified slightly by Dr. Annette Payne. Dr. Alisa Vollmer undertook the adaptation to a small group format.

or how to use cognitive therapy with a variety of human problems. Instead, this manual assumes that the user is familiar with the writings of Meichenbaum (1977, 1985), Beck (1976), Beck et al. (1980), and Persons (1989) and is generally experienced in cognitive therapy and comfortable with this approach to human problems. This chapter is not designed to teach the basic skills.

It should be remembered that the three therapists whose studies support this approach to IBS were each fourth year doctoral students in clinical psychology. Each had had three years of course work and supervised practicum from a cognitive–behavioral perspective and each had had some experience with IBS clients. As was noted earlier, this level of experience is in contrast to Blanchard, Schwarz et al., 1992, Study 2, for which some of the therapists had only 6 months of graduate training before treating clients with the CBT package described in Chapter 17.

The treatment program described below is based on ten 90-min sessions. Our individual cognitive therapy regimen has varied from 12 to 10 sessions of 50 to 60 min duration. For the 12 session regimen, it was twice per week for 4 weeks, followed by once per week for 4 additional weeks. The 10-session regimen (which yielded slightly weaker results), was once per week for 10 weeks.

Clinical Hint

I believe contracting for 12 individual sessions would be better than 10 sessions, and spreading them over 10 weeks [twice per week for 2 weeks, then weekly sessions for 8 weeks] would be optimum. The somewhat more intense contact may help by correcting errors early on rather than waiting a week. Some clients clearly will not need the full 12 sessions, and can be discharged early, whereas others will undoubtedly need more. We have no empirical data on this issue, only an opinion.

The once-per-week schedule for small groups seems the only regimen which would work. It is hard enough to get 4 or 5 clients together for one weekly session; trying for more intensive contact seems unrealistic.

ALBANY COGNITIVE THERAPY MANUAL

Treatment Session 1

Materials needed

Diagram of 3 components of IBS (Exhibit 18.1)
Diagram of 2-level analysis (Exhibit 18.2)
Cognitive monitoring sheets (Form 1) (Table 18.1)

Goals

1. Introduce group members and rules of the group (confidentiality)
2. Introduce treatment schedule
3. Introduce treatment rationale
4. Describe stress-appraisal model of IBS and obtain problem list
5. Define three components of IBS
6. Describe two-level analysis of psychological problems
7. Describe specificity and automaticity of cognitions
8. Introduce "downward arrow" technique
9. Introduce cognitive monitoring
10. Assign homework

Have group members introduce themselves, first names only, for this session. Explain that what happens and what is said in the group is strictly *confidential.* Although it is acceptable to tell one's spouse or partner what you said and what the therapist said if needed, *it is NOT appropriate to discuss what any other group member said or who they are.*

Possible script for introduction:

> Some of you may be a bit uncomfortable in this small group setting and a bit embarrassed talking about your GI problems and your private thoughts, in front of others. This is understandable at first, over time you should become more comfortable.
>
> Also remember that each of you has IBS and you are not alone with your problem—the other group members have it also. Because IBS comes in many varieties with different symptoms, each person's experience of it may be unique, but there are commonalities.

Protocol

1. Explain the treatment schedule: There will be ten 1 1/2 hour treatment sessions spread out over 10 weeks with sessions

held once per week. Posttreatment evaluation will take place 2 weeks after the last treatment session. (Discuss and resolve any conflicts with the treatment schedule.)

2. Give treatment rationale:

Possible script:

> IBS is a disorder whose symptoms often appear as a reaction to stress. Stress is a natural part of life. It is basically an interaction between you and your environment. Something happens and you interpret its meaning, how you feel about it, and how equipped you feel to cope with it. Sometimes you can underestimate your capabilities for dealing with tough situations or make the situation worse by worrying about it.
>
> People who are under stress often engage in self-defeating thoughts that only make the stress worse. If you see some problem as being overwhelming to the resources that you have available for coping with it, the result is a bodily stress reaction. Your body reacts as if that stressor is actually some kind of danger to your life.
>
> You have two types of nervous systems in your body. One is the central nervous system, with which you control your arms, legs, and all the other muscles you normally use voluntarily. The other nervous system is called the autonomic nervous system. It is the automatic nervous system that controls the smooth muscle of your body. The smooth muscles are the ones which you don't normally purposely control like your heart, your lungs and your intestinal muscles.
>
> When you become very stressed, and your body starts reacting as if it is in danger, your autonomic system becomes active. This is known as the *fight or flight* response, where your system is getting ready for you to either defend yourself or get away from the danger. Adrenaline starts pumping, your breathing becomes shallower, your heart beats faster, and your blood pressure increases. Another reaction useful to the animal about to fight or escape is the dumping of waste in the bowel, so the muscles in the bowel spasm in order to get rid of this waste.
>
> People with IBS feel these spasms and will experience diarrhea if the spasms all go one way, and constipation if the spasms go up and down the intestine, essentially trapping the stools in the bowel. The pain and symptoms are like urges to have a bowel movement and are very real

but often, IBS clients are told that their symptoms are "all in your head," which refers to the symptoms being a stress reaction.

IBS is difficult to manage when viewed as a global thing. It is very easy for people to say "stop being so anxious," but it is very difficult to use that as a method of control.

When IBS is viewed in terms of its components, the job of learning to control it is much easier (use the 3-component diagram, Exhibit 18.1). IBS seems to consist of a combination of three major components: physiological, cognitive and behavioral. Problems exist across all three of these systems. The physiological component involves the physical feelings or symptoms such as abdominal pain, nausea, constipation, diarrhea, and so on. The behavioral system includes what you actually do: your ability to work on the job, your ability to enjoy leisure activities, and your tendency to avoid certain places where IBS symptoms are expected to occur. The cognitive component involves thoughts that you have in certain stressful situations. You may think that something terrible is about to happen, you are helpless, or you may worry a great deal about the present as well as the future, or you may think all three things.

All three aspects play some role in the IBS experience. (The therapist should ask clients to identify the things that he or she thinks, feels, and does when IBS hits.)

The therapist then reviews the three components of IBS using the diagram and the clients' own examples.

Possible script:

These three systems are very closely related. Thoughts or cognitions can bring about heightened physical arousal and GI arousal, which in turn can interfere with behavior. These systems interact in ways that serve to create more intense IBS symptoms. In addition, how you feel emotionally will be largely a reflection of these three systems. (Elicit examples from the clients' own experiences.)

Our treatment is essentially a training program designed to help you cope with stress before it becomes a full blown IBS attack. Over the next few weeks you will learn to pay more attention to how you deal with stressful situations and to change whatever may be leading up to an attack. The basic strategy in this treatment program is a cognitive technique. Due to the interactive nature of the three systems of IBS, changing the cognitive element will in turn affect the physiological (GI tract) and behavioral (escape–avoidance) components. You will also experience changes in emotions from negative to more positive ones. You will be taught methods of *identifying, questioning*, and *challenging* your *thoughts, appraisals, interpretations*, and *assumptions*. Once you are able to isolate the particular thoughts that often precipitate IBS, you will learn to change them.

In addition to working with these automatic thoughts, we will also search for your more basic attitudes and your underlying beliefs (use the 2-level analysis diagram, Exhibit 18.2). You may think of these two types of thoughts, automatic and the more basic ones, as representing two levels. Automatic thoughts lie on the first level, the surface. You may recognize these thoughts as your real life problems, such as thinking "I'm trapped, I don't want to be here," "I can't cope with this, this IBS is just too much," "I'll never solve this problem, I'll be fired," and "These kids are driving me crazy."

On the second level are the underlying beliefs. You may think of these as underlying psychological mechanisms which is a long term meaning the thoughts or fuel which runs your thinking system. Underlying mechanisms are not as obvious and as easy to identify as your automatic thoughts. They can be expressed in terms of one (or a few) irrational beliefs or maladaptive ideas you hold about yourself. These beliefs produce your overt, level one, difficulties.

For example, a young female IBS client who was anxious about a new job, socially withdrawn, and depressed held the belief that "Unless I'm perfect in everything I do, I'll fail." This basic underlying belief fueled her automatic thoughts; "I can't do this job" and "I don't look good enough to date men," which produced her problems. It led her to avoid social interactions and inhibited her from searching for solutions to her work difficulties. Her fear of making mistakes was rooted in her more basic underlying belief that she must be perfect and this led to increased anxiety and IBS symptoms, more depression and impaired performance. (The therapist emphasizes the interaction between cognitions, behaviors, physiology, and emotions using the 3-component diagram).

Coping with stressful situations also includes changing the environment as well as your thoughts. Remember, stress is an interaction between you and your environment. Sometimes, making changes in your environment can be just as important as changing how you think about it. Examples of this could be as drastic as quitting a job you hated or hiring a babysitter once a week so you and your spouse can enjoy a night out.

(The therapist should begin a general inquiry into each client's primary IBS symptoms asking for an initial volunteer. The focus is upon identifying the pattern of IBS symptoms, cognitions, behaviors, and feelings and the situations in which these are likely to occur. For clients who have difficulty, reporting that IBS symptoms can occur at almost any time and that there seems to be very little relationship between situation and IBS symptoms, attempt to identify internal cues that may trigger IBS, particularly negative cognitions. Go through this with each group member in turn. If someone is reluctant to talk or says the ideas do not fit their situation, ask them to try to bear with you and the group and come back to them later.)

3. Teach the case formulation approach:
   a. Teach the relationship between behaviors, cognitions, and mood (use 3-component sheet);
   b. Teach relationship between behavior problems and irrational beliefs. Point to how behaviors reinforce negative irrational beliefs and point to underlying problem (use 2-level analysis sheet);
   c. Emphasize how behaviors reflect and support underlying irrational beliefs.
4. Begin inquiry into clients' problems and obtain a problem list from each client. Transform vague, general complaints into discrete problems. Remember to look for mood, behavior, and cognitive components.
5. Discuss specificity and automaticity of cognitions.

   Possible script:

   > We view maladaptive thoughts as having two major characteristics: first, they are automatic, and second, they are discrete predictions or interpretations of a given situation.
   >
   > The term "automatic" means that these cognitions or thoughts occur very rapidly in certain situations and

they may be outside of your direct awareness. The term 'discrete' refers to the fact that these thoughts are very specific in content.

(The implication for treatment is that the client must become clearly aware of the kind of self-talk going on situations and must learn to pursue the thought until arriving at the very specific content of prediction. Proceeding no further than "I feel terrible and anxious" is not therapeutic and indeed may serve to intensify anxiety by virtue of its global and nondirective nature.)

(During sessions, the therapist can model and coach for this kind of self-monitoring and critical analysis of anxiety-provoking thoughts. For example, a client may say "I'm afraid to go out to dinner." In responding to such a statement, the therapist should ask questions which are designed to elicit specific interpretations and predictions being made by the client in that situation. The therapist could ask *"What do you think would happen?" "What are you telling yourself about this situation?"* In response to questions such as these, the client may produce more specific statements.)

6. Help the client make cognitions as specific as possible by implementing the downward arrow technique. Explain that this technique is useful in identifying specific thoughts that the client may not even be aware of and that once he or she identifies these thoughts, changing them is easier. Demonstrate this technique by asking the client to become more and more specific with his or her thoughts by asking questions such as "What does it mean when you say you feel ____?" and "What do you imagine happening that is so terrible?" Continue questioning until the client identifies specific cognitions. The therapist begins working to identify underlying psychological mechanisms, the "working hypotheses" from central themes of thoughts revealed from clients' responses to questioning.
7. Review the 2-level model of psychological problems: the overt difficulties including problematic thoughts and associated maladaptive behaviors, negative emotions and physiological responses (using any actual examples the client has been able to identify thus far whenever possible), and the underlying basic beliefs. Emphasize the close relation between the two levels. Explain to the client that you will be working with him or her to identify their own underlying psychological mechanisms by exploring specific situations and thoughts. Remember to highlight the fact that automatic

thoughts are viewed as derivatives of underlying irrational beliefs.

Explain to the client.

Possible script:

> Focusing on and questioning specific thoughts that arise in certain stressful situations will eventually reveal central themes that indicate your underlying mechanisms. The therapeutic work will be directed at challenging your automatic thoughts and helping you to restructure any distorted thoughts into more adaptive ones. By working on changing the level one surface thoughts through various cognitive techniques, change in underlying beliefs is expected. We will proceed one step at a time. The first step is just to identify the automatic thoughts.

8. Introduce cognitive monitoring. Show the client the cognitive monitoring sheet and explain how to use it (Table 18.1). Use an example from the client's recent experience and fill out the form. Answer any questions about the use of the form.
9. Assign homework. "Homework until the next session (for individual therapy, later this week) is to monitor any stressful situations as well as GI symptoms." Ask the clients to recall activities or be aware of activities that they find stressful and to identify thoughts, physical feelings, behaviors, and emotions related to the anxiety in those situations. Instruct clients to use the downward arrow technique. Also, ask them to simply note these on the form and not to try to change them yet. Explain that it is important for them to first learn simply to identify cognitions and that this can be a difficult task at first because automatic thoughts can be subtle and they occur almost like a reflex.

Treatment Session 2

Materials needed

Cognitive Monitoring sheets (Form 1, Table 18.1)
4 Patterns of Maladaptive Thinking Sheet (Exhibit 18.3)

Goals

1. Review rationale
2. Review homework
3. Identify and refine cognitions
4. Begin to identify working hypotheses
5. Introduce 4 patterns of maladaptive thinking
6. Assign homework

Protocol

1. Review treatment rationale. Make sure that the clients understand the treatment rationale. If a client does not understand, review session 1 rationale. Review the 3 components of IBS and the 2-level analysis of thoughts. This is a replay of session 1 for those who did not understand the first time.
2. Review homework. Go over the clients' cognitive monitoring sheets and confirm that the clients understand the directions. If a client has not filled out the form, ask him or her to remember a situation that was stressful and fill out the form during the session using that situation. Check for clients' use of the downward arrow technique. Also, check symptom diaries and encourage their continued use.
3. Identify and refine problems, particularly cognitions. Refine cognitions to specifics using downward arrow. Review this technique with the clients so that it can be effectively used without help. Describe the principle of automaticity and specificity to the client. Select examples from the cognitive monitoring sheets to identify and refine thoughts relevant to the specific situation that has occurred.

   If a client has difficulty identifying specific cognitions, refer to the notion of automatic cognitions, which can become more clearly identifiable with practice, especially when attempts are made to record self-talk during anxiety.
4. Emphasize the relationship between cognitions, GI symptoms, negative emotions, and behaviors.
5. The therapist begins to identify central themes from the client's list of monitored cognitive responses and from auto-

matic thoughts and chief complaints, antecedents and consequences. The therapist may discuss these with the client.

6. Introduce the 4 patterns of maladaptive thinking (use Exhibit 18.3). Explain self-criticism, poor coping, rumination, and cognitive avoidance.
7. Assign homework. Until the next session, the client is to continue to monitor IBS symptoms and automatic cognitions in anxious situations. Make an appointment for next week.

Treatment Session 3

Materials needed

Cognitive Monitoring sheets (Form 2, Table 18.2)

Goals

1. Review homework
2. Identify central themes
3. Introduce catastrophic consequences and countering
4. Relate catastrophic cognitions to possible underlying beliefs
5. Assign homework

Protocol

1. Review homework. Inquire about the success of cognitive monitoring and refining cognitions. Identify and refine cognitions relevant to specific situations that occurred.
2. Identify central themes and working hypotheses.
3. Introduce catastrophic consequences. Explain that you will be introducing the first type of cognitive error that many people make. Inform the clients that unnecessary anxiety arises from viewing an event as dangerous, insufferable, or catastrophic when in actuality it is not.

   Hence, typical types of catastrophic errors are: "If I have IBS symptoms, it is terrible and it will ruin my entire day," "If everything is not perfect tonight, I will be a total failure."

   Point out to the clients that if these consequences were to happen, these occurrences are not as catastrophic as the clients see them. Ask the clients about the worst thing that they can envision happening. Help them to identify whether any of the cognitions associated with events of the past week satisfy the criteria for catastrophic thinking: using such statements as "This is unbearable," "I can't stand it," and so on. Apply this method of analysis to past and future predictions regarding panic and anxiety in general and IBS attacks in particular.

   Describe the method for countering catastrophic thinking. The client must learn to critically evaluate the actual severity of the consequences of an event that is being viewed catastrophically.

   Decatastrophizing asks the client to imagine the worst possible outcome of a situation, and then evaluate the severity of that consequence.

Possible script:

> You might ask yourself "Well, what if this worst possible thing were to happen?" "What if I did fail?" You may find that when you think carefully and critically about these assumptions, you prematurely assume them to be catastrophic. For instance, ask yourself what would really happen if you did fail. You may automatically assume that your life will be ruined. As you begin focusing in on these thoughts, you will probably experience an increase in anxiety because the thoughts themselves are anxiety provoking. These kinds of thoughts can be subjected to a more logical counter-thought that reduces anxiety.

Ask the clients to think of a logical counter to the illogical belief that if everything is not perfect, he or she is a total failure. Then give another example situation for the clients to use decatastrophizing techniques. Explain that as he or she continues to practice logical countering, the thoughts will become less salient and less anxiety provoking.

The clients and therapist then evaluate whether the cognitions that are viewed as catastrophic would indeed be as intolerable as each client believes or whether, in contrast, the client's anxiety or distress would be time limited and manageable. This strategy should be applied to both IBS anxiety and general anxiety.

4. Relate catastrophic thinking to possible underlying beliefs and test out your working hypotheses by questioning the clients about specific complaints, difficulties, and problematic situations. Try to tell a story about how the proposed mechanism might lead to problems that may be on a client's list. Test out predictions by collecting data on family history. Ask for each client's reaction.
5. Assign homework. The client should be instructed to continue monitoring GI symptoms and cognitions, paying particular attention to catastrophic thoughts. The client should begin countering catastrophic thoughts, using Cognitive Form 2 (Table 18.2).

Treatment Session 4

Materials needed

Cognitive Monitoring Sheets (Form 2, Table 18.2)

Goals

1. Review homework
2. Introduce Polarized Thinking
   a. Identification
   b. Countering
3. Relate Polarized Thinking to working hypotheses
4. Assign homework

Protocol

1. Review cognitive monitoring sheets and GI diaries and check on any problems the client may have. Discuss the catastrophic thoughts that the clients may have identified and review the use of the downward arrow technique.
2. Continue exploring and testing your working hypotheses.
3. Introduce Polarized Thinking.

   Possible script:

   > Last time we talked about catastrophizing, or blowing things out of proportion, and how to identify those types of thoughts. There are other types of thoughts which can lead to a stress reaction. I want to talk about one of these other types of thoughts today.
   >
   > Polarized Thinking is when you see things as either *all* good or *all* bad. This is also called *thinking in black and white*. There is no middle ground, you think you have to be perfect and see yourself as either being wonderful or just awful. Again, you can see nothing in between.
4. Identify examples of polarized thinking in the clients' lives. Try to have clients recall events, thoughts, feelings, and behavior associated with polarized thinking, or use the clients' monitoring sheets.
5. Introduce countering for polarized thinking.

   Possible script:

   > The way to counter this type of polarized thinking is to think in terms of percentages instead of thinking in absolute terms. A person is not either totally good or totally bad, the person will fall somewhere along a contin-

uum. When you see yourself thinking that you are completely stupid and cannot handle yourself, change that to "I can be pretty stupid about 5% of the time, but the rest of the time I can handle myself O.K."

6. Relate polarized thoughts to underlying beliefs (again, by questioning the client about specific complaints and problematic situations while fitting precipitants with your formulation, collecting historical data, and asking for client's reactions).
7. Assign homework. Instruct clients to continue monitoring GI symptoms and cognitions, paying special attention to catastrophic thoughts and polarized thinking.

Clinical Hint

The manual for the remaining sessions are written as if you are dealing with an individual. You do need to work with each person in the group *on an individual basis* at each group session.

Of course, this also makes it easier to adapt the manual to use in individual therapy.

Treatment Session 5

Materials needed

Cognitive Monitoring Sheets (Form 2, Table 18.2)
Cognitive Distortion Sheet (Exhibit 18.3)
Cognitive Coping Strategies (Exhibit 18.4)

Goals

1. Review homework
2. Introduce other cognitive distortions
3. Relate cognitive distortions to working hypotheses
4. Introduce cognitive coping strategies
5. Assign homework

Protocol

1. Review homework. Check the client's cognitive monitoring sheets and GI symptom diaries. Inquire about and resolve difficulties. Check for the client's identification of and countering of catastrophic and polarized thoughts.
2. Continue to explore underlying beliefs and working hypotheses.
3. Give the client the cognitive distortion sheet and discuss. Review his or her identification of catastrophic and polarized thinking and tell the client that you are now going to discuss other types of dysfunctional thoughts. Ask the client to provide examples of each type of distortion that he or she has thought of and discuss countering methods for each type of distortion.
4. Give the client the cognitive coping strategies and discuss. Use situations from the client's life and apply the strategies.
5. a. Try Old Plan/New Plan to aid the client in changing cognitions and underlying beliefs by trying out behavioral plans. Make sure the client's desired behavior is in his or her best interest and do NOT reinforce pathological or irrational beliefs. Examine the relationship between the proposed behavioral plan and the underlying belief.
   b. Try following strategies for behavior change. These new behaviors are anti-belief behaviors (they attack the underlying beliefs): Rewards and punishments, breaking tasks into small parts, exposure, stimulus control, exercise.
6. Relate the client's cognitive distortions to underlying irrational beliefs (again, by asking the client about specific complaints and problematic situations while fitting precipitants

with formulation, collecting history data, and asking for the client's reaction).

7. Assign homework. The client should continue to record symptoms and cognitions and should actively apply countering techniques and coping skills. Ask the client to record the use of countering and coping.
8. Consider switching to the alternate Form 2 at this point (Table 18.3). It has a slightly better format to prompt countering of negative automatic thoughts.

Treatment Session 6

Materials needed

Cognitive Monitoring Sheets (Form 2, Table 18.2)
Problem Solving Outline (Exhibit 18.5)

Goals

1. Review homework
2. Introduce problem solving outline
3. Assign homework

Protocol

1. Check diaries and self-monitoring sheets. Discuss any difficulties the client may have had using countering and cognitive coping skills.
2. Introduce problem solving. Give the client the problem solving outline (Exhibit 18.5) and explain the principles of problem solving as in Meichenbaum (1985):
3. Instruct the client in the use of self-statements during stress reactions and during problem solving. Use relevant examples from the client's life and go through the problem solving technique with him or her.
4. Assign homework. The client should continue to monitor IBS symptoms and cognitions and continue using countering and coping skills. The client should also use and record problem solving techniques at least once during the next week.

Treatment Session 7

Materials needed

Cognitive Monitoring Sheets (Form 2, Table 18.2)

Goals

1. Review homework
2. Discuss and role play the application of cognitive coping strategies
3. Discuss and role play problem solving
4. Assign homework

Protocol

1. Review homework. Check IBS symptom diaries and cognitive monitoring sheets. Review the client's use of countering and coping skills. Also, review the client's use of problem solving over the past week and make sure that he or she understands the technique and the use of self-statements.
2. Relate the client's specific automatic cognitions to his or her possible underlying beliefs.
3. Discuss in more detail the application of coping strategies and countering. Give the client several scenarios of stressful events that are meaningful in his or her life, and ask about automatic thoughts and self-statements in those situations. Point out progress that the client has made.
4. Discuss problem solving and again give the client scenarios of stressful situations in his or her life, and use the problem solving technique. Explain that the use of this technique may be awkward at first, but with continued use becomes easier, much like using cognitive coping skills.
5. Assign homework. The client is to continue to monitor IBS symptoms and cognitions and use countering and coping skills. Ask client to also continue to use the problem solving method.

Treatment Session 8

Materials needed

Cognitive Monitoring Sheets (Form 2, Table 18.2)

Goals

1. Review homework
2. Introduce causal analysis
3. Assign homework

Protocol

1. Review and discuss cognitive monitoring, cognitive coping, and problem solving. Discuss any difficulties the client may be having with the homework.
2. Introduce causal analysis. Causal analysis involves detection of possible precipitants to generalized anxiety and IBS. This is a useful technique because understanding precipitants:
   a. removes anxiety associated with uncertainty and helps to lower the tendency to search for illogical reasons;
   b. helps develop a sense of personal control and removes the sense that the person is a victim of their emotions or that anxiety or an IBS attack can occur unexpectedly at any time in any place.
3. Describe the two kinds of anxiety: Anxiety that is associated with particular situations and is usually expected, and anxiety which does not seem to be related to any obvious external situations. Ask the client to identify situations in which he or she anticipates feeling anxious, including IBS attacks and generalized anxiety relevant to personal, social, and occupational areas of life. Pay attention to the situations in which he or she expects to feel anxious. Explain how anxiety can be more intense if it is associated with fearful, expectant thoughts.
4. Inform the client that cues can always be found for feelings of anxiety. Sometimes they are very subtle:
   a. Physical state: feeling natural sensations (GI) that are associated with anxiety and therefore can trigger an anxious mode of thinking and feeling.
   b. Thoughts: Worries can precipitate feeling anxious.
   c. General stressors: subtle pressures and hassles can build to create a feeling of anxiety (e.g., dealing with hostile people, being caught in traffic, attempting to meet a deadline).

5. Discuss behavioral and cognitive strategies of handling antecedents of anxiety and IBS symptoms. (The therapist continues to try to tie proposed central mechanism to precipitants of IBS as a test of the hypothesis.)
6. Assign homework. The client should continue to monitor IBS symptoms and cognitions and continue to use coping and problem solving techniques. The client should also apply causal analysis and attend to antecedents.

Treatment Session 9

Materials needed

Cognitive Monitoring Sheets (Tables 18.2 and 18.3)

Goals

1. Review homework
2. Review the use of cognitive coping strategies, countering, problem solving, and identification of antecedents
3. Assign homework

Protocol

1. Review the client's homework. Discuss any difficulties with monitoring, the use of coping and countering, problem solving, or the identification of antecedents.
2. Discuss the client's progress using the above techniques. If there are any areas in which he or she does not show mastery of the techniques, review as necessary. Be sure to review the use of causal analysis.
3. Assign homework. The client should continue monitoring symptoms and cognitions, and the use of coping and problem solving.
4. Schedule the last appointment for next week. Explain that treatment is ending and check for any concerns regarding the termination of treatment.

Treatment Session 10

Materials needed

Cognitive Monitoring Sheets (Tables 18.2 and 18.3)

Goals

1. Review homework
2. Discuss client's progress and success emphasizing the 2-level analysis of automatic thoughts and underlying psychological mechanisms

Protocol

1. Review the client's homework. Explain that therapy is ending, but it is still useful to write down thoughts and the problem solving process for personal use rather than for homework.
2. Discuss the client's progress throughout treatment. Review treatment rationale and encourage the continued use of the techniques he or she has learned. Review the client's particular level one cognitive distortions and level two underlying psychological mechanisms.

Clinical Hints

Two issues frequently arise with the group treatment of IBS: Almost inevitably, group members progress *at different rates* in understanding and then implementing the various ideas presented, such as how to access and record their automatic thoughts and how to recognize and then counter various irrational beliefs and schemas. My best advice is to pitch the pace of group to the group average.

Thus, for the person who is very psychologically minded and grasps the ideas quickly, the group will probably move at too slow a pace. One way to keep clients like this involved is by enlisting their help as a junior partner (but not as a cotherapist). This can be done by asking the quick client for ideas while another client is going through a situation on the latter's diary.

The danger to this, of course, is that the quick client may make an unhelpful suggestion or interpretation. You need to counter it while continuing to be supportive of your helper. You can say something like, "That may not be the only interpretation. Another way to look at this is . . . ." Your approval and verbal reinforcement are probably powerful with both the helper and the other clients.

A different problem is presented by the client who seems to have trouble understanding the ideas and who does a very poor job of monitoring and recording. This client will need some extra attention and support to help him or her understand. However, you need to be careful that this client does not use his or her "slowness" in a manipulative fashion to gain too much of your and the group's attention and time. These extremes are part of the downside of conducting the therapy in small groups.

Some time should be spent with each client's homework monitoring and on each client's application of the lesson for the day. This means that individual clients probably get less individual attention to their idiosyncratic issues. One hopes there is vicarious learning from the discussion of another client's situation. You, as the therapist, should be trying to maximize this vicarious learning by asking different group members what we would label a certain fallacy and then asking for help from the group members on how the client could counter the fallacy.

The hypothetical sequence should be: ask the focus client for his or her ideas, then ask different group members for additional suggestions, with care taken to reinforce good ones and gently question poor ones.

Another problem that arises occasionally is that a client will claim to have no stress in his or her life or will claim to have no thoughts in a stressful situation or will claim that psychological distress does not lead to IBS attacks.

For the purportedly stress-free client (usually a man), the first step is to ask the client to *try a bit harder* to identify stressful situations and thoughts. (It is probably the case that onset of GI symptoms is stressful, otherwise he or she would not be in treatment.) The next step is to ask the person to go along with the program and to try to examine the ideas and constructs being presented and how they may fit his or her situation. The last step is to agree with the client after 4 or 5 weeks that stress does not seem related to his or her IBS and to raise the issue of the client's stopping treatment early after he or she has given it a good try.

TABLE 18.1
Cognitive Monitoring—Form 1

For each IBS attack or stressful/anxious event this week, please describe your reactions on this form.

Situation	Automatic Thoughts	*Physical Feelings* Abdominal pain, constipation, diarrhea, headache, etc.	*Negative Emotions* Anxiety, depression (Rate 1–10)	*Behavior* What did you do?

TABLE 18.2
Cognitive Monitoring—Form 2

For each IBS attack or stressful/anxious event this week, please describe your reactions on this form.

Situation	Automatic Thoughts	Alternative	*Physical Feelings* Abdominal pain, constipation, diarrhea, headache, etc.	*Negative Emotions* Anxiety, depression (Rate 1–10)	*Behavior* What did you do?

TABLE 18.3
Daily Record of Dysfunctional Thoughts (Alternate Form 2)

	Situation (describe)	Emotion(s)	Automatic thought(s)	Rational response	Outcome
DATE	1. Actual event leading to unpleasant emotion, or 2. Stream of thought, daydreams, or recollection leading to unpleasant emotion.	1. Specify sad, anxious, angry, etc. 2. Rate degree of emotion 1–100.	1. Write automatic thought(s) that preceded emotion(s). 2. Rate belief in automatic thought 0–100%.	1. Write rational response to automatic thought(s). 2. Rate belief in rational response 0–100%.	1. Rerate belief in automatic thoughts. 2. Specify and rate subsequent emotions.

Note. When you experience an unpleasant emotion, note the situation that seemed to stimulate the emotion. If the emotion occurred while you were thinking, daydreaming, etc., then note the automatic thought associated with the emotion. Record the degree to which you believe this thought: 0% = not at all; 100% = completely. In rating the emotion: 1 = a trace; 100 = the most intense possible.

EXHIBIT 18.1
The Three Components of IBS

Physiological—physical symptoms such as:
abdominal pain
nausea
bloating
constipation
diarrhea

Behavioral—what you actually do (and what you *avoid* doing because of fear of IBS)

Cognitive—thoughts that occur in stressful situations; times when IBS symptoms elicit fears and expectations.

EXHIBIT 18.2
Two Levels of Analysis of Thoughts

Automatic Thoughts (which we can capture with attention in a situation).

Underlying Thoughts or Schemas (basic ways of viewing self, life, and the future).

EXHIBIT 18.3
Distorted Thoughts

Distorted thoughts present an unrealistic view of reality, involve illogical reasoning, or are maladaptive.

Here are some common cognitive distortions:

1. *Emotional Reasoning*
   You make an inference about yourself, your world, or your future on the basis of an emotional experience.
   "I feel hopeless, therefore I am hopeless and my life will never improve."
   "Because I feel incompetent and inadequate, this means I do a poor job."
   To counter this type of thought, remember: Feelings are NOT facts!

2. *Overgeneralization*
   Using a single piece of evidence or one isolated experience to draw an unwarranted generalized conclusion.
   A depressed man, turned down for a date, concludes "This means I'll never find a date."

3. *Illogical Thinking*
   Unwarranted connections between ideas that are unrelated.
   "If I'm offered a job, I'll have to accept it even if its not right for me."
   After three treatment sessions, a patient concludes, "If I haven't shown subjective improvement by now, I'll never get well."

4. *All or Nothing Thinking*
   Seeing things as black or white, never gray.
   Using terms like always, never, completely, totally, or perfectly.
   "Unless I do it perfectly, it's not worth doing at all."
   If your performance falls short of perfect, you see yourself as a total failure.

EXHIBIT 18.4
Coping Strategies Outline

1. For potentially stressful *situations*
   a. Plan ahead.
   b. Try to avoid the situation.

2. Within stress situations
   a. Try to relax and calm yourself.
   b. Try breaking task down into smaller parts.
   c. Tell yourself "I can manage this situation."

3. Ask internal questions
   a. Is this situation worth developing a stomach problem over?
   b. How responsible am I for this situation?
   c. If I am not responsible for it and if I cannot change it, can I just accept it?

4. Examine internal conversation (thoughts) for *catastrophic thoughts* and *logical fallacies.*

EXHIBIT 18.5
Problem Solving Outline

1. Define the stressor or stress reaction as a problem to be solved.
2. Set realistic goals as concretely as possible by stating the problem in behavioral terms and by delineating steps necessary to reach each goal.
3. Generate a wide range of possible alternative courses of action.
4. Imagine and consider how others might respond if asked to deal with a similar stress problem.
5. Evaluate the pros and cons of each proposed solution and rank order the solutions from the least to the most practical and desirable.
6. Rehearse strategies and behaviors by means of imagery, behavioral rehearsal, and graduated practice.
7. Try out the most acceptable and feasible solution.
8. Expect some failures but reward yourself for having tried.
9. Reconsider the original problem in light of the attempt at problem solving and in reference to hypothesized underlying basic beliefs.

19

HYPNOTHERAPY TREATMENT MANUAL FOR IRRITABLE BOWEL SYNDROME

As was summarized in Chapter 15, hypnotherapy has been used for quite some time in the U.K. as a treatment for IBS, especially by Dr. Peter Whorwell. In fact, according to Whorwell, hypnotherapy for IBS is recognized and thus reimbursable by the U.K. National Health Insurance. Whorwell was kind enough to send us detailed descriptions of his hypnotherapy treatment procedures and these are included in this chapter.

Using these protocols, we recently completed and published a replication of the use of hypnotherapy with IBS (Galovski & Blanchard, 1999) using 12 IBS patients in 6 matched pairs, multiple baseline across-subjects experiments. As was noted in that paper, treatment was superior to symptom monitoring in a comparison of Composite Primary Symptom Reduction (CPSR) scores (hypnotherapy: 55; symptom monitoring: −32, $t(9) = 2.95$, $p = .016$). After the symptom monitoring controls were treated, bringing the total treated to 11, 6 (55%) were improved, 2 (18%) were somewhat improved, and 3 (27%) were unimproved.

Our success rate was not as good as has been reported by Whorwell, but was on a par with another replication conducted in the U.K. by Harvey et al. (1989). Thus, we believe hypnotherapy, as described here, is a highly viable treatment for IBS among an American population.

Clinical Hint

We should also note that degree of initial hypnotic susceptibility as measured by Scale A of the Stanford Hypnotic Susceptibility Scale (SHSS) (Weitzenhoffer & Hilgard, 1959) did not correlate with outcome. Initial pretreatment SHSS scores ranged from 2 (very low susceptibility) to 12 (very high susceptibility). Thus, we believe that this treatment can be offered to any IBS client who is willing to give it a try. There will probably be some clients who are so suspicious of hypnosis that they will refuse treatment. For them, one of the other cognitive or cognitive–behavioral treatments could be an alternative.

Clinical Hint

We believe that some background and experience in the clinical use of hypnosis is needed by the therapist who wishes to use the treatments in this chapter. This is similar to our belief that the therapist who wishes to use cognitive therapy with IBS should have a background in, and some experience with, cognitive therapy before applying it to IBS clients.

These treatment manuals are not designed to train a therapist in hypnotherapy nor is the manual in Chapter 18 designed to train one in cognitive therapy. A reasonable level of clinical experience and training in the basic modality are assumed.

INTRODUCTORY MATERIAL

Some clients will be worried about hypnosis and about losing control to the therapist. Reassure the client that he or she will *always* be in control of all that he or she does and that much of hypnosis is suggestion and focusing of attention.

Treatment Rationale

Possible script:

> IBS is a disorder of colonic motility. The smooth musculature of the gut, primarily the colon or large bowel, normally works in smooth, rhythmic fashion to move material through it. With IBS, this smooth rhythmic motion is disrupted.
>
> Ordinarily one does not have voluntary control of the musculature of the gut; it is involuntary but it is responsive to thoughts and to stress. With training, one can bring back the smooth rhythmic motion and thus decrease pain and bloating, and normalize bowel habit.

Home Practice

Tell the client that he or she will have to practice the calming and relaxing exercises at home each day between visits. This is very important and treatment may not help without the regular home practice.

Outline Treatment Regimen

Possible script:

> In the first two sessions you will learn to become relaxed and calm as a result of the hypnosis and also begin to learn to focus attention. After those sessions and the home practice, I would expect you to be able to become relaxed and enter the hypnotic state fairly readily.
>
> The next 10 sessions will focus on calming and controlling gut or colonic motility. There will continue to be regular homework practice between visits. Just like it can take a while to learn to relax and to enter the hypnotic state quickly, so it will take a while and a lot of home practice to calm and gain control of gut motility. Thus, we expect gradual progress over time, not a sudden change like a medicine might bring.

The therapist should then try to answer any remaining questions.

Guided Imagery

Before starting the hypnotic induction, tell the client you will want him or her to engage in an imagery exercise (called guided imagery) while he or she is relaxed. Review the alternatives from Exhibit 19.1 with the client and pick the one he or she prefers and finds most pleasant and relaxing.

Closing Comments

As best as we can determine, 12 weekly sessions is the standard length of treatment for hypnotherapy for IBS. Obviously, there will be some clients who have not responded after 12 sessions. My advice is to stop at that point unless the client has recently seemed to be improving somewhat, as

EXHIBIT 19.1
Scenes for Guided Imagery

I	*Garden Scene*—Flowers, pond, birds, grass, smells, sun on face
II	*Beach Scene*—Salt, sun, wind, sand, warmth
III	*Waterfall*—Water lilies, frogs, sun sparkling, rushing water, cool, wet
IV	*Mountain Scene*—Tall, breathtaking, cool air, sparkling brook, eagle soaring

indicated by the GI symptom diary (not the client global report). In this case, I would suggest contracting for up to four more weekly visits with a strong emphasis on continued regular home practice. There is no good empirical guidance on this point.

Likewise, some clients may be noticeably improved (again as shown by the GI symptom diary) by 8 sessions; in this case I would suggest stopping the weekly sessions and having the client go for two weeks before returning, and then 4 weeks before returning. If improvement is maintained (as it usually is), so much the better.

In any event, we would suggest a follow-up, booster visit, 1 to 2 months after the last session to reinforce practice and to encourage the client as well as to wean him or her away from therapy.

Treatment Sessions 1 and 2

The primary foci of these two sessions are:

1. A lengthy hypnotic induction
2. Providing the client with a thorough sense of relaxation
3. Introduction of guided imagery
4. Introduction of the ego-strengthening material

The sessions are designed to familiarize the client with the experience of hypnosis while beginning some gut-directed focus. A primary induction is relaxation-based and is found below. It carries the client all the way through, including suggestions at the end for home practice of relaxation and autohypnosis and a final reorientation (awakening) script.

An alternative induction is included if there are difficulties with the relaxation induction. It begins on page 289 and involves eye closure, achieved in one of two ways.

BASIC INDUCTION SCRIPT (RELAXATION METHOD)

[Script 1]

[Subject's hands resting on lap]

Just choose a spot on the back of your right hand to look at . . . and just look at the back of your hand . . . and make yourself very, very aware of that right hand. . . . Try and concentrate on that right hand to the exclusion of everything else going on around you. . . .

Concentrate hard on feeling everything going on in that right hand . . . the muscular movements, changes in sensation. . . .

Make that hand very sensitive so that it can pick up anything going on around . . . differences in temperature at the back of your hand being different to the palm of your hand with heat coming through from your leg . . . you can become very, very aware of the quality of your [skirt/trousers] . . . feeling every fiber in the [skirt/trousers] . . . just make that hand extremely sensitive. . . .

And as you become more and more aware of that hand, you can become less and less aware of everything else going on around you . . . and then inducing that hand to a state of weightlessness . . . think about it wanting to float off your lap, getting lighter and lighter . . . and lighter, lighter and lighter . . . and you become more and more aware of just that hand . . . and nothing else at all. . . .

[Repeat until client's hand lifts.]

And in a moment or two I am going to count up to 3 . . . and when I get to 3 that hand will become really heavy again and flop back onto your lap . . . your eyes will close and you are going to go into a restful state of relaxation. . . .

One, two, three

So just let your hand drop back onto your lap . . . close your eyes and drift off into a restful state of deep, deep relaxation . . . the deeper you go the nicer you feel and the nicer you feel, the deeper you go . . . just feel comfortable and relaxed. . . . I'm just going to go through all the muscles of your body to make these relax a little bit more as well. . . .

Just think of all your feet muscles relaxing . . . all the muscles in your feet relaxing . . . and your calf muscles becoming all calm . . . and relaxed . . . and neutral . . . your thigh muscles calm and relaxed and calm . . . no tension in any of your muscles at all, so your legs feel comfortable, heavy and relaxed. . . .

Then your arms . . . think of your hands becoming relaxed and heavy on your lap . . . your forearms all calm and relaxed . . . your upper arms comfortable and relaxed . . . so your arms feel relaxed and heavy on your lap . . . and you can just go deeper and deeper into this comfortable state. . . .

Shoulder muscles . . . chest muscles . . . tummy muscles . . . back muscles . . . all calm and relaxed . . . all the muscles in your body are relaxed . . . your neck muscles comfortable and relaxed . . . no tension anywhere . . . and lastly your facial muscles relaxing . . . so you have a lovely serene expression on your face as all the muscles in your body relax . . . so think about every single muscle in your body relaxing . . . a beautiful state of relaxation . . . not a trace of tension left anywhere in your body . . . Every single muscle in a calm state of balance and neutrality. . . .

Just sit there in a comfortable state of deep . . . deep . . . deep relaxation . . . and the deeper you go the nicer you feel . . . and the nicer you feel the deeper you go . . . deeper . . . deeper and deeper. . . . You feel really . . . really relaxed, and the more relaxed your body becomes the calmer your mind becomes . . . so think about your mind being calm . . . calm and relaxed . . . tranquil . . . and calm and peaceful. . . . A state of peace of mind. . . . A state of harmony between body and mind . . . Just go deeper . . . deeper and deeper into this comfortable state of relaxation. . . . Deeper, deeper and deeper. . . . You can feel really nice . . . really calm and really peaceful. . . .

[Visual imagery/experiencing peaceful scene]

Now think of a peaceful scene. . . . Think of a peaceful scene which makes you feel wonderful. . . . Make it as realistic as you can. . . . Just as relaxed as you can. . . . As rewarding as you can. . . . Feel wonderful . . . and make that scene as realistic as you can . . . just feeling wonderful . . . blissfully content, calm and happy. . . . Just sit there relaxing deeper . . . deeper and deeper into this comfortable state where you feel so confident . . . so strong . . . so in control. . . .

Your mind is strong . . . your body is healthy and relaxed . . . and you feel beautiful because you are so in control. . . . Enjoy feeling like this . . . it does you good to feel like this . . . so let it do you the world of good . . . and let yourself go deeper . . . deeper and deeper into this state where you can cope with anything . . . where you can overcome anything . . . and nothing is beyond your ability to control. . . .

You can cope with anything . . . you control anything . . . you can deal with anything. . . .

You feel strong . . . and in control . . . and you feel wonderful. . . .

Your whole being is in a calm state of harmony . . . your whole being is very healthy and invigorating. . . . Everything is working perfectly. . . .

Your body is really healthy . . . your mind is strong . . . and you can cope with anything. . . . You can control anything . . . and you are strong. . . .

So there, with every system in your body working normally and your body feeling revitalized . . . invigorated . . . rejuvenated . . . refreshed . . . feeling wonderful . . . not a care in the world. . . . Blissfully relaxed . . . blissfully relaxed and at peace. . . . A lovely state of peace in your mind . . . and calm in your body. . . .

Feel peaceful . . . calm and tranquil . . . and just go deeper . . . deeper and deeper. and feel wonderful . . . with not a care in the world. . . .

[EGO STRENGTHENING—Script 1]

Because you are relaxing so well . . . when this session is over you will keep as much as you need of this feeling of calmness and relaxation that you have now . . . and this inner feeling of calmness and relaxation will remain with you. . . . You can call on it at any time. . . . It's there for you at any time in the future. . . . Whenever you are troubled . . . by situations or events . . . or by people . . . you will be able to deal with them in so calm a way as you choose . . . drawing on the experience you have achieved today. . . . And as each day goes by . . . you will feel yourself becoming more and more mentally calm . . . your mind will become crystal clear . . . and calm . . . like a clear, beautiful lake that reflects the sky without a ripple. . . . So calm and more and more at ease. . . . And it can feel so good . . . as if nothing matters . . . nothing at all. It's so nice to be alive to have peace of mind . . . to be calm and relaxed. Floating so peacefully . . . so at ease, so calm. . . . Your mind becoming more and more open . . . just so at ease . . . feeling so good. . . .

And you can feel this way whenever you wish, by taking a few long, slow deep breaths . . . and as you breathe out each deep breath, slowly all the way out, saying to yourself silently, in your mind, the word "CALM" . . . "CALM". . . .

[Synchronize these words with client breathing out.]

Starting now, in any situation . . . . whenever you feel tense . . . any bother . . . you can take these few deep breaths, and as you breathe slowly all the way out, you can say to yourself "CALM" . . . and hear it in the back of your mind. . . . And you will feel calm and relaxation calm washing over you, like water in a hot bath or shower. . . . You can feel so calm, so relaxed . . . in every aspect of your life . . . every day . . . all the time . . . no matter what you're doing . . . no matter who's with you . . . no matter where you are. . . . And the more you practice using this way to feel calm and relaxed, the stronger that feeling of calm and relaxation will become each time you use it. . . .

And as the days go by and you feel yourself becoming more and more relaxed . . . more and more mentally calm . . . you will also feel yourself becoming more and more confident. You will be more confident in yourself . . . more confident about whatever you're doing . . . more confident in your ability to do . . . not only what it is you have to do each day, but more and more confident in your ability to do the things you want to be able to do . . . and you'll be more confident in your ability to cope with things and people . . . but above all . . . more confident and more optimistic about the future. . . . Yes, you'll be able to handle any situation . . . cope with anyone . . . no matter how difficult or trying things may seem, drawing on the inner strengths and resources and abilities that you have within you . . . inner strengths and resource and abilities that you have, that perhaps you didn't know that you have. . . . For you have, deep within you . . . that part we call the unconscious mind . . . all the strengths and resources, all the power that you need to cope with anyone, to handle anything that happens. . . .

The key to your success is confidence . . . confidence in yourself . . . confidence in your ability to do . . . whatever you truly want to do . . . confidence that you can and will accomplish your goals through the power of your mind . . . the power of your thoughts. . . .

And what you tell yourself has the greatest of power over your life. . . . What you tell yourself determines whether you feel cheerful, or gloomy and worried . . . and the way you feel, whether you feel full of joy, or sad and worried, determines, to a great extent, the health and well-being of your physical body, When you are bothered and unhappy, your body simply cannot function properly. What you tell yourself has an enormous impact on your life . . . What you tell yourself ultimately determines what you are and are not able to do.

And so . . . now you can tell yourself that your life is just starting, and that from this day on you are beginning to live fully . . . moment by moment . . . and you can really appreciate and enjoy being alive each moment. . . . You will no longer worry unnecessarily . . . either about things that happened in the past . . . or about what might happen in the future, unless there is something constructive that you can do to change them . . . because the past and the future exist only in our thoughts . . . life exists only in each moment. If you spend your moments worrying about the past or the future . . . these moments, which are your life . . . pass you by. So, with each day that passes, you become more and more deeply involved in everything that is happening around you . . . less conscious of yourself . . . and more at peace with yourself . . . and with the world. . . . Tell yourself that with each passing day . . . you will feel happier . . . more content . . . more joyous . . . more cheerful . . . because you choose to feel this way by controlling your thinking. . . . And because you feel this way . . . life will be more fun . . . you will enjoy each day . . . and you will become more and more healthy . . . as your body functions easily . . . free of tension. . . .

Starting now . . . you can start a new life. . . . Ready to live in a new way . . . to enjoy everything around you . . . to be aware of all the beauty of the world, the beauty and goodness of being alive . . . more and more . . . enjoying life more and more. . . . Starting now . . . you'll be able to flow comfortably and easily with everything around you so much better . . . more and more all the time . . . just flowing comfortably . . . experiencing . . . not hung up . . . not bothered . . . just enjoying a calm . . . relaxed mind . . . able to face life with its problems in a relaxed way. . . . Flowing comfortably with the problems. . . . Any worries will seem less significant . . . At times, things and people may still annoy and upset you . . . that's only natural . . . and it's OK to experience these different emotions . . . and to express them if you choose to and need to, in a way that is useful and appropriate . . . but nothing and no one will worry you to the same extent . . . nothing and no one will upset you to the same extent. . . .

And as you continue to relax . . . you can allow your inner mind to work for you. . . . And as the days go by, you will find yourself becoming more and more physically relaxed . . . more and more mentally calm . . . more and more confident . . . and you will find yourself increasingly able to achieve what it is you want. . . . Your unconscious mind will provide you with all the inner resources, inner strengths, the power that you need to achieve what it is you want. . . .

[Specific instructions for IBS clients]

And one of the things you want is to bring your gut under control . . . to be in control of your body. not your body in control of you. . . . Now, there are several things you know about that problem with your gut which you do not know that you know . . . One is that you already know very well how to solve the problem . . . your unconscious mind knows how to eliminate that problem. . . . Your unconscious mind knows all about you . . . and it controls so much of your body. . . . You know that it can alter heart rate when you are relaxed or anxious . . . and your breathing . . . and it controls your digestion . . . and so much more. . . . And so, your unconscious mind knows how to eliminate the problem you are having. . . . You know this . . . because the problem has occurred so many times . . . and yet, those unpleasant sensations which you have experienced have, at times . . . discontinued . . . they have gone away . . . maybe for only a few seconds at a time . . . maybe for longer. . . . Your mind and body know exactly how to create that problem . . . and they also know how to eliminate that problem. . . .

So as you are sitting there, allowing yourself to drift deeper and deeper into relaxation . . . with each breath you are taking . . . and listening to what I say . . . you know, with each word that I speak, that you are relaxing well at this moment . . . and because you know you are relaxing well at this moment . . . deep,

deep down inside of you . . . deep, deep down inside your unconscious mind that knows all about you . . . you know that you are achieving what it is you want. . .

And as you're continuing to relax . . . you know you are learning to listen to your body and what it is saying to you . . . and you are also learning to listen to, to trust . . . and to use all that your unconscious mind can provide. . . . All you have to do is ask your unconscious mind for what it is you want . . . and relax. . . . No need to know how these things will happen . . . no need to worry how these things will happen . . . your unconscious mind will provide the means . . . the ways . . . the opportunities. . . .

And you're beginning a process . . . which may take days, weeks or maybe months . . . and I don't know just when you'll turn around sometime in the future, and look back at this time . . . and see just how far you've come, how much has changed . . . .

And so, day by day . . . as you continue to relax . . . and you are more and more mentally calm . . . you feel less tense . . . less nervous . . . less worried . . . less anxious. And as a consequence, you are starting to feel much more energetic. . . . For a lot of energy is tied up in a useless way in stress and tension . . . and as you are relaxed . . . and calm and at ease . . . and you are at peace with the universe . . . you will have much more energy, and you will be able to do many more things that you want to do and you will be able to see any problems in a different light. . . . For most of our problems are really challenges . . . opportunities to learn . . . to change . . . to adjust . . . to develop . . . to grow. . . . And any mistakes we may make are opportunities to learn . . . to change . . . to adjust . . . to develop . . . to grow. . . . So, any problems you will be able to handle them easily . . . efficiently . . . effectively . . . and confidently . . . without becoming bothered or tired out . . . for you have all you need within you to deal with anything, to handle any situation and so you are also finding that you are sleeping better . . . sleeping for a normal length of time . . . and waking up refreshed . . . ready to face the challenges of the coming day. . . .

And so . . . as you are becoming more and more physically relaxed . . . and more and more mentally calm . . . you can receive what you most need right now . . . your deep inner mind, that part we call the unconscious mind, knows all about you, how to solve your problems and what you most need your unconscious mind knows all about you and everything that has ever happened to you . . . and it knows how to solve your problems . . . resolve any conflict even without your being consciously aware of this happening. . . .

Now your inner mind can continue working all by itself to solve your problems in a way that fully meets all of your needs, answering your needs in a way that is more useful for you than at present . . . [pause]. . . . You have memories, life experiences, and abilities that your inner mind can use in many ways that you may not have realized before . . . [pause]. . . . And you can allow your inner mind to scan through your abilities . . . and with time you'll become aware of a very deep sense . . . of just who you are and what you are capable of doing. . . .

And you already know how to use the power of your unconscious mind . . . without even realizing it. . . . I'm sure, like many of us, you have wrestled with a problem . . . no matter what that might be . . . trying to find the answer, the solution . . . and yet, however hard you try, you just can't solve it. . . . And finally, you put the problem to one side . . . you put it out of your conscious mind . . . and turn your mind to other things, other thoughts, and get on with something else. . . . And a little later . . . or the next morning, the next day perhaps . . . the answer to that problem pops into your mind . . . seemingly from nowhere . . . from deep down inside. . . . And you have the answer because your unconscious mind has continued working on your problem, without you consciously being aware of it . . . and in a quiet moment, the answer has been able to come into your conscious mind. . . . And so you already know very well how to use the power of your unconscious mind. . . .

[SUGGESTIONS FOR SELF-HYPNOSIS & RELAXATION—to use at end of relaxation]

Each day I want you to practice this relaxation technique: all you need to do is find a comfortable time and place, then when you are ready, you can close your eyes, take a deep breath in, and as you breathe out RELAX. Then I would like you to repeat to yourself, not out loud, the sound of "CALM" with each breath that you are taking, don't bother to give it any meaning, just repeat it like the sound of a distant bell. And as you repeat the sound of "CALM" with each breath you are taking, your mind and body will quickly begin to feel calm, just as calm as it is now, so calm that your body will feel as if it's no longer a part of you. And because this is such a pleasant, comfortable feeling, you can allow yourself to go further into relaxation, any thoughts that come into your head, just let them go, and bring back the sound of "CALM," and as you allow yourself to sink into the feeling of calm, let this feeling of calm wash over you, let yourself become aware of the vastness of calm. There are no boundaries, no frontiers. Calm goes on . . . and on . . . and on . . . as you allow yourself to drift deeper and deeper into relaxation, listening to the silence that whispers calm . . . calm . . . calm. . . .

In a few moments' time, I shall stop speaking, and you can either remain in this lovely state of relaxation, or you can just count up to 5 in your mind and open your eyes. When you are ready to open your eyes, they will automatically open, you will feel calm and relaxed and refreshed. All heaviness will leave your muscles and they will feel better for the rest. You will feel invigorated and healthy, and have an inner feeling of confidence. And the next time we work like this, you can enter this state of relaxation quickly and easily. When I stop speaking, you decide when you open your eyes—it's your decision—do whatever you like, you are in control.

[REORIENTATION—use if client is resistant to previous reorientation.]

In a moment or two I am going to count to 5 and ask you to wake up . . . and when you do wake up, you will feel calm and refreshed and invigorated . . . calm and content and happy . . . in control of everything . . . and very, very relaxed . . . you are going to feel very relaxed.

So on the count of 5 . . . wide awake, refreshed, and in control . . . feeling wonderful

One . . . two . . . three . . . four . . . five. . . .

[EYE FIXATION AND CLOSURE—Script 2]

I'd like you to pick a spot on the ceiling, any spot will do . . . and keep on staring at it. . . . Let your eyes rise up to that spot but keeping your head straight, not tilted back. . . . And just concentrate all your attention on that spot . . . if your eyes wander, then just bring your eyes back again . . . focusing all your attention on that spot . . . and as you keep concentrating on that spot . . . your eyes will begin to feel . . . more and more tired . . . as you continue to look at that spot . . . heavier and heavier . . . until you just want to let your eyes close . . . gently . . . to feel more comfortable . . . and when they feel heavy . . . becoming really, really heavier . . . heavier and heavier . . . then you can let them close.

[Repeat as necessary]

[PROGRESSIVE RELAXATION]

As you rest in the chair . . . you can begin to allow relaxation and comfort to flow through you, however that feels to you. . . .

Starting from your eyelids . . . allowing relaxation to flow up over your forehead . . . over the top of your head . . . spreading through all of your scalp . . . and down the back of your head, into the muscles at the back of the neck . . . all those muscles just beginning to relax in their own way . . . as you allow comfort and relaxation to flow through . . . and down now . . . down from your eyelids, down through your face . . . relaxation trickling down, rather like rain on a window pane . . . relaxation flowing down through your cheeks . . . your jaw . . . so you're not clenching your teeth together . . . and into the muscles at the front of the neck . . . all of the muscles in your head . . . your face . . . and neck . . . just beginning to relax. . . . And it may be that your head feels a little heavier . . . and, if you wish, you can allow it to move into its most comfortable position . . . to one side or the other . . . or to be supported even more by the back of the chair. . . .

And you can allow that same feeling of relaxation and comfort to begin to spread . . . and flow out across your shoulders . . . and down into your arms . . . following its path in your mind's eye . . . flowing all the way down . . . down through all the muscles at the top of your arms . . . across your elbows . . . down through your lower arms . . . into your hands . . . even into your fingers . . . right to the tips of your fingers . . . all the muscles in your arms beginning to relax, beginning to let go of any tension . . . that relaxation and feeling of comfort flowing all the way down . . . all of the muscles beginning to feel looser . . . more comfortable. . . .

And you can allow that relaxed feeling and comfort . . . to flow down through your body . . . down from the back of your neck . . . through all the muscles in your back . . . flowing all the way down, like a stream, through those muscles either side of the spine . . . all the way down to the base of the back . . . and as those muscles begin to relax, then your body can sink a little more into the comfort of the chair. . . .

And going down from the front of the neck . . . allowing that relaxation to flow down through all the muscles in and around your chest . . . so that you're only using the muscles you need to use to breathe easily and comfortably . . . down through all the muscles around the waist . . . your tummy . . . your abdomen . . . all those muscles beginning to relax . . . to feel more comfortable, and you can gradually become aware of a deeper sense of comfort. . . .

And allowing that same relaxation to flow down now into your legs . . . flowing all the way down . . . down through your thighs . . . through the muscles at the front . . . at the back . . . and the sides of your thighs . . . flowing all the way through . . . all of those muscles gradually beginning to feel looser . . . more relaxed . . . down across your knees . . . into your calf muscles . . . flowing all the way down . . . into your feet . . . right to the ends of your toes . . . so that even the tiniest muscles are beginning to relax . . . letting go of any tension . . . and your feet can feel as though you've been wearing a pair of tight shoes and you've just taken them off . . . and your feet can spread out a little. . . .

And as you just rest . . . relaxing more and more with each breath you take . . . all of the muscles letting go of any tension . . . any remaining tension draining down and down . . . and out through the soles of your feet . . . feeling more and more comfortable . . . more and more relaxed . . . feeling safe and secure . . . more and more deeply relaxed . . . every muscle which you don't need to use right now relaxing . . . relaxing more and more . . . feeling so comfortable and relaxed . . . and calm. . . .

TREE METAPHOR

This is useful to include as an ego-strengthener, disguised as a deepener. When using visual imagery to deepen the hypnotic state, such as a garden, a forest, the countryside, even a tropical beach, the weather being pleasant, warm and sunny, and then one can introduce a tree as follows:

> And I'd like you to notice that there is a tall, strong tree. . . . Its branches are reaching up to the sky. . . . I'd like you to look at this tree . . . tall and strong, and notice the branches and how they reach up to the sky . . . growing up to the sky. . . . Then bring your eyes down onto the trunk. . . . Notice how wide and thick the trunk is . . . how strong it is . . . and the texture of the bark on the trunk . . . imagine how it might feel if you were to touch it with your fingertips. . . . Then let your eyes travel down to the bottom of the tree . . . and notice the roots running into the ground . . . and knowing that it is these

roots which provide the tree with all the nutrients and water that the tree needs . . . and how they firmly anchor that tree into the ground . . . holding it firm and steady . . . so that the rest of the tree can bend and sway in the winds and storms . . . for it is not always warm and sunny here. . . . And know that it is the winds and storms which have made this tree grow strong. . . . And this tree provides shade against the sun, and shelter from the wind and rain and storms, not only for birds and perhaps small animals, but also for human beings. . . .

And in many ways, we are like that tree . . . and when we are firmly rooted . . . rooted within ourselves, within the very essence of our own being . . . strong and steady . . . we can receive all that we need from deep within us . . . all the nourishment we need . . . and we are able to be flexible and to bend with the storms and struggles of life . . . and these storms and struggles are what make us grow strong . . . all our experiences are opportunities to learn . . . to change and to adjust . . . to develop . . . to GROW . . . to become all that we are capable of becoming . . . and any mistakes we may make are opportunities to learn . . . to change and adjust as necessary . . . to develop . . . to GROW. . . .

Just as an acorn has the potential to become a tall, strong oak tree . . . in the right soil, fed, and watered . . . then we have within us the seed of our own great potential . . . to become all that we are capable of becoming . . . to become our own true person . . . firmly grounded, firmly rooted within ourselves . . . deep within ourselves . . . and as we feed and nurture that seed . . . using all that we have within us . . . we grow . . . becoming all that we are capable of becoming. . . .

[Use reorienting script from end of first induction (page 289).]

Clinical Hint

A direct or authoritarian approach can challenge subjects who are not easily compliant and responsive to the clinician's requests, e.g., those who are very tense and anxious, or need to feel in control. It is, therefore, useful to build in indirect and permissive suggestions which focus the subject's attention and allow them to respond in their own way. The degree of indirection should be directly proportional to the degree of resistance encountered or anticipated.

[Permissive suggestions for eye closure—Script 2]

You can pick a spot, maybe on the ceiling, any spot will do . . . and keep on staring at it. If your eyes should wander, then you can just go back to the same spot. . . . Just keep on staring at it until you find your eyes becoming tired of it . . . and then when you're ready, you can let your eyes close. . . . But while you stare at that spot . . . just notice what you see and experience. . . . Some people experience a blurring of their vision . . . for others the spot moves . . . pulsates . . . or disappears. Some people see a halo or aura around the spot. . . . Others just experience heaviness in their eyelids. So, just notice what it is that you experience . . . noticing how that spot may change as you continue watching it . . . and just enjoy it . . . knowing that when you're ready, and your eyes become tired . . . when they begin to blink a little more . . . you can just close them when you're ready. . . .

[Carry on with rest of induction without waiting for eye closure.]

[To focus attention: making reference to sensory experiences.]

Just be aware of what sounds you can hear at the moment . . . then relax to any sounds you hear . . . don't worry, they won't disturb you.

And with your eyes gently closed . . . just notice what it is that you can see behind your eyelids . . . any light or patches of light and shade . . . any colors, perhaps . . . whatever it is that you can see behind your eyelids . . . and you know that there isn't anything that your eyes really have to do, and so you can allow them to rest. . . .

And be aware of how your body feels as it rests in the chair . . . how the chair feels beneath you and behind you . . . your arms as they rest . . .

[on the arms of the chair]

. . . how your hands feel as they rest on your lap . . . you may even be able to sense the texture of the material of your clothes beneath your fingertips . . . and noticing how your feet feel inside your shoes. . . .

[as they rest on the floor]

. . . and how your chest rises . . . and falls . . . as you breathe in . . . and out. . . .

[in time with respiration]

... and you can allow yourself to breathe just as slowly, just as deeply as you're comfortable with....

[MANTRA Example]

And each time that you breathe out, I'd like you to repeat the word "CALM" silently in your mind ... "CALM" ... "CALM"....

[in time with expiration]

repeating it as a sound ... like the sound of a distant bell ... not giving it any meaning ... and you can repeat the sound of "CALM" silent in your mind each time that you breathe out ... and gradually your whole mind and body are becoming more calm ... more comfortable.... And if you should find the sound of "CALM" fades from your mind, then you can gently bring it back and keep repeating it ... until the time comes when it begins to fade from your mind and you can't be bothered to bring it back ... then you can let it go ... putting yourself into a calm and comfortable state.

[FOCUSING ON THE BREATH]

And you can notice how cool the breath feels as you breathe in through your nose ... aware of the journey of the breath ... down ... down into your lungs ... [pause] ... and the parts of the body that expand and dilate as you breathe in....

[in time with inspiration]

and then becoming aware of the breath, warmer now, as you breathe out

[in time with expiration]

... and I will remain quiet for just a little while, while you continue to concentrate on your breath, as you breathe in and out, and as you do so, you can find yourself becoming more relaxed ... noticing the breath, cool as you breathe in ... warmer as you breathe out....

[in time with respiration]

[REASSURANCE ABOUT RELAXATION AND THE HYPNOTIC STATE—These can be inserted near the end of either induction before the reorienting. Use them based on your judgment of the client's skepticism.]

[I] And you may wonder how it feels to be relaxed . . . something you may not have known much in your busy life, perhaps . . . but just notice what sensations you experience, and how these may change and be different from before. . . . And I don't know just how you experience relaxation . . . some people tell me that they have a sense of heaviness in their limbs and others a sensation of lightness . . . and others still have a feeling a tiredness . . . so I don't know just how you experience relaxation . . . but you can just notice what sensations you experience. . . .

[II] There's nothing in particular that you really have to do right now . . . nothing in particular that you really need to expect . . . you're just allowing yourself this time to experience yourself a little differently . . . to be aware of yourself just a little differently . . . allowing yourself the opportunity to become familiar with yourself at a different level of your being . . . to feel more comfortable . . . in your own way . . . and there's nothing that you really have to try to do . . . as you listen to my voice . . . .

[III] And it may be that you have wondered how it feels to be relaxed . . . and to focus inwardly. . . . That is something that we all know how to do . . . and we probably do it many, many times a day without realizing it . . . Many of us can become so absorbed in a good film we are watching, becoming involved in the story, in the characters, that we seem to switch off from whatever is going on around us. . . . And I expect you have had the experience of having to listen to a talk by someone with a boring, monotonous voice . . . and you begin to daydream. . . . Or when you've had a conversation with someone who is so interesting that an hour seems to fly by in less than five minutes. . . . And have you ever driven the car, especially along a very familiar route, and found you have driven all that way and yet been thinking of something else and hardly been aware of driving there? . . . And most of us have experienced that curious in between state at bedtime or first thing in the morning when you're neither fully awake, not fully asleep . . . and you're wondering which state you would like to enter. . . .

[Reassurance regarding using the power of the unconscious mind]

Give examples of our everyday experiences, e.g., solving a problem, when we put it out of our mind, get on with something else, and then the answer pops into the mind later.

[Reassurance regarding ability to turn off pain]

And our minds have the greatest ability to turn off sensations . . . our minds turn off sensations all the time . . . without you even consciously knowing it, and you only notice those sensations again when you turn your attention to them. . . . Just like first thing in the morning, when you get dressed . . . you pull on your clothes . . . and you can feel your clothes touching your skin, and yet within a very short space of time, you are no longer aware of these sensations . . . your mind has turned them off. and you only notice your clothes touching your skin when you turn your attention to them again. . . .

And so you already know very well how to turn off sensations . . . your mind is very good at turning off sensations no matter what these sensations are. . . .

And so, using the power of your mind, you can turn off any sensation, including pain . . . using the power of your mind, you can remove any pain, you can remove any discomfort. . . .

GUT-DIRECTED THERAPY (FOR IBS)

Sessions 3+

At the beginning of each session inquire about home practice and ability to become calm and relaxed. If there are difficulties, try to troubleshoot with the client.

[WARMING TECHNIQUE]

In a few moments' time, I'm going to count up to 3 and ask you to place a hand on your tummy. . . . So ready . . . 1 . . . 2 . . . 3 . . . place a hand on your tummy. . . . I'd like you to concentrate on that hand on your tummy . . . be aware of how it feels . . . is it cooler on the back than on the palm? . . .

As your hand rests on your tummy . . . you will begin to feel a sense of warmth and comfort spreading around the muscles and tissues of this area . . . This feeling will become warmer . . . warmer . . . and warmer as you channel the energies of your mind into your tummy. . . . Yes, warmer . . . warmer . . . and . . . warmer . . . a soothing feeling in your gut. . . . Going right inside your tummy . . . right through to every nook and cranny of your tummy . . . every muscle and fiber of your bowel is becoming warm . . . soothed . . . and comfortable. Yes, warmer . . . and warmer . . . a soothing feeling in your gut. . . .

[Check if client can regenerate that feeling him- or herself; take hand off and put back and ask if he or she got it.]

And on a count of 3, I'd like you to put your other hand on top of the hand and your tummy . . . and reinforce that feeling. . . . So ready . . . 1 . . . 2 . . . 3 . . . hand on your tummy. Now make that feeling really strong . . . warmer . . . warmer . . . and warmer . . . a soothing feeling in your gut. Yes, warmer . . . and warmer . . . a special feeling you can identify with . . . going right inside your tummy . . . and with each breath that you take . . . and with each word that I speak, this feeling of warmth and comfort will steadily increase. . . . Yes, warmer . . . and warmer . . . a comforting glow . . . soothing your gut. . . .

Yes, this feeling is a healing glow, indicating that your unconscious mind is directing all the inner resources of your own mind . . . and your own body to the areas where the need is the greatest. . . . You know how your feelings and thoughts affect the muscles of your gut . . . we have discussed this previously . . . and so it follows that you . . . [say client's name] . . . can control your own gut muscles . . . you can remove pain . . . remove bloating . . . remove discomfort . . . and make your bowel habit normal to your own satisfaction. . . .

Yes, all this is happening to you as a result of your relaxing so well at this moment . . . a result of the treatments you have had . . . but most of all as a result of your own efforts, your own determination to get your gut under control. . . . So feel the strength of your mind . . . feel the determination growing stronger and stronger . . . Feel you're going to win.

You will find you can continue to control the muscles of your gut by placing your hands in this same position whenever you feel the need. . . . If at any time you place your hands in this position . . . you will feel the same sense of warmth and comfort. . . . This will be a signal to your unconscious mind for you to take control of the muscles of your gut. . . . To remove pain . . . remove bloating . . . remove discomfort . . . and make your bowel habit normal to your own satisfaction.

[Can use river analogy as well, if diarrhea is involved . . .]

Now I would like you to picture a river in your mind . . . flowing through beautiful countryside. . . . Picture the clean, clear water . . . and the steady . . . calm . . . peaceful . . . tranquil . . . rhythmic . . . orderly . . . flow of the water. No rushing . . . no hurry . . . no delays . . . no hold ups . . . just a steady . . . calm . . . peaceful . . . rhythmic . . . tranquil . . . orderly flow of the water. . . .

Now I would like you to picture your gut in the same way . . . just like the river. . . .

[can also use river analogy again]

> . . . a steady . . . rhythmic . . . calm . . . peaceful . . . tranquil . . . orderly . . . normal . . . movement through your bowel. . . . No rushing . . . no hurry . . . no delays . . . no hold ups . . . just a steady . . . calm . . . rhythmic . . . peaceful . . . orderly . . . normal movement through your gut.
>
> As you sink deeper and deeper into this image . . . feel the strength of your mind . . . because the stronger your mind becomes the more and more control you will acquire . . . and consequently your tummy will feel better . . . and better . . . and better. . . . No pain . . . no bloating . . . no discomfort . . . and a normal regular bowel habit. Soon you will hardly be aware that you have a tummy . . . it's working so well . . . so normally . . . You can achieve this . . . you can and you will. . . . So feel you're going to win . . . feel a sense of control . . . feel the strength of your mind. . . .

[Elaborate on this]

> Let me draw your attention once more to the hands on your stomach . . .
>
> . . . Feel another surge of warmth and comfort beneath your hands . . . and think of that healing glow . . . indicating that you are in control of your gut . . . rather than your gut . . . you are in control. . . .

Clinical Hint

At times the flowing river analogy will not seem to be working or the client may seem "stuck." You can learn this by your brief beginning of session inquiry and checking the symptom diary. If this seems to be the case, try this alternative for one or two sessions. It is directed more at the client's taking control of gut function.

SUGGESTIONS FOR SELF-HYPNOSIS & RELAXATION

[To use at end of relaxation]

> Each day, I want you to practice this relaxation technique—all you need to do is find a comfortable time and place, then when you are ready, you can close your eyes, take a deep breath in, and as you breathe out—RELAX. Then I would like you to repeat to yourself, not out loud, the sound of "CALM" with each breath that you are taking, don't bother to give it any

meaning, just repeat it like the sound of a distant bell. And as you repeat the sound of "CALM" with each breath you are taking, your mind and body will quickly begin to feel calm, just as calm as it is now, so calm that your body will feel as if it's no longer a part of you. And because this is such a pleasant, comfortable feeling, you can allow yourself to go further into relaxation; any thoughts that come into your head, just let them go, and bring back the sound of "CALM," and as you allow yourself to sink into the feeling of calm, let this feeling of calm wash over you, let yourself become aware of the vastness of calm. There are no boundaries, no frontiers. Calm goes on . . . and on . . . and on . . . as you allow yourself to drift deeper and deeper into relaxation, listening to the silence that whispers calm . . . calm . . . calm. . . .

In a few moments' time, I shall stop speaking, and you can either remain in this lovely state of relaxation, or you can just count up to 5 in your mind and open your eyes. When you are ready to open your eyes, they will automatically open, you will feel calm and relaxed and refreshed. All heaviness will leave your muscles and they will feel better for the rest. You will feel invigorated and healthy, and have an inner feeling of confidence. And next time we work like this, you can enter this state of relaxation quickly and easily When I stop speaking, you decide when you open your eyes it's your decision do whatever you like, you are in control.

GUT-DIRECTED THERAPY (2) Alternative

[Use after Script 2—Eye Fixation and Relaxation Induction]

That's good . . . as you drift deeper and deeper into relaxation, just allow a sense of calmness and tranquility to come over you . . . but at the same time a strengthening of your mind, as you become more able to channel the energy of your mind into whatever you want to, and gaining the ability to control your body to your own satisfaction.

Feel calm . . . feel tranquil . . . feel strong and in control. . . . This is a lovely, secure, comfortable state to be in. Your mind is feeling a sense of calm, your body is feeling a pleasant sense of well-being. In this state, you will find good health and a greater sense of personal well-being.

In a few moments' time, I would like to help you relax even more. Yes, I'd like to help you to relax as deeply as you can relax today, as deeply as you would like to relax today. In a few moments' time, I shall count backwards from ten to zero . . . and as I count backwards from ten to zero, you can allow yourself to drift even deeper into the most relaxed state you wish to experience this session. So, ready. . . .

10 . . . 9 . . . 8 . . . 7 . . . 6 . . . 5 . . . 4 . . . 3 . . . 2 . . . 1 . . . zero.

That's good . . . you are entering the deepest, most relaxed state you wish to experience this session . . . just allowing yourself to enjoy this comfortable, calm, relaxed state you have allowed yourself to enter. . . . Just enjoy it . . . this is your time . . . with each breath that you're taking, with each word that I'm saying, you can feel utterly relaxed and comfortable, just drifting deeper and deeper into relaxation. . . . You are breathing freely, easily, naturally. Your mind is becoming really, really calm . . . really, really tranquil . . . but at the same time, more and more strong, more and more in control, more and more able to control your body. . . .

Now in a few moments' time, I'm going to count up to 3 and ask you to place a hand on your abdomen, and as you place a hand on your tummy, feel a sense of comfort and well-being in your abdomen.

So ready . . . 1 . . . 2 . . . 3 . . . place a hand on your tummy. As your hand rests on your abdomen, feel the warmth . . . the comfort of the palm of your hand on your tummy . . . and now feel a sense of comfort and well-being spreading around to muscles and tissues in this area as you channel the energy of your mind into your abdomen. It is the energy which is putting things to right . . . which is balancing everything in your abdomen . . . energy which is removing spasm and removing any abnormal contractions.

You know, it's the spasm that causes all the problems . . . it causes pain, it causes bloating, it causes problems in your bowel movements. But with the power of your mind, and as you practice, you can begin to prevent the spasm. So feel a sense of well-being in your abdomen, think of the power of your mind reducing spasm and so relieving pain . . . relieving bloating . . . reducing any discomfort . . . and normalizing your bowel habit.

Concentrate now on feeling the energy of your mind gradually channeling into your tummy . . . making it feel warm, making it feel comfortable, making it feel better. Feel a sense of CONTROL.

And on a count of 3, place your other hand on top of the

hand already on your tummy, to reinforce that feeling and make it stronger. . . .

So ready . . . 1 . . . 2 . . . 3 . . . hand on your tummy. Now reinforce that lovely, comfortable, soothing feeling in your abdomen, feel a sense of well-being in your abdomen, putting your abdomen under your control . . . to take away spasm, to take away pain, to take away bloating, and returning your bowel habit to normal, returning everything to normal, achieving a state of balance in your abdomen, making all the systems, in your abdomen work normally. Think of your guts and all the systems inside working absolutely normally, so that you are no longer controlled by your gut. You are able to control your gut, rather than your gut controlling you.

BE DETERMINED to overcome your gut and your bowel problems. You can and you will do it . . . it will take time, but you can achieve it. Not all at once, but with practice over the days . . . over the weeks . . . over the months. . . . You'll get better and better at controlling your gut. With determination, you can get rid of your stomach problem completely, but you have to practice. You have to be determined. With practice and determination, you can make your mind so strong that it can overcome anything.

You'll gradually become more confident in the strength of your mind and your ability to overcome your gut problem, and you will also find that you have more confidence in yourself.

You'll have the confidence to apply your mind to your gut problem, to overcome your abdominal trouble and feel good again . . . back in control of your life again, feeling invigorated, feeling mentally calm, physically relaxed, more and more confident.

So relax there, feeling confident in your mind, confident in yourself . . . with a lovely feeling of well-being in your abdomen . . . and as you gradually get your gut under control and restore normality to your abdomen, so you can achieve a state of balance and well-being . . . to take away pain, to take away bloating, to take away discomfort. . . . You, yes you, can take away spasm and return your gut to normal. To achieve this, you need to be quiet, you need to be determined . . . you need to practice.

But, with practice and determination, you'll be able to achieve whatever you want to achieve. The more you practice, the more your mind will be able to overcome your abdominal problems. The more you practice, the more your feeling of well-being will increase, your strength of mind will increase, your confidence in yourself will increase.

Yes, the more you practice, the greater your ability to overcome your problem. So, feel full of confidence, feel full of optimism about the future.

You'll feel a greater sense of health and well-being in your body, because your body will benefit from regular deep relaxation . . . your mind will become stronger and stronger. . . . You'll feel better and better in all sorts of ways, and you'll find you are able to apply your mind to all sorts of problems more and more easily. So feel confident . . . feel determined . . . feel strong. And the more you practice, the more you'll want to practice . . . and as you do, you'll feel better and better . . . healthier and healthier.

Yes, as you practice, you'll find you gradually achieve a greater and greater depth of relaxation . . . wanting to go deeper because the feeling is so pleasant, so comfortable, so secure, so relaxed there now . . . allowing yourself to go deeper, wanting to go deeper . . . feeling well, feeling a lovely sense of well-being in your tummy, and a sense of peace and tranquility in your mind. So, now your mind feels calm and tranquil . . . your tummy feels soothed and comfortable . . . your body feels well and healthy.

Just enjoy this feeling . . . allow it to happen, wanting to relax more and more . . . and the more you do so, the more you will achieve, the more control you will acquire. Feel in control . . . feel confident . . . feel at peace with yourself . . . and with the world. Just relax there now with a lovely feeling of control in your tummy and a lovely feeling of peace in your mind.

Your body, calm, relaxed, and healthy. . . . Your mind at peace, calm, and tranquil . . . yet very much in control, getting stronger . . . stronger and stronger. Feel your mind growing stronger . . . more and more confident . . . more and more in control . . . overcoming your abdominal problem. Yes, with practice and determination you will overcome your gut problem . . . no more pain, no more bloating, no more discomfort, no more trouble with your bowel. You are no longer ruled by your gut. You are in control . . . you can apply yourself to anything because with practice, your mind will become so strong, so confident, that you can overcome anything you want to . . .

[Do alerting exercise and then remind of home practice.]

20

PREDICTION OF TREATMENT RESPONSE AMONG PATIENTS WITH IRRITABLE BOWEL SYNDROME

The preceding five chapters have all dealt with psychological treatment of IBS, demonstrating the relative efficacy of the various treatment regimens. For all of these treatments, with only one exception, there has always been a range of response to treatment from patients who seem symptom free by the end of treatment to patients who are unchanged or, even worse, more symptomatic. Only the initial report by Whorwell et al. (1984) on hypnotherapy for IBS claimed clinical success with the entire treated sample.

Given this situation, a question of obvious interest is whether there are individual difference variables which predict, from pretreatment assessment data or from early in-session treatment response, who will be a responder to treatment and who will not. This chapter presents a summary of what we know from the many treatment studies summarized in Chapter 15 and also what we know from the Albany studies summarized in Chapter 16.

PREDICTION OF TREATMENT OUTCOME

There are six reports on the prediction of treatment outcome. Fortunately, three of the four primary forms of psychological treatment de-

TABLE 20.1
Summary of Research on Prediction of Outcome from Psychological Treatments of IBS

Authors	Sample Size	% Female	Age	Diagnosis Criteria	Treatment	How Outcome Assessed	Significant Predictors
Whorwell et al., 1987	50	88	N/R	Clinical	Hypnotherapy	Patient daily diary	95% of classical cases respond vs. 43% of atypical cases (intractable abdominal pain with little bloating or bowel habit disturbance) vs. 60% with significant psychopathology (GHQ score of 14+). 25% of patients over age 50 respond vs. 100% of classical cases under age 50
Harvey et al., 1989	33	75	38	Rome	Hypnotherapy	Patient daily diary	Presence of more psychological problems (GHQ score of 5+) associated with poorer outcome. Percent with psychological problems who are unimproved–38%, improved–33%, symptom-free–0%
Galovski & Blanchard, 1999	12	83	39	Rome	Hypnotherapy	Patient daily diary	Significant correlation (r = .59) between number Axis I diagnoses and CPSR scores indicating better response with less pathology. No correlation between hypnotic susceptibility and improvement.

Study	N	Col. 3	Col. 4	Sample	Treatment	Outcome measure	Predictors
Guthrie et al., 1991	43	85	49	Clinical	Dynamic Psychotherapy	Physician global rating	Presence of anxiety or depression predicts better outcome, 65% vs. 25% success. Presence of constant pain predicts poorer outcome, 23% vs. 75% success. Presence of abdominal pain from stressful events predicts better outcome, 65% vs. 17% success. Longer duration of symptoms predicts poorer outcome, 2 years (successes) vs. 4.5 years. More lost time from work predicts poorer outcome 2 weeks (successes) vs. 6.5 weeks.
Blanchard, Schwarz, Neff, & Gerardi, 1988	45*	73	41	Clinical	CBT (see Chapter 17)	Patient daily diary	Higher STAI trait anxiety score predicts poorer outcome (CPSR) ($r = -.39$). Female gender predicts poorer outcome: female successes–50%, males–70%. More symptom-free days in 2 weeks baseline predicts better outcome ($r = .32$). No significant prediction from MMPI or BDI or age.
Blanchard, Scharff, et al., 1992	90**	67	44	Clinical	CBT (see Chapter 17)	Patient daily diary	Presence of Axis I diagnosis predicts poorer outcome (CPSR): 64% success with no Axis I, 29% success with at least one Axis I diagnosis.

Note. GHQ = General Health Questionnaire; CPSR = Composite Primary Symptom Reduction; STAI = State–Trait Anxiety Inventory; BDI = Beck Depression Inventory. *Patients from Neff and Blanchard, 1987; Blanchard & Schwarz, 1987; Blanchard, Schwarz, et al., Study 1 treated with CBT; **Patients from Blanchard, Schwarz, et al., 1992, Study 2, treated with CBT or attention–placebo condition.

scribed in Chapters 15 and 16 are represented: hypnotherapy, short term dynamic psychotherapy, and cognitive–behavioral therapy (CBT). The results are summarized in Table 20.1.

Examining the table, we find three separate reports by three independent research teams predicting the outcome from hypnotherapy (Galovski & Blanchard, 1999; Harvey et al., 1989; Whorwell et al., 1987). One finding is consistent across all three studies: *The presence of psychopathology*, either number of Axis I diagnoses (Galovski & Blanchard, 1999) or elevated scores on the General Health Questionnaire (GHQ; Goldberg, 1972) indicative of psychiatric caseness (Harvey et al., 1989; Whorwell et al., 1987), are all associated with poorer outcome. Whorwell identified two other factors associated with poorer outcome, namely older age (over 50) and an atypical presentation of IBS (intractable abdominal pain with few or no other symptoms).

Blanchard, Scharff, et al. (1992) reported a similar finding on the presence of psychopathology and outcome in the treatment of IBS with CBT: The presence of one or more Axis I diagnoses was significantly related to poorer outcome. Those who were diagnosis-free had a 64% success rate (CPSR greater than 50), whereas those with any Axis I diagnosis had only a 29% success rate. Other data are somewhat in agreement with this finding: Blanchard et al. (1987) combining the data from several small studies of CBT found higher trait anxiety scores associated with poorer outcome.

In stark contrast, Guthrie et al. (1991), in their study of short term psychodynamic psychotherapy, found the presence of anxiety and depression was associated with better outcome instead of poorer outcome. This inconsistency could easily be because of different treatment modalities and certainly deserves further investigation.

Another predictor variable that is fairly consistent across studies is the negative role of chronic, unremitting abdominal pain. Whorwell et al. (1987) found very poor response to hypnotherapy for patients with intractable abdominal pain who had little or no bloating or bowel habit disturbance. Likewise, Guthrie et al. (1991), using psychodynamic psychotherapy, found constant abdominal pain predicted a poorer outcome. Finally, Blanchard et al. (1987) found CBT was more likely to be successful in patients who had some symptom free days during baseline (thus, those with abdominal pain every day would tend to respond more poorly). No other reports support this finding but the consistency across therapy types is impressive.

Other potential predictor variables which have been identified in only a single study are: (1) *older age* (over 50) is associated with poorer outcome in hypnotherapy (Whorwell et al., 1987); (2) *female* gender is associated with poorer outcome in CBT (Blanchard et al., 1987); (3) longer duration of symptoms and more disability from symptoms (loss of work days) are associated with poorer outcome in psychodynamic psychotherapy (Guthrie et al., 1991).

One last interesting point has been the absence of significant predictors from the MMPI clinical scales and the Beck Depression Inventory as reported for CBT by Blanchard et al. (1987; Blanchard, Scharff, et al., 1992), and the absence of a relation between outcome and hypnotic susceptibility with hypnotherapy (Galovski & Blanchard, 1999). Clearly more research is needed on this topic so as to optimize the matching of patient to treatment.

Clinical Hints

Given the extent to which poor outcome is associated with diagnosable psychopathology and the high likelihood of finding diagnosable pathology among IBS patients (see Chapter 7), it seems clear that one would be well advised to conduct a psychiatric or psychological diagnostic evaluation with the new IBS patient. A problem then arises as to what to do if one finds diagnosable psychiatric conditions.

My first recommendation would be not to use hypnotherapy or CBT. Instead, our work with pure cognitive therapy (Greene & Blanchard, 1994; Payne & Blanchard, 1995) suggests that the presence of an Axis I disorder does not affect outcome. We found an 80% success rate in Greene and Blanchard when, 90% of the sample had an Axis I diagnosis; in Payne and Blanchard, we had a 75% success rate when 83% of the sample had an Axis I diagnosis. One could also use short term dynamic psychotherapy: Guthrie et al. (1991) reported that the presence of anxiety and depression are associated with good outcome.

At a more general level, if you find from pretreatment assessment that your IBS patient is a poor candidate for the treatment you plan, what do you then do? One can switch treatment approaches, selecting from those described in Chapters 17, 18, and 19. Above all, I believe you treat the patient nevertheless because there are no perfect predictors. I would not tell the patient he or she is a poor candidate in this instance because a pessimistic patient will probably fail or drop out. Instead, I would be forewarned as the therapist and thus be prepared to extend treatment longer than usual, or perhaps switch approaches.

21

LONG-TERM FOLLOW-UP OF PSYCHOLOGICAL TREATMENTS FOR IRRITABLE BOWEL SYNDROME

The last chapter of this book deals with what is possibly the most important clinical and research topic that has been addressed: long-term outcome of psychological treatments.

It almost goes without saying that one needs to be interested in the long-term outcome of psychological treatments for IBS. Several factors combine to make this the case. First, as was noted in Chapter 2, IBS tends to be a chronic, long-term disorder with periods of exacerbation and periods of improvement. Second, with drug treatments one typically expects improvement after a brief period of time on the medication. Then, the study ends with no long-term follow-up of the patient as he or she continues the medication for months, or even years. There is an implicit assumption that the patient will need to continue the medication for years or forever (although this is rarely examined on an empirical basis). Third, and most important for psychological treatments, one expects relatively permanent changes to occur in the IBS patient undergoing psychological treatment. That is, one expects the patient to have learned something in the psychological treatment and to have been permanently altered, psychologically, by that experience. Last, it is well known (Klein, 1988) that there is a large placebo effect among IBS patients who take part in drug

TABLE
Summary of Long Term Follow-up of

Authors	Sample Size	% Female	Mean Age	Diagnosis Criteria	Treatment	FU (months)
Svedlund et al., 1983 (Sweden)	50	70	33	Clinical	Dynamic short term psychotherapy, 10 sessions	12
Guthrie et al., 1991 (UK)	53 (46 completers) 33 of controls treated	85	49	Clinical	Dynamic psychotherapy, 7 session + home practice in relaxation	9 For initial Tx. 6 For treated controls
Whorwell et al., 1987 (UK)	15	87	39	Clinical	Hypnotherapy, 7 sessions over 3 months	14–21 mean: 18
Shaw et al., 1991 (UK)	18	61	50	Clinical	Stress management, relaxation training, & education, 6 sessions over 6 months	6
van Dulmen et al., 1996 (Netherlands)	45	53	46	Clinical	CBT in groups, 8 sessions over 3 months	6 to 48 mean: 28

Note. CBT = Cognitive–behavioral therapy; P = Patient; FU = Follow-up.

trials. One might expect something similar in psychological treatments, thus we want to see if treatment effects endure. (If a placebo response leads to relatively permanent improvement in the patient then, clinically, one wants to capitalize on this result!)

For the purposes of this chapter, long-term follow-up is defined as any systematic assessment of patients 6 months or more after the completion of treatment. In Table 21.1 are summarized the results from long-term follow-ups of various psychological treatments. In Table 21.2 are summarized the results from long-term follow-ups from our Albany studies.

As can be seen in Table 21.1, only five of the controlled trials reported in Chapter 15 had follow-ups of 6 months or more. In two instances, Guthrie et al. (1991) and van Dulmen et al. (1996), patients from a waiting list control condition were crossed over after completion of the initial experimental comparison to receive the primary treatment, either short term psychodynamic psychotherapy or group cognitive–behavioral therapy, respectively. Even though this tactic has the advantage of increasing the size of treated sample and meets the obvious ethical obligation one has to the patients on the waiting list, it eliminates the ability to make long-term comparisons.

For the most part, retention rates have been very good, with only

21.1
Psychological Treatments for IBS

Assessed	% at FU	Intermed. Treatments	% Improved	Other Results
Physician global ratings & P global ratings	100	None	N/R	Treated P showed improvement from end of treatment to FU on abdominal pain and bowel dysfunction. Tx. superior to controls on abdominal pain, bowel dysfunction, overall somatic symptoms; trends on anxiety and depression.
P global ratings (diary at post-tx)	92	None	72.6%	P showed significant reduction in outpatient clinic visits.
P symptom diary	100	1 additional session for 2 cases	100	2 relapses (13.3%) responded to single booster session of hypnosis.
P global ratings over telephone	100	None	50	67% reported fewer and less severe symptom attacks at end of treatment. These gains were mostly maintained.
Symptoms diary & P questionnaire	71	5 Pts. received CBT for other problems	37 of FU sample based on Symptom diary	Significant reductions in diary on GI symptoms from pretreatment to follow-up. No difference in benefit based on length of FU.

van Dulmen et al. (1996) falling below 90%. The 100% retention rates reported by Svedlund et al. (1983), Whorwell et al. (1987) and Shaw et al. (1991) are truly outstanding!

Unfortunately, in only two instances were follow-up results evaluated by means of symptom diaries, Whorwell et al. (1987) and van Dulmen et al. (1996). Others relied on patient global reports, sometimes collected during a telephone interview. Guthrie et al. (1991) evaluated the initial effects of treatment by patient symptom diaries but relied on global ratings for the follow-up data. We know from our work in Albany (Meissner et al., 1997) that patient global report *overestimates* improvement documented by a daily symptom diary.

The fraction of the sample who met criteria for being called improved at follow-up was highly variable, ranging from 100% in Whorwell et al.'s (1987) sample of 15 patients receiving hypnotherapy to 37% for those receiving cognitive–behavioral therapy on a group basis (van Dulmen et al., 1996). The latter value is disappointing when one realizes it represents only 27% of those initially treated. Interestingly, these two extreme values were those confirmed by patient symptom diary and represented the longer-term follow-ups.

It would appear that those using cognitive–behavioral treatment ap-

TABLE 21.2
Summary of Long Term Follow-up of Albany Treatment Studies of IBS

Authors	Sample Size	% Female	Mean Age	Diagnosis Criteria	Treatment	FU (months)	Assessed	% at FU	% Improved	Other Results
Schwarz et al., 1986	17	65	39	Clinical	CBT, 12 sessions/8 wks	12	16 global report 14 daily symptom diary	94 82	69 by global report 57 by diary	Average CPSR at FU = 46% Average global report at FU = 71% improvement. Significant reductions on abdominal pain, diarrhea, constipation, flatulence.
Blanchard et al., 1988	17	65	39	Clinical	CBT, 12 sessions/8 wks	24	15 global report 14 daily symptom diary	88 82	80 by global report 57 by diary	Average CPSR at FU = 46% Significant reductions on abdominal pain, diarrhea, constipation, flatulence.
*Schwarz et al., 1990	27	74	41	Clinical	CBT, 12 sessions/8 wks	Avg. 47, 39–55	19 global report 12 daily symptom diary	70 44	89.5 by global report 50 by diary	Average CPSR at FU = 44% Significant reduction on abdominal pain, diarrhea, flatulence.
Blanchard, Schwartz, et al., 1992 Study 2	31	68	44	Clinical	CBT	6	Daily symptom diary	64	49	Significant reduction on abdominal pain, constipation, flatulence, belching.
Radnitz & Blanchard, 1989	5	60	31	Clinical Diarrhea predominant	Bowel Sound Biofeedback, 10 sessions/5 wks	12 24	Symptom diary Symptom diary	100 80	60 75	N/R

Note. CBT = Cognitive–Behavioral Therapy; CPSR = Composite Primary Symptom Reduction; FU = follow up. *This follow-up was of the 17 patients in Neff and Blanchard (1987) plus the 10 CBT treated patients from Blanchard, Schwartz, et al. (1992), Study 1.

proaches might want to include either some relapse prevention work in the treatment regimen or else schedule booster treatments when relapses occur (as was done by Whorwell et al., 1987).

LONG-TERM FOLLOW-UP OF THE ALBANY STUDIES

In our work at Albany, we have been able to follow-up our initial sample treated with a combination of cognitive and behavioral techniques (Neff & Blanchard, 1987) at 1-year and 2-years posttreatment. These patients, as well as another set of patients treated with the same protocol, were also followed up at four years posttreatment. Furthermore, we obtained 6-month follow-up data on part of the sample in our large-scale evaluation of the cognitive–behavioral treatment protocol (Blanchard, Schwarz, et al., 1992, study 2).

We also obtained 1-year and 2-year follow-up on the small sample of diarrhea-predominant IBS patients treated with bowel sound biofeedback (Radnitz & Blanchard, 1989). Results from these follow-ups are summarized in Table 21.2.

As one can see from the table, we were able to gather follow-up symptom diary data on 82% of our first CBT treated sample out to 2 years. These results showed 57% of the treated patients maintaining their improved status based on a CPSR score of 50% or greater. The global patient ratings were notably higher at 69% and 80% for the one and two year follow-ups, respectively. This is another example of how patient global ratings may *overestimate* improvement substantially in comparison to the daily diary, a point to be remembered in interpreting the results in Table 21.1.

At 4 years, our retention of diary completers was only 44%. We did gather patient global ratings on 70% of the sample. This latter subsample showed 89.5% of patients reporting substantial, sustained improvement (but remember it is probably an overestimate).

For the large-scale evaluation of CBT (Blanchard, Schwarz, et al., 1992, study 2), our follow-up retention was poor at only 64% at 6 months. The fraction of the sample who were improved (49%) was comparable to the end of treatment results (51.6%). I suspect that patients having multiple therapists, some of whom were not very experienced, hurt the retention results.

The follow-up data from the small trial of bowel sound biofeedback (Radnitz & Blanchard, 1989) show good retention at 1- and 2-years and fairly stable levels of improvement in the primary target, diarrhea.

Overall, our follow-up data from individually administered CBT seem noticeably stronger than the one partially comparable data set, the results of group CBT reported by van Dulmen et al. (1996). It is unfortunate that we never obtained long-term follow-up on those patients treated with cognitive therapy. In those studies, the 3-month follow-ups showed good maintenance of GI symptom reduction and continued improvement in psychological state (Greene & Blanchard, 1994; Payne & Blanchard, 1995).

CONCLUSIONS

By far, the strongest follow-up data come from hypnotherapy: Whorwell et al.'s (1984) initial sample of 15 refractory IBS patients were all substantially improved at end of treatment and maintained those gains at 18 months posttreatment. The results from the short-term dynamic psychotherapy trials are good and on a par with the data from our initial CBT trial (Neff & Blanchard, 1987). Thus, unlike drugs, for which return of symptoms when the drug is discontinued is an expected effect, the effects of the psychological treatments seem to lead to relatively enduring improvement.

Clinical Hint

One might want to build in a program of regular (every 6 months or so for a couple of years) callbacks to check on patient status and remind them of their newly acquired skills in the event of a brief relapse or symptom flare.

Patients have told us that after regular treatment ends, they discontinue the regular practice and application of the cognitive and behavioral techniques they learned in treatment. They add, however, that they feel more confident and know they can return to practicing and using the treatment techniques if the need arises. It is as if they have learned new ways to cope and apply them as necessary. That seems a good outcome for therapy to me!

APPENDIX A: PSYCHOEDUCATIONAL SUPPORT GROUP FOR IRRITABLE BOWEL SYNDROME

ANNETTE PAYNE AND EDWARD B. BLANCHARD

SUPPORT GROUP

This group was designed to focus specifically on IBS and those issues related to the development and maintenance of IBS such as stress, anxiety, and diet. The group format consisted of 10 weekly group sessions that focused on specific topics introduced by the therapist as well as an open group discussion about each group member's experience or reaction to the topic of discussion.

Each week the group session consisted of two parts. The first part included information about the specific topic for that week. Within this, participants were encouraged to provide examples from their experiences to enhance the groups understanding of the given topic. The therapist facilitated discussion and answered questions as they arose. The purpose of the group was for the participants to help each other understand the different aspects of IBS. Participants were informed that the certain topics were more relevant for some than others and that each participant suggested more salient issues than others. In addition, it was the responsibility of each member to participate and take from the discussion the information that was most relevant for him or her.

In addition to the informational part of group, each group member was asked to participate and support each other. Discussion centered on how each topic related to the participants specifically and each participant provided personal examples. The goal of the second part of group was for each participant to recognize the similarities and differences among the group members' experiences with IBS. In the process of sharing experiences, it became apparent that each participant was not the only individual who suffered with these types of problems and issues. Thus, in the group format, the participants spent much of each session learning from each other and providing support.

In sum, the group attempted to gather as much information about IBS as possible from both the therapist and each other to further understand the development and maintenance of IBS. That is, through the information provided by the therapist and the experiences shared with each other, the group developed a better understanding of IBS. Armed with information and the support of the group, each member of the group had an increased confidence to face his or her own specific difficulties.

An outline of the treatment manual follows.

SOCIAL SUPPORT/EDUCATION MANUAL

Group Session 1

Forms needed

IBS Symptom Diaries
Pretreatment Rationale
Confidentiality Form
Outline of Session Topics

Goals

1. Introductions, name tags (first name only)
2. Sign consent form, confidentiality form
3. Introduce treatment rationale, treatment schedule
4. Group expectancies for outcome
5. Introduce group members, brief description of concerns
6. Assign homework

Protocol

1. *Introductions*. The therapist should introduce self and other members of the group. Ask clients to say a few things about themselves (e.g., age, marital status, employment, school, hobbies). Following initial introductions, therapist hands out name tags explaining that it is difficult to remember everyone's name and name tags will initially reduce awkwardness.
2. *Confidentiality Forms*. The therapist should make a confidentiality statement.

   In a group format, confidentiality becomes an important topic. Therefore, I strongly suggest that in order to respect each other's privacy, you do not discuss each other by name or any of the information shared by group members outside of the clinic. Each of you will only feel comfortable sharing private information if he or she believes it will be kept in confidence.
3. *Treatment Rationale and Consent for Treatment*. The therapist should explain why the client has come, the session format, what he or she can expect to get from the group, what is expected of each client in the group, and the role the therapist will play in discussion.

   This social support and education group will be similar to other support groups you may have heard of before, such as cancer support groups, etc. However, in this group, we will focus specifically on IBS and issues related to IBS such as stress, anxiety, and diet. Each week we will discuss different topics as described. I will provide some information but much of the burden for discussion will fall on you.

Every week, the group session will consist of two parts. The first part will include information and education about the specific topic for that week. Within this, clients will be encouraged to provide examples from their experiences to enhance the group's understanding of the given topic. I will help facilitate discussion and answer questions as they arise. However, let me say from the very beginning that I do not have all of the answers or even many of the answers. The purpose of the group is for you to help each other discover answers. It is also the case that there may be a different answer for different ones of you.

Some of the topics will be more relevant for some participants than others. Therefore, it is the responsibility of each member to participate and take from the discussion the information that is most relevant for him or her. Because IBS is often a very different experience for each person, I will not take a position on the topics.

In addition to the educational part of the group, we will encourage group participation and support. Discussion will center on how each topic relates to the group members specifically and each client can provide personal examples. The goal is for each client to recognize the similarities and differences among the group members' experiences with IBS. In the process of sharing our experiences, it will become apparent that each client is not the only one who suffers with these types of problems and issues. Thus, we will spend much of each session learning from each other and providing support.

To sum up, the group will attempt to gather as much information about IBS as possible to further understand IBS. That is, through the information provided by me and the experiences shared with each other, the group will develop a better understanding of IBS. Armed with information and the support of the group, each member of the group will have an increased confidence to face his or her own specific difficulties.

4. *Expectancy for Treatment Outcome.* Each client should introduce him- or herself. The client should discuss his or her reasons for coming to treatment and what he or she hopes to learn and get from it. In addition, each may offer specific information regarding his or her difficulties with IBS. In gen-

eral, clients may discuss several issues: (1) what he or she hopes or expects to be different following treatment, (2) how he or she feels about group treatment, and/or (3) concerns regarding how he or she fits into the group.

5. *Assign Homework.* Each client will monitor GI symptoms in his or her diary. In addition, clients will be given IBS terms to think about and define. The following week, the group will discuss these terms and the relationship with IBS. The therapist should tell clients that each week more group participation will be expected, so it is important that each client makes a sincere effort on the homework.

Group Session 2

Forms needed

IBS Symptom Diaries
Definitions of Terms Sheet

Goals

1. Review rationale
2. Review homework
3. Discussion of IBS terms
4. Encourage disclosure by group members
5. Provide forum for discussion and support of peers
6. Assign homework

Protocol

1. *Introductions.* Introduce each group member and have clients wear name tags. Ask for comments or questions from the previous week or reactions to this week's session.
2. *Review Treatment Rationale.* Make sure that the clients understand the treatment rationale. If clients are not sure, review session one rationale. Review the educational and support components of the group treatment.
3. *Address the "IBS" Problem.* The therapist should explain that bowel functioning is not something that people typically talk about with anyone.

   Sometimes people will say that a certain food did not agree with them, but people don't typically talk about diarrhea or constipation. One of the goals for today's session is to become more comfortable discussing these issues. Therefore, we will discuss IBS terms. Remember back to session one when I asked you to explain in detail what you meant by certain terms. That was because I wondered exactly what you meant and if everyone's definitions were the same.
4. *Review Homework.* Go over the client's IBS terms and definitions. Discuss similarities and differences among the client's definitions. Discuss how IBS is a mixture of symptoms, just as the word syndrome suggests. Mention that IBS can produce a wide variety of bothersome gastrointestinal symptoms although not all of these symptoms occur at the same time or in the same person. It would be helpful to refer to a chart of the human body to discuss the following terms.
   a) *Abdominal pain:* Abdominal pain is perhaps the most com-

mon and recognizable symptoms of IBS. It is the reason most IBS patients initially go to see their physicians. Although IBS pain most typically occurs in the lower left abdominal area, it may be felt on the right side, or much higher up. In fact, one type of IBS pain is actually felt in the chest area (the shoulders and arms). IBS pain may take the form of aching, cramping, or of abdominal tenderness. It may be constant or it may be felt on and off and be relieved by passage of stool or gas.

b) *Constipation*: Constipation may be characterized by the passage of small hard fecal balls or small soft stools. In a typical pattern, several days of constipation will lead to passage of hard stools, followed by several softer ones, and finally, watery excretion. Strands of mucus and spots of bright red blood may be noticed in stool but are usually the result of rectal irritation. Any increased or persistent bleeding should be discussed immediately with your physician.

c) *Diarrhea:* Diarrhea most commonly occurs in the morning before or after breakfast and is often accompanied by a strong sense of urgency. Stools are usually soft, watery, and only partially formed. The urge to defecate may also be quite strong immediately following other meals during the day. However, only a few watery stools may be passed at each bowel movement. Diarrhea will rarely awaken an IBS sufferer at night, although sleep may occasionally be interrupted by cramping. Not uncommon, IBS may produce both diarrhea and constipation with or without pain intermittently in the same person.

d) *Flatulence*: Flatulence is a common symptom of IBS. Within IBS, it is defined as the presence of excessive gas in the digestive tract.

e) *Bloating*: Bloating is described as a sensation of swelling up or inflating with gas or liquid. Often, bloating is noted after ingesting food or liquid, especially after a large meal.

f) *Anxiety*: Anxiety seems to be a general, vague term. It refers to an experience of uncertainty, apprehension, and dread—a prediction of a negative outcome.

g) *Fear*: Fear means sudden danger; a normal response to an active or imagined threat with accompanied physical symptoms such as increased heart rate, tension in muscles, increased breathing, and a burst of energy.

h) *Stress*: Stress is a mentally or emotionally disruptive or disquieting influence, distress.

5. *Discuss How These Terms Relate to IBS.*

    You have two types of nervous systems in your body. One is the central nervous system that controls your arms, legs, and all the other muscles that you normally use voluntarily. The other nervous system is the autonomic nervous system, that controls the smooth muscles of the body. The smooth muscles are the ones that you do not normally purposely control like your heart, your lungs, and your intestinal muscles.

    When you become very stressed and your body starts reacting as if it is in danger, your autonomic system becomes active. This is known as the *fight or flight* response, when your system is getting ready to either defend itself or get away from the danger. Adrenaline is released, your breathing becomes shallower, and your heart beats faster. Another reaction that is useful to the animal about to fight or escape is the dumping of waste in the intestine, so the muscles in the intestine spasm in order to get rid of this waste.

    People with IBS feel these spasms and will experience diarrhea if the spasms all go one way and will experience constipation if the spasms go up and down the intestine, essentially trapping the stools in the intestine. The pain and symptoms are very real, but often IBS patients are told that their symptoms are "all in your head," which refers to the symptoms being a stress reaction.

6. *Group Discussion.*

    Now that we have some information about IBS, let's talk about these terms and how they relate to IBS. Many of you share the same experience of suffering in silence with your IBS. Nevertheless, sharing common experiences within a supportive group is often helpful.

    Open up discussion for each client to discuss situations that are stressful, their common experiences, etc. Therapist will facilitate discussion but will maintain a distance from the group allowing group members to initiate topics and control the flow of discussion.

7. *Assign Homework.* Clients should continue to monitor IBS symptoms. Note that the following week, the group will discuss theories of how IBS begins. Tell the clients to spend this week reflecting on the possible origins of their IBS so the group can compare these. (Give handout for next week.)

Group Session 3

Forms needed

IBS Symptom Diaries

Goals

1. Review homework.
2. Identify causes of IBS.
3. Discuss emotional triggers of IBS.
4. Group discussion.
5. Assign homework.

Protocol

1. *Review Homework.* Inquire about each client's homework and his or her belief about the origin of their IBS.
2. *Causes of IBS.* (Use a long, narrow balloon, if possible, to illustrate movement of material in GI tract.)
   a) Discuss how researchers have determined that most symptoms of IBS are directly related to an abnormal pattern of motion (motility) of the large intestine (colon).

      The colon is a 5-foot area of bowel between the small intestine and the anus. Its main function is to remove water and salts from digestive products coming from the small intestine and hold the remaining residue until defecation. This fecal material then passes through the colon by means of a very delicate process of motion.

      The motility of the colon is controlled by the body's nervous system. There are nerve impulses that stimulate activity, others that inhibit it—and with a fine balance between the two types of impulses, gastrointestinal contents are propelled forward smoothly and without problems.

      In persons with IBS, however, this delicate balance is disturbed. In addition to the regular contractions that propel colon contents along, there are irregular, nonpropulsive contractions that can upset normal rhythm.

      Constipation occurs when the propulsive movements are inhibited and absorption of water in the colon is increased, leaving the feces dry and hard. Diarrhea results when the propulsive movements are excessive, and there is little chance for water absorption. Abdominal pain and cramping result from the spasm of the colon and a buildup of gas that fills the bowel.

b) Discuss the emotional triggers that bring about IBS symptoms.

Why the nerve impulses that control colonic motility are out of balance in persons with IBS has been the subject of much investigation. All the answers are still not known. However, it has become obvious that both emotional factors and dietary habits play a very important role. By measuring colon contractions in patients under stressful and nonstressful conditions, scientists have demonstrated that emotional stress clearly helps trigger abnormal motility. This is further borne out by the fact that many persons who suffer from IBS are sometimes tense, anxious and given to emotional ups and downs. There is usually a history of overwork, inadequate sleep, and hurried and irregular meals.

c) Explain dietary abuses and their role in IBS symptoms.

Colon contractions are also regulated by the amount and types of food consumed. High caloric meals and meals high in fat content can produce exaggerated contractions in persons with IBS, leading to cramps and diarrhea. Fats in the form of oils, animal fat, or butter are particularly important culprits, while carbohydrates, dietary protein, and blander foods usually have a minimal effect on the colon.

d) Discuss biological predisposition (how IBS tends to run in families). Note that some researchers believe that people may be predisposed to develop IBS as a reaction to stress.

3. *Group Discussion.* The therapist will facilitate discussion about each patient's belief of how their IBS began. In addition, discussion of how stress, emotional triggers, and dietary abuses affect IBS should be encouraged. Allow each client to discuss his or her individual difficulties.
4. *Assign Homework.* The clients should be instructed to continue to monitor GI symptoms with the diaries. Tell the clients that the following week's session will focus on going to doctors and the medical tests that have been performed. Have clients reflect on what this has been like for them and think about their reactions to the tests.

Group Session 4

Forms needed

IBS Symptom Diaries

Goals

1. Review homework
2. Discuss difficulties with doctors:
   a) Medical tests
   b) Medications
3. Group discussion
4. Assign homework

Protocol

1. *Review Homework.* Discuss any concerns expressed by clients that are associated with doctors and/or medical tests. Clients may have concerns about medical procedures or tests that need to be addressed. Therefore, allow each client to ask questions, offer suggestions, or provide information.

   Many clients complain about the number of doctors they have seen and the number of medical tests they have gone through. In this session, we will discuss some of the issues that surround this process. For example, many clients will first begin by going to their family physician or primary care physician. If the doctor cannot discover the reason for the GI symptoms, often doctors refer to other doctors with more expertise in GI functioning. Nevertheless, even these doctors sometimes cannot determine what is going on. I am sure many IBS clients have had the experience of their doctor telling them that he or she does not know what is wrong or what treatment to offer the IBS client. Thus, many IBS clients have seen many different doctors such as internists, OB/GYN doctors, primary care doctors, and gastroenterologists with few positive outcomes or much information about their GI symptoms.

   Besides seeing many different doctors, many clients have had an extensive battery of medical tests. In fact, some of these medical tests are very uncomfortable and time-consuming, including tests such as upper GI series, lower GI series, and flexible sigmoidoscopy. Not only are these medical tests unpleasant, clients must often repeat these tests for each new doctor they are referred to. Nevertheless, these medical tests often yield negative results; they often do not offer any specific information about why the client is experiencing the GI symptoms that he or she is experiencing. Therefore, the client goes through invasive and uncomfortable medical tests, repeats these tests for many different doctors, and still the client may not receive information about why he or she is experiencing the GI symptoms.

It is understandable that clients suffering from IBS become easily frustrated with medical doctors and medical tests. IBS clients tend to receive multiple medical evaluations from many doctors from different medical specialties. In addition to multiple medical evaluations, IBS clients will go through repeated medical tests to try to understand why they experience their symptoms. Nevertheless, the medical field does not have all the answers about IBS and this makes for frustrated IBS clients.

2. Identify hypothetical examples of an IBS client and the process that he or she could go through with medical evaluations and medical tests. Note potential difficulties with doctors and referrals. Also, specifically discuss the types of tests and the progression of tests (i.e., least invasive to most invasive) that an IBS client might experience.
3. *Group Discussion.* Allow each client to discuss his or her experiences with medical doctors and medical tests. The therapist should note that each person is different, thus different doctors may order different tests and different treatment regimens. It is important that each client recall specifics of the situations and tests. The therapist will facilitate discussion.

   It is important to note that during the group discussion, it is possible that discussion may turn into a "doctor-bashing" session. It is important that the therapist diffuse this counterproductive trend. The therapist should point out that everyone may have problems with a doctor, and other professionals as well, for many different reasons including poor communication regarding the client's physical problems and/or the doctor's prescribed treatment. Therefore, it is conceivable that misunderstandings might occur, especially with a multifaceted physical problem such as IBS.
4. *Assign Homework.* The clients should be instructed to continue filling out their GI symptom diaries. At the next session, the group will discuss the possibility that IBS clients are concerned that they may have cancer or another serious

medical condition that has not been properly diagnosed, prompting the client to continue seeking medical treatment and testing. Have each client comment on his or her experiences with these concerns.

Group Session 5

Forms needed

IBS Symptom Diaries

Goals

1. Review homework
2. Discuss medical concerns
3. Group discussion
4. Assign homework

Protocol

1. *Review Homework.* Address the discussion topic and how each client did with his or her homework, if there were any questions, etc.
2. *Address Client's Fears.*

   For many clients, the diagnosis of IBS does not reassure them. That is, when a client receives a diagnosis of IBS, often it is because the doctor cannot find anything physically wrong with the client. Therefore, based on the symptoms described by the client plus the lack of physical findings based on medical examination and medical tests, the doctor makes an IBS diagnosis. Nevertheless, many clients still wonder if there is a physical abnormality or problem that the tests or the doctor just did not find yet. Thus, a diagnosis of IBS does not always assist the client's understanding of why or how their symptoms have occurred.

   One of the common concerns that IBS clients express is that they may have cancer of some type. For example, many doctors suggest that a person be evaluated for cancer if blood or mucus is passed through the stool. For IBS patients with symptoms of constipation and/or hemorrhoid, blood or mucus in the stool may be a relatively common occurrence secondary to straining while trying to defecate. Therefore, concern about cancer may be high for these clients.

   There are other diseases that IBS clients have been concerned about. Some of these diseases may be autoimmune difficulties, parasites, etc. Because of the concerns about other diseases, clients continue to seek medical evaluations and tests to ensure that an IBS client does not have a serious medical problem.

   Another difficulty IBS clients must deal with is that

sometimes IBS symptoms are very different for different people. Moreover, for an individual IBS client, the symptom picture may change over time. That is, at another time the predominant symptom may be alternating diarrhea and constipation. When a symptom picture changes, clients may feel compelled to have their physical condition reevaluated. Therefore, this process of a changing symptom presentation may facilitate general concern about potential disease processes.

3. *Group Discussion.* Have each client discuss his or her concerns with other physical difficulties including cancer. Encourage discussion of difficulties and problems with changing symptom pictures and how this process supports concerns about other diseases. Address each client and elicit specific diseases or concerns he or she may have.
4. *Assign Homework.* Clients should continue to record symptoms in GI diaries. At the next session, plan to discuss different dietary problems each client may have noted. For example, some IBS clients notice that to reduce their symptoms, they should not ingest dairy products. Have clients make a list of foods and/or drinks that they have noticed cause them problems. (Hand out homework sheets.)

Group Session 6

Forms needed

IBS Symptom Diaries
Physiological Symptoms Handout
Homework Handout
Therapist Rating Form

Goals

1. Review homework
2. Discuss dietary difficulties associated with IBS
3. Group discussion
4. Assign homework

Protocol

1. *Review Homework.* Discuss the different dietary restrictions clients mention. Allow each client to offer suggestions and solutions for IBS symptoms associated with different foods or drinks.

   It is important to learn which foods are the right foods for each IBS client and how to avoid the foods that exacerbate IBS symptoms. If your situation warrants it, your physician may recommend a special diet for you. In general, IBS clients should try to stay away from heavy meals and lean toward blander foods. Avoid very fatty foods. Cut down on your intake of fried foods, milk, and any milk products. Do not drink a lot of coffee. Stay away from very hot or very cold drinks. It sometimes also helps to have a high fiber diet with plenty of bulk.

   Try to learn what foods are most irritating to your own digestive system. Keep a log of your IBS episodes and note the foods you ingested prior to the attacks. After a few weeks you may find that certain foods are more likely than others to set off symptoms. Tell your doctor what they are and avoid or cut down on these foods if your physician so advises.

   In some IBS clients, particularly when constipation is the dominant problem, a diet high in fiber has been useful. Your doctor can tell you if increased fiber intake will help your case.
2. *Group Discussion.* Encourage each client to discuss the physical symptoms he or she experiences from different foods and

drinks. The therapist should facilitate the discussion to include sensitivity to and specific reactions to different foods.

3. *Assign Homework.* Clients should be instructed to continue filling out their GI symptom diaries. At the next session, discussion will center around how family members and friends understand IBS symptoms. Instruct clients to reflect on how people in their life understand their IBS symptoms.

Group Session 7

Forms needed

IBS Symptom Diaries

Goals

1. Review homework
2. Discuss family/friends' understanding of IBS
3. Group discussion
4. Assign homework

Protocol

1. *Review Homework.* Address each client's homework and examples provided. Discuss any problems or concerns expressed by clients about family or friends.

   IBS clients have important people in their lives who do not suffer from IBS. For many clients, it is important to try to help these people understand what they are going through. That is, IBS clients want those close to them to understand what they are going through.

   Because IBS clients do not show physical signs of distress (e.g., broken leg, cast), often loved ones to not understand the difficulties the IBS client must face. Therefore, it is important for IBS clients to try to explain this to important people in their lives.

   However, as many of you know, often those we care about do not understand our situations. Because they cannot see the physical discomfort, they often do not understand it. In addition, they can become impatient or upset with us when we cannot do what they would like us to. When someone shows they have difficulties (e.g., wheelchair), others are usually more sympathetic and patient. IBS clients tend to have difficulty receiving the support and understanding from their important others because they do not seem to be suffering.
2. *Group Discussion.* Have each client discuss how important people in his or her life understand the client's IBS symptoms. Encourage discussion of difficulties and problems with others' understanding of IBS symptoms.
3. *Assign Homework.* Clients should continue to monitor their

GI symptoms in their diary. In addition, the client should complete the questions on the handout. Clients should reflect on issues from the group that are personally relevant and helpful.

Group Sessions 8 and 9

Forms needed

IBS Symptom Diaries

Goals

1. Review homework and the past week
2. General discussion of IBS and how members are coping with it
3. Group discussion

Protocol

1. Remind group members that this session and the next are more general sessions without a specific topic. Instead, therapist should explicitly remind group members that this is *their* group and each member should share concerns about IBS and how he or she is coping with it.

   In addition, it is important that group members provide each other with support to let others know that they are not alone, that other group members understand the concerns and problems.
2. *Group Discussion.* Have each client discuss how he or she is dealing with major concerns surrounding IBS. Encourage discussion of difficulties, especially those of an interpersonal nature.
3. At Session 9, remind clients that the next session is the last session. Note that the group will be evaluating past sessions, discussing individual changes, and saying good-byes.
4. *Assign Homework.* Clients should continue to monitor GI symptoms in his or her diary. Clients should also reflect on issues from the group that are personally relevant and helpful.

Group Session 10

Forms needed

IBS Symptom Diaries

Goals

1. Review homework
2. Discuss the end of treatment
3. Obtain posttreatment rating
4. Review follow-up schedule
5. Make appointment for posttreatment assessment

Protocol

1. *Review Homework.* Address any questions or concerns about the ending of treatment. Discuss the progress throughout treatment for each client. Review rationale and encourage the continued use of things learned from the group.
2. *Group Discussion.* Allow each client to discuss what benefit they received from treatment and what they still hope to accomplish. Take time to share any changes that have come about during the past 10 weeks of treatment.
3. *Follow-Up.* Address the follow-up schedule and review what the process will entail. Explain that there will be a meeting of the group and there will be brief individual interviews to assess progress.
4. Give the clients 2 weeks of diaries and psychological tests.

APPENDIX B: IDEAS ON APPROACHING GASTROENTEROLOGISTS AND OTHER PHYSICIANS FOR IBS REFERRALS

There are five points I believe you should try to make with a potential referral source.

1. IBS, as they probably know, is a widespread disorder affecting upwards of 20-million Americans.
2. A portion of the IBS population, probably 25 to 30%, seems refractory to dietary and drug therapies. Mention the Drossman and Thompson (1992) article from the *Annals of Internal Medicine, 116*, 1009–1016, and leave a copy of it with the physician.
3. There have been reports in respected medical journals about successful psychological treatments of IBS.
4. Let the referral source know you are prepared to take IBS patient referrals. Emphasize that you will rely on their diag-

---

This whole section can described as a *Clinical Hint* because I have no data to back up any of this advice.

noses since you know competing diagnoses such as IBD and lactose malabsorption need to be ruled out.

5. Emphasize that you know the patient is more likely to follow-up on the referral if the physician makes a pointed referral but does not infer that the patient is crazy.

I would advise having copies of the following three articles to leave with the physician. They are chosen because of the journal in which they were published. Unfortunately, none of the CBT or cognitive therapy articles have been published in top rated medical journals.

Guthrie, E., Creed, F., Dawson, D., & Tomenson, B. (1991). A controlled trial of psychological treatment for the irritable bowel syndrome. *Gastroenterology, 100*, 450–457.

Svedlund, J., Sjodin, I., Ottosson, J. O., & Dotevall, G. (1983). Controlled study of psychotherapy in irritable bowel syndrome. *Lancet*, 589–592.

Whorwell, P. J., Prior, A., & Faragher, E. B. (1984). Controlled trial of hypnotherapy in the treatment of severe refractory irritable bowel syndrome. *Lancet*, 1232–1234.

APPENDIX C: INFORMATION ABOUT IRRITABLE BOWEL SYNDROME

IRRITABLE BOWEL SYNDROME: A COMMON DISORDER

A Mixture of Symptoms

Just as the word "syndrome" suggests, IBS can produce a wide variety of bothersome gastrointestinal symptoms. Usually, though, not all of these symptoms occur at the same time or in the same person.

Abdominal Pain

Abdominal pain is perhaps the most common and recognizable symptom of irritable bowel syndrome (IBS). It is the reason most IBS patients initially come to see their physicians.

Although IBS pain most typically occurs in the lower left abdominal area, it may be felt on the right side, or much higher up. In fact, one type of IBS pain is actually felt in the chest, shoulders, and arms. IBS pain may take the form of aching or cramping. It may be constant, or it may be felt on and off and be relieved by passage of stool or gas.

Constipation and Diarrhea

At times, even more distressing than pain are the disturbances in bowel function that occur with IBS. Not uncommonly, IBS may produce both diarrhea and constipation (with or without pain) intermittently in the same person.

Constipation may be characterized by the passage of small hard fecal balls or small soft stools. In a typical pattern, several days of constipation will lead to passage of hard stools, followed by several softer ones, and finally, watery excretion. Strands of mucus and spots of bright red blood may be noticed in stool but are usually the result of rectal irritation. Any increased or persistent bleeding should be discussed immediately with your physician.

Diarrhea most commonly occurs in the morning before or after breakfast and is often accompanied by a strong sense of urgency. Stools are usually soft, watery, and only partially formed. The urge to defecate may also be quite strong immediately following other meals during the day. However, only a few watery stools may be passed at each bowel movement. Diarrhea will rarely awaken an IBS sufferer at night, although sleep may occasionally be interrupted by cramping.

Other Complaints

Other symptoms of IBS may include indigestion, bloating, belching, excess gas, nausea, vomiting, and loss of appetite. Headache, heart palpitations, dizziness, fatigue, shortness of breath, and tingling of the hands and feet may also be experienced by the person with IBS.

Causes Of IBS

What causes IBS? Well, researchers have determined that most symptoms are directly related to an abnormal pattern of motion (motility) of the large intestine (colon).

The colon is a 5-foot area of bowel between the small intestine and the anus. Its main function is to remove water and salts from digestive products coming from the small intestine and hold the remaining residue until defecation. This fecal material then passes through the colon by means of a very delicate process of motion.

The motility of the colon is controlled by the body's nervous system. There are nerve impulses that stimulate activity, others that inhibit it—and with a fine balance between the two types of impulses, gastrointestinal contents are propelled forward smoothly and without problems.

In persons with IBS, however, this delicate balance is disturbed. In addition to the regular contractions that propel colon contents along, there are irregular, nonpropulsive contractions that can upset normal rhythm.

Constipation occurs when the propulsive movements are inhibited and absorption of water in the colon is increased, leaving the feces dry and hard. Diarrhea results when the propulsive movements are excessive, and there is little chance for water absorption. Abdominal pain and cramping result from the spasm of the colon and a buildup of gas that fills the bowel.

Emotional Triggers

Why the nerve impulses that control colonic motility are out of balance in persons with IBS has been the subject of much investigation. All the answers are still not known. However, it has become obvious that both emotional factors and dietary habits play a very important role.

By measuring colon contractions in patients under stressful and nonstressful conditions, scientists have demonstrated that emotional stress clearly helps trigger abnormal motility. This is further borne out by the fact that many persons who suffer from IBS are sometimes tense, anxious and given to emotional ups and downs. There is usually a history of overwork, inadequate sleep, and hurried and irregular meals.

Dietary Abuse

Colon contractions are also regulated by the amount and types of food consumed. High caloric meals and meals high in fat content can produce exaggerated contractions in persons with IBS, leading to cramps and diarrhea. Fats in the form of oils, animal fat, or butter are particularly important culprits, while carbohydrates, dietary protein, and blander foods usually have a minimal effect on the colon.

A Vicious Cycle You Can Break

Once you understand why irritable bowel syndrome occurs you can begin to do something about it. For example, it is important to recognize that there is a distinct cycle of events that takes place during a bout with IBS.

First, the attack may be triggered by anxiety, tension, and emotional stress. This causes the pain and diarrhea or constipation. In turn, these symptoms produce even more anxiety and the cycle begins all over again.

Stay Calm

It's obvious, then, that reducing emotional stress will reduce the frequency and severity of irritable bowel syndrome and help break the vicious cycle. Of course, none of us can change our personalities or the way we react to people or events in our lives overnight. However, try to keep things in perspective and learn to deal with any anger, hostility, or anxieties you may have. Also remember that, although the symptoms of IBS are very real and often very distressing, they are not usually the result of any serious organic disease. That is why your doctor has fully examined you before making the diagnosis. If you get an attack, stay calm and try to ride it out. You will be surprised at the positive results you'll get.

Exercise and Get Plenty of Rest

One good way to get rid of any bottled up hostilities or anxiety you may have is regular, vigorous, and enjoyable physical exercise. Exercise clears the mind and tones the body.

Get plenty of rest, too, and if possible, try to live according to a regular daily schedule. That means working, sleeping, and eating at the same times during each 24-hour period. Try to eat the same number of meals each day always at evenly spaced intervals. Be sure to get enough sleep—all at one time, if possible, rather than catnaps. And try to avoid alcohol and tobacco.

Eat the Right Foods and Learn Which Foods Bother You

If your situation warrants it, your physician may recommend a special diet for you. In general, you should try to stay away from heavy meals and lean toward blander foods. Avoid very fatty foods. Cut down on your intake of fried foods, milk, and any milk products. Don't drink a lot of coffee and stay away from very hot or very cold drinks.

Try to learn which foods are most irritating to your own digestive system. Keep a log of your IBS episodes and note the foods you ingested prior to the attacks. After a few weeks you may find that certain foods are more likely than others to set off symptoms. Tell your doctor what they are and avoid or cut down on these foods if your physician so advises.

In some IBS patients, particularly where constipation is the dominant problem, a diet high in fiber has been useful. Your doctor can tell you if increased fiber intake will help in your case.

Medication

There are a number of medications your physician may elect to prescribe for you if your case warrants. Two of the most common types are tranquilizers and antispasmodics. Tranquilizers are designed to help calm you down a little so that unusual stresses are less likely to trigger or perpetuate an attack of IBS. Antispasmodics are intended to help normalize colon contractions by regulating the chemicals that help produce the rhythm-controlling impulses. For your convenience, your doctor may sometimes prescribe a medication that contains both an antispasmodic and a tranquilizer.

Whatever medications your doctor prescribes, take them exactly as he or she directs. Timing of medication doses can be very important in treating IBS. Also, if you experience any side effects be sure to tell your physician.

Keep Your Chin Up

Remember, the WORST thing you can do is WORRY. IBS is controllable but it takes some positive thinking and positive effort. So keep your chin up. Smile! Your doctor is there to help you, and you're there to help yourself!

REFERENCES

Agras, W. S., Chapin, H. N., & Oliveau, D. C. (1972). The natural history of phobia: Course and prognosis. *Archives of General Psychiatry, 26*, 315–317.

Alexander, F. (1950). *Psychosomatic Medicine: Its principles and applications.* New York: Norton.

Almy, T. P., Kern, F., & Tulin, M. (1949). Alterations in colonic functioning in man under stress: II. Experimental production of sigmoid spasm in healthy persons. *Gastroenterology, 12*, 425–436.

American Psychiatric Association. (1968). *Diagnostic and statistical manual of mental disorders* (2nd ed.). Washington, DC: American Psychiatric Press.

American Psychiatric Association. (1980). *Diagnostic and statistical manual of mental disorders* (3rd ed.). Washington, DC. American Psychiatric Press.

American Psychiatric Association. (1987). *Diagnostic and statistical manual of mental disorders* (3rd ed., rev.). Washington, DC. American Psychiatric Press.

American Psychiatric Association. (1994). *Diagnostic and statistical manual of mental disorders* (4th ed.). Washington, DC. American Psychiatric Press.

Apley, J., & Hale, B. (1973). Children with recurrent abdominal pain: How do they grow up? *British Medical Journal, 3*, 7–9.

Apley, J., & Naish, N. (1958). Recurrent abdominal pains: A field study of 1,000 school children. *Archives of Disease in Childhood, 33*, 165–170.

Arapakis, G., Lyketsos, C. G., Gerolymatos, K., Richardson, S. C., & Lyketsos, G. C. (1986). Low dominance and high intropunitiveness in ulcerative colitis and irritable bowel syndrome. *Psychotherapy and Psychosomatics, 46*, 171–176.

Attanasio, V., Andrasik, F., Blanchard, E. B., & Arena, J. G. (1984). Psychometric properties of the SUNY Revision of the Psychosomatic Symptom Checklist. *Journal of Behavioral Medicine, 7*, 245–259.

Azrin, N., Naster, B., & Jones, R. (1973). Reciprocity counseling: A rapid learning-based procedure for marital counseling. *Behaviour Research and Therapy, 11*, 365–382.

Beck, A. T. (1976). *Cognitive therapy and the emotional disorders.* New York: International Universities Press.

Beck, A. T., Rush, J. A., Shaw, B. F., & Emery, G. (1980). *Cognitive therapy of depression.* New York: Guilford Press.

Beck, A. T., Ward, C. H., Mendelson, M., Mock, J., & Erbaugh, J. (1961). An inventory for measuring depression. *Archives of General Psychiatry, 5*, 561–571.

Bennett, E. J., Piesse, C., Palmer, K., Badcock, C. A., Tennant, C. C., & Kellow, J. E. (1998). Functional gastrointestinal disorders: Psychological, social, and somatic features. *Gut, 42*, 414–420.

Bennett, P., & Wilkinson, S. (1985). Comparison of psychological and medical treatment of the irritable bowel syndrome. *British Journal of Clinical Psychology, 24,* 215–216.

Bergeron, C. N. (1983). *A comparison of cognitive stress management, progressive muscle relaxation, and biofeedback in the treatment of irritable bowel syndrome.* Unpublished doctoral dissertation, University of Missouri-Columbia. Available from University Microfilms International: Ann Arbor, MI.

Best, W. R., Becktel, J. M., Singleton, J. W., & Kern, F. (1976). Development of a Crohn's Disease Activity Index: National Cooperative Crohn's Disease Study. *Gastroenterology, 70,* 439–444.

Blanchard, E. B. (1992). Psychological treatment of benign headache disorders. *Journal of Consulting and Clinical Psychology, 60,* 537–551.

Blanchard, E. B., & Andrasik, F. (1985). *Management of chronic headache: A psychological approach.* Elmsford, NY: Pergamon Press.

Blanchard, E. B., Andrasik, F., Appelbaum, K. A., Evans, D. D., Myers, P., & Barron, K. D. (1986). Three studies of the psychological changes in chronic headache patients associated with biofeedback and relaxation therapies. *Psychosomatic Medicine, 48,* 73–83.

Blanchard, E. B., & Epstein, L. H. (1978). *A biofeedback primer.* Reading, MA: Addison-Wesley.

Blanchard, E. B., Greene, B., Scharff, L., & Schwarz-McMorris, S. P. (1993). Relaxation training as a treatment for irritable bowel syndrome. *Biofeedback and Self-Regulation, 18,* 125–132.

Blanchard, E. B., Martin, J. E., & Dubbert, P. M. (1988). *Non-drug treatments for essential hypertension.* Elmsford, NY: Pergamon Press:

Blanchard, E. B., Radnitz, C., Evans, D. D., Schwarz, S. P., Neff, D. F., & Gerardi, M. A. (1986). Psychological comparisons of irritable bowel syndrome to chronic tension and migraine headache and non-patient controls. *Biofeedback and Self-Regulation, 11,* 221–230.

Blanchard, E. B., Radnitz, C., Schwarz, S. P., Neff, D. F., & Gerardi, M. A. (1987). Psychological changes associated with self-regulatory treatments of irritable bowel syndrome. *Biofeedback and Self-Regulation, 12,* 31–38.

Blanchard, E. B., Scharff, L., Payne, A., Schwarz, S. P., Suls, J. M., & Malamood, H. (1992). Prediction of outcome from cognitive–behavioral treatment of irritable bowel syndrome. *Behaviour Research and Therapy, 30,* 647–650.

Blanchard, E. B., Scharff, L., Schwarz, S. P., Suls, J. M., & Barlow, D. H. (1990). The role of anxiety and depression in the irritable bowel syndrome. *Behaviour Research and Therapy,* 28, 401–405.

Blanchard, E. B., & Schwarz, S. P. (1987). Adaptation of a multi-component treatment program for irritable bowel syndrome to a small group format. *Biofeedback and Self-Regulation, 12,* 63–69.

Blanchard, E. B., & Schwarz, S. P. (1988). Clinically significant changes in behavioral medicine. *Behavioral Assessment, 10,* 171–188.

Blanchard, E. B., Schwarz, S. P., & Neff, D. F. (1988). Two-year follow-up of behavioral treatment of irritable bowel syndrome. *Behavior Therapy, 19,* 67–73.

Blanchard, E. B., Schwarz, S. P., Neff, D. F., & Gerardi, M. A. (1988). Prediction of outcome from the self-regulatory treatment of irritable bowel syndrome. *Behaviour Research and Therapy, 26*(3), 187–190.

Blanchard, E. B., Schwarz, S. P., Suls, J. M., Gerardi, M. A., Scharff, L., Greene, B., Taylor, A. E., Berreman, C., & Malamood, H. S. (1992). Two controlled evaluations of multicomponent psychological treatment of irritable bowel syndrome. *Behaviour Research and Therapy, 30,* 175–189.

Blewett, A., Allison, M., Calcraft, B., Moore, R., Jenkins, P., & Sullivan, G. (1996). Psychiatric disorder and outcome in irritable bowel syndrome. *Psychosomatics, 37,* 155–160.

Brantley, P. J., & Jones, G. N. (1989). *Daily Stress Inventory.* Odessa, FL: Psychological Assessment Resources, Inc.

Budzynski, T. H. (1973). Biofeedback procedures in the clinic. *Seminars in Psychiatry, 5,* 537–547.

Bueno-Miranda, F., Cerulli, M., & Schuster, M. M. (1976). Operant conditioning of colonic motility in irritable bowel syndrome (IBS). *Gastroenterology, 70,* 867.

Burns, D. D. (1980). *Feeling good: The new mood therapy.* New York: Signet.

Bury, R. G. (1987). A study of 111 children with recurrent abdominal pain. *Australian Paediatric Journal, 23,* 117–119.

Christensen, M. F., & Mortensen, O. (1975). Long-term prognosis in children with recurrent abdominal pain. *Archives of Disease in Childhood, 50,* 110–114.

Corney, R. H., & Stanton, R. (1990). Physical symptom severity, psychological and social dysfunction in a series of outpatients with irritable bowel syndrome. *Journal of Psychosomatic Research, 34,* 483–491.

Corney, R. H., Stanton, R., Newell, R., Clare, A., & Fairclough, P. (1991). Behavioural psychotherapy in the treatment of irritable bowel syndrome. *Journal of Psychosomatic Research, 35,* 461–469.

Costa, Jr., P. T., & McCrae, R. R. (1985). *The NEO Personality Inventory Manual.* Odessa, FL: Psychological Assessment Resources.

Craig, T. K. J., & Brown, G. W. (1984). Goal frustration and life events in the aetiology of painful gastrointestinal disorder. *Journal of Psychosomatic Research, 28,* 411–421.

Dancey, C. P., Taghavi, M., & Fox, R. J. (1998). The relationship between daily stress and symptoms of irritable bowel: A time-series approach. *Journal of Psychosomatic Research, 44,* 537–545.

Dancey, C. P., Whitehouse, A., Painter, J., & Backhouse, S. (1995). The relationship between hassles, uplifts, and irritable bowel syndrome: A preliminary study. *Journal of Psychosomatic Research, 39,* 827–832.

DeLongis, A., Coyne, J. C., Dakoif, G., Folkman, S., & Lazarus, R. S. (1982). Relation of daily hassles, uplifts, and major life events to health status. *Health Psychology, 1,* 119–136.

DeLongis, A., Folkman, S., & Lazarus, R. S. (1988). The impact of daily stress on health and mood: Psychological and social resources as mediators. *Journal of Personality and Social Psychology, 54*, 486–495.

Delvaux, M., Denis, P., Allemand, H., & the French Club of Digestive Motility. (1997). Sexual abuse is more frequently reported by IBS patients than by patients with organic digestive diseases or controls. Results of a multicentre inquiry. *European Journal of Gastroenterology and Hepatology*, 9, 345–352.

Derogatis, L. R. (1994). *The SCL-90-R: Administration, scoring, and procedures manual* (3rd ed.). Minneapolis, MN: Minneapolis National Computer Systems, Inc.

Derogatis, L. R., Lipman, R. S., & Covi, L. (1973). SCL-90: An outpatient psychiatric rating scale. Preliminary report. *Psychopharmacology Bulletin*, 9, 13–28.

Derogatis, L. R., Lipman, R. S., Rickels, K., Uhlenhuth, E. H., & Covi, L. (1974). The Hopkins Symptom Checklist (HSCL): A self-report symptom inventory. *Behavioral Science, 19*, 1–15.

Dewsnap, P., Gomborone, J., Libby, G., & Farthing, M. (1996). The prevalence of symptoms of irritable bowel syndrome among acute psychiatric inpatients with an affective diagnosis. *Psychosomatics*, 37, 385–389.

Dill, B., Sibcy, G. A., Dill, J. E., & Brende, J. O. (1997). Abuse, threat, and irritable bowel syndrome: What is the connection? *Gastroenterology Nursing, 20*, 211–215.

DiNardo, P. A., & Barlow, D. H. (1988). *Anxiety Disorders Interview Schedule—Revised* (ADIS-R). Available from the Center for Anxiety and Related Disorders, Boston, MA.

Drossman, D. A. (1995). Diagnosing and treating patients with refractory functional gastrointestinal disorders. *Annals of Internal Medicine, 123*, 688–697.

Drossman, D. A., Leserman, J., Nachman, G., Li, Z., Gluck, H., Toomey, T. C., & Mitchell, C. M. (1990). Sexual and physical abuse in women with functional or organic gastrointestinal disorders. *Annals of Internal Medicine, 113*, 828–833.

Drossman, D. A., Li, Z., Andruzzi, E., Temple, R. D., Talley, N. J., Thompson, W. G., Whitehead, W. E., Janssens, J., Funch-Jensen, P., Corazziari, E., Richter, J. E., & Koch, G. G. (1993). U.S. Householder Survey of Functional Gastrointestinal Disorders: Prevalence, sociodemography, and health impact. *Digestive Diseases and Sciences*, 38, 1569–1580.

Drossman, D. A., Li, Z., Toner, B. B., Diamant, N. E., Creed, F. H., Thompson, D., Read, N. W., Babbs, C., Barreiro, M., Bank, L., Whitehead, W. E., Schuster, M. M., & Guthrie, E. A. (1995). Functional bowel disorders: A multicenter comparison of health status and development of illness severity index. *Digestive Diseases and Sciences*, 40, 1–9.

Drossman, D. A., McKee, D. C., Sandler, R. S., Mitchell, C. M., Cramer, E. M., Lowman, B. C., & Burger, A. L. (1988). Psychosocial factors in the irritable bowel syndrome: A multivariate study of patients and non-patients with irritable bowel syndrome. *Gastroenterology*, 95, 701–708.

Drossman, D. A., Sandler, R. S., McKee, D. C., & Lovitz, A. J. (1982). Bowel patterns among subjects not seeking health care: Use of a questionnaire to identify a population with bowel dysfunction. *Gastroenterology*, *83*, 529–534.

Drossman, D. A., Talley, N. J., Leserman, J., Olden, K. W., & Barreiro, M. A. (1995). Sexual and physical abuse and gastrointestinal illness. *Annals of Internal Medicine*, *123*, 782–794.

Drossman, D. A., & Thompson, G. (1992). The irritable bowel syndrome: Review and a graduated multicomponent treatment approach. *Annals of Internal Medicine*, *116*, 1009–1016.

Drossman, D. A., Thompson, W. G., Talley, N. J., Funch-Jensen, P., Janssens, J., & Whitehead, W. E. (1990). Identification of sub-groups of functional gastrointestinal disorders. *Gastroenterology International*, *3*, 159–174.

Engel, G. L. (1977). The need for a new medical model: A challenge for biomedicine. *Science*, *196*, 129–136.

Esler, M. D., & Goulston, K. J. (1973). Levels of anxiety in colonic disorders. *New England Journal of Medicine*, *288*, 16–20.

Eysenck, H. J., & Eysenck, S. B. G. (1968). *Eysenck Personality Inventory*. San Diego: Educational and Industrial Testing Service.

Faull, C., & Nicol, A. R. (1986). Abdominal pain in six year olds: An epidemiological study in a new town. *Journal of Child Psychology, Psychiatry, and Allied Disciplines*, *27*, 251–260.

Feighner, J. P., Robins, E., Guze, S. B., Woodruff, R. A., Winokur, G., & Munoz, R. (1972). Diagnostic criteria for use in psychiatric research. *Archives of General Psychiatry*, *26*, 57–63.

Feliti, V. J. (1991). Long-term medical consequences of incest, rape, and molestation. *Southern Medical Journal*, *84*, 328–331.

Fielding, J. F. (1977). A year in out-patients with the irritable bowel syndrome. *Irish Journal of Medical Science*, *146*, 162–166.

Fielding, J. F., & Regan, R. (1984). Excessive cold pressor responses in the irritable bowel syndrome. *Irish Journal of Medical Science*, *153*, 348–350.

Finney, J. W., Lemanek, K. L., Cataldo, M. F., Katz, H. P., & Fuqua, R. W. (1989). Pediatric psychology in primary health care: Brief targeted therapy for recurrent abdominal pain. *Behavior Therapy*, *20*, 283–291.

Ford, M. J., Miller, P. McC., Eastwood, J., & Eastwood, M. A. (1987). Life events, psychiatric illness and the irritable bowel syndrome. *Gut*, *28*, 160–165.

Fordyce, W. E. (1974). Behavioral science and rehabilitation. *Rehabilitation Psychology*, *21*, 82–85.

Fordyce, W. E. (1976). *Behavioral methods for chronic pain and illness*. St. Louis: Mosby.

Fossey, M. D., & Lydiard, R. B. (1990). Anxiety and the gastrointestinal system. *Psychiatric Medicine*, *8*, 175–186.

Fowlie, S., Eastwood, M. A., & Ford, M. J. (1992). Irritable bowel syndrome: The influence of psychological factors on the symptom complex. *Journal of Psychosomatic Research, 36*, 169–173.

Freedman, R. R. (1993). Raynaud's disease and phenomenon. In R. J. Gatchel & E. B. Blanchard (Eds.), *Psycho-physiological disorders: Research in clinical applications* (pp. 245–267). Washington, DC: American Psychological Association.

Furman, S. (1973). Intestinal biofeedback in functional diarrhea: A preliminary report. *Journal of Behavior Therapy and Experimental Psychiatry, 4*, 317–321.

Galovski, T. E., & Blanchard, E. B. (1999). The treatment of irritable bowel syndrome with hypnotherapy. *Applied Psychophysiology and Biofeedback, 23*, 219–232.

Gick, M. L., & Thompson, G. (1997). Negative affect and the seeking of medical care in university students with irritable bowel syndrome: A preliminary study. *Journal of Psychomatic Research, 43*, 535–540.

Giles, S. L. (1978). *Separate and combined effects of biofeedback training and brief individual psychotherapy in the treatment of gastrointestinal disorders*. Unpublished doctoral dissertation, Department of Psychology, University of Colorado. Available from University Microfilms International: Ann Arbor, MI.

Goldberg, D. P. (1972). *The detection of psychiatric illness by questionnaire*. Maudsley Monograph No. 21, London: Oxford University Press.

Goldberg, D. P., Cooper, B., Eastwood, M., Kedward, H., & Shepherd, M. (1970). A psychiatric interview suitable for using in community surveys. *British Journal of Preventive Medicine, 24*, 18–26.

Gomborone, J., Dewsnap, P., Libby, G., & Farthing, M. (1995). Abnormal illness attitudes in patients with irritable bowel syndrome. *Journal of Psychosomatic Research, 39*, 227–230.

Greenbaum, D. S., Mayle, J. E., Vanegeren, L. E., Jerome, J. A., Mayor, J. W., Greenbaum, R. B., Matson, R. W., Stein, G. E., Dean, H. A., Halvorsen, N. A., & Rosen, L. W. (1987). Effects of desipramine on irritable bowel syndrome compared with atropine and placebo. *Digestive Diseases and Sciences, 32*, 257–266.

Greene, B., & Blanchard, E. B. (1994). Cognitive therapy for irritable bowel syndrome. *Journal of Consulting and Clinical Psychology, 62*, 576–582.

Guthrie, E., Creed, F., Dawson, D., & Tomenson, B. (1991). A controlled trial of psychological treatment for the irritable bowel syndrome. *Gastroenterology, 100*, 450–457.

Guthrie, E., Moorey, J., Margison, R., Barker, H., Palmer, S., McGrath, G., Tomenson, B., & Creed, F. (1999). Cost-effectiveness of brief psychodynamic-interpersonal therapy in high utilizers of psychiatric services. *Archives of General Psychiatry*, 56, 519–526.

Hamilton, M. A. (1959). The assessment of anxiety states by rating. *British Journal of Medical Psychology, 32*, 50–55.

Hamilton, M. A. (1960). A rating scale for depression. *Journal of Neurology, Neurosurgery, and Psychiatry, 23*, 56–61.

Harvey, R. F., Hinton, R. A., Gunary, R. M., & Barry, R. E. (1989). Individual and group hypnotherapy in treatment of refractory irritable bowel syndrome. *The Lancet, i*, 424–425.

Harvey, R. F., Mauad, E. C., & Brown, A. M. (1987). Prognosis in the irritable bowel syndrome: A 5-year prospective study. *The Lancet*, 963–965.

Harvey, R. F., Salih, S. Y., & Read, A. E. (1983). Organic and functional disorders in 2000 gastroenterology outpatients. *The Lancet, 2*, 632–634.

Heaton, K. W., O'Donnell, L. J. D., Braddon, F. E. M., Mountford, R. A., Hughes, A. O., & Cripps, P. J. (1992). Symptoms of irritable bowel syndrome in a British urban community: Consulters and nonconsulters. *Gastroenterology, 102*, 1962–1967.

Hermann, C., Peters, M. L., & Blanchard, E. B. (1995). Use of hand-held computers for symptom-monitoring: The case of chronic headache. *Mind/Body Medicine, 1*, 59–69.

Hersen, M., & Barlow, D. H. (1976). *Single case experimental designs: Strategies for studying behavior change*. New York: Pergamon Press.

Hislop, I. G. (1971). Psychological significance of the irritable colon syndrome. *Gut*, 12, 452–457.

Hollon, S. D., & Kendall, P. E. (1980). Cognitive self-statements in depression: Development of an Automatic Thoughts Questionnaire. *Cognitive Therapy and Research, 4*, 383–396.

Holmes, K. M., & Salter, R. H. (1982). Irritable bowel syndrome—a safe diagnosis? *British Medical Journal*, 285, 1533–1534.

Holmes, T. H., & Rahe, R. H. (1967). The Social Readjustment Rating Scale. *Journal of Psychosomatic Research*, 11, 213–218.

Holroyd, K. A., Andrasik, F., & Noble, J. (1980). Comparison of EMG biofeedback and a credible pseudotherapy in treating tension headache. *Journal of Behavioral Medicine*, 3, 29–39.

Holroyd, K. A., Andrasik, F., & Westbrook, T. (1977). Cognitive control of tension headache. *Cognitive Therapy and Research, 1*, 121–133.

Houghton, L. A., Heyman, D. J., & Whorwell, P. J. (1996). Symptomatology, quality of life and economic features of irritable bowel syndrome: The effect of hypnotherapy. *Alimentary Pharmacology and Therapeutics, 10*, 91–95.

Irwin, C., Falsetti, S. A., Lydiard, R. B., Ballenger, J. C., Brock, C. D., & Brener, W. (1996). Comorbidity of posttraumatic stress disorder and irritable bowel syndrome. *Journal of Clinical Psychiatry, 57*, 576–578.

Jarrett, M., Heitkemper, M., Cain, K. C., Tuftin, M., Walker, E. A., Bond, E. F., & Levy, R. L. (1998). The relationship between psychological distress and gastrointestinal symptoms in women with irritable bowel syndrome. *Nursing Research, 47*, 154–161.

Joachim, G. (1983). The effects of two stress management techniques on feelings of well-being in patients with inflammatory bowel disease. *Nursing Papers, 15*, 5–18.

Kanner, A. D., Coyne, J. C., Schaefer, C., & Lazarus, R. S. (1981). Comparison of two modes of stress management: Minor daily hassles and uplifts versus major life events. *Journal of Behavioral Medicine, 4,* 1–39.

Keeling, P. W. N., & Fielding, J. F. (1975). The irritable bowel syndrome: A review of 50 consecutive cases. *Journal of the Irish Colleges of Physicians and Surgeons, 4,* 91–94.

Kellner, R. (1981). Manual of the IAS (Illness Attitudes Scale). Albuquerque: University of New Mexico.

Klein, K. B. (1988). Controlled treatment trials in the irritable bowel syndrome: A critique. *Gastroenterology,* 95, 232–241.

Kovacs, M. (1980/1981). Rating scales to assess depression in school-aged children. *Acta Paedo Psychiatrica, 46,* 305–315.

Kruis, W., Thieme, C. H., Weintzierl, M., Schussler, P., Holl, J., & Paulus, W. (1984). A diagnostic score for the irritable bowel syndrome: Its value in the exclusion of organic disease. *Gastroenterology,* 87, 1–7.

Lange, A. J., & Jakubowski, P. (1976). *Responsible assertive behavior.* Champaign, IL: Research Press.

Latimer, P. R. (1983). *Functional gastrointestinal disorders: A behavioral medicine approach.* New York: Springer Publishing Co.

Latimer, P., Campbell, D., Latimer, M., Sarna, S., Daniel, E., & Waterfall, W. (1979). Irritable bowel syndrome: A test of the colonic hyperalgesia hypothesis. *Journal of Behavioral Medicine,* 2, 285–295.

Latimer, P., Sarna, S., Campbell, D., Latimer, M., Waterfall, W., & Daniel, E. E. (1981). Colonic motor and myoelectrical activity: A comparative study of normal subjects, psychoneurotic patients, and patients with irritable bowel syndrome. *Gastroenterology,* 80, 893–901.

Lazarus, R. (1966). *Psychological stress and the coping process.* New York: McGraw-Hill.

Leserman, J., Drossman, D. A., Li, Z., Toomey, T. C., Nachman, G., & Glogau, L. (1996). Sexual and physical abuse history in gastroenterology practice: How types of abuse impact health status. *Psychosomatic Medicine,* 58, 4–15.

Levine, B. S., Jarrett, M., Cain, K. C., & Heitkemper, M. M. (1997). Psychophysiological response to a laboratory challenge in women with and without diagnosed irritable bowel syndrome. *Research in Nursing and Health, 20,* 431–441.

Levy, R. L., Cain, K. C., Jarrett, M., & Heitkemper, M. M. (1997). The relationship between daily life stress and gastrointestinal symptoms in women with irritable bowel syndrome. *Journal of Behavioral Medicine,* 20, 177–193.

Liss, J. L., Alpers, D. H., & Woodruff, R. A. (1973). The irritable colon syndrome and psychiatric illness. *Diseases of the Nervous System, 34,* 151–157.

Longstreth, G. F., & Wolde-Tsadik, G. (1993). Irritable bowel-type symptoms in HMO examinees: Prevalence, demographics, and clinical correlates. *Digestive Diseases and Science, 38,* 1581–1589.

Lydiard, R. B. (1992). Anxiety and the irritable bowel syndrome. *Psychiatric Annals, 22,* 612–618.

Lydiard, R. B., Greenwald, S., Weissman, M. M., Johnson, J., Drossman, D. A., & Ballenger, J. C. (1994). Panic disorder and gastrointestinal symptoms: Findings from the NIMH Epidemiologic Catchment Area Project. *American Journal of Psychiatry, 151,* 64–70.

Lydiard, R. B., Laraia, M. T., Howell, E. F., & Ballenger, J. C. (1986). Can panic disorder present as irritable bowel syndrome? *Journal of Clinical Psychiatry, 47,* 470–473.

Lynch, P. M., & Zamble, E. (1987). Stress management training for irritable bowel syndrome: A preliminary investigation. *Clinical Biofeedback and Health, 10,* 123–134.

Lynch, P. M., & Zamble, E. (1989). A controlled behavioral treatment study of irritable bowel syndrome. *Behavior Therapy,* 20, 509–523.

MacDonald, A. J., & Bouchier, I. A. D. (1980). Non-organic gastrointestinal illness: A medical and psychiatric study. *British Journal of Psychiatry,* 136, 276–283.

Malton, M. (1982). *The behavioral assessment of stress: The Queen's Stress Inventory.* Kingston, Ontario, Canada: Queen's University.

Manning, A. P., Thompson, W. G., Heaton, K. W., & Morris, A. F. (1978). Towards positive diagnosis of the irritable bowel. *British Medical Journal,* 2, 653–654.

Masand, P. S., Kaplan, D. S., Gupta, S., Bhandary, A. N., Nasra, G. S., Kline, M. D., & Margo, K. L. (1995). Major depression and irritable bowel syndrome: Is there a relationship? *Journal of Clinical Psychiatry,* 56, 363–367.

McGrath, P. A. (1990). *Pain in children: Nature, assessment, and treatment.* New York: Guilford Press.

McIllmurray, M. B., & Langman, M. J. S. (1975). Causation and management. *Gut, 17,* 815–820.

McNicol, D. (1972). *A primer of signal detection theory.* London: George Allen & Unwin Ltd.

Meichenbaum, D. (1977). *Cognitive behavior modification: An integrative approach.* New York: Plenum.

Meichenbaum, D. (1985). *Stress innoculation training.* Elmsford, NY: Pergamon Press.

Meissner, J. S., Blanchard, E. B., & Malamood, H. S. (1997). Comparison of treatment outcome measures for irritable bowel syndrome. *Applied Psychophysiology and Biofeedback,* 22, 55–62.

Melzack, R. (1975). The McGill Pain Questionnaire: Major properties and scoring methods. *Pain,* 7, 277–299.

Melzack, R., & Wall, P. D. (1965). Pain mechanisms: A new theory. *Science, 150,* 971–980.

Mendeloff, A. I., Monk, M., Siegel, C. I., & Lilienfeld, A. (1970). Illness experience and life stresses in patients with irritable colon and with ulcerative colitis. *New England Journal of Medicine,* 282, 14–17.

Mertz, H., Naliboff, B., Munakata, J., Niazi, N., & Mayer, E. A. (1995). Altered rectal perception is a biological marker of patients with irritable bowel syndrome. *Gastroenterology, 109*, 40–52.

Meyer, T. J., Miller, M. L., Metzger, R. L., & Borkovec, T. D. (1990). Development and validation of the Penn State Worry Questionnaire. *Behaviour Research and Therapy, 28*, 487–495.

Milne, B., Joachim, G., & Niedhardt, J. (1986). A stress management programme for inflammatory bowel disease patients. *Journal of Advanced Nursing, 11*, 561–567.

Mitchell, C. M., & Drossman, D. A. (1987). Survey of the AGA Membership relating to patients with functional gastrointestinal disorders. *Gastroenterology, 92*, 1281–1284.

Morris-Yates, A., Talley, N. J., Boyce, P. M., Nandurkar, S., & Andrews, G. (1998). Evidence of a genetic contribution to functional bowel disorder. *The American Journal of Gastroenterology, 93*, 1311–1317.

Mueller-Lissner, S. A. (1988). Effect of wheat bran on weight of stool and gastrointestinal transit time: A meta analysis. *British Medical Journal, 296*, 615–617.

Naliboff, B. D., Munakata, J., Fullerton, S., Gracely, R. H., Kodner, A., Harraf, F., & Mayer, E. A. (1997). Evidence for two distinct perceptual alterations in irritable bowel syndrome. *Gut, 41*, 505–512.

Neff, D. F., & Blanchard, E. B. (1987). A multi-component treatment for irritable bowel syndrome. *Behavior Therapy, 18*, 70–83.

NIDDK. (1992). Workshop on Irritable Bowel Syndrome (IBS): State-of-the-Art and Research Objectives (September 9–11). Bethesda, MD.

Noyes, Jr., R., Cook, B., Garvey, M., & Summers, R. (1990). Reduction of gastrointestinal symptoms following treatment for panic disorder. *Psychosomatics, 31*, 75–79.

O'Connell, M. F., & Russ, K. L. (1978). *A case report comparing two types of biofeedback in the treatment of irritable bowel syndrome*. Ninth Annual Meeting of the Biofeedback Society of America, Albuquerque, NM.

Overall, J. E., & Gorham, D. R. (1962). The Brief Psychological Rating Scale. *Psychological Reports, 10*, 799–812.

Palmer, R. L., Stonehill, E., Crisp, A. H., Waller, S. L., & Misiewicz, J. J. (1974). Psychological characteristics of patients with the irritable bowel syndrome. *Postgraduate Medical Journal, 50*, 416–419.

Patterson, G. R. (1976). *Living with children*. Champaign, IL: Research Press.

Payne, A., & Blanchard, E. B. (1995). A controlled comparison of cognitive therapy and self-help support groups in the treatment of irritable bowel syndrome. *Journal of Consulting and Clinical Psychology, 63*, 779–786.

Payne, A., Blanchard, E. B., Holt, C. S., & Schwarz, S. P. (1992). Physiological reactivity to stressors in irritable bowel syndrome patients, inflammatory bowel disease patients, and non-patient controls. *Behaviour Research and Therapy, 30*, 293–300.

Payne, A., Blanchard, E. B., Vollmer, A. J., & Brown, T. A. (1993). *Early sexual and physical abuse in irritable bowel syndrome: Replication and extension.* Unpublished manuscript. Center for Stress and Anxiety Disorders, Albany, NY.

Persons, J. B. (1989). *Cognitive therapy in practice: A case formulation approach.* New York: Norton.

Plotkin, W. B., & Rice, K. M. (1981). Biofeedback as a placebo: Anxiety reduction facilitated by training in either suppression or enhancement of alpha brain waves. *Journal of Consulting and Clinical Psychology, 49,* 590–596.

Prior, A., Colgan, S. M., & Whorwell, P. J. (1990). Changes in rectal sensitivity after hypnotherapy by patients with irritable bowel syndrome. *Gut, 31,* 896–898.

Radnitz, C. L., & Blanchard, E. B. (1988). Bowel sound biofeedback as a treatment for irritable bowel syndrome. *Biofeedback and Self-Regulation, 13,* 169–179.

Radnitz, C. L., & Blanchard, E. B. (1989). A one- and two-year follow-up study of bowel sound biofeedback as a treatment for irritable bowel syndrome. *Biofeedback and Self-Regulation, 14,* 333–338.

Rathus, S. A. (1973). A 30-item schedule for assessing assertive behavior. *Behavior Therapy, 4,* 398–406.

Read, N. S. (1985). *Irritable Bowel Syndrome.* Greene & Stratton: London.

Rice, K. M., Blanchard, E. B., & Purcell, M. (1993). Biofeedback treatments of generalized anxiety disorder: Preliminary results. *Biofeedback and Self-Regulation, 18,* 93–105.

Ritchie, J. (1973). Pain from distension of the pelvic colon by inflating a balloon in the irritable colon syndrome. *Gut, 14,* 125–132.

Robins, L. N., Helzer, J. E., Croughan, J., & Ratcliff, K. S. (1981). National Institute of Mental Health Diagnostic Interview Schedule: Its history, characteristics, and validity. *Archives of General Psychiatry, 38,* 381–389.

Robins, L. N., & Regier, D. A. (Eds.). (1991). *Psychiatric disorders in America: The Epidemiological Catchment Area Study.* New York: The Free Press.

Robins, L. N., Wing, J. K., & Wittchen, H. V. (1988). The Composite International Diagnostic Interview. *Archives of General Psychiatry, 45,* 1069–1078.

Robinson, J. O., Alverez, J. H., & Dodge, J. A. (1990). Life events and family history in children with recurrent abdominal pain. *Journal of Psychosomatic Research, 34,* 171–181.

Sanders, M. R., Rebgetz, M., Morrison, M., Bor, W., Gordon, A., Dadds, M., & Shepherd, R. (1989). Cognitive–behavioral treatment of recurrent nonspecific abdominal pain in children: An analysis of generalization, maintenance, and side effects. *Journal of Consulting and Clinical Psychology, 57,* 294–300.

Sanders, M. R., Shepherd, R. W., Cleghorn, G., & Woolford, H. (1994). The treatment of recurrent abdominal pain in Children: A controlled comparison of cognitive–behavioral family intervention and standard pediatric care. *Journal of Consulting and Clinical Psychology, 62,* 306–314.

Sandler, R. S., Drossman, D. A., Nathan, H. P., & McKee, D. C. (1984). Symptom complaints and health care seeking behavior in subject with bowel dysfunction. *Gastroenterology, 87,* 314–318.

Sarason, I. G., Johnson, J. H., & Siegel, J. M. (1978). Assessing the impact of life changes: Development of the Life Experience Survey. *Journal of Consulting and Clinical Psychology*, 46, 932–946.

Scharff, L., & Blanchard, E. B. (1996). *Behavioral treatment of recurrent abdominal pain: The effects of parent training and self-control in the management of symptoms.* Unpublished manuscript, Center for Stress and Anxiety, Albany, NY.

Schwartz, M. S. (1987). *Biofeedback: A practitioner's guide.* New York: Guilford Press.

Schwarz, S. P., & Blanchard, E. B. (1990). Inflammatory bowel disease: A review of the psychological assessment and treatment literature. *Annals of Behavioral Medicine*, *12*, 95–105.

Schwarz, S. P., & Blanchard, E. B. (1991). Evaluation of a psychological treatment for inflammatory bowel disease. *Behaviour Research and Therapy*, *29*, 167–177.

Schwarz, S. P., Blanchard, E. B., Berreman, C. F., Scharff, L., Taylor, A. E., Greene, B. R., Suls, J. M., & Malamood, H. S. (1993). Psychological aspects of irritable bowel syndrome: Comparisons with inflammatory bowel disease and nonpatient controls. *Behaviour Research and Therapy*, *31*, 297–304.

Schwarz, S. P., Blanchard, E. B., & Neff, D. F. (1986). Behavioral treatment of irritable bowel syndrome: A 1-year follow-up study. *Biofeedback and Self-Regulation*, *11*, 189–198.

Schwarz, S. P., Taylor, A. E., Scharff, L., & Blanchard, E. B. (1990). A four-year follow-up of behaviorally treated irritable bowel syndrome patients. *Behaviour Research and Therapy*, *28*, 331–335.

Shaw, G., Srivastava, E. D., Sadlier, M., Swann, P., James, J. Y., & Rhodes, J. (1991). Stress management for irritable bowel syndrome: A controlled trial. *Digestion*, *50*, 36–42.

Shaw, L., & Ehrlich, A. (1987). Relaxation training as a treatment for chronic pain caused by ulcerative colitis. *Pain*, *29*, 287–293.

Snaith, R. P., Baugh, S. J., Clayden, A. D., Hussain, A., & Sipple, M. A. (1982). The Clinical Anxiety Scale: An instrument derived from the Hamilton Anxiety Scale. *British Journal of Psychiatry*, *141*, 518–523.

Spielberger, C. D. (1973). *Manual for the State–Trait Anxiety Inventory for Children (Form Y).* Palo Alto, CA: Consulting Psychologists Press.

Spielberger, C. D. (1979). *Preliminary manual for State–Trait Anger Scale (STAS).* Unpublished manuscript, University of South Florida, Tampa.

Spielberger, C. D., Gorsuch, R. L., & Lushene, R. E. (1970). *STAI Manual for the State–Trait Anxiety Inventory.* Palo Alto, CA: Consulting Psychologists Press.

Spitzer, R. L., & Endicott, J. (1977). *Schedule for Affective Disorders and Schizophrenia-Life-time Version (SADS-L).* (Available from New York State Psychiatric Institute, 722 West 168th Street, New York, NY 10032)

Spitzer, R. L., & Williams, J. B. W. (1982). *Structured Clinical Interview for DSM-III.* New York: Biometrics Research Department, New York State Psychiatric Institute.

Spitzer, R. L., Williams, J. B. W., Gibbon, M., & First, M. B. (1990a). *Structured*

Clinical Interview for DSM-III-R Personality Disorders (SCID-II) (Version 1.0). Washington, DC: American Psychiatric Press.

Spitzer, R. L., Williams, J. B. W., Gibbon, M., & First, M. B. (1990b). *Structured Clinical Interview for DSM-III-R Non-patient Edition (SCID-NP) (Version 1.0).* Washington, DC: American Psychiatric Press.

Stickler, G. B., & Murphy, D. B. (1979). Recurrent abdominal pain. *American Journal of Diseases in Childhood, 133,* 486–489.

Sullivan, G., Jenkins, P. L., & Blewett, A. E. (1995). Irritable bowel syndrome and family history of psychiatric disorder: A preliminary study. *General Hospital Psychiatry, 17,* 43–46.

Suls, J., Wan, C. K., & Blanchard, E. B. (1994). A multilevel data-analytic approach for evaluation of relationships between daily life stressors and symptomatology: Patients with irritable bowel syndrome. *Health Psychology, 13,* 103–113.

Svedlund, J., Sjodin, I., Ottosson, J.-O., & Dotevall, G. (1983). Controlled study of psychotherapy in irritable bowel syndrome. *The Lancet,* 589–592.

Svendsen, H., Munck, L. K., & Andersen, J. R. (1983). Irritable bowel syndrome —Prognosis and diagnostic safety. *Scandinavian Journal of Gastroenterology, 20,* 415–418.

Switz, D. N. (1976). What the gastroenterologist does all day. *Gastroenterology, 70,* 1048–1050.

Talley, N. J., Fett, S. L., & Zinsmeister, A. R. (1995). Self-reported abuse and gastrointestinal disease in outpatients: Association with irritable bowel-type symptoms. *American Journal of Gastroenterology,* 90, 366–371.

Talley, N. J., Fett, S. L., Zinsmeister, A. R., & Melton, III., L. J. (1994). Gastrointestinal tract symptoms and self-reported abuse: A population-based study. *Gastroenterology, 107,* 1040–1049.

Talley, N. J., Gabriel, S. E., Harmsen, W. S., Zinsmeister, A. R., & Evans, R. W. (1995). Medical costs in community subjects with irritable bowel syndrome. *Gastroenterology, 109,* 1736–1741.

Talley, N. J., Phillips, S. F., Bruce, B., Twomey, C. K., Zinsmeister, A. R., & Melton, III, L. J. (1990). Relation among personality and symptoms in nonulcer dyspepsia and the irritable bowel syndrome. *Gastroenterology,* 99, 327–333.

Talley, N. J., Phillips, S. F., Melton, L. J., Mulvihill, C., Wiltgen, C., & Zinsmeister, A. R. (1986). Diagnostic value of the Manning criteria in irritable bowel syndrome. *Gut, 31,* 77–81.

Talley, N. J., Phillips, S. F., Melton, L. J., Wiltgen, C., & Zinsmeister, A. R. (1989). A patient questionnaire to identify bowel disease. *Annals of Internal Medicine, 111,* 671–674.

Talley, N. J., Weaver, A. L., Zinsmeister, A. R., & Melton, III, L. J. (1992). Onset and disappearance of gastrointestinal symptoms and functional gastrointestinal disorders. *American Journal of Epidemiology, 136,* 165–177.

Talley, N. J., Zinsmeister, A. R., & Melton, III, L. J. (1995). Irritable bowel syndrome in a community: Symptom subgroups, risk factors, and health care utilization. *American Journal of Epidemiology*, *142*, 76–83.

Talley, N. J., Zinsmeister, A. R., Van Dyke, C., & Melton, L. J. (1991). Epidemiology of colonic symptoms and the irritable bowel syndrome. *Gastroenterology*, *101*, 927–934.

Thompson, W. G., Creed, F., Drossman, D. A., Heaton, K. W., & Mazzacca, G. (1992). Functional bowel disease and functional abdominal pain. *Gastroenterology International*, *5*, 75–91.

Thompson, W. G., & Heaton, K. W. (1980). Functional bowel disorders in apparently healthy people. *Gastroenterology*, *79*, 283–288.

Thompson, W. G., Longstreth, G. F., Drossman, D. A., Heaton, K. W., Irvine, E. J., & Muller-Lissner, S. A. (1999). Functional bowel disorders and functional abdominal pain. *Gut*, *45*, 1143–1147.

Thornton, S., McIntyre, P., Murray-Lyon, I., & Gruzelier, J. (1990). Psychological and psychophysiological characteristics in irritable bowel syndrome. *British Journal of Clinical Psychology*, *29*, 343–345.

Tollefson, G. D., Tollefson, S. L., Pederson, M., Luxenberg, M., & Dunsmore, G. (1991). Comorbid irritable bowel syndrome in patients with generalized anxiety and major depression. *Annals of Clinical Psychiatry*, *3*, 215–222.

Toner, B. B., Garfinkel, P. E., Jeejeebhoy, K. N., Scher, H., Shulhan, D., & Gasbarro, I. D. (1990). Self-schema in irritable bowel syndrome and depression. *Psychosomatic Medicine*, *52*, 149–155.

Toner, B. B., Segal, Z. V., Emmott, S., Myran, D., Ali, A., DiGasbarro, I., & Stuckless, N. (1998). Cognitive–behavioral group therapy for patients with irritable bowel syndrome. *International Journal of Group Psychotherapy*, *48*, 215–243.

van Dulmen, A. M., Fennis, J. F. M., & Bleijenberg, G. (1996). Cognitive–behavioral group therapy for irritable bowel syndrome: Effects and long-term follow-up. *Psychosomatic Medicine*, *58*, 508–514.

Vollmer, A., & Blanchard, E. B. (1998). Controlled comparison of individual versus group cognitive therapy for irritable bowel syndrome. *Behavior Therapy*, *29*, 19–33.

Walker, E. A., Gelfand, A. N., Gelfand, M. D., & Katon, W. J. (1995). Psychiatric diagnoses, sexual and physical victimization, and disability in patients with irritable bowel syndrome or inflammatory bowel disease. *Psychological Medicine*, *25*, 1259–1267.

Walker, E. A., Katon, W. J., Jemelka, R. P., & Roy-Byrne, P. P. (1992). Comorbidity of gastrointestinal complaints, depression, and anxiety in the Epidemiologic Catchment Area (ECA) study. *The American Journal of Medicine*, *92*, 26S–30S.

Walker, E. A., Katon, W. J., Roy-Byrne, P. P., Jemelka, R. P., & Russo, J. (1993). Histories of sexual victimization in patients with irritable bowel syndrome or inflammatory bowel disease. *American Journal of Psychiatry*, *150*, 1502–1506.

Walker, E. A., Roy-Byrne, P. P., & Katon, W. J. (1990). Irritable bowel syndrome and psychiatric illness. *American Journal of Psychiatry, 147*, 565–572.

Walker, E. A., Roy-Byrne, P. P., Katon, W. J., Li, L., Amos, D., & Jiranek, G. (1990). Psychiatric illness and irritable bowel syndrome: A comparison with inflammatory bowel disease. *American Journal of Psychiatry, 147*, 1656–1661.

Walker, L. S., Garber, J., & Greene, J. W. (1993). Psychosocial correlates of recurrent childhood pain: A comparison of pediatric patients with recurrent abdominal pain, organic illness, and psychiatric disorders. *Journal of Abnormal Psychology, 102*, 248–258.

Walker, L. S., Guite, J. W., Duke, M., Barnard, J. A., & Greene, J. W. (1998). Recurrent abdominal pain: A potential precursor of irritable bowel syndrome in adolescents and young adults. *The Journal of Pediatrics, 132*, 228–237.

Waller, S. L., & Misiewicz, J. J. (1969). Prognosis in the irritable-bowel syndrome. *The Lancet*, 753–756.

Ware, J. E. (1993). *SF-36 Health Survey: Manual and interpretation guide*. Boston: The Health Institute, New England Medical Center.

Weinstock, S. A. (1976). The reestablishment of intestinal control in functional colitis. *Biofeedback and Self-Regulation, 1*, 324.

Weissman, A., & Beck, A. T. (1978, November). *Development and validation of the Dysfunctional Attitude Scale: A preliminary investigation*. Presented at the annual meeting of the American Educational Research Association, Toronto, Ontario, Canada.

Weitzenhoffer, A. M., & Hilgard, E. R. (1959). *Stanford Hypnotic Susceptibility Scale, Forms A and B*. Palo Alto, CA: Consulting Psychologists Press.

Welch, G. W., Hillman, L. C., & Pomare, E. W. (1985). Psychoneurotic symptomatology in the irritable bowel syndrome: A study of reporters and nonreporters. *British Medical Journal, 291*, 1382–1384.

Welgan, P., Meshkinpour, H., & Hoehler, F. (1985). The effect of stress on colon motor and electrical activity in irritable bowel syndrome. *Psychosomatic Medicine, 47*, 139–149.

Wender, P. H., & Kalm, M. (1983). Prevalence of attention deficit disorder, residual type, and other psychiatric disorders in patient with irritable colon syndrome. *American Journal of Psychiatry, 140*, 1579–1582.

Whitehead, W. E. (1985). Psychotherapy and biofeedback in the treatment of irritable bowel syndrome. In N. S. Read (Ed.), *Irritable bowel syndrome* (pp. 245–263). London: Grune & Stratton.

Whitehead, W. E. (1994). Assessing the effects of stress on physical symptoms. *Health Psychology, 13*, 99–102.

Whitehead, W. E. (1999, April). *Psychological and cognitive influence on visceral pain perception*. Presented at the 3rd International Symposium on Functional Gastrointestinal Disorders, Milwaukee, WI.

Whitehead, W. E., Bosmajian, L., Zonderman, A. B., Costa, Jr., P. T., & Schuster, M. M. (1988). Symptoms of psychologic distress associated with irritable bowel syndrome. *Gastroenterology, 95*, 709–714.

Whitehead, W. E., Burnett, C. K., Cook, III, E. W., & Taub, E. (1996). Impact of irritable bowel syndrome on quality of life. *Digestive Diseases and Sciences, 41*, 2248–2253.

Whitehead, W. E., Crowell, M. D., Davidoff, A. L., Palsson, O. S., & Schuster, M. M. (1997). Pain from rectal distention in women with irritable bowel syndrome: Relationship to sexual abuse. *Digestive Diseases and Sciences, 42*, 796–804.

Whitehead, W. E., Crowell, M. D., Robinson, J. C., Heller, B. R., & Schuster, M. M. (1992). Effects of stressful life events on bowel symptoms: Subjects with irritable bowel syndrome compared with subjects without bowel dysfunction. *Gut, 33*, 825–830.

Whitehead, W. E., Engel, B. T., & Schuster, M. M. (1980). Irritable bowel syndrome: Physiological and psychological differences between diarrhea-predominant and constipation-predominant patients. *Digestive Diseases and Sciences, 25*, 404–413.

Whitehead, W. E., Holtkotter, B., Enck, P., Hoelzi, R., Holmes, K. D., Anthony, J., Shabsin, H. S., & Schuster, M. M. (1990). Tolerance for rectosigmoid distention in irritable bowel syndrome. *Gastroenterology*, 98, 1187–1192.

Whitehead, W. E., & Palsson, O. S. (1998). Is rectal pain sensitivity a biological marker for irritable bowel syndrome? Psychological influences on pain perception. *Gastroenterology, 115*, 1263–1271.

Whitehead, W. E., Winget, C., Fedoravicius, A. S., Wooley, S., & Blackwell, B. (1982). Learned illness behavior in patients with irritable bowel syndrome and peptic ulcer. *Digestive Diseases and Sciences, 27*, 202–208.

Whorwell, P. J., Prior, A., & Colgan, S. M. (1987). Hypnotherapy in severe irritable bowel syndrome: Further experience. *Gut, 28*, 423–425.

Whorwell, P. J., Prior, A., & Faragher, E. B. (1984). Controlled trial of hypnotherapy in the treatment of severe refractory irritable bowel syndrome. *The Lancet*, 1232–1234.

Wing, J. K., Cooper, J. E., & Sartorious, N. (1974). *Measurement and classification of psychiatric symptoms*. Cambridge: Cambridge University Press.

Wise, T. N., Cooper, J. N., & Ahmed, S. (1982). The efficacy of group therapy for patients with irritable bowel syndrome. *Psychosomatics, 23*, 465–469.

Wolpe, J. (1958). *Psychotherapy by reciprocal inhibition*. Berkeley, CA: Stanford University Press.

Young, S. J., Alpers, D. H., Norland, C. C., & Woodruff, Jr., R. A. (1976). Psychiatric illness and the irritable bowel syndrome: Practical implications for the primary physician. *Gastroenterology, 70*, 162–166.

Zigmund, A. S., & Snaith, R. P. (1983). The Hospital Anxiety and Depression Scale. *Acta Psychiatrica Scandinavia, 67*, 361–370.

AUTHOR INDEX

SUBJECT INDEX

ABOUT THE AUTHOR

Edward B. Blanchard, PhD, received his doctoral degree in clinical psychology from Stanford University in 1969. After holding faculty positions at the University of Georgia, the University of Mississippi Medical Center, and the University of Tennessee Center for Health Sciences, Dr. Blanchard accepted a position at the University at Albany, State University of New York, in 1977 and has remained there ever since. He is currently director of the Center for Stress and Anxiety Disorders at the University at Albany. In 1989, Dr. Blanchard was named Distinguished Professor of Psychology by the Board of Trustees of the State University of New York.

Dr. Blanchard began his work on irritable bowel syndrome in the early 1980s with a series of Albany doctoral students. This work has been supported at times by the National Institutes of Health.